Fodor's 99

Costa Rica

The complete guide, thoroughly up-to-date

Packed with details that will make your trip

The must-see sights, off and on the beaten path

What to see, what to skip

Mix-and-match vacation itineraries

City strolls, countryside adventures

Smart lodging and dining options

Essential local do's and taboos

Transportation tips, distances and directions

Key contacts, savvy travel tips

When to go, what to pack

Clear, accurate, easy-to-use maps

Fodor's Travel Publications, Inc.
New York • Toronto • London • Sydney • Auckland
www.fodors.com

D0404048

Fodor's Costa Rica 99

EDITOR: Caragh Rockwood

Editorial Contributors: Robert Blake, David Brown, David Dudenhoefer, Justin Henderson, Christina Knight, Helayne Schiff, M.T. Schwartzman (gold guide editor)

Editorial Production: Melissa Klurman

Maps: David Lindroth, *cartographer*; Steven Amsterdam, *map editor*

Design: Fabrizio La Rocca, *creative director*; Guido Caroti, *associate art director*; Jolie Novak, *photo editor*

Production/Manufacturing: Mike Costa

Cover Photograph: Buddy Mays/Travel Stock

Copyright

ISBN 0–679–00124–7

Special Sales

PRINTED IN THE UNITED STATES OF AMERICA

10 9 8 7 6 5 4 3 2 1

CONTENTS

ON THE ROAD WITH FODOR'S

WHEN I PLAN A VACATION, the first thing I do is cast around among my friends and colleagues to find someone who's just been where I'm going. That's because there's no substitute for a recommendation from a good friend who knows your tastes, your budget, and your circumstances, someone who's just been there. Unfortunately, such friends are few and far between. So it's nice to know that there's *Fodor's Costa Rica*.

In the first place, this book won't stay home when you hit the road. It will accompany you every step of the way, steering you away from wrong turns and wrong choices and never expecting a thing in return. It includes a wonderful, full-color map from Rand McNally, the world's largest commercial mapmaker. Most important of all, it's written and assiduously updated by the kind of people you *would* hit up for travel tips if you knew them. They're as choosy as your pickiest friend, except they've probably seen a lot more of Costa Rica. In these pages, they don't send you chasing down every town and sight in Costa Rica but have instead selected the best ones, the ones that are worthy of your time and money. Just tear out the map at the perforation, and join us on the road in Costa Rica.

About Our Writers

Our success in helping to make your trip the best of all possible vacations is a credit to the hard work of our extraordinary writers.

Freelance hack **David Dudenhoefer** has spent the better part of the past decade in Central America. Based in San José, he travels regularly within the isthmus, writing about everything from surfing to presidential summits. His articles have appeared in about two dozen publications in North, Central, and South America. He is a regular Fodor's contributor and is the author of *The Panama Traveler*. When not chained to his computer, he can usually be found wandering through the woods, playing in the waves, or propping up the bar at one of San José's seedier nightspots.

Surfing through Guanacaste every winter and dodging man-eating crocodiles, photogenic turtles, and ill-mannered gringo surfers, **Justin Henderson** still finds time to uncover new territory for Fodor's when not tearing up Costa Rica's epic waves. Back home in Seattle, he writes books and magazine articles on travel, architecture, and design, and lives happily ever after with photographer Donna Day and Clyde the wonder dog, the smartest standard poodle in this sector of the galaxy.

In *Costa Rica 99* we've expanded coverage of Guanacaste and the Central Valley areas, plus created some new maps to help you get around. We've also added some fun "Close-Up" features to give you more background info—they highlight bird- and turtle-watching (grab your binoculars!), volunteer vacations, and Costa Rican coffee (for all you coffee achievers!). Check them out.

Connections

We're pleased that the American Society of Travel Agents continues to endorse Fodor's as its guidebook of choice. ASTA is the world's largest and most influential travel trade association, operating in more than 170 countries, with 27,000 members pledged to adhere to a strict code of ethics reflecting the Society's motto, "Integrity in Travel." ASTA shares Fodor's devotion to providing smart, honest travel information and advice to travelers, and we've long recommended that our readers—even those who have guidebooks and traveling friends—consult ASTA member agents for the experience and professionalism they bring to your vacation planning.

On the Web, check out Fodor's site (http://www.fodors.com) for information on major destinations around the world and travel-savvy interactive features that are replete with hot links to complementary on-line resources. The Web site also lists the 85-plus radio stations across the United States that carry *Fodor's Travel Show*, a live call-in program that airs every weekend. Tune in to hear the writers of this book and other guests discuss their adventures, and call in to get answers to your most pressing travel questions.

How to Use This Book

Organization

Up front is the **Gold Guide,** an easy-to-use section arranged alphabetically by topic. Under each listing you'll find tips and information that will help you accomplish what you need to in Costa Rica. You'll also find addresses and telephone numbers of organizations and companies that offer destination-related services and detailed information and publications.

The first chapter in the guide, Destination: Costa Rica helps get you in the mood for your trip. New and Noteworthy cues you in on trends and happenings, What's Where gets you oriented, Pleasures and Pastimes describes the activities and sights that make Costa Rica unique, and Fodor's Choice showcases our top picks.

The second chapter in *Fodor's Costa Rica '99* covers San José, with all of the following chapters after Chapter 3 circling counterclockwise around the capital. The San José chapter begins with an Exploring section subdivided by neighborhood; each subsection recommends a walking or driving tour and lists sights in alphabetical order. Each regional chapter is divided by geographical area; within each area, towns are covered in logical geographical order, and attractive stretches of road and minor points of interest between them are indicated by the designation *En Route.* And within town sections, all restaurants and lodgings are grouped.

To help you decide what to visit in the time you have, all chapters begin with our recommended itineraries. The A to Z section that ends all chapters covers getting there and getting around. It also provides helpful contacts and resources. At the end of the book you'll find Portraits, with a wonderful essay about the biodiversity of Costa Rica.

Icons and Symbols

★   Our special recommendations
✕   Restaurant
🏠 Lodging establishment
✕🏠 Lodging establishment whose restaurant warrants a special trip
⛺ Campgrounds
🐤 Good for kids (rubber duck)

☞   Sends you to another section of the guide for more information
✉   Address
☎   Telephone number
🕓 Opening and closing times
💲 Admission prices (those we give apply to adults; substantially reduced fees are almost always available for children, students, and senior citizens)

Numbers in white and black circles ③ ❸ that appear on the maps, in the margins, and within the tours correspond to one another.

Dining and Lodging

The restaurants and lodgings we list are the cream of the crop in each price range. Price categories are as follows:

For restaurants:

CATEGORY	COST*
$$$$	over $20
$$$	$10–$20
$$	$5–$10
$	under $5

Dining prices are for cost of a dinner entrée and a nonalcoholic beverage.

For hotels:

CATEGORY	COST*
$$$$	over $90
$$$	$50–$90
$$	$25–$50
$	under $25

Lodging prices are for a double room, excluding service and 18.4% tax (in Costa Rica) or 10% tax (in Panama).

Hotel Facilities

We always list the facilities that are available—but we don't specify whether you'll be charged extra to use them: When pricing accommodations, always ask what's included. In addition, assume that all rooms have private baths unless noted otherwise. In addition, when you book a room, be sure to mention if you have a disability or are traveling with children, if you prefer a private bath or a certain type of bed, or if you have specific dietary needs or other concerns.

Restaurant Reservations and Dress Codes

Reservations are always a good idea; we mention them only when they're essential or are not accepted. Book as far ahead as you can, and reconfirm as soon as you arrive. Unless otherwise noted, the restaurants listed are open daily for lunch and dinner. We mention dress only when men are required to wear a jacket or a jacket and tie. Look for an overview of local dining-out habits in the Gold Guide.

Credit Cards

The following abbreviations are used: **AE,** American Express; **DC,** Diners Club; **MC,** MasterCard; and **V,** Visa.

Don't Forget to Write

You can use this book in the confidence that all prices and opening times are based on information supplied to us at press time; Fodor's cannot accept responsibility for any errors. Time inevitably brings changes, so always confirm information when it matters—especially if you're making a detour to visit a specific place.

Were the restaurants we recommended as described? Did our hotel picks exceed your expectations? Did you find a museum we recommended a waste of time? Keeping a travel guide fresh and up-to-date is a big job, and we welcome your feedback, positive *and* negative. If you have complaints, we'll look into them and revise our entries when the facts warrant it. If you've discovered a special place that we haven't included, we'll pass the information along to our correspondents and have them check it out. So send us your thoughts via e-mail at editors@fodors.com (specifying the name of the book on the subject line) or on paper in care of the Costa Rica editor at Fodor's, 201 East 50th Street, New York, New York 10022. In the meantime, have a wonderful trip!

Karen Cure

Karen Cure
Editorial Director

Costa Rica

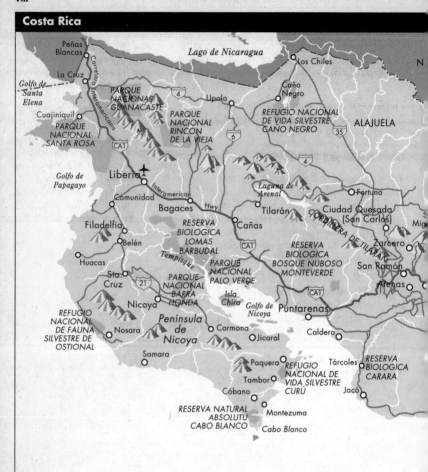

Peñas Blancas
Los Chiles
Lago de Nicaragua
La Cruz
N
Golfo de Santa Elena
Carretera Interamericana
PARQUE NACIONAL GUANACASTE
4
Upala
Caño Negro
Cuajiniquil
PARQUE NACIONAL SANTA ROSA
PARQUE NACIONAL RINCON DE LA VIEJA
6
REFUGIO NACIONAL DE VIDA SILVESTRE CAÑO NEGRO
35
ALAJUELA
CAT
4
Golfo de Papagayo
Liberia
Interamerican
Laguna de Arenal
Fortuna
Comunidad
Bagaces
Hwy.
Tilarán
Ciudad Quesada (San Carlos)
Filadelfia
RESERVA BIOLOGICA LOMAS BARBUDAL
Cañas
CORDILLERA DE TILARAN
Mig
Belén
CAT
Zarcero
Huacas
Tempisque
PARQUE NACIONAL PALO VERDE
RESERVA BIOLOGICA BOSQUE NUBOSO MONTEVERDE
San Ramón
Sta. Cruz
21
PARQUE NACIONAL BARRA HONDA
Isla Chira
CAT
Atenas
Nicoya
Península de Nicoya
Golfo de Nicoya
Puntarenas
REFUGIO NACIONAL DE FAUNA SILVESTRE DE OSTIONAL
Nosara
Carmona
Caldera
Jicaral
Samara
Paquera
REFUGIO NACIONAL DE VIDA SILVESTRE CURÚ
Tárcoles
RESERVA BIOLOGICA CARARA
Tambor
Cóbano
Jacó
RESERVA NATURAL ABSOLUTU CABO BLANCO
Montezuma
Cabo Blanco

PACIFIC

OCEAN

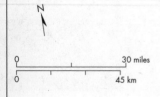

N

| 0 | | 30 miles |
| 0 | | 45 km |

Central America

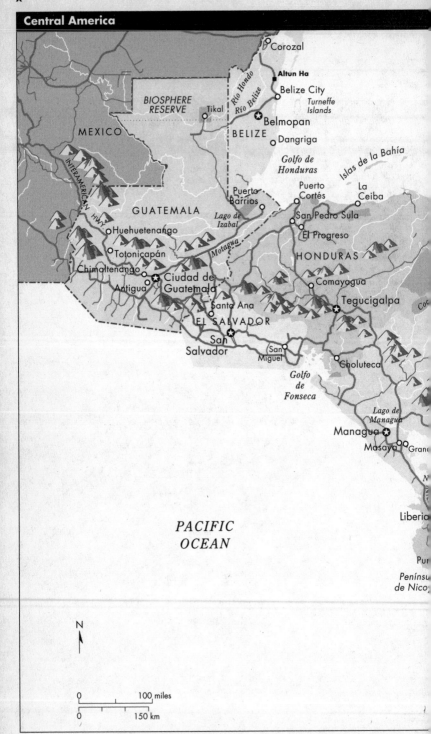

Corozal

Altun Ha
Belize City
Turneffe
Islands

BIOSPHERE
RESERVE
Tikal

Río Hondo
Río Belize

★ Belmopan

MEXICO
BELIZE

Dangriga

Golfo de
Honduras

Islas de la Bahía

INTERAMERICAN HWY

Puerto
Barrios

Puerto
Cortés

La
Ceiba

GUATEMALA
Lago de
Izabal

San Pedro Sula

Huehuetenango

El Progreso

Motagua

HONDURAS

Totonicapán

Chimaltenango
Antigua

Ciudad de
Guatemala

Comayagua

Tegucigalpa

Santa Ana

Coc

Santo Ana

EL SALVADOR

San
Salvador

San
Miguel

Choluteca

Golfo
de
Fonseca

Lago de
Managua

Managua

Masaya
Grand

N

Liberia

*PACIFIC
OCEAN*

Pu

Penínsu
de Nico

N

| 0 | | 100 miles |
| 0 | 150 km | |

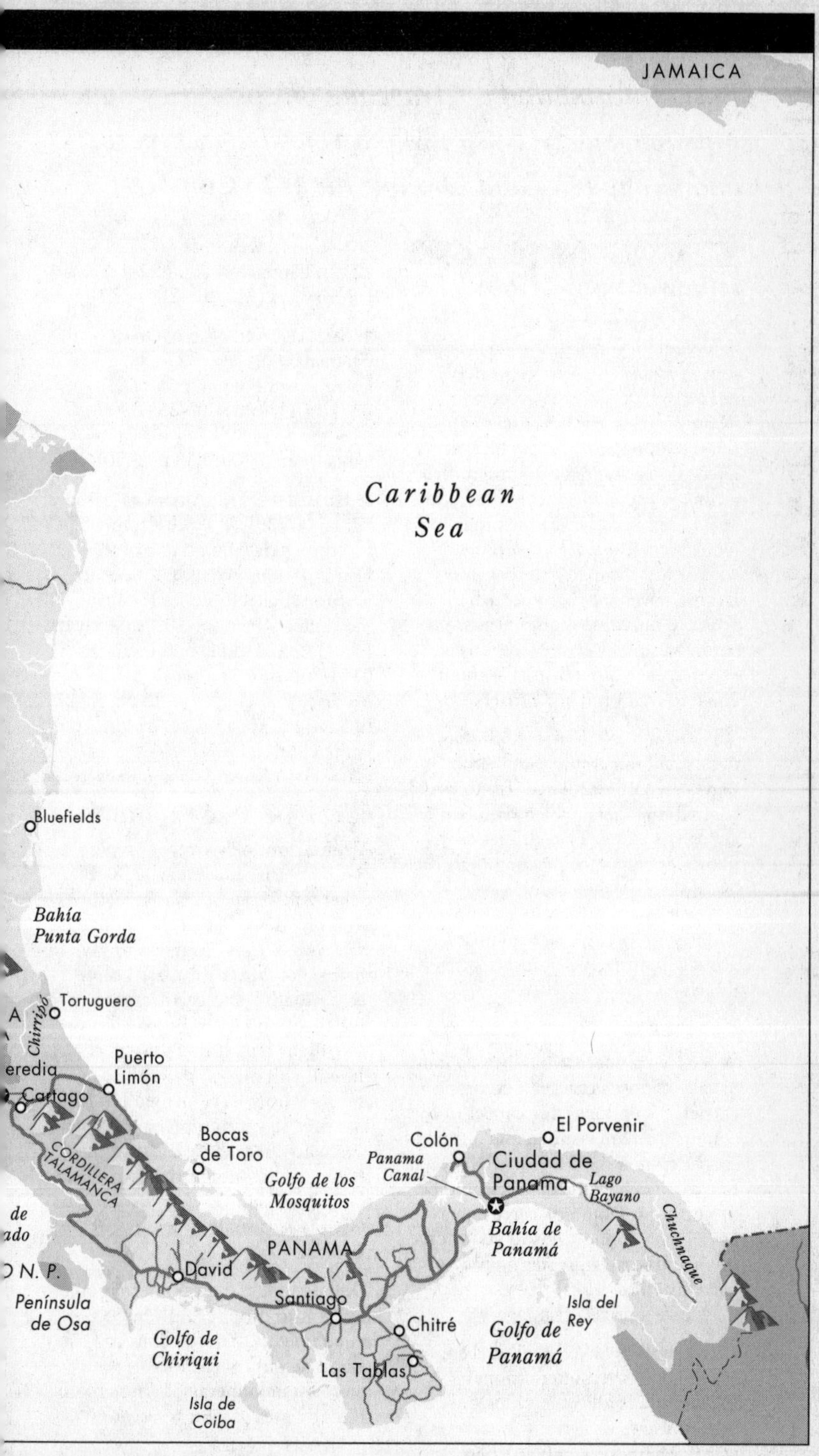

JAMAICA

*Caribbean
Sea*

Bluefields

*Bahía
Punta Gorda*

Chirripó

Tortuguero

A

eredia

Puerto
Limón

Cartago

CORDILLERA
TALAMANCA

Bocas
de Toro

Colón

El Porvenir

*Panama
Canal*

Ciudad de
Panama

*Golfo de los
Mosquitos*

*Lago
Bayano*

*de
ado*

PANAMA

*Bahía de
Panamá*

Chichnaque

N. P.

David

*Península
de Osa*

Santiago

Chitré

*Isla del
Rey*

*Golfo de
Chiriqui*

Las Tablas

*Golfo de
Panamá*

*Isla de
Coiba*

SMART TRAVEL TIPS A TO Z

Basic Information on Traveling in Costa Rica and Panama, Savvy Tips to Make Your Trip a Breeze, and Companies and Organizations to Contact

AIR TRAVEL

BOOKING YOUR FLIGHT

Price is just one factor to consider when booking a flight: frequency of service and even a carrier's safety record are often just as important. Major airlines offer the greatest number of departures. Smaller airlines—including regional and no-frills airlines—usually have a limited number of flights daily. On the other hand, so-called low-cost airlines usually are cheaper, and their fares impose fewer restrictions, such as advance-purchase requirements. Safety-wise, low-cost carriers as a group have a good history—about equal to that of major carriers.

When you book, **look for nonstop flights** and **remember that "direct" flights stop at least once.** Try to **avoid connecting flights,** which require a change of plane. Two airlines may jointly operate a connecting flight, so ask if your airline operates every segment. International flights on a country's flag carrier are almost always nonstop; U.S. airlines often fly direct.

CARRIERS

When flying internationally, you must usually choose between a domestic carrier, the national flag carrier of the country you are visiting, and a foreign carrier from a third country. National flag carriers have the greatest number of nonstops. Domestic carriers may have better connections to your home town and serve a greater number of gateway cities. Third-party carriers may have a price advantage.

Many carriers have prohibited smoking on all of their international flights; others allow smoking only on certain routes or certain departures, so **ask about the smoking policy.**

➤ Major Airlines: **American** (☎ 800/433–7300). **Continental** (☎ 800/

231–0856). **Delta** (☎ 800/221–1212). **United** (☎ 800/827–7777). **US Airways** (☎ 800/428–4322).

➤ Smaller Airlines: **Aviateca Guatemala** (☎ 800/327–9832). **Lacsa Costa Rican** (☎ 800/225–2272). **LTU** (☎ 800/888–0200). **Mexicana** (☎ 800/531–7921). **TACA Salvadoran** (☎ 800/535–8780).

➤ From the U.K.: **American Airlines** (☎ 0345/789–789) flies from Heathrow via Miami, one of the fastest options given that there are no nonstop flights to Costa Rica from the United Kingdom. **British Airways** (☎ 0345/222–111) and **Iberia** (☎ 0171/830–0011) offer flights to Madrid, changing to an Iberia flight to San José, Costa Rica. **Virgin Atlantic** (☎ 01293/747–747) goes from Gatwick to Miami, changing there.

CHECK IN & BOARDING

Airlines routinely overbook planes, assuming that not everyone with a ticket will show up, but sometimes everyone does. When that happens, airlines ask for volunteers to give up their seats. In return these volunteers usually get a certificate for a free flight and are rebooked on the next flight out. If there are not enough volunteers, the airline must choose who will be denied boarding. The first to get bumped are passengers who checked in late and those flying on discounted tickets, so **get to the gate and check in as early as possible,** especially during peak periods.

Although the trend on international flights is to drop reconfirmation requirements, many airlines still ask you to reconfirm each leg of your international itinerary. Failure to do so may result in your reservation being canceled.

Always **bring a government-issued photo ID to the airport.** You may be asked to show it before you are allowed to check in.

CONSOLIDATORS

Consolidators buy tickets for scheduled international flights at reduced rates from the airlines, then sell them at prices that beat the best fare available directly from the airlines, usually without restrictions. Sometimes you can even get your money back if you need to return the ticket. Carefully read the fine print detailing penalties for changes and cancellations, and **confirm your consolidator reservation with the airline.**

➤ CONSOLIDATORS: **Cheap Tickets** (☎ 800/377–1000). **Up & Away Travel** (☎ 212/889–2345). **Discount Travel Network** (☎ 800/576–1600). **Unitravel** (☎ 800/325–2222). **World Travel Network** (☎ 800/409–6753).

COURIERS

When you fly as a courier, you trade your checked-luggage space for a ticket deeply subsidized by a courier service. It's all perfectly legitimate, but there are restrictions: You can usually book your flight only a week or two in advance, your length of stay may be set for a certain number of days, and you may not be able to book a companion on the same flight.

CUTTING COSTS

The main tourist season (the dry season) in Costa Rica and Panama, from mid-December to April, coincides with Thanksgiving, Christmas, and Easter. Flights are sometimes fully booked well ahead of time. Check fares from your city to San José, as well as fares from your city to a U.S. gateway city and from that gateway into San José; the latter can be cheaper. If your ticket combines airlines, try to get it issued on the ticket stock of the airline that has an office in San José, making it easier to make changes on the return leg. Also, flexibility on dates makes it more likely that a consolidator (☞ *above*) can find you a less-expensive ticket. At press time, there were weekly charters from Dallas and Atlanta, and more charter flights were expected for the high season, from other United States and Canadian ports.

The least-expensive airfares to Costa Rica and Panama are priced for round-trip travel and usually must be purchased in advance. It's smart to **call a number of airlines, and when you are quoted a good price, book it on the spot**—the same fare may not be available the next day. Airlines generally allow you to change your return date for a fee. If you don't use your ticket, you can apply the cost toward the purchase of a new ticket, again for a small charge. However, most low-fare tickets are nonrefundable. To get the lowest airfare, **check different routings.** Compare prices of flights to and from different airports if your destination or home city has more than one gateway. Also price off-peak flights, which may be significantly less expensive.

Travel agents, especially those who specialize in finding the lowest fares (☞ Discounts & Deals, *below*), can be especially helpful when booking a plane ticket. When you're quoted a price, **ask your agent if the price is likely to get any lower.** Good agents know the seasonal fluctuations of airfares and can usually anticipate a sale or fare war. However, waiting can be risky: The fare could go *up* as seats become scarce, and you may wait so long that your preferred flight sells out.

FLYING TIMES

From New York, flights to San José are 5½ hours (via Miami); from Los Angeles, 8½ hours (via Mexico); from Houston, 4½ hours (via Guatemala); and from Miami, 2 hours (direct).

FLYING WITHIN COSTA RICA AND PANAMA

Given the nations' often difficult driving conditions—what may appear to be a small distance on a map can represent hours of driving time on dirt roads pocked with moon-craters—**consider flying, which, depending on your itinerary, may not cost that much more than renting a car. Expansion of flights between different regions of Costa Rica means that you can see much of the country via domestic flights, which could save days of driving or busing**

Two domestic airlines—Sansa and Travelair—serve Costa Rica, and the

Panamanian domestic airline, Aeroperlas, connects major cities within that country and also has several flights a week between Costa Rica and Panama. Travelair also offers charter flights, as do several other air-charter companies in San José that will fly you to places that don't have scheduled flights. Sansa is considerably cheaper but its planes sometimes take off late.

➤ COSTA RICAN CARRIERS: **Sansa** (✉ C. 24, between Avda. Central and Avda. 1, San José, ☎ 506/221−9414 or 506/441−8035) flies out of Juan Santamaría International Airport, near Alajuela, to the following destinations: Barra del Colorado, Coto 47, Golfito, La Fortuna, Liberia, Nosara, Palmar Sur, Puerto Jiménez, Punta Islita, Quepos, Samara, San Vito, Tamarindo, Tambor, and Tortuguero. They are also flights between Quepos, Tamarindo, and La Fortuna. One-way fares range from $30 to $50.

Travelair (✉ Aeropuerto Tobías Bolaños, in Pavas, just west of San José, ☎ 506/220−3054, 506/232−7883) has daily flights from Tobias Bolaños Airport, in the San José suburb of Pavas, to the following destinations: Carrillo, Golfito/Puerto Jiménez, Jaco, La Fortuna, Liberia, Palmar Sur, Punta Islita, Quepos, Tamarindo, Tambor, and Tortuguero. They also have flights between Tamarindo, Liberia, La Fortuna, and Tortuguero; between Tambor, Quepos, and Jacó, and between Palmar Sur and Quepos. Prices range from $48 for the one-way hop to Quepos up to $88 for one way to Liberia.

➤ COSTA RICAN CHARTER COMPANIES: **Aero Costa Sol** (☎ 506/440−1444, FAX 506/440−2671). **Aerolineas Turisticas** (☎ 506/232−1125, FAX 506/232−5802). **Aeronaves** (☎ 506/282−4033, FAX 503/232−1176) also has an office in Golfito (☎ FAX 506/775−0278). **Alas Anfibias** (☎ FAX 506/232−9567) is a seaplane service offering charter flights to spots that lie far from airfields, such as Drake Bay, Lake Arenal, and distant Cocos Island. **Helicópteros de Costa Rica** (☎ 506/232−7534) rents helicopters.

➤ PANAMANIAN CARRIERS: **Aeroperlas** (Costa Rica ☎ 506/440−0093, FAX 506/442−9103; Panama ☎ 507/269−4555, FAX 507/269−4564), Panama's main domestic airline, Aeroperlas has five direct flights per week (Mon.−Fri.), between David and San José, which connect to direct flights to Bocas del Toro, Changuinola, and Panama City. Aeroperlas also has daily flights between David, Changuinola, Bocas del Toro, and Panama City, from where flights depart to Contadora and the Darien Gap. **Aerotaxi** (☎ 507/264−8844, FAX 507/269−7210) has daily flights to about a dozen airstrips in the San Blas Islands region.

HOW TO COMPLAIN

If your baggage goes astray, complain right away. Most carriers require that you **file a claim immediately.**

➤ AIRLINE COMPLAINTS: U.S. Department of Transportation **Aviation Consumer Protection Division** (✉ C-75, Room 4107, Washington, DC 20590, ☎ 202/366−2220). **Federal Aviation Administration Consumer Hotline** (☎ 800/322−7873).

AIRPORTS

All flights arriving in Costa Rica from the United States and Canada land at Juan Santamaría International Airport, 16 km (10 mi) north of downtown San José. At press time, a small number of flights were continuing on to the new Daniel Oduber International Airport at Liberia in Guanacaste. **If your destination is in the northwest, look into a direct flight to Liberia**—you might save yourself several hard hours on the road.

➤ AIRPORTS: **Aeropuerto Internacional Juan Santamaría** (☎ 011−506/443−2682). **Aeropuerto Internacional Daniel Oduber** (☎ 011−506/667−0014).

BIKE TRAVEL

BIKES IN FLIGHT

Most major airlines will accommodate bikes as luggage, provided they are dismantled and put into a box; Costa Rica's domestic airlines Sansa and Travelair will usually allow disassembled mountain bikes (and 7-ft surfboards) aboard for $15, space provided. Call to see if your airline sells bike boxes (about $5; bike bags are at least $100) although you can often pick them up free at bike shops. International travelers can sometimes substitute a bike for a piece of checked luggage for free; otherwise, it will cost about $100.

BOAT & FERRY TRAVEL

WITHIN COSTA RICA

Regular passenger and/or car ferries connect Playa Naranjo, Tambor, and Paquera on the south end of the Nicoya Peninsula with Puntarenas. A car and passenger ferry crosses the Río Tempisque, about a one-hour drive north and west from Puntarenas, from 5 AM to 7 PM. The Arco Iris Passenger Ferry makes daily runs between Golfito and Puerto Jiménez, and the Zancudo's passenger ferry makes a daily round-trip to Golfito. During the holidays and the high season, waits of up to three hours are common.

WITHIN PANAMA

Water taxis travel regularly between Almirante and Bocas del Toro, and make several trips daily between Almirante and Chiriquí Grande. A car ferry also makes one trip daily between Almirante and Chiriquí Grande, stopping at Bocas del Toro twice a week, but water taxis make the same trip in a fraction of the time. Several ferries run daily between Panama City and the Island of Taboga.

BUS TRAVEL

WITHIN COSTA RICA

There is reliable, inexpensive bus service throughout much of the country. A patchwork of private companies operates out of San José from a variety of departure points; for schedules and San José departure points, ☞ Getting Around sections *in* A to Z sections of individual chapters. On longer routes, buses stop midway at inexpensive restaurants. Tickets are sold at the bus station or on the buses themselves. The only way to reserve a seat is to buy your ticket ahead of time and/or get there early. Near the ends of their runs many nonexpress buses turn into large taxis, dropping passengers off one by one once they reach their destinations. To save time, take a *directo* (express bus). Due to frequent schedule changes, it is worthwhile to call the tourist office in San José or the bus company for an update.

WITHIN PANAMA

The widespread use of microbuses means that there is very regular service between most Panamanian towns. Buses depart about every 30 minutes between Changuinola and Almirante, and slightly less frequently between Changuinola and the border with Costa Rica. About five buses a day run between Chiriquí Grande and David, from where buses leave every 20 minutes for the Costa Rican border, Volcán and Cerro Punta, and Boquete. Old "Greyhound" buses leave every hour between David and Panama City; it's a seven-hour trip. Direct service also runs daily between Panama City and Chiriquí Grande, departing Panama City at 5 AM, and Chiriquí Grande at 1 PM, when the ferry arrives from Almirante.

BETWEEN COSTA RICA AND PANAMA

Tica Bus buses leave Panama City daily at noon and arrive in San José at 5 AM the next morning, with buses leaving San José for Panama at 10 PM and arriving the following day at 4 PM. Round-trip fare is about $36. **Panaline** has a new daily luxury express service that departs from the Hotel Cocorí at 2 PM and arrives in Panama City at 6 AM the next day, returning from Panama City at 1 PM and arriving in San José at 3 AM. The round-trip fare is about $42. **Tracopa** buses leave San José daily at 7:30 AM, arriving at David, Panama, at 5:30 PM. From there, buses head on to Panama City, seven hours away. The round-trip fare at is around $14. **Bernardo Fumero** runs a daily bus from San José to Changuinola, in northeast Panama, at 10 AM. Leaving from the Hotel Cocorí, the eight-hour trip costs about $6 (each way).

➤ BUS LINES: **Tica Bus** (✉ C. 9 and Avda. 4, San José, ☎ 507/221–8954). **Panaline** (✉ Hotel Cocorí, C. 14 between Avdas. 5 and 7, ☎ 506/255–1205). **Tracopa** (✉ Avda. 18 and C. 4, ☎ 506/221–4214). **Bernardo Fumero** (Hotel Cocorí, ☞ *above,* ☎ 506/556–1432).

THE GOLD GUIDE / SMART TRAVEL TIPS

BUSINESS HOURS

BANKS

Most of Costa Rica's state banks are open weekdays 9–3. Several branches of Banco Nacional (behind the main post office in San José and in the San José suburb of San Pedro) are open until 6. The growing cadre of private banks tend to keep longer hours. Panamanian banks keep similar hours, though many are also open Saturday mornings.

MUSEUMS

Generalizing about Costa Rican museum opening times is unwise, though most public museums are closed Monday. Most Panamanian museums are open 9–4, Monday–Friday.

SHOPS

Most shops are open weekdays 9–6, though a few older ones still observe the long lunch hour from noon to 2 PM. Most shops open Saturday, though some close at noon. A handful of stores, especially souvenir shops, have Sunday hours.

CAMERAS & COMPUTERS

EQUIPMENT PRECAUTIONS

Always **keep your film, tape, or computer disks out of the sun.** Carry an extra supply of batteries, and **be prepared to turn on your camera, camcorder, or laptop** to prove to security personnel that the device is real. Always **ask for hand inspection of film,** which becomes clouded after successive exposure to airport X-ray machines, and **keep videotapes and computer disks away from metal detectors.**

➤ PHOTO HELP: **Kodak Information Center** (☎ 800/242–2424). **Kodak Guide to Shooting Great Travel Pictures,** available in bookstores or from Fodor's Travel Publications (☎ 800/533–6478; $16.50 plus $4 shipping).

ONLINE ON THE ROAD

➤ INTERNET CAFÉS: **Internet Cafe Costa Rica** (✉ 50 meters west of the Banco Popular, San Pedro, ☎ 283–5375. **Racsa office** (✉ C. 1 at Avda. 5, ☎ 287–0087).

CAR RENTALS

Renting cars is not common among Central American travelers. The reasons are clear: In capital cities, traffic is bad and car theft is rampant (look for guarded parking lots or hotels with lots); in rural areas, roads are often unpaved, muddy, and dotted with potholes; and often the cost of gas can be steep. However, with your own wheels you don't have to worry about unreliable bus schedules, and you have a lot more control over your itinerary and the pace of your trip.

Decide which type of vehicle you want to rent: a *doble-tracción* (four-wheel-drive) vehicle is often essential to reach the more remote parts of Costa Rica, especially during the rainy season. They can cost roughly twice as much as an economy car and should be booked well in advance. Most destinations are easily reached with a standard vehicle. **Reserve several months ahead of time if you plan to rent any kind of vehicle between December 15 and January 3, or during Holy Week.**

Costa Rica has approximately 50 international and local car-rental firms, the larger of which have several offices around San José. There are at least a dozen offices on Paseo Colón, and the most large hotels have representatives. Ads in *The Tico Times* and other publications often offer discounts. Panama has fewer car-rental companies, but rates are often lower than in Costa Rica. For a complete listing, look in local phone directories under *alquiler de automóviles.*

Rates in San José begin at $28 a day and $168 a week for an economy car with air conditioning, a manual transmission, and unlimited mileage. When renting a car in San José, **ask if the price includes the mandatory $15 daily fee for collision insurance.**

➤ MAJOR AGENCIES: **Budget** (☎ 800/527–0700, 0800/181181 in the U.K.). **Dollar** (☎ 800/800–4000, 0990/565656 in the U.K., where it is known as Eurodollar). **Hertz** (☎ 800/654–3001, 800/263–0600 in Canada, 0345/555888 in the U.K., 03/9222–2523 in Australia, 03/358–6777 in New Zealand). **National InterRent** (☎ 800/227–3876, 0345/

222525 in the U.K., where it is known as Europcar InterRent).

➤ OFFICES IN COSTA RICA: **Ada** (☎ 506/233–7733). **Alfa** (☎ 506/233–1537). **Avis** (☎ 506/232–9922). **Budget** (☎ 506/223–3284). **Elegante** (☎ 506/221–0066). **Economy** (☎ 506/232–9130). **Hertz** (☎ 506/223–5959). **National InterRent** (☎ 506/233–4044).

➤ OFFICES IN PANAMA: **Alamo** (☎ 507/260–0822). **Avis** (☎ 507/264–0722). **Budget** (☎ 507/263–8777). **Dollar** (☎ 507/225–3455). **Hertz** (☎ 507/226–7110). **National InterRent** (☎ 507/264–8277).Budget, Dollar, and Hertz have offices in David.

INSURANCE

When driving a rented car you are generally responsible for any damage to or loss of the vehicle. You also are liable for any property damage or personal injury that you may cause while driving. Before you rent, **see what coverage you already have** under the terms of your personal auto-insurance policy and credit cards.

REQUIREMENTS

In both countries your own driver's license is acceptable. You will also need a valid passport and credit card.

SURCHARGES

Before you pick up a car in one city and leave it in another, **ask about drop-off charges or one-way service fees,** which can be substantial. Note, too, that some rental agencies charge extra if you return the car before the time specified in your contract. To avoid a hefty refueling fee, **fill the tank just before you turn in the car,** but be aware that gas stations near the rental outlet may overcharge.

CAR TRAVEL

Driving in a developing nation may be a bit of a challenge, but it's a great way to explore certain regions, especially the Northwest and the Atlantic Zone apart from the Tortuguero Canals. Keep in mind that mountains and poor road conditions make most trips take longer than you would expect. If you want to visit several far-flung areas, domestic flights may be a better option.

AUTO CLUBS

Information**Australian Automobile Association** (☎ 06/247–7311). **Canadian Automobile Association** (CAA, ☎ 613/247–0117). **New Zealand Automobile Association** (☎ 09/377–4660). (In the U.K.)**Automobile Association** (AA, ☎ 0990/500–600); **Royal Automobile Club** (RAC, ☎ 0990/722–722 for membership, 0345/121–345 for insurance). **American Automobile Association** (☎ 800/564–6222).

BETWEEN COSTA RICA AND PANAMA

It possible to drive between Costa Rica and Panama, but it must be done in a private vehicle, since a car rented in one country cannot be taken into the next.

EMERGENCY SERVICES

911 is a nationwide number for accidents. Traffic police are scattered around the country, but Costa Ricans are very good about stopping for people with car trouble. Local car rental companies can provide you with a list of numbers to call in case of accidents or car trouble.

GASOLINE

Gas costs about $1.50 per gallon.

INSURANCE

Don't leave home without valid insurance: This may mean having to insure through a Mexican company.

➤ INSURANCE AGENTS: **Sanborn's** (☎ 210/686–0711), in McAllen, Texas, will write insurance for trips of any length south of the border—talk to "Mexico" Mike Nelson.

PARKING

Car theft is rife in Costa Rica and Panama. Be certain to **park overnight in a locked garage or lot, as Central American insurance may hold you liable if your rental car is stolen.** Most hotels, except for the least expensive, therefore offer secure parking with a guard or locked gates.

ROAD CONDITIONS

Road conditions in Costa Rica are lamentable: you'll run into plenty of potholes and many stretches with no

THE GOLD GUIDE / SMART TRAVEL TIPS

pavement at all. Roads are considerably better in Panama.

RULES OF THE ROAD

There are plenty of would-be Mario Andrettis on Costa Rican and Panamanian highways; **be prepared for harebrained passing on blind corners, tailgating, and failures to signal.** Watch out, too, for two-lane roads that feed into one-lane bridges with specified rights of way. And finally, look out for potholes, even in the smoothest sections of the best roads.

CHILDREN & TRAVEL

FLYING

If your children are two or older, **ask about children's airfares.** As a general rule, infants under two not occupying a seat fly at greatly reduced fares or even for free.

In general the adult baggage allowance applies to children paying half or more of the adult fare. When booking, **ask about carry-on allowances for those traveling with infants.** In general, for babies charged 10% of the adult fare you are allowed one carry-on bag and a collapsible stroller, which may have to be checked; you may be limited to less if the flight is full.

Experts agree that it's a good idea to use safety seats aloft for children weighing less than 40 pounds. Airlines, however, can set their own policies: U.S. carriers allow FAA-approved models but usually require that you buy a ticket, even if your child would otherwise ride free, since the seats must be strapped into regular seats. Airline rules vary, so it's important to **check your airline's policy about using safety seats during takeoff and landing.** Safety seats cannot obstruct the movement of other passengers in the row, so get an appropriate seat assignment as early as possible.

When making your reservation, **request children's meals or a free-standing bassinet** if you need them; the latter are available only to those seated at the bulkhead, where there's enough legroom. Remember, however, that bulkhead seats may not have their own overhead bins, and there's no storage space in front of you—a major inconvenience.

CONSUMER PROTECTION

Whenever possible, **pay with a major credit card** so you can cancel payment or get reimbursed if there's a problem, provided that you have documentation. This is the best way to pay, whether you're buying travel arrangements before your trip or shopping at your destination.

If you're buying a package or tour, always **consider travel insurance** that includes default coverage (☞ Insurance, *below*).

➤ LOCAL BBBs: **Council of Better Business Bureaus** (✉ 4200 Wilson Blvd., Suite 800, Arlington, VA 22203, ☎ 703/276–0100, FAX 703/525–8277).

CRUISE TRAVEL

Cruises are the most restful way of traveling. The U.S.–Panama/Costa Rica cruise season runs September–May, with trips lasting from three days to a week. Your travel agent will be able to give you details of prices, which range from $1,000 to $5,000. Luxury liners equipped with swimming pools and gymnasiums sail from Fort Lauderdale, Florida, to Limón, or through the Panama Canal to Caldera, south of Puntarenas. There are also some cruises that head out of Los Angeles to Caldera, continuing to the canal. Aboard the ship you can sign up for shore excursions and tours. Packages include the cost of flying to the appropriate port in the United States.

➤ CRUISE LINES: **Carnival** (☎ 800/327–9501). **Crystal Cruises** (☎ 800/446–6645). **Cunard** (☎ 800/221–4770). **Holland America** (☎ 800/426–0327), **Ocean Cruise** (☎ 800/556–8850). **Royal Viking** (☎ 800/422–8000). **Seabourn** (☎ 800/351–9595). **Sitmar Cruise** (☎ 305/523–1219). **Sunline** (☎ 800/872–6400).

CUSTOMS & DUTIES

When shopping, **keep receipts** for all of your purchases. Upon reentering the country, **be ready to show customs officials what you've bought.** If you feel a duty is incorrect, appeal the assessment. If you object to the way your clearance was handled, get the inspector's badge number. In either case, first ask to see a supervisor, then write to the appropriate authorities, beginning with the port director at your point of entry.

IN COSTA RICA

Visitors entering Costa Rica may bring in 500 milligrams of tobacco, 3 liters of wine or spirits, 2 kilos of sweets and chocolates, and the equivalent of $100 worth of merchandise. Two cameras, six rolls of film, binoculars, and electrical items for personal use only are also allowed. Customs officials at the international airport rarely examine tourists' luggage. If you enter by land, however, customs officials will probably look through your bags.

IN PANAMA

Visitors entering Panama may bring in 500 cigarettes, 3 liters of wine or spirits, two cameras, and personal electronic equipment. Just as in Costa Rica, luggage revision is a rare occurrence with airport arrivals, but standard procedure at land crossings.

IN AUSTRALIA

Australia residents who are 18 or older may bring back $A400 worth of souvenirs and gifts (including jewelry), 250 cigarettes or 250 grams of tobacco, and 1,125 ml of alcohol (including wine, beer, and spirits). Residents under 18 may bring back $A200 worth of goods.

➤ INFORMATION: **Australian Customs Service** (✉ Regional Director, Box 8, Sydney, NSW 2001, ☎ 02/9213–2000, FAX 02/9213–4000).

IN CANADA

Canadian residents who have been out of Canada for at least seven days may bring in C$500 worth of goods duty-free. If you've been away less than seven days but more than 48 hours, the duty-free allowance drops to C$200; if your trip lasts 24–48 hours, the allowance is C$50. You may not pool allowances with family members. Goods claimed under the C$500 exemption may follow you by mail; those claimed under the lesser exemptions must accompany you. Alcohol and tobacco products may be included in the seven-day and 48-hour exemptions but not in the 24-hour exemption. If you meet the age requirements of the province or territory through which you reenter Canada, you may bring in, duty-free, 1.14 liters (40 imperial ounces) of wine or liquor or 24 12-ounce cans or bottles of beer or ale. If you are 16 or older you may bring in, duty-free, 200 cigarettes and 50 cigars.

You may send an unlimited number of gifts worth up to C$60 each duty-free to Canada. Label the package UNSOLICITED GIFT—VALUE UNDER $60. Alcohol and tobacco are excluded.

➤ INFORMATION: **Revenue Canada** (✉ 2265 St. Laurent Blvd. S, Ottawa, Ontario K1G 4K3, ☎ 613/993–0534, 800/461–9999 in Canada).

IN NEW ZEALAND

Although greeted with a "Haere Mai" ("Welcome to New Zealand"), homeward-bound residents with goods to declare must present themselves for inspection. If you're 17 or older, you may bring back $700 worth of souvenirs and gifts. Your duty-free allowance also includes 4.5 liters of wine or beer; one 1,125-ml bottle of spirits; and either 200 cigarettes, 250 grams of tobacco, 50 cigars, or a combo of all three up to 250 grams.

➤ INFORMATION: **New Zealand Customs** (✉ Custom House, 50 Anzac Ave., Box 29, Auckland, New Zealand, ☎ 09/359–6655).

IN THE U.K.

From countries outside the EU, including Costa Rica and Panama, you may import, duty-free, 200 cigarettes or 50 cigars; 1 liter of spirits or 2 liters of fortified or sparkling wine or liqueurs; 2 liters of still table wine; 60 milliliters of perfume; 250 milliliters of toilet water; plus £136 worth of other goods, including gifts and souvenirs.

➤ INFORMATION: **HM Customs and Excise** (✉ Dorset House, Stamford St., London SE1 9NG, ☎ 0171/202–4227).

IN THE U.S.

U.S. residents may bring home $400 worth of foreign goods duty-free if they've been out of the country for at least 48 hours (and if they haven't used the $400 allowance or any part of it in the past 30 days).

U.S. residents 21 and older may bring back 1 liter of alcohol duty-free. In addition, regardless of your age, you are allowed 200 cigarettes and 100 non-Cuban cigars. Antiques, which the U.S. Customs Service defines as objects more than 100 years old, enter duty-free, as do original works of art done entirely by hand, including paintings, drawings, and sculptures.

You may also send packages home duty-free: up to $200 worth of goods for personal use, with a limit of one parcel per addressee per day (and no alcohol or tobacco products or perfume worth more than $5); label the package PERSONAL USE, and attach a list of its contents and their retail value. Do not label the package UNSOLICITED GIFT, or your duty-free exemption will drop to $100. Mailed items do not affect your duty-free allowance on your return.

➤ INFORMATION: **U.S. Customs Service** (Inquiries, ✉ Box 7407, Washington, DC 20044, ☎ 202/927–6724; complaints, Office of Regulations and Rulings, ✉ 1301 Constitution Ave. NW, Washington, DC 20229; registration of equipment, Resource Management, ✉ 1301 Constitution Ave. NW, Washington, DC 20229, ☎ 202/927–0540).

DINING

Though neither Costa Rican nor Panamanian food compares with the world's great cuisines, both countries have some interesting local dishes well worth trying. There are also plenty of foreign-owned restaurants offering everything from French and Italian to Cantonese and Peruvian cuisine. Eating hours in both Costa Rica and Panama are noon–3 and 7–10.

DISABILITIES & ACCESSIBILITY

ACCESS IN COSTA RICA AND PANAMA

Accessibility in Costa Rica and Panama is extremely limited. Wheelchair ramps are practically nonexistent, and outside major cities, roads are unpaved, making wheelchair travel difficult. Exploring most of the area's attractions involves walking down cobblestone streets and, sometimes, steep trails and muddy paths, though there are some attractions that require little or no walking. Buses are not equipped to carry wheelchairs, so wheelchair users should hire a van to get about and have someone with them to help out. There is a growing awareness of the needs of people with disabilities, and some hotels and attractions in Costa Rica have made the necessary provisions.

➤ LOCAL RESOURCES: **Costa Rican Tourist Institute** (✉ Avda. 4, C. 5 y 7, 11th floor, San José, Costa Rica, ☎ 506/223–1733), known locally as the ICT, has information on accessibility.

MAKING RESERVATIONS

When discussing accessibility with an operator or reservations agent, **ask hard questions.** Are there any stairs, inside *or* out? Are there grab bars next to the toilet *and* in the shower/tub? How wide is the doorway to the room? To the bathroom? For the most extensive facilities meeting the latest legal specifications, **opt for newer accommodations,** which are more likely to have been designed with access in mind. Older buildings or ships may have more limited facilities. Be sure to **discuss your needs before booking.**

TRANSPORTATION

Costa Rica and Panama present serious challenges to travelers with disabilities. Though developed areas, especially San José and the Central Valley, can be managed in a wheelchair, most rural areas are tougher. The tour company *Vaya con Silla de Ruedas* (Go with Wheelchair) provides transportation and guided tours.

➤ TOUR COMPANY: **Vaya con Silla de Ruedas** (✉ Apdo. 1146-2050, San Pedro Montes de Oca, ☎ 225–8561, ℻ 253–0931).

➤ COMPLAINTS: **Disability Rights Section** (✉ U.S. Department of Justice, Civil Rights Division, Box 66738, Washington, DC 20035–6738, ☎ 202/514–0301 or 800/514–0301, TTY 202/514–0383 or 800/

514–0383, FAX 202/307–1198) for general complaints. **Aviation Consumer Protection Division** (☞ Air Travel, *above*) for airline-related problems. **Civil Rights Office** (✉ U.S. Department of Transportation, Departmental Office of Civil Rights, S-30, 400 7th St. SW, Room 10215, Washington, DC 20590, ☎ 202/366–4648, FAX 202/366–9371) for problems with surface transportation.

TRAVEL AGENCIES & TOUR OPERATORS

The travel industry has become more aware of the needs of travelers with disabilities. In the U.S., the Americans with Disabilities Act requires that travel firms serve the needs of all travelers. Note, though, that some agencies and operators specialize in making travel arrangements.

➤ TRAVELERS WITH MOBILITY PROBLEMS: **Access Adventures** (✉ 206 Chestnut Ridge Rd., Rochester, NY 14624, ☎ 716/889–9096), run by a former physical-rehabilitation counselor. **Accessible Journeys** (✉ 35 W. Sellers Ave., Ridley Park, PA 19078, ☎ 610/521–0339 or 800/846–4537, FAX 610/521–6959), for escorted tours exclusively for travelers with mobility impairments. **Flying Wheels Travel** (✉ 143 W. Bridge St., Box 382, Owatonna, MN 55060, ☎ 507/451–5005 or 800/535–6790, FAX 507/451–1685), a travel agency specializing in customized tours and itineraries worldwide. **Hinsdale Travel Service** (✉ 201 E. Ogden Ave., Suite 100, Hinsdale, IL 60521, ☎ 630/325–1335), a travel agency that benefits from the advice of wheelchair traveler Janice Perkins.

DISCOUNTS & DEALS

Be a smart shopper and **compare all your options** before making any choice. A plane ticket bought with a promotional coupon may not be cheaper than the least expensive fare from a discount ticket agency. For high-price travel purchases, such as packages or tours, keep in mind that what you get is just as important as what you save.

CREDIT-CARD BENEFITS

When you use your credit card to make travel purchases you may get free travel-accident insurance, collision-damage insurance, and medical or legal assistance, depending on the card and the bank that issued it. American Express, MasterCard, and Visa provide one or more of these services, so **get a copy of your credit card's travel-benefits policy.** If you are a member of an auto club, always **ask hotel and car-rental reservations agents about auto-club discounts.** Some clubs offer additional discounts on tours, cruises, and admission to attractions.

PACKAGE DEALS

Packages and guided tours can save you money, but don't confuse the two. When you buy a package, your travel remains independent, just as though you had planned and booked the trip yourself. Fly/drive packages, which combine airfare and car rental, are often a good deal.

ECOTOURISM

Ecotourism, green tourism, environmental tourism: these buzzwords and catch phrases have been flying around Costa Rica for well more than a decade. Many of the tour companies currently operating in Costa Rica and Panama have evolved a high level of environmental awareness in their business practices. **Find out whether or not a tour company you're interested in practices "eco-friendly" policies,** such as hiring and training local people as guides, drivers, managers, and office workers; teaching people as much as possible about the plant and animal life, the geography, and the history they are experiencing; controlling the numbers of people allowed daily onto a given site; restoring watersheds or anything else damaged by trail-building, visitors, or overuse; or discouraging wildlife feeding or any other unnatural or disruptive behavior (i.e., making loud noises to scare birds into flight). All of this can mitigate the effects of intense tourism; and, after all, it is better to have a hundred people walking through a forest than to cut the forest down.

There are numerous environmental organizations in Costa Rica and Panama, and most of them are heavily dependent on private donations and dedicated volunteers. To obtain a list of Costa Rican groups that might need a hand and/or donation, consult the *Directorio de Organizaciones, Instituciones y Consultores en El Sector de Recursos Naturales en Costa Rica,* published in Spanish by the Costa Rican Federation for the Preservation of the Environment (FECON). Also, for locally generated advice about ecotourism, consult the *Sustainable Tourism Newsletter,* published by the Eco-Institute of Costa Rica.

➤ ECOTOUR COMPANIES IN COSTA RICA: **Costa Rica Expeditions** (☎ 506/222–0333, FAX 506/257–0766). **Explore Costa Rica** (☎ 506/220–2121). **Horizontes** (☎ 506/222–2022, FAX 506/255–4513). **Tikal Tours** ☎ 506/223–2811, FAX 506/223–1916). **Sun Tours** (☎ 506/255–3418, FAX 506/233–6890). *M/V Temptress* (☎ 506/220–1679, 800/336–8423 in the U.S.) is a 185-ft ship that offers three-day natural-history cruises along the Southern Pacific coast.

➤ ECOTOUR COMPANIES IN PANAMA: **Pesántez Tours** (☎ 507/263–8771). **Ecotours de Panama** (☎ 507/263–3076, FAX 507/263–3089). **Río Monte Ecological Tours** (☎ 507/720–1536, FAX 507/720–2055), in the western province of Chiriquí in Boquete, belongs to the Collins family, which has been involved in ecotourism since long before the term was coined. **Expediciones Tierras Altas** (☎ 507/720–1342, in Boquete, is a small operation offering low-budget nature and hiking tours. **Turtle Divers** (☎ FAX 507/757–9594), in Bocas del Toro, runs tours to dive spots, islands and indigenous communities, and supports environmental education in local schools.

LOCAL ENVIRONMENTAL ORGANIZATIONS

Neotropica Foundation (☎ 506/253–2130). **APREFLOFAS** (☎ 506/240–6087).

ELECTRICITY

The electrical current in Central America, 110 volts (AC), and plugs are the same as in the United States.

GAY & LESBIAN TRAVEL

While harassment of gays and lesbians is infrequent in Costa Rica and Panama, so are public displays of affection—discretion is advised. As a result of its history of tolerance, Costa Rica has attracted many gays from other Latin American nations and, consequently, has a large gay community. Panama, on the other hand, doesn't have as extensive a gay population, but gays who practice a little discretion should encounter no problems there.

➤ LOCAL RESOURCES: **Costa Rica Human Rights Commission** (☎ 506/226–2658 or 506/226–2081) in San José gives legal advice to gays and lesbians who feel their rights have been violated. **Abraxas** (✉ Apartado Postal 1619–4050, Alajuela, Costa Rica) is a gay association that organizes activities every Sunday near Alajuela.

➤ GAY- AND LESBIAN-FRIENDLY TOUR OPERATORS: **Toto Tours** (✉ 1326 W. Albion Ave., Suite 3W, Chicago, IL 60626, ☎ 773/274–8686 or 800/565–1241, FAX 773/274–8695).

➤ GAY- AND LESBIAN-FRIENDLY TRAVEL AGENCIES: **Corniche Travel** (✉ 8721 Sunset Blvd., Suite 200, West Hollywood, CA 90069, ☎ 310/854–6000 or 800/429–8747, FAX 310/659–7441). **Islanders Kennedy Travel** (✉ 183 W. 10th St., New York, NY 10014, ☎ 212/242–3222 or 800/988–1181, FAX 212/929–8530). **Now Voyager** (✉ 4406 18th St., San Francisco, CA 94114, ☎ 415/626–1169 or 800/255–6951, FAX 415/626–8626). **Yellowbrick Road** (✉ 1500 W. Balmoral Ave., Chicago, IL 60640, ☎ 773/561–1800 or 800/642–2488, FAX 773/561–4497). **Skylink Travel and Tour** (✉ 3577 Moorland Ave., Santa Rosa, CA 95407, ☎ 707/585–8355 or 800/225–5759, FAX 707/584–5637), serving lesbian travelers.

HEALTH

ENGLISH-SPEAKING DOCTORS

Many of the doctors at San José's Clinica Biblica speak English well.

➤ LOCAL MEDICAL HELP: **Clinica Biblica** (✉ Avda. 14 at C. 1, San José, ☎ 221–3922).

FOOD & DRINK

Although the Costa Rican and Panamanian food and water supplies are sanitary for the most part, in rural areas there is some risk posed by the contamination of drinking water, fresh fruit, and vegetables by fecal matter, which causes the intestinal ailment known variously as Montezuma's Revenge (traveler's diarrhea), and leptospirosis (another disease borne on contaminated food or water that can be treated by antibiotics if detected early). In remote areas, **watch what you eat.** Stay away from ice, uncooked food, and unpasteurized milk and milk products, and **drink only bottled water** or water that has been boiled for at least 20 minutes. Mild cases may respond to Imodium (known generically as loperamide) or Pepto-Bismol (not as strong), both of which can be purchased over the counter; paregoric, another antidiarrheal agent, requiring a doctor's prescription in Costa Rica. Drink plenty of purified water or tea—chamomile is a good folk remedy. In severe cases, rehydrate yourself with a salt-sugar solution (½ teaspoon salt and 4 tablespoons sugar per quart of water).

MEDICAL PLANS

No one plans to get sick while traveling, but it happens, so **consider signing up with a medical-assistance company.** Members get doctor referrals, emergency evacuation or repatriation, 24-hour telephone hot lines for medical consultation, cash for emergencies, and other personal and legal assistance. Coverage varies, so **review the benefits of each carefully.**

➤ MEDICAL-ASSISTANCE COMPANIES: **International SOS Assistance** (✉ 8 Neshaminy Interplex, Suite 207, Trevose, PA 19053, ☎ 215/245–4707 or 800/523–6586, FAX 215/244–9617; ✉ 12 Chemin Riantbosson, 1217 Meyrin 1, Geneva, Switzerland, ☎ 4122/785–6464, FAX 4122/785–6424; ✉ 10 Anson Rd., 14-07/08 International Plaza, Singapore, 079903, ☎ 65/226–3936, FAX 65/226–3937).

SHOTS & MEDICATIONS

According to the Centers for Disease Control (CDC), there is a limited risk of malaria, hepatitis A and B, dengue fever, typhoid fever, and rabies in Central America. Travelers in most urban or easily accessible areas need not worry. However, if you plan to visit remote regions or stay for more than six weeks, check with the CDC's International Travelers Hotline (☞ Health Warnings, *below*). In areas with malaria and dengue, both of which are carried by mosquitoes, **take mosquito nets, wear clothing that covers the body, apply repellent containing DEET, and use a spray against flying insects in living and sleeping areas.** Mild repellents, such as those contained in certain skin softeners, are not adequate for the intense levels of mosquito activity that occur in the hot, humid regions of the Atlantic Lowlands. Also, note that perfume, after-shave, and other body lotions and potions can attract mosquitoes. The CDC recommends chloroquine (analen) as an antimalarial agent; no vaccine exists against dengue.

Though dengue and malaria are less of a problem in Panama, the threat of infection exists there as well, especially in the country's western and eastern extremes and along the Atlantic coast. The threat of malaria is the worst during the May to mid-December rainy season.

Children traveling to Central America should have current inoculations against measles, mumps, rubella, and polio.

➤ HEALTH WARNINGS: **National Centers for Disease Control** (✉ CDC, National Center for Infectious Diseases, Division of Quarantine, Traveler's Health Section, 1600 Clifton Rd. NE, M/S E-03, Atlanta, GA 30333, ☎ 404/332–4559, FAX 404/332–4565).

HOLIDAYS

National holidays are known as *feriados;* Costa Rica has 15 each year, and Panama has 11. On these days government offices, banks, and post offices are closed, and public transport is restricted. Religious festivals are characterized by colorful processions. Panama's annual carnival celebrations feature some spectacular costumes.

January 1: New Year's Day; January 9: Day of the Martyrs (Panama only); March 19: St. Joseph's Day (San José's patron saint—Costa Rica only); February 16: Shrove Tuesday, Carnival Tuesday (Panama); April 2–4: Good Friday–Easter Sunday; April 11: Anniversary of Battle of Rivas (Costa Rica); May 1: Labor Day; July 25: Annexation of Guanacaste (Costa Rica); August 2: Virgin of Los Angeles (Costa Rica's patron saint); August 15: Mother's Day (Costa Rica); September 15: Independence Day (Costa Rica); October 12: Columbus Day (Día de la Raza); November 3: Independence from Colombia (Panama); November 10: Call for Independence (Panama); November 28: Independence from Spain (Panama); December 8: Immaculate Conception; December 25: Christmas.

INSURANCE

Travel insurance is the best way to **protect yourself against financial loss.** The most useful plan is a comprehensive policy that includes coverage for trip cancellation and interruption, default, trip delay, and medical expenses (with a waiver for preexisting conditions).

Without insurance, you will lose all or most of your money if you cancel your trip, regardless of the reason. Default insurance covers you if your tour operator, airline, or cruise line goes out of business. Trip-delay covers unforeseen expenses that you may incur due to bad weather or mechanical delays. It's important to compare the fine print regarding trip-delay coverage when comparing policies.

For overseas travel, one of the most important components of travel insurance is its medical coverage. Supplemental health insurance will pick up the cost of your medical bills should you get sick or injured while traveling. U.S. residents should note that Medicare generally does not cover health-care costs outside the United States, nor do many privately issued policies. Residents of the United Kingdom can buy an annual travel-insurance policy valid for most vacations taken during the year in which the coverage is purchased. If you are pregnant or have a preexisting condition, make sure you're covered. British citizens should buy extra medical coverage when traveling overseas, according to the Association of British Insurers. Australian travelers should buy travel insurance, including extra medical coverage, whenever they go abroad, according to the Insurance Council of Australia.

Always **buy travel insurance directly from the insurance company;** if you buy it from a cruise line, airline, or tour operator that goes out of business you probably will not be covered for the agency or operator's default, a major risk. Before you make any purchase, **review your existing health and home-owner's policies** to find out whether they cover expenses incurred while traveling.

➤ TRAVEL INSURERS: In the U.S., **Access America** (✉ 6600 W. Broad St., Richmond, VA 23230, ☎ 804/285–3300 or 800/284–8300). **Travel Guard International** (✉ 1145 Clark St., Stevens Point, WI 54481, ☎ 715/345–0505 or 800/826–1300). In Canada, **Mutual of Omaha** (✉ Travel Division, 500 University Ave., Toronto, Ontario M5G 1V8, ☎ 416/598–4083, 800/268–8825 in Canada).

➤ INSURANCE INFORMATION: In the U.K., **Association of British Insurers** (✉ 51 Gresham St., London EC2V 7HQ, ☎ 0171/600–3333). In Australia, the **Insurance Council of Australia** (☎ 613/9614–1077, FAX 613/9614–7924).

LANGUAGE

Spanish is the official language of both Costa Rica and Panama, although some people speak English, especially along the Caribbean coast. Your stay in Central America will be much better if you learn some basic Spanish before you go and bring a phrase book with you. At the very least, attempt to **learn the rudiments of polite conversation—such phrases as *por favor* (please) and *gracias* (thank you) are sure to be appreciated.**

LANGUAGES FOR TRAVELERS

A phrase book and language tape set can help get you started.

➤ PHRASE BOOKS AND LANGUAGE-TAPE SETS: *Languages for Travelers: Fodor's Spanish for Travelers* (audio set; $16.95, $23.50 Canada; U.S. 800/733–4247, Canada 800/668–4247, international 212/572–6045; Fodor's Web site: www.fodors.com).

LODGING

Hotels are going up fast in Costa Rica, to keep pace with the country's growing popularity as a vacation destination. Development is moving more slowly in Panama, which is still a fairly unknown destination. For Costa Rica's popular beach and mountain resorts, Panama City's best hotels, and the Chiriquí highlands, **reserve well in advance for the dry season** (mid-December–April)—you'll need to give credit card information or send a deposit to confirm the reservation. During the rainy season—May to mid-December—most hotels drop their rates considerably, which sometimes puts them into a lower price category.

Luxury international hotels are found mainly in San José and Panama City. Many visitors will prefer the smaller one-of-a-kind hotels in colonial bungalows with verdant courtyards; these are numerous in and around San José. Except for the northwest beaches of Guanacaste's "Gold Coast," where a number of large-scale projects have recently been completed or are in the works, lodging in outlying areas is often in *cabinas* (cabins) or *cabañas*, as they are called in Panama—rustic equivalents of U.S. motels (motels here, by the way, are mostly short-stay sex hotels). Cabinas range from very basic huts with few creature comforts to flashier units with all the modern conveniences. In Costa Rica, there are nature lodges (often within private biological reserves) that cater to naturalist vacationers. Though most of these lodges have only rustic accommodations, a few of the newer ones are luxurious. Some national parks have campsites with facilities.

APARTMENT & VILLA RENTALS

If you want a home base that's roomy enough for a family and comes with cooking facilities, **consider a furnished rental.** These can save you money, especially if you're traveling with a large group of people. Home-exchange directories list rentals (often second homes owned by prospective house swappers), and some services search for a house or apartment for you (even a castle if that's your fancy) and handle the paperwork. Some send an illustrated catalog; others send photographs only of specific properties, sometimes at a charge. Up-front registration fees may apply.

➤ RENTAL AGENTS: **Europa-Let/Tropical Inn-Let** (✉ 92 N. Main St., Ashland, OR 97520, ☎ 541/482–5806 or 800/462–4486, FAX 541/482–0660). **Property Rentals International** (✉ 1008 Mansfield Crossing Rd., Richmond, VA 23236, ☎ 804/378–6054 or 800/220–3332, FAX 804/379–2073). **Rent-a-Home International** (✉ 7200 34th Ave. NW, Seattle, WA 98117, ☎ 206/789–9377 or 800/488–7368, FAX 206/789–9379). **Vacation Home Rentals Worldwide** (✉ 235 Kensington Ave., Norwood, NJ 07648, ☎ 201/767–9393 or 800/633–3284, FAX 201/767–5510). **Villas and Apartments Abroad** (✉ 420 Madison Ave., Suite 1003, New York, NY 10017, ☎ 212/759–1025 or 800/433–3020, FAX 212/755–8316). **Villas International** (✉ 950 Northgate Dr., Suite 206, San Rafael, CA 94903, ☎ 415/499–9490 or 800/221–2260, FAX 415/499–9491). **Hideaways International** (✉ 767 Islington St., Portsmouth, NH 03801, ☎ 603/430–4433 or 800/843–4433, FAX 603/430–4444; membership $99) is a club for travelers who arrange rentals among themselves.

B&BS

There is an overabundance of B&Bs in San José, many set in former homes in the historic Amon and Otoya neighborhoods (☞ Chapter 2).

CAMPING

Many, though not all, national parks have camping areas. Some of the popular beaches have private camping areas with bathrooms and showers. If you camp on the beach or in other unguarded areas, **don't leave belongings unattended in your tent.**

HOSTELS

No matter what your age, you can **save on lodging costs by staying at hostels.** In some 5,000 locations in more than 70 countries around the world, Hostelling International (HI), the umbrella group for a number of national youth hostel associations, offers single-sex, dorm-style beds and, at many hostels, "couples" rooms and family accommodations. Membership in any HI national hostel association, open to travelers of all ages, allows you to stay in HI-affiliated hostels at member rates (one-year membership is about $25 for adults; hostels run about $10–$25 per night). Members also have priority if the hostel is full; they're eligible for discounts around the world, even on rail and bus travel in some countries.

➤ HOSTEL ORGANIZATIONS: **Hostelling International—American Youth Hostels** (✉ 733 15th St. NW, Suite 840, Washington, DC 20005, ☎ 202/783–6161, FAX 202/783–6171). **Hostelling International—Canada** (✉ 400-205 Catherine St., Ottawa, Ontario K2P 1C3, ☎ 613/237–7884, FAX 613/237–7868). **Youth Hostel Association of England and Wales** (✉ Trevelyan House, 8 St. Stephen's Hill, St. Albans, Hertfordshire AL1 2DY, ☎ 01727/855215 or 01727/845047, FAX 01727/844126); membership in the U.S. $25, in Canada C$26.75, in the U.K. £9.30.

HOTELS

There are a few big hotels found on the outskirts of San José and on some of the more popular beaches, but most of them are smaller, offering more personalized service. Remember that most hotels drop their rates during the "green season," from May to December.

NATURE LODGES

Since Mother Nature's wonders are Costa Rica's biggest attractions, it should come as no surprise that there is an abundance of nature lodges offering guests an ecologically educational experience.

MAIL

Mail from the States or Europe can take two–three weeks to arrive in Costa Rica or Panama (occasionally it never does); within these countries, mail service is even less reliable. Outgoing mail is marginally quicker, especially when sent from the capitals. **Always use airmail for overseas cards and letters;** delivery may take anywhere from five days to two weeks or more. Mail theft is a chronic problem, so **do not mail checks, money, or anything else of value.**

POSTAL RATES

Rates are low; letters sent from Costa Rica to the United States and Canada cost just 50 colones; to the United Kingdom, 60 colones. Letters sent from Panama to the United States cost 35¢; to Canada 40¢; to the United Kingdom, 45¢.

RECEIVING MAIL

You can have mail sent to your hotel or use poste restante at the post office (Lista de Correos). Most Costa Ricans and Panamanians have to go to the post office to pick up their mail, because of the absence of both street names and any house-to-house service. *Apartado* (abbreviated *apdo.*) means post-office box.

Anyone with an American Express card or traveler's checks can have mail sent to them at the American Express offices in San José and Panama City.

A faster and more functional alternative for nonpersonal letters, particularly those confirming reservations and the like, is the fax machine, which is nearly ubiquitous in Costa Rica and Panama.

If you need to send important documents, checks, or other noncash valuables, you can use one of the courier services, such as Federal Express, DHL, or one of the less expensive airline courier services.

MONEY

COSTS

Here is an approximation of what costs what in Costa Rica: Bottle of Coca-Cola, 200–300 colones; cup of coffee, 150–250 colones; bottle of beer, 250–400 colones; sandwich, 500–900 colones; daily U.S. newspaper, 300–600 colones.

CREDIT & DEBIT CARDS

Major credit cards are accepted at most of the larger hotels and more expensive restaurants in both countries. As the phone system improves and expands, many budget hotels, restaurants, and other facilities are accepting credit cards. Still, **don't count on using plastic**—it is essential, especially when traveling away from San José and Panama City, to **carry enough cash or traveler's checks** for the many businesses without phones or credit-card capabilities. Also, some hotels, restaurants, tour companies, and other businesses will give you a 5%–15% discount if you pay cash.

Should you use a credit card or a debit card when traveling? Both have benefits. A credit card allows you to delay payment and gives you certain rights as a consumer (☞ Consumer Protection, *above*). A debit card, also known as a check card, deducts funds directly from your checking account and helps you stay within your budget. When you want to rent a car, though, you may still need an old-fashioned credit card. Although you can always *pay* for your car with a debit card, some agencies will not allow you to *reserve* a car with a debit card.

Otherwise, the two types of plastic are virtually the same. Both will get you cash advances at ATMs worldwide if your card is properly programmed with your personal identification number (PIN). For use in Costa Rica, your PIN must be four digits long.) Both offer excellent, wholesale exchange rates. And both protect you against unauthorized use if the card is lost or stolen. Your liability is limited to $50, as long as you report the card missing.

CURRENCY

All prices in this guide are quoted in U.S. dollars, due to the following:

The Costa Rican currency is the colón (plural: colones). However, the colón is subject to continual, small devaluations; at press time (spring 1998), the colón had topped 260 to the dollar and was still rising.

Panama's national currency is the balboa, which has been out of print for decades—they use the U.S. dollar instead, and simply call it a balboa. The Panamanian government mints its own coins, which are the same size as U.S. coins, and circulate together with their American counterparts. Since the dollar is currency, and traveler's checks are accepted by most businesses, there is little need to go to the bank. Carry lots of $10 and $20 bills; the abundance of counterfeit dollars has caused many businesses to stop accepting $50 and $100 bills.

EXCHANGING MONEY

For the most favorable rates, **change money through banks.** Although fees charged for ATM transactions may be higher abroad than at home, Cirrus and Plus exchange rates are excellent, because they are based on wholesale rates offered only by major banks. You won't do as well at exchange booths in airports or rail and bus stations, in hotels, in restaurants, or in stores, although you may find their hours more convenient. To avoid lines at airport exchange booths, **get a bit of local currency before you leave home.** It's best to **avoid people on the city streets who offer to change money:** Most of the guys who change money at the airport are legit, thought they might not be above shortchanging you. The money changers in the streets of San José are notorious for shortchanging people and passing counterfeit bills.

➤ EXCHANGE SERVICES: **Chase *Currency To Go*** (☎ 800/935–9935; 935–9935 in NY, NJ, and CT). **International Currency Express** (☎ 888/842–0880 on the East Coast, 888/278–6628 on the West Coast). **Thomas Cook Currency Services** (☎ 800/287–7362 for telephone orders and retail locations).

GETTING CASH

In San José the Banco Popular near the National Theater and the Parque Central has several 24-hour access ATMs which at press time gave cash advances—in colones—on Visa cards utilizing American PINs. Cash advances are also available through the Credomatic office, on Calle Central between Avenidas 3 and 5, or the Banco de San José, across the street, which also has an American Express office on the third floor.

There are ATMs connected to the Cirrus system all over San José and the Central Valley, as well as in most other cities—Liberia, Puerto Limón, San Isidro—at branches of the Banco de San José. The Plus system is less prevalent, but can be found outside San José, at branches of the Banco Popular.

In Panama, the Banco del Istmo, which has branches in Changuinola and David, gives cash advances on MasterCard and Visa.

➤ ATM LOCATIONS: **Cirrus** (☎ 800/424–7787). **Plus** (☎ 800/843–7587) for locations in the U.S. and Canada, or visit your local bank.

➤ REPORTING LOST CARDS: **American Express** (☎ 336/393–1111 collect to U.S.). **Diners Club** (☎ 303/799–1504 collect to U.S.). **Mastercard** (☎ 0800/011–0184 toll-free to U.S.). **Visa** (☎ 0800/011–0030 toll-free to U.S.; ☎ 410/581–9994 collect to U.S.).

TRAVELER'S CHECKS

Do you need traveler's checks? It depends on where you're headed. If you're going to rural areas and small towns, go with cash; traveler's checks are best used in cities. Lost or stolen checks can usually be replaced within 24 hours. To ensure a speedy refund, buy your own traveler's checks—don't let someone else pay for them: irregularities like this can cause delays. The person who bought the checks should make the call to request a refund.

Travelers who have an American Express card and money in a U.S. checking account can purchase traveler's checks at the American Express office in San José, or Panama City; there's a 1% service charge.

OUTDOOR ACTIVITIES & SPORTS

BIKING

Although much of this region is mountainous, there are also many ideal-for-cycling flatlands in Costa Rica. A number of Costa Rican companies currently offer mountain-biking tours out of San José; tours range in length from a single day to a week. In La Fortuna de San Carlos, Desafío rents bikes and offers guided tours. You can also hire your own bicycles in most Costa Rican and Panamanian mountain and beach resorts.

➤ BIKE TOUR OPERATORS: **Costaricabike** (☎ 506/224–0899). **Desafío** (☎ 506/479–9464). (☎ 202/647–0518). **Dos Montañas** (☎ 506/233–6455).

BIRD-WATCHING

➤ BIRD-WATCHING TOUR OPERATORS: **Horizontes** (☎ 506/222–2022). **Costa Rica Expeditions** (☎ 506/222–0333). **Ecotours de Panama** (☎ 507/263–3079). **Pesántez Tours** (☎ 507/263–8771).

WATER SPORTS

Costa Rica and Panama are worth visiting for their water-sports' opportunities alone. Wild rivers provide plenty of white water for rafting, and Costa Rica's Lake Arenal is acclaimed as one of the best places in the world to windsurf. Skin diving excursions are available out of Costa Rica's Drake Bay, Flamingo, Ocotal, and Playa del Coco. The country's best dive spot, Cocos Island, can be visited on 10-day scuba safaris on the *Okeanos Aggressor* and the *Undersea Hunter*. Panama has even more diving options, and with plenty of dive centers at Caribbean and Pacific locations.

➤ DIVE OPERATORS: **Bill Beard's Diving Safaris** (☎ 506/672–0012). **El Ocotal Diving Safaris** (☎ 506/222–4259). *Okeanos Aggressor* (☎ 506/232–6672). *Undersea Hunter* (☎ 506/228–6535). **Turtle Divers** (☎ 507/757–9594) leads dives in Panama's Bocas del Toro. **Captain Morgan's** (☎ 507/250–4029), on Contadora, organizes dives around the Pacific's Pearl Islands. **Scuba Panama** (☎ 507/261–3841) can arrange scuba safaris off either coast in a 65-ft yacht. *See* regional sections for details.

➤ RAFTING OUTFITTERS: **Aventuras Naturales** (☎ 506/225–3939). **Costa Rica Expeditions** (☎ 506/222–0333). **Ríos Tropicales** (☎ 506/233–6455). **Chiriquí River Rafting** (☎ 507/236–5217) runs two rivers, a class III and a class IV, in western Panama.

➤ WINDSURFING OUTFITTERS: **Tilawa** (☎ 506/695–5050) on Lake Arenal is a windsurfing specialist.

PACKING

LUGGAGE

How many carry-on bags you can bring with you is up to the airline. Most allow two, but the limit is often reduced to one on certain flights. Gate agents will take excess baggage—including bags they deem oversize—from you as you board and add it to checked luggage. To avoid this situation, make sure that everything you carry aboard will fit under your seat. Also, get to the gate early, and request a seat at the back of the plane; you'll probably board first, while the overhead bins are still empty. Since big, bulky baggage attracts the attention of gate agents and flight attendants on a busy flight, make sure your carry-on is really a carry-on. Finally, a carry-on that's long and narrow is more likely to remain unnoticed than one that's wide and squarish.

On international flights, baggage allowances may be determined not by piece but by weight—generally 88 pounds (40 kilograms) in first class, 66 pounds (30 kilograms) in business class, and 44 pounds (20 kilograms) in economy.

Airline liability for baggage is limited to $1,250 per person on flights within the United States. On international flights it amounts to $9.07 per pound or $20 per kilogram for checked baggage (roughly $640 per 70-pound bag) and $400 per passenger for unchecked baggage. You can buy additional coverage at check-in for about $10 per $1,000 of coverage, but it excludes a rather extensive list of items, shown on your airline ticket.

Before departure, **itemize your bags' contents** and their worth, and label the bags with your name, address, and phone number. (If you use your home address, cover it so that potential thieves can't see it readily.) Inside each bag, **pack a copy of your itinerary**. At check-in, **make sure that each bag is correctly tagged** with the destination airport's three-letter code. If your bags arrive damaged or fail to arrive at all, file a written report with the airline before leaving the airport.

PACKING LIST

Pack light: Bring comfortable, hand-washable clothing. T-shirts and shorts are acceptable near the beach and in heavily touristed areas. Loose-fitting long-sleeve shirts and pants are good in smaller towns (where immodest attire is frowned upon) and to protect your skin from the ferocious sun and mosquitoes. **Bring a large hat to block the sun from your face and neck.** Pack a light sweater or jacket for cool nights, early mornings, and trips up volcanoes; you'll need even more warm clothes if you plan on descending Chirripó or Barú Volcano, or spend a night in San Gerardo de Dota or La Providencia. Sturdy sneakers or hiking boots are essential for sightseeing and hiking. Waterproof hiking sandals or other footwear that lets your feet breathe are good for strolling about town, and also for beach walking, fording streams, and navigating the myriad mud holes you'll find on rain and cloud forest trails.

Insect repellent, sunscreen, sunglasses, and umbrellas (during the rainy season) are musts. Other handy items—especially if you will be traveling on your own or camping—include toilet paper, facial tissues, a plastic water bottle, and a flashlight (for occasional power outages or use at campsites). Snorkelers should consider bringing their own equipment unless traveling light is a priority, though gear can be rented at most beach resorts. Some beaches, such as Playa Grande, do not have shade trees, so if you're planning a stay at the beach you might consider investing in a stirdy, shade-making tarpaulin. For long-term stays in remote rural areas, *see* Health, *above*.

In your carry-on luggage **bring an extra pair of eyeglasses or contact lenses** and **enough of any medication you take** to last the entire trip. You may also want your doctor to write a spare prescription using the drug's generic name, since brand names may vary from country to country. **Never put prescription drugs or valuables in luggage to be checked.** To avoid customs delays, carry medications in their original packaging. And don't forget to copy down and carry addresses of offices that handle refunds of lost traveler's checks.

PASSPORTS & VISAS

Carry a passport even if you don't need one (it's always the best form of I.D.), and make **two photocopies of the data page** (one for someone at home and another for you, carried separately from your passport). If you lose your passport, promptly call the nearest embassy or consulate and the local police.

ON ARRIVAL

U.S. CITIZENS

Although U.S. citizens do not need a valid passport to enter Costa Rica for stays of up to 30 days—you can enter using a Tourist Card if you have a photo ID and a copy of your birth certificate—we recommend that you **bring your passport**: for passage from Costa Rica into Panama, for emergencies, for longer stays, and because it is the most recognizable form of identification for changing money, renting hotel rooms, or any other transaction. U.S. citizens with valid passports are allowed to stay in Costa Rica for 90 days, after which they must leave for at least 72 hours.

A valid passport is needed to visit Panama, either with a visa issued by a Panamanian embassy or consulate (free of charge) or on a tourist card that can be purchased at the border, airport or the tourist board offices in Paso Canoas and Sixaola (cost $5). In Costa Rica, you can get a visa from the Panamanian Consul, 350 North of the Centro Colon in western San José (☎ 202/256–8160); you'll need a round-trip ticket and photocopy of the photo page of your passport; drop it off on a weekday morning, and it will be ready the next workday.

AUSTRALIAN AND NEW ZEALAND CITIZENS

Citizens of Australia and New Zealand need only a valid passport to enter Costa Rica for stays of up to 30 days (once in the country, you can go to the Migracion office in La Uruca and get it extended to 90 days). A 30-day visa for Panama can be purchased

for US$10 at a Panamanian consulate (☞ U.S. Citizens, *above*). Tourist cards, also good for 30 days, can be purchased for $5 at the border, airport, Paso Canoas, or Sixaola.

CANADIANS

You need only a valid passport to enter Costa Rica for stays of up to 90 days. A 30-day visa for Panama can be purchased for $10 U.S. at a Panamanian consulate (☞ U.S. Citizens, *above*). Tourist cards, also good for 30 days, can be purchased for $5 at the border, airport, Paso Canoas, or Sixaola.

U.K. CITIZENS

Citizens of the United Kingdom need only a valid passport to enter Costa Rica for up to 90 days, and to enter Panama for stays of up to 30 days.

PASSPORT OFFICES

➤ Australian Citizens: **Australian Passport Office** (☎ 131–232).

➤ Canadian Citizens: **Passport Office** (☎ 819/994–3500 or 800/567–6868).

➤ New Zealand Citizens: **New Zealand Passport Office** (☎ 04/494–0700 for information on how to apply, 0800/727–776 for information on applications already submitted).

➤ U.K. Citizens: **London Passport Office** (☎ 0990/21010), for fees and documentation requirements and to request an emergency passport.

➤ U.S. Citizens: **National Passport Information Center** (☎ 900/225–5674; calls are charged at 35¢ per minute for automated service, $1.05 per minute for operator service).

SENIOR-CITIZEN TRAVEL

To qualify for age-related discounts, **mention your senior-citizen status up front** when booking hotel reservations (not when checking out) and before you're seated in restaurants (not when paying the bill). Note that discounts may be limited to certain menus, days, or hours. When renting a car, **ask about promotional car-rental discounts,** which can be cheaper than senior-citizen rates.

➤ Adventures: **Overseas Adventure Travel** (✉ Grand Circle Corporation,

625 Mt. Auburn St., Cambridge, MA 02138, ☎ 617/876–0533 or 800/221–0814, FAX 617/876–0455).

➤ EDUCATIONAL PROGRAMS: **Elderhostel** (✉ 75 Federal St., 3rd floor, Boston, MA 02110, ☎ 617/426–8056). **Interhostel** (✉ University of New Hampshire, 6 Garrison Ave., Durham, NH 03824, ☎ 603/862–1147 or 800/733–9753, FAX 603/862–1113).

SHOPPING

Some of the most popular handicrafts are made from the country's varied hardwoods: everything from jewelry boxes to salad bowls, decorative fruit, statues, and miniature oxcarts. You can also pick up some nice leather goods, ceramics, rope hammocks, jewelry, an array of T-shirts and, of course, coffee.

STUDENT TRAVEL

Central America is a fantastic place for students and youths on a budget. Although prices are on the rise in Costa Rica, it is still possible to travel on $20 a day. There are youth hostels all over Costa Rica, and though Panama lacks hostels, it has its share of inexpensive hotels. One of the cheapest ways to spend the night is camping. As long as you have your own tent, it's easy to set up camp anywhere. (If it looks like you're near someone's home, it's always a good idea to inquire first.) Central America is popular with adventurous backpackers, so you'll have no problem hooking up with other like-minded travelers in major cities or along popular travel routes. To get good tips and advice on traveling within a budget, chat with other backpackers.

STUDYING ABROAD

The University of Costa Rica has exchange programs with at least half a dozen U.S. universities, the oldest of which is the University of Kansas program. Many of the private language institutes offer Spanish courses for college credit.

TRAVEL AGENCIES

To save money, **look into deals available through student-oriented travel agencies.** To qualify you'll need a bona fide student I.D. card. Members of international student groups are also eligible.

➤ STUDENT I.D.s & SERVICES: **Council on International Educational Exchange** (CIEE, ✉ 205 E. 42nd St., 14th floor, New York, NY 10017, ☎ 212/822–2600 or 888/268–6245, FAX 212/822–2699), for mail orders only, in the United States. **Travel Cuts** (✉ 187 College St., Toronto, Ontario M5T 1P7, ☎ 416/979–2406 or 800/667–2887) in Canada.

TAXES

A $16.50 airport tax is payable on departure from the José Santamaría Airport. Individuals may offer to sell the exit stamp to departing tourists as they climb out of taxis and buses. Look for properly displayed credentials, and **make sure you get the appropriate stamp in exchange for your dollars or colones.** The Panamanian airport tax is $20, which must be paid at a booth in the Tocumen International Airport, near Panama City.

TELEPHONES

The Costa Rican and Panamanian phone systems are very good by Third World standards. Calls within the country are also very cheap, but you will pay more if you use a hotel's phone, and more still from your room. Many hotels now have fax machines. In rural areas, where pay phones don't exist as such, **look for the yellow TELÉFONO PÚBLICO signs,** indicating phones from which you can make calls for the same rates as pay phones. You will often find them in the village *pulpería* (grocery).

COUNTRY CODES

The country code for Costa Rica is 506; for Panama, 507. We list these codes only in chapters with both Costa Rican and Panamanian phone numbers.

DIRECTORY & OPERATOR INFORMATION

Call ☎ 113 for domestic directory inquiries in Costa Rica, ☎ 102 in Panama, and ☎ 110 for domestic collect calls in Costa Rica.

INTERNATIONAL CALLS

The *guía telefónica* (phone book) contains numbers for various services as well as rates for calling different countries. To call overseas direct, dial 00, then the country code (1 for the United States and Canada, 44 for Great Britain), the area code, and the number. It is more expensive to phone from your hotel. Calls through the operator are more than twice as expensive, the only advantage being that if the person you need to speak to isn't in, there is no charge even if somebody answers. Discount times for calling the United States and Canada are weekdays 10 PM–7 AM and weekends; for calling the United Kingdom the only discounted time is between Friday at 10 PM and Monday at 7 AM.

AT&T, MCI, and Sprint international access codes make calling the United States relatively convenient, but you may find the local access number blocked in many hotel rooms. First ask the hotel operator to connect you. If the hotel operator balks, ask for an international operator, or dial the international operator yourself. One way to improve your odds of getting connected to your long-distance carrier is to travel with more than one company's calling card (a hotel may block Sprint, for example, but not MCI). If all else fails, call from a pay phone in the hotel lobby.

➤ ACCESS CODES: **AT&T Direct** (☎ 0800/011–4114, 800/435–0812 for other areas). **MCI WorldPhone** (☎ 0800/012–2222, 800/444–4141 for other areas). **Sprint International Access** (☎ 0800/013–0123, 800/877–4646 for other areas).

➤ TELEPHONE OFFICES: ICE (✉ Avda. 2 between C. 1 and 3), open daily 7 AM–11 PM, is the best place to make international calls and to send faxes in San José. **Radiográfica Costarricense** (✉ Avda. 5 between C. 1 and 3), open daily 7 AM–10 PM, also has phone, fax, and Internet facilities. **INTEL** (✉ C. Manuel María Icaza, 100 m south of the Vía España), open daily 8 AM–10 PM, is the phone office of choice in Panama City.

PUBLIC PHONES

There are two types of public phones in Costa Rica: those which accept change—10 or 20 colón coins—and those that require calling cards, which are sold at a variety of stores. Either phone can be used for direct service with a U.S. operator.

TIPPING

Meal prices range enormously from the *sodas* (cafés) to the sophisticated restaurants of San José and Panama City. In Costa Rican restaurants, a 13% tax and 10% service charge is added to the prices on the menu, so additional gratuity is not expected, though if the service is good, it's nice to leave something extra. In Panamanian restaurants, only the 5% tax is added, which means you are expected to leave at least 10% gratuity.

TOUR OPERATORS

Buying a prepackaged tour or independent vacation can make your trip to Costa Rica or Panama less expensive and more hassle-free. Because everything is prearranged, you'll spend less time planning.

Operators that handle several hundred thousand travelers per year can use their purchasing power to give you a good price. Their high volume may also indicate financial stability. But some small companies provide more personalized service; because they tend to specialize, they may also be more knowledgeable about a given area.

BOOKING WITH AN AGENT

Travel agents are excellent resources. In fact, large operators accept bookings made only through travel agents. But it's a good idea to **collect brochures from several agencies,** because some agents' suggestions may be influenced by relationships with tour and package firms that reward them for volume sales. If you have a special interest, **find an agent with expertise in that area;** ASTA (☞ Travel Agencies, *below*) has a database of specialists worldwide.

Make sure your travel agent knows the accommodations and other services. Ask about the hotel's location, room size, beds, and whether it has a pool, room service, or programs for children, if you care about these. Has your agent been there in person or sent others you can contact?

Do some homework on your own, too: Local tourism boards can provide information about lesser-known and small-niche operators, some of which may sell only direct.

BUYER BEWARE

Each year consumers are stranded or lose their money when tour operators—even very large ones with excellent reputations—go out of business. So **check out the operator.** Find out how long the company has been in business, and ask several travel agents about its reputation. If the package or tour you are considering is priced lower than in your wildest dreams, **be skeptical.** Try to **book with a company that has a consumer-protection program.** If the operator has such a program, you'll find information about it in the company's brochure. If the operator you are considering does not offer some kind of consumer protection, then ask for references from satisfied customers.

In the U.S., members of the National Tour Association and United States Tour Operators Association are required to set aside funds to cover your payments and travel arrangements in case the company defaults. It's also a good idea to choose a company that participates in the American Society of Travel Agent's Tour Operator Program (TOP). This gives you a forum if there are any disputes between you and your tour operator; ASTA will act as mediator.

➤ TOUR-OPERATOR RECOMMENDATIONS: **American Society of Travel Agents** (☞ Travel Agencies, *below*). **National Tour Association** (NTA, ✉ 546 E. Main St., Lexington, KY 40508, ☎ 606/226–4444 or 800/ 755–8687). **United States Tour Operators Association** (USTOA, ✉ 342 Madison Ave., Suite 1522, New York, NY 10173, ☎ 212/599–6599 or 800/468–7862, FAX 212/599– 6744).

COSTS

The more your package or tour includes, the better you can predict the ultimate cost of your vacation. Make sure you know exactly what is covered, and **beware of hidden costs.** Are taxes, tips, and service charges included? Transfers and baggage handling? Entertainment and excursions? These can add up.

Prices for packages and tours are usually quoted per person, based on two sharing a room. If traveling solo, you may be required to pay the full double-occupancy rate. Some operators eliminate this surcharge if you agree to be matched with a roommate of the same sex, even if one is not found by departure time.

GROUP TOURS

Among companies that sell tours to Costa Rica and Panama, the following have a proven reputation and offer plenty of options. The classifications used below represent different price categories, and you'll probably encounter these terms when talking to a travel agent or tour operator. The key difference is usually in accommodations, which run from budget to better, and better-yet to best.

➤ SUPER-DELUXE: **Abercrombie & Kent** (✉ 1520 Kensington Rd., Oak Brook, IL 60521-2141, ☎ 630/954– 2944 or 800/323–7308, FAX 630/ 954–3324). **Travcoa** (✉ Box 2630, 2350 S.E. Bristol St., Newport Beach, CA 92660, ☎ 714/476–2800 or 800/ 992–2003, FAX 714/476–2538).

➤ DELUXE: **Globus** (✉ 5301 S. Federal Circle, Littleton, CO 80123- 2980, ☎ 303/797–2800 or 800/ 221–0090, FAX 303/347–2080). **Maupintour** (✉ 1515 St. Andrews Dr., Lawrence, KS 66047, ☎ 913/ 843–1211 or 800/255–4266, FAX 913/843–8351). **Tauck Tours** (✉ Box 5027, 276 Post Rd. W, Westport, CT 06881-5027, ☎ 203/226–6911 or 800/468–2825, FAX 203/221– 6866).

➤ FIRST-CLASS: **Brendan Tours** (✉ 15137 Califa St., Van Nuys, CA 91411, ☎ 818/785–9696 or 800/ 421–8446, FAX 818/902–9876). **Caravan Tours** (✉ 401 N. Michigan Ave., Chicago, IL 60611, ☎ 312/ 321–9800 or 800/227–2826, FAX 312/321–9845). **Collette Tours** (✉ 162 Middle St., Pawtucket, RI 02860, ☎ 401/728–3805 or 800/340–5158, FAX 401/728–4745).

➤ BUDGET: **Cosmos** (☞ Globus, *above*).

PACKAGES

Like group tours, independent vacation packages are available from major tour operators and airlines. The companies listed below offer vacation packages in a broad price range.

➤ AIR-HOTEL: **American Airlines Vacations** (☎ 800/321–2121). **United Vacations** (☎ 800/328–6877).

➤ FROM THE U.K.: **South American Experience** (✉ 47 Causton St., London SW1P 4AT, ☎ 0171/976–5511, FAX 0171/976–6908). **Journey Latin America** (✉ 16 Devonshire Rd., Chiswick, London W4 2HD, ☎ 0181/747–8315, FAX 0181/742–1312). **Steamond Holidays** (✉ 278 Battersea Park Rd., London SW11 3BS, ☎ 0171/924–4008, FAX 0171/978–5603).

THEME TRIPS

➤ ADVENTURE: **American Wilderness Experience** (✉ Box 1486, Boulder, CO 80306, ☎ 303/444–2622 or 800/444–0099, FAX 303/444–3999). **Himalayan Travel** (✉ 110 Prospect St., Stamford, CT 06901, ☎ 203/359–3711 or 800/225–2380, FAX 203/359–3669). **Mountain Travel-Sobek** (✉ 6420 Fairmount Ave., El Cerrito, CA 94530, ☎ 510/527–8100 or 888/687–6235, FAX 510/525–7710). **Safaricentre** (✉ 3201 N. Sepulveda Blvd., Manhattan Beach, CA 90266, ☎ 310/546–4411 or 800/223–6046, FAX 310/546–3188).

➤ BIKING: **Backroads** (✉ 801 Cedar St., Berkeley, CA 94710-1800, ☎ 510/527–1555 or 800/462–2848, FAX 510/527–1444).

➤ CUSTOMIZED TOURS: **Avanti Destinations** (✉ 851 SW 6th St., Ste. 1010, Portland, OR, 97204, ☎ 503/295–1100 or 800/422–5053, FAX 503/295–2723). **4th Dimension Tours** (✉ 7101 S.W. 99th Ave., #106, Miami, FL 33173, ☎ 305/279–0014 or 800/343–0020, FAX 305/273–9777). **Ladatco Tours** (✉ 2220 Coral Way, Miami, FL 33145, ☎ 305/854–8422 or 800/327–6162, FAX 305/285–0504).

➤ FISHING: **Anglers Travel** (✉ 1280 Terminal Way, #30, Reno, NV 89502, ☎ 702/324–0580 or 800/624–8429, FAX 702/324–0583). **Cutting Loose Expeditions** (✉ Box 447, Winter Park, FL 32790, ☎ 407/629–4700 or 800/533–4746, FAX 407/740–7816). **Fishing International** (✉ Box 2132, Santa Rosa, CA 95405, ☎ 707/539–3366 or 800/950–4242, FAX 707/539–1320). **Rod & Reel Adventures** (✉ 566 Thomson Ln., Copperopolis, CA 95228, ☎ 209/785–0444, FAX 209/785–0447).

➤ HORSEBACK RIDING: **Equitour FITS Equestrian** (✉ Box 807, Dubois, WY 82513, ☎ 307/455–3363 or 800/545–0019, FAX 307/455–2354).

➤ HORTICULTURE: **Expo Garden Tours** (✉ 70 Great Oak, Redding, CT 06896, ☎ 203/938–0410 or 800/448–2685, FAX 203/938–0427).

➤ LEARNING: **Earthwatch** (✉ Box 9104, 680 Mount Auburn St., Watertown, MA 02272, ☎ 617/926–8200 or 800/776–0188, FAX 617/926–8532) for research expeditions. **National Audubon Society** (✉ 700 Broadway, New York, NY 10003, ☎ 212/979–3066, FAX 212/353–0190). **Natural Habitat Adventures** (✉ 2945 Center Green Ct., Boulder, CO 80301, ☎ 303/449–3711 or 800/543–8917, FAX 303/449–3712). **Nature Expeditions International** (✉ 6400 E. El Dorado Cir. #210, Tucson, AZ 85715, ☎ 520/721–6712 or 800/869–0639). **Naturequest** (✉ 934 Acapulco St., Laguna Beach, CA 92651, ☎ 714/499–9561 or 800/369–3033, FAX 714/499–0812). **Oceanic Society Expeditions** (✉ Fort Mason Center, Bldg. E, San Francisco, CA 94123-1394, ☎ 415/441–1106 or 800/326–7491, FAX 415/474–3395). **Questers** (✉ 381 Park Ave. S, New York, NY 10016, ☎ 212/251–0444 or 800/468–8668, FAX 212/251–0890). **Smithsonian Study Tours and Seminars** (✉ 1100 Jefferson Dr. SW, Room 3045, MRC 702, Washington, DC 20560, ☎ 202/357–4700, FAX 202/633–9250). **Wilderness Travel** (✉ 1102 Ninth St., Berkeley, CA 94710, ☎ 510/558–2488 or 800/368–2794). **Victor Emanuel Nature Tours** (✉ Box 33008, Austin, TX 78764, ☎ 512/328–5221 or 800/328–8368, FAX 512/328–2919).

➤ SCUBA DIVING: **Rothschild Dive Safaris** (✉ 900 West End Ave., #1B,

New York, NY 10025-3525, ☎ 212/662-4858 or 800/359-0747, FAX 212/749-6172). **Tropical Adventures** (⊠ 111 2nd Ave. N, Seattle, WA 98109, ☎ 206/441-3483 or 800/247-3483, FAX 206/441-5431).

➤ WALKING/HIKING: **Backroads** (☞ Biking, *above*). **Country Walkers** (⊠ Box 180, Waterbury, VT 05676-0180, ☎ 802/244-1387 or 800/464-9255, FAX 802/244-5661). **Walking the World** (⊠ Box 1186, Fort Collins, CO 80522, ☎ 970/498-0500 or 800/340-9255, FAX 970/498-9100) specializes in tours for ages 50 and older.

➤ YACHT CHARTERS: **Ocean Voyages** (⊠ 1709 Bridgeway, Sausalito, CA 94965, ☎ 415/332-4681, FAX 415/332-7460).

TRAVEL AGENCIES

A good travel agent puts your needs first. Look for an agency that has been in business at least five years, emphasizes customer service, and has someone on staff who specializes in your destination. In addition, **make sure the agency belongs to a professional trade organization,** such as ASTA in the United States. If your travel agency is also acting as your tour operator, *see* Buyer Beware *in* Tour Operators, *above*).

➤ LOCAL AGENT REFERRALS: **American Society of Travel Agents** (ASTA, ☎ 800/965-2782 24-hr hot line, FAX 703/684-8319). **Association of Canadian Travel Agents** (⊠ Suite 201, 1729 Bank St., Ottawa, Ontario K1V 7Z5, ☎ 613/521-0474, FAX 613/521-0805). **Association of British Travel Agents** (⊠ 55-57 Newman St., London W1P 4AH, ☎ 0171/637-2444, FAX 0171/637-0713). **Australian Federation of Travel Agents** (☎ 02/9264-3299). **Travel Agents' Association of New Zealand** (☎ 04/499-0104).

TRAVEL GEAR

Travel catalogs specialize in useful, space-saving items, such as compact alarm clocks and travel irons. They also offer dual-voltage appliances and currency converters.

➤ CATALOGS: **Magellan's** (☎ 800/962-4943, FAX 805/568-5406). **Orvis Travel** (☎ 800/541-3541, FAX 540/

343-7053). **TravelSmith** (☎ 800/950-1600, FAX 800/950-1656).

VISITOR INFORMATION

TOURIST INFORMATION

➤ COSTA RICA INFORMATION IN THE U.S.: **Costa Rica Tourist Board** (☎ 800/343-6332). **Embassy of Costa Rica** (⊠ 2114 S St., NW, Washington, DC 20008, ☎ 202/234-2945). **Brochures nationwide** (☎ 800/343-6332). **Chicago Consulate** (⊠ 185 N. Wabash Ave., Ste. 1123, Chicago, IL 60603, ☎ 312/263-2772). **Houston Consulate** (⊠ 2901 Wilcrest Dr., Suite 275, Houston, TX 77042, ☎ 713/266-0484). **Los Angeles Consulate** (⊠ 3450 Wilshire Blvd., Suite 404, Los Angeles, CA 90010, ☎ 213/380-6031). **Miami Consulate** (⊠ 1600 N.W. Le June Rd., Ste 102, Miami, FL 33126, ☎ 305/871-7485, FAX 305/871-0860). **New York City Consulate** (⊠ 80 Wall St., New York, NY 10005, ☎ 212/425-2620).

➤ COSTA RICA INFORMATION IN CANADA: **Ottawa Consulate** (⊠ 150 Argyle Ave., Suite 115, Ottawa, Ontario K2P 1 B7, ☎ 613/562-2855).

➤ COSTA RICA INFORMATION IN THE U.K.: **Costa Rica Tourist Services** (⊠ 47 Causton St., London SW1P 4AT, ☎ 0171/976-5511, FAX 0171/976-6908).

➤ PANAMA INFORMATION IN THE U.S.: **Panamian Embassy** (⊠ 2862 McGill Terr., NW, Washington, DC 20008, ☎ 202/483-1407).

U.S. GOVERNMENT

➤ ADVISORIES: **U.S. Department of State** (⊠ Overseas Citizens Services Office, Room 4811 N.S., Washington, DC 20520, ☎ 202/647-5225 or FAX 202/647-3000 for interactive hot line, ☎ 301/946-4400 for computer bulletin board); enclose a self-addressed, stamped, business-size envelope.

VOLUNTEER & EDUCATIONAL TRAVEL

Some, but not many, Costa Ricans have smartened up of late in realizing the need to preserve the country's precious, eye-opening biodiversity. Volunteer and educational efforts have been created by natives and far-flung environmentalists, and you, too, can have an impact. You do, however, pay for the privilege. ☞ Close-Up: Volunteer Vacations *in* Chapter 10.

➤ OPERATORS: **ATEC** (✉ Puerto Viejo de Talamanca, Puerto Limón,, ☎ 750–0188). **CCC** (✉ 4424 Northwest 13th St., Suite A-1, Gainseville, FL 32609, ☎ 800/678–7853, FAX 352/375–2449). **Earthwatch Institute** (✉ 680 Mt. Auburn St., Box 9104, Watertown, MA 02272–9104, ☎ 800/776–0188, FAX 617/926–8532).

WHEN TO GO

The most popular time to visit Costa Rica and Panama is during the dry season, which runs from mid-December through April. From mid-December until early February, you have the combined advantages of good weather and lush vegetation. If you want to visit the beach during the rainy season, it is often dry and sunny in the morning and rainy in the afternoon. Much of the region experiences sunnier weather during July and August, whereas the Caribbean coast around Cahuita and Bocas del Toro tends to enjoy a short dry season from around September to late October, when the Pacific slope is being drenched by daily storms. Remember that hotels are much more likely to be booked up during the dry season.

Despite the fact that temperatures in Costa Rica and Panama vary little from season to season, the dry season (mid-December–April) is referred to as *verano* (summer) and the rainy season (May–mid-December) as *invierno* (winter).

To escape the tourist crowds and prices, visit during the rainy season, which has been promoted in recent years as the "Green" season. Green it is. The vegetation is at its lushest and most gorgeous, but some roads—those without asphalt—are washed out, and thus require four-wheel drive. Bear in mind, that during a visit in April, some areas, especially Guanacaste, are drier and dustier for lack of enriching rains, and some landscapes may resemble the frontier. Visit during either July and August, when the storms let up a bit, or early December, when the rains are tapering off, but the high tourist season has yet to kick in. Keep in mind that during the rainiest months—September and October—some rural hotels simply shut down. The majority stay open, however, and not only are reservations easy to get, even at top establishments, you'll also have the beaches to yourself.

CLIMATE

Central America's climate varies greatly between the lowlands and the mountains. Tropical temperatures generally hover between 70°F and 85°F. The high humidity, especially in the dense jungle of the Caribbean coast, is the true sweat culprit. Guanacaste, on the more arid Pacific coast, is perhaps the hottest region, with dry-season temperatures frequently up in the 90s. Remember to drink plenty of bottled water to avoid dehydration. The following are average daily maximum and minimum temperatures for cities in Costa Rica.

GOLFITO, COSTA RICA

Jan.	91F	33C	May	91F	33C	Sept.	91F	33C
	72	22		73	23		72	22
Feb.	91F	33C	June	90F	32C	Oct.	90F	32C
	72	22		73	23		72	22
Mar.	91F	33C	July	90F	32C	Nov.	91F	32C
	73	23		72	22		72	22
Apr.	91F	33C	Aug.	90F	32C	Dec.	91F	33C
	73	23		72	22		72	22

Golfito, which lies at sea level, has a climate similar to that of most coastal and lowland towns, such as Panama City, David, Manuel Antonio, Jacó, Puntarenas, and the better part of Guanacaste.

SAN JOSÉ, COSTA RICA

Jan.	75F	24C	May	80F	27C	Sept.	79F	26C
58	14		62	17		61	16	
Feb.	76F	24C	June	79F	26C	Oct.	77F	25C
58	14		62	17		60	16	
Mar.	79F	26C	July	77F	25C	Nov.	77F	25C
59	15		62	17		60	16	
Apr.	79F	26C	Aug.	78F	26C	Dec.	75F	24C
62	17		61	16		58	14	

San José's average temperatures are similar to those of other highland towns, such as Monteverde and Panama's Boquete and Cerro Punta.

➤ FORECASTS: **Weather Channel Connection** (☎ 900/932–8437), 95¢ per minute from a Touch-Tone phone.

WORLD WIDE WEB

Do check out the World Wide Web when you're planning. You'll find everything from up-to-date weather forecasts to virtual tours of famous cities. Fodor's Web site, www.fodors.com, is a great place to start your on-line travels.

➤ COSTA RICA AND PANAMA WEB SITES: Costa Rica: There are plenty of Web sites, which are best sorted out using one of the following internet directories: http://www.info.co.cr and http://www.cr. For current events, check out http://www.ticotimes.co.cr. For Panama's Bocas del Toro, visit http://www.bocas.com.

THE GOLD GUIDE / SMART TRAVEL TIPS

1 Destination: Costa Rica

COSTA RICA: LAND OF PLEASANT SURPRISES

T USED TO BE THAT WHEN YOU asked Americans and Europeans where Costa Rica was, the reply would invariably be, "Um. It's that island in the Caribbean. Right?" Times have certainly changed. Mention Costa Rica to someone today and most likely they'll conjure up visions of rain forests, tropical beaches, and exotic wildlife. The reason perceptions about Costa Rica have changed is simple: the country has become one of the hottest destinations on the map.

You don't need to spend too long contemplating Costa Rica's attractions to understand why it's such a popular place to visit. Tucked away in the Central American isthmus, with Nicaragua to the north and Panama to the south, Costa Rica is about the same size as the state of West Virginia. But packed into this small country is incredible biological diversity, equally varied landscapes, and a seemingly endless selection of outdoor diversions. From its exemplary system of parks and preserves to its sun-drenched Pacific beaches, and from the tropical jungles of the Caribbean coast to the bustling towns of the Central Valley, Costa Rica is full of pleasant surprises.

Visitors are astonished by the cleanliness of the country, its incredible natural beauty, the panoramic views, colorful mountain towns, and even by the fact that you can drink water straight from the tap. Though more famous for its flora, fauna, and spectacular scenery, Costa Rica's greatest asset is actually its people. Ticos, as Costa Ricans call themselves, are fiercely proud of their history, culture, and achievements, but they are also a remarkably polite and accommodating people.

Perhaps what makes Ticos so special is their desire to *"quedar bien"*—"to leave a good impression." Or it could be the exuberant friendliness they express so naturally, with a marked willingness to get to know visitors and help them where they can. Whatever the reason, one thing is for sure—it is a rare visitor who does not return home impressed with the Ticos' warmth and hospitality.

Costa Rica was never an important part of the Spanish empire, which is one of the reasons why the country developed along lines very different from Spain's other colonies. Largely neglected during the colonial era, Costa Rica experienced most of its growth after independence from Spain. It is consequently a nation of immigrants, who came to work and prospered. Although most Latin American countries remain dominated by families that were granted vast tracts of land by the Spanish Crown, Costa Rica is more of a workingman's republic, and the consequent economic and political democracy results in citizens who believe in their country. This can be seen today in the strong sense of national identity—Ticos pride themselves first on being Costa Ricans rather than Central Americans, or even Latin Americans—and in the fact that the country has largely avoided the political turmoil that has beset so much of the region.

However, it is a fact that the strife and upheaval that rocked Central America during much of the past two decades painted a less than rosy picture of the area in the minds of most Americans and Europeans. People not well acquainted with Costa Rica often equate the problems in countries such as El Salvador and Nicaragua with all of Central America. In the midst of political unrest, Costa Rica managed to remain an island of stability and peace. The country has no army, for example—it was abolished in 1949. Costa Rica is also the region's most stable democracy, and the country has a deep-rooted respect for human rights.

When visiting, you'll hear a wide variety of superlative statistics, such as "Costa Rica has more teachers than policemen," and "The only thing that doesn't grow is what you don't plant," among others. In education, for example, Costa Rica ranks with many developed countries (the literacy rate is a very respectable 93%). Its telecommunications system is probably the best in the region.

The country's most striking feature, however, is the amazing variety of flora, fauna, landscape, and climate within its frontiers. Its national parks and biological preserves protect a vast array of habitats, covering more than 13% of the national territory, which should ensure the survival of its 850 species of birds, 205 species of mammals, 376 types of reptiles and amphibians, and more than 9,000 different species of flowering plants, among them 1,200 varieties of orchids. That spectacular biological diversity is distributed through an equally impressive array of landscapes, which include cool mountain valleys, sultry mangrove forests, and massive volcanoes draped with lush forests and topped with desolate craters.

The rivers that wind down the country's valleys churn through steep stretches that are popular white-water rafting routes, whereas others end up as languid jungle waterways appropriate for both animal watching and sportfishing. With mile upon mile of beaches backdropped by coconut palms and thick forest, the Caribbean and Pacific coasts are ideal for shell collectors and sun worshipers, and when the sun goes down, many beaches are visited by nesting sea turtles. The oceans that hug those coasts hold intricate coral formations, rugged islands, colorful schools of fish, and plentiful waves, which provide the perfect playground for skin divers, anglers, surfers, and sea kayakers. What more could you want?

A BRIEF HISTORY

First Encounters with the Old World

In mid-September 1502, on his fourth and last voyage to the New World, Christopher Columbus was sailing along the Caribbean coast of Central America when his ships were caught in a violent tropical storm. Seeking shelter, he found sanctuary in a bay protected by a small island; ashore, he encountered natives wearing heavy gold disks and gold bird-shape figures who spoke of great amounts of gold in the area. Sailing farther south, Columbus encountered more natives, also wearing pendants and jewelry fashioned in gold. He was convinced that he had discovered a land of great wealth to be claimed for the Spanish empire. The land itself was a vision of lush greenery; popular legend has it that, on the basis of what he saw and encountered, Columbus named the land Costa Rica, the rich coast.

The Spanish Colonial Era

The first Spaniard to attempt conquest of Costa Rica was Diego de Nicuesa in 1506. But he found serious difficulties due to sickness, hunger, and Indian raids. Similar hardships were encountered by other Spaniards who visited the region. The first successful expedition to the country was made by Gil González de Ávila in 1522. Exploring the Pacific coast, he converted more than 6,000 Indians of the Chorotega tribe to Catholicism. A year later he returned to his home port in Panama with the equivalent of $600,000 in gold, but more than 1,000 of his men had died on the exhausting journey. Many other Spanish expeditions were undertaken, but all were less than successful, often because of rivalries between various expeditions. By 1560, almost 60 years after its discovery, no permanent Spanish settlement existed in Costa Rica (this name was then in general use, although it incorporated an area far larger than its present-day boundaries), and the natives had not been subdued.

Costa Rica remained the smallest and poorest of Spain's Central American colonies, producing little wealth for the empire. It tended to be largely ignored in terms of the conquest and instead began to receive a wholly different type of settler—hardy, self-sufficient individuals who had to work to maintain themselves. The population stayed at less than 20,000 for centuries (even with considerable growth in the 18th century) and was mainly confined to small, isolated farms in the highland Central Valley and the Pacific lowlands. Intermixing with the native Indians was not a common practice, and the population remained largely European.

By the end of the 18th century, however, Costa Rica had begun to emerge from isolation. Some trade with neighboring Spanish colonies was carried out—in spite of constant harassment by English pirates, both at sea and on land—and the population had begun to expand across the Central Valley.

Seeds of political discord, which were soon to affect the colony, had been planted in Spain when Napoléon defeated and removed King Charles IV in 1808 and installed his brother Joseph on the Spanish throne. Costa Rica pledged support for the old regime, even sending troops to Nicaragua in 1811 to help suppress a rebellion against Spain. By 1821, though, sentiment favoring independence from Spain was prevalent throughout Central America, and Costa Rica supported the declaration of independence issued in Guatemala on September 15 of that year. Costa Rica did not become a fully independent sovereign nation until 1836, after annexation to the Mexican empire and 14 years as part of the United Provinces of Central America. The only major threat to that sovereignty took place in 1857 when the mercenary army of U.S. adventurer William Walker invaded the country from Nicaragua, which they had conquered the year before. Walker's plan to turn the Central American nations into slave states was cut short by Costa Rican president Juan Rafael Mora, who raised a volunteer army and repelled the invaders, pursuing them into Nicaragua, and joining troops from various Central American nations to defeat the mercenaries.

Foundations of Democracy

The 19th century saw dramatic economic and political changes in Costa Rica. For the major part of that century, the country was ruled by a succession of wealthy families whose grip was partially broken only toward the end of the century. The development of agriculture included the introduction of coffee in the 1820s and bananas in the 1870s, both of which became the country's major sources of foreign exchange.

In 1889 the first free popular election was held, characterized by full freedom of the press, frank debates by rival candidates, an honest tabulation of the vote, and the first peaceful transition of power from a ruling group to the opposition. This event provided the foundation of political stability that Costa Rica enjoys to this day.

During the early 20th century each successive president fostered the growth of democratic liberties and continued to expand the free public school system, started during the presidency of Bernardo Soto in the late 1880s. By the 1940s economic growth was healthy due to agricultural exports, but the clouds of discontent were again gathering. In 1948 the president refused to hand over power after losing the election; the result was a civil uprising by outraged citizens, led by the still-revered José Figueres Ferrer. In a few short weeks the rebellion succeeded and an interim government was inaugurated.

New Beginnings

On May 8, 1948, Figueres accepted the position of president of the Founding Junta of the Second Republic of Costa Rica. One of his first acts was to disband the army, creating in its stead a national police force.

Significant changes took place during the 1950s and 1960s, including the introduction of new social-welfare policies, greater expansion of the public school system, and greater involvement by the state in economic affairs. The early 1970s saw further growth, but then an economic crisis introduced Costa Ricans to hyperinflation. By the mid-1980s, Costa Rica began pulling out of its economic slump, in part thanks to efforts to diversify the economy, which had long been dominated by coffee and bananas. Still, the country's currency continues to be devalued on a regular basis.

Today the challenge facing Costa Rica is how best to cope with its booming tourism industry, which has surpassed coffee and banana exports as the country's top moneymaker. Although tourism provides a much needed injection of foreign exchange into the flagging economy, it has yet to be fully decided which direction it should take. The buzzwords now are "ecotourism" and "sustainable development," and with so much in the way of natural beauty to protect, it is hoped that Costa Rica will find it possible to continue down these roads rather than opt for something akin to the Acapulco or Cancún style of development.

NEW AND NOTEWORTHY

Costa Rica has recently experienced a bit of a golf boom, with several new courses open on the Pacific coast, and several more either under construction or in planning. Golf resorts in the Parque Nacional Marino Las Baulas's backyard, behind Playa Grande's turtle preserve, and Playa Conchal—replete with two golf courses, 310 luxury hotel rooms, and the "largest swimming pool in Central America"—are complete, and other courses are on the way near Playa Hermosa, just up the coast, and in Caldera, between Puntarenas and Jacó.

The Aeropuerto Internacional Daniel Oduber, near the Guanacaste city of Liberia, now offers easier access to the beach resorts of the northern Nicoya Peninsula and nearby national parks. The Costa Rican carrier Lacsa Costa Rican has direct flights to Liberia from Miami on Wednesday and Saturday, continuing to San José, and return Miami flights Thursday and Sunday. A number of charter operations also fly to Liberia sporadically from such cities as New York, Detroit, and Toronto; ask your travel agent about charters. The country's two domestic airlines also have several flights daily between Liberia and San José.

The Costa Rican government made good on its promise to mark routes leading to major tourist destinations—you'll find road signs up at most important crossroads, some of which point the way to large hotels. Unfortunately, most of the country's roads remain in poor repair, even those to the country's most popular beaches, and it remains to be seen if the incoming government would be willing and able to do something about that perennial problem.

Improved phone service in such areas as Dominical, Tamarindo, and Puerto Viejo de Limón has allowed most properties to install their own phones. As a result, reservations are easier to make, and more places are taking credit cards.

WHAT'S WHERE

Costa Rica can be divided into several distinct territories, each of which possesses its own unique qualities and defining characteristics. San José, for example, is a bustling, cosmopolitan city with a population of more than a million; it is the political, social, historical, and cultural center of the entire country. Each of the other regions has its own special features as well, from the northwest with its rolling plains to the cool mountains of the Central Valley and the humid jungles of the Atlantic Lowlands.

Our coverage of Panama concentrates on two regions, each of which makes for an easy excursion from Costa Rica: the Bocas del Toro Archipelago, where spectacular coral reefs and deserted beaches are complemented by laid-back island towns, and Chiriquí Province, a largely undiscovered area that is home to raging rivers, verdant highland valleys, and protected cloud forests.

San José

The capital of Costa Rica has several good museums, a varied cultural calendar, and many of the country's best hotels and restaurants. Located in the approximate center of the country, and sitting more than 3,000 ft above sea level in the Meseta Central, or Central Valley, San José offers a surprisingly pleasant climate for the capital of a tropical country. From almost any location within the city, you can catch a glimpse of the green hills and volcanoes that surround it—and which hold tranquil agricultural communities and natural attractions that can be visited on a variety of day trips. And since it is the transportation hub of a conveniently compact country, many of Costa Rica's other destinations lie just a short drive, flight, or bus ride from the capital.

Central Valley: Around San José

The Meseta Central, or Central Valley, is a broad bowl planted with neat rows of coffee, dotted with traditional towns, and surrounded by a ring of stunning volcanoes and mountains. Its altitude of more than 3,000 ft above sea level assures a pleasant mixture of warm days and cool nights, whereas the upper slopes can often become quite cold. The mountains hold some of the valley's great attractions, such as active volcanic craters, luxuriant cloud forests, and hotels and restaurants with unforgettable vistas. Costa Rica's most accessible volcanoes—Poás and Irazú—define the valley's northern edge. The Central Valley also has some interesting small cities and towns, such as Cartago, Escazú, Heredia, and neighboring communities, with their handsome churches and provincial charm. To the east lies the smaller Orosí Valley, which holds two historical monuments and lovely scenery, and the agricultural community of Turrialba, near which is the country's most important archaeological site, the Monumento Nacional Guayabo.

Northern Guanacaste and Alajuela

This region encompasses the mountainous chain of volcanoes in the northern center of the country, along with the hot, dry, cattle-grazing plains to the west of the mountains, and the upland and lowland jungles, forests, and plains to the east. At the heart of the Northwest Guanacaste zone lies the perfect cone of the Volcán Arenal, the country's most active. South of Arenal can be found the magnificent cloud forests of Monteverde and the other preserves. Laguna de Arenal's powerful winds create conditions for some of the best windsurfing in all the Americas, while the Refugio Nacional de Vida Silvestre Caño Negro (Caño Negro Wildlife Refuge) in the far north is a bird-watchers' delight, for it lies in the migratory flyway of hundreds of thousands of birds. Farther west the national parks of Rincón de la Vieja and Guanacaste offer uncrowded miles of dry, cloud forest, and rain-forest mountain trails for hiking and bird-watching as well as close-up views of geothermal activity.

Nicoya Peninsula

The country's driest region, the Nicoya Peninsula is a land of contrast where dry cattle ranches give way to lush river deltas. Along the northwest coast lie most of Costa Rica's most popular beaches, made so by the reliably rain-free dry season. The fine weather and beautiful settings have also turned the northwest's beaches into a "Gold Coast," and so it is here that development of overscale resorts most threatens the country's tranquil way of life and magnificent scenery. But there are still miles of uncrowded beach; the national parks are endowed with an abundance of flora and fauna, and some are remote and little visited. There are party towns like Montezuma, Coco, and Tamarindo, but it's easy to get away and find a secret place, an uncrowded shore where the only footprints are the trucklike tracks of the leatherback turtles, who come ashore to lay their eggs on a beach at the end of a trail through a forest full of howler monkeys and raccoonlike coatis.

Central Pacific Costa Rica

Though a relatively small region, the Central Pacific packs in many of the attractions that have made Costa Rica famous. Two of the country's most popular beaches—Jacó and Manuel Antonio—are found here, but there is more to the region than surf and sand. Although Jacó is a surfer's mecca with an array of accommodations, it lies very close to the Reserva Biológica Carara, where birdwatchers can spot such striking species as the scarlet macaw and roseate spoonbill. Manuel Antonio features beaches and rain forest side by side in the national park, plus diversions such as sportfishing charters and horseback riding trips into the mountains. For travelers who want to stray from the crowd, the Central Pacific is also home to secluded luxury resorts and nature lodges.

Southern Pacific Costa Rica

The southwest corner of Costa Rica is a wild and varied region containing an array of ecosystems ranging from the cloud forests of the Cordillera de Talamanca to the lowland rain forests of the Osa Peninsula. It comprises some of the country's more pristine, less accessible regions—which happen to be some of its most beautiful—but many of its attractions are actually quite easy to reach. Amateur naturalists head there to look for such rare creatures as the tapir, resplendent quetzal, scarlet macaw, and Central American squirrel monkey, or to wander the paths of one of the best botanical gardens in Latin America. Active travelers are drawn to this region by its world-class conditions for fishing, hiking, bird-watching, skin diving, white-water rafting, and surfing. And to top it off, many of these natural wonders are complemented by first-class accommodations, some surrounded by rain forest and overlooking the blue Pacific.

Atlantic Lowlands and the Caribbean Coast

Costa Rica's Atlantic Lowlands region is a world apart, separated from the rest of the country by towering mountains and volcanoes. Long isolated from the rest of Costa Rica, the residents of the Atlantic Lowlands have turned in other directions to find commonality: most of the blacks of the region claim Jamaica as their ancestral home, while the Indians that live here have more in common with the peoples of western Panama. Their language partakes of both English and Spanish, with a little spice provided by regional Indian dialects. The lifestyle is slower and more laid-back, reflecting the reality of a hot, wet climate, for this is a land dominated by the intense heat of a tropical sun interspersed with frequent bouts of torrential rain. Closer to San José, you'll find rivers for rafting with rapids in every category and the jungle preserves of La Selva and Rara Avis amidst the farmlands and banana plantations of the region.

Excursions to Panama

The archipelago of Bocas del Toro, off the northwest coast of Panama, is among the most remote places in the Americas. It soon may become another hot spot on the international vagabond circuit, because it has much to offer: great beaches, jungle-covered islands, friendly indigenous peoples, low-priced hotels, and, best of all, an abundance of pristine coral reefs for skin divers to explore. The most popular snorkeling area is around the Zapatilla Cays, which are protected within the confines of the Parque Nacional Marina Isla Bastimentos, but there are at least a dozen other dive spots in the area, each of which has its own marine attractions. And for those who have no interest in skin diving, there are plenty of pristine beaches, trails through the rain forest, Indian villages, and the laid-back town of Bocas. The town is in serious need of a face-lift, and it will probably take tourist dollars to make it happen—but the tourists with the dollars will forever change this charming place.

The Panamanian province of Chiriquí boasts impressive landscapes, tranquil mountain towns, traditional cultures, and the flora and fauna of the cloud forest. The upper reaches of the Cordillera de Talamanca Mountains, which stretch out of Costa Rica to the southeast, are largely covered with pristine forest, home to everything from jaguars to quetzals. The mountains' lower slopes and valleys contain tranquil agricultural communities, Guaymí Indian villages, and pleasant pastoral scenery. The mountain forests are the perfect playground for hikers and birders, and the rivers that flow from them are exciting white-water-rafting routes. But probably the best thing about western Panama is the fact that it is still relatively undiscovered, so you won't have to share its attractions with crowds of tourists.

PLEASURES AND PASTIMES

Archaeological Treasures

Though Costa Rica was never part of the Maya empire and has nothing to compare with the ruins of Guatemala and Mexico, it was home to some sophisticated cultures prior to the arrival of Christopher Columbus. Those people may never have erected temples to rival those of Tikal and Palenque, but they left behind a treasure trove of gold, jade, ceramics, and stonework, which can be admired at several San José museums. Pre-Columbian Costa Rica was home to some incredibly talented artisans, and thanks to good laws prohibiting the export of their works, museums such as the Museo de Jade and the Museo de Oro house collections that could be envied by the nations of the former Maya realm. Though the country's most impressive pre-Columbian heritage is found in the museums, there is one noteworthy archaeological site: Monumento Nacional Guayabo, a partially excavated city of 20,000 surrounded by protected rain forest.

Dining

Costa Rica and Panama are veritable gardens of fresh vegetables and fruit, which means that most cooking is tasty regardless of the recipe. Just don't expect anything spicy, since the local fare tends to be mild. Typical Costa Rican food is available from the ubiquitous and inexpensive *sodas* (small cafés). In San José, a string of higher-priced restaurants serve an international smorgasbord of recipes— Italian, French, Spanish, Chinese, Peruvian, you name it. Panamanian food is similar, though a bit greasy, and that country boasts an even greater selection of international cuisine than Costa Rica.

The typical Costa Rican main course is called a *casado*, which consists of rice, black beans, a shredded raw cabbage and tomato salad, meat or fish, and sometimes fresh cheese, a fried egg, and *plátanos* (fried plantains); this is standard fare at most sodas and small restaurants. The national breakfast dish is *gallo pinto* (fried rice and beans), usually served with a fried or scrambled egg, sour cream, and tortillas. Panamanians tend to eat eggs or meat for breakfast, often served with a deep-fried, unleavened bread called *ojaldre*. Maize is a popular staple in both countries, especially for snacks: options include *guiso de maíz* (corn stew), empanadas (corn turnovers filled with beans, cheese, potatoes, and meat), *gallos* (meat, beans, or cheese in a sandwich of tortillas or maize pancakes), and *elote* (corn on the cob), served *asado* (roasted) or *cocinado* (boiled). Delicious seviche is made from raw fish, or other seafood, cured in lime juice with onions, peppers, and coriander; the acid in the lime juice actually cooks the fish. In Costa Rica, chicken is often roasted using coffee wood. Panamanians tend to eat chicken *guisado* (served in a red sauce), or in a soup called *sancocho*. You can find good-quality *lomito* (beef tenderloin) at amazingly low prices in both countries. Popular fish include dorado, mahimahi, and corvina, which are sautéed or panfried. Small corvina fish are often deep fried whole and served as *pescado entero*.

Fried plátanos, *yuca* (cassava), and boiled *pejibaye* (palm fruit that tastes like a cross between avocado, chestnut, and pumpkin) are also popular and often eaten on their own. Common fruits are mango, papaya, *piña* (pineapple), and the ubiquitous banana. Lesser-known and therefore more exciting options include the *marañon* (the fruit of the cashew tree), *granadilla* (passion fruit), *guanabana* (soursop), *mamón chino* (similar to a litchi with a spiky red skin), and *carambola* (star fruit). You can get many of these in the form of delicious juices, called *refrescos,* made with either water or milk. Recommended desserts include *tres leches,* a Nicaraguan specialty made of treacle sponge and three kinds of milk; *arroz con leche* (rice pudding); *queque seco* (dry cake, like pound cake); and *flan de coco* (a sweet coconut flan).

Horseback Riding

Because horses remain one of the most common forms of transportation in Costa Rica, you can ride just about everywhere in that country. Experienced equestrians should be pleased with the spirit of the horses in Costa Rica, but even if you can't remember when you were last in the saddle, exploring a bit of the countryside on horseback is recommended. Horses are available for rent at most of the popular beach towns and mountain resorts, and guided trail rides often head to waterfalls, scenic overlooks, and other landmarks that you might otherwise never visit. The most interesting places to ride are the many farms and ranches that have been converted to nature lodges, several of which border national parks. There are also dozens of day trips available out of San José, which usually take you up into the mountains for a morning of trail riding followed by a typical Costa Rican lunch.

Flora and Fauna

Costa Rica and Panama possess an almost unfathomable wealth of natural treasures, with more species of plants and animals than scientists have been able to count, and a variety of scenery that ranges from barren mountain peaks to luxuriant lowland forests. Because Costa Rica is such a small country, it is easy to visit many different ecosystems, and see some of the plants and animals that are contained in them, in a short period of time. Costa Rica has made a concerted effort to preserve its natural heritage, and it has paid off: more than 13% of Costa Rica's national territory is under the aegis of the parks system, which contains nearly all the country's ecosystems. The most pristine of those protected areas lie in remote locations, which can take some time and effort to reach, but whether you hike in, take a four-wheel-drive vehicle, or board a boat or small plane, the trip there is often half the adventure. There are also a growing number of private nature reserves, many of which are just as wild and beautiful as the national parks, and which often have better facilities and easier access. Western Panama holds the larger half of the binational Parque Internacional La Amistad, best visited from the highland community of Cerro Punta, and the abundant marine life of the Parque Nacional Marina Isla Bastimentos.

Snorkeling and Scuba Diving

The options for observing the marine life off the coasts of Costa Rica and Panama range from simple snorkeling sessions off the beach near your hotel to a full-fledged scuba diving safari. Coastal reefs submerged off Costa Rica's southern Caribbean coast are home to colorful coral gardens and hundreds of species of fish and invertebrates. The country's most extensive reef is protected within Parque Nacional Cahuita, but there are several other good diving spots spread between Puerto Viejo and Manzanillo. The Pacific has less coral diversity, but more big animals, such as manta rays, sea turtles, and even whale sharks. The northwest is a popular diving area, with dozens of diving spots in sheltered Bahía Culebra (Snake Bay) and around Santa Catalina and the Islas Murcielagos (Bat Islands), all of which can be visited from the area's beach resorts. The snorkeling is good off such popular beaches as Montezuma and Manuel Antonio, but the best diving spot along the Pacific coast is Isla del Caño, in the southwest. Even better diving, however, is found at distant Isla del Coco, some 530 km (330 mi) southwest of the mainland. Two commercial boats offer 10-day trips to Cocos, which feature three daily dives and the opportunity to swim with hammerhead sharks, dolphins, and occasional whales.

In the Parque Nacional Marina Isla Bastimentos, near the faded town of Bocas del Toro in northeast Panama, the tropical fish are bountiful, and there are at least 25 different kinds of coral to gawk at, not to mention an even greater diversity of sponges. Much of the water is shallow, precluding the need for the complications of scuba equipment (although here, as in any good diving area, a regulator and a set of tanks open up a whole new world), and it is fairly easy to book a ride to the best snorkeling sites. Several dive shops in the town of Bocas del Toro rent scuba and snorkeling equipment and run regular excursions to the Cayos Zapatillas and half a dozen other interesting spots.

Sportfishing

Anglers have long flocked to Costa Rica, drawn by phenomenal offshore fishing all along its Pacific coast and the abundance of snook and tarpon in the rivers and coastal canals of the northern Caribbean. The Pacific charter fleet is scattered along the ports and beach towns from Playa del Coco, in the northwest, to Zancudo, deep within the Golfo Dulce, making sportfishing possible from almost every resort on the west coast. Those fully equipped boats usually head a few miles out to troll for marlin and sailfish, but they also catch plenty of tuna, dolphin, wahoo, and roosterfish. Though the Pacific fishing is good year-round, it drops off a bit during the rainiest months (September–November). The balmy Caribbean offers a more languid type of angling—casting into the murky waters of canals and rivers, where silvery snook and tarpon lurk, waiting to burst into the air when hooked. Several lodges in the northeast specialize in fishing packages. The best months for tarpon are January to August, whereas the snook fishing is best from September to February.

Surfing

Both Costa Rica's east and west coasts are dotted with innumerable surfing spots, from the radical, experts-only reef break at Puerto Viejo, on the Atlantic Coast, to the mellower waves off the town of Tamarindo in northern Guanacaste. Together with Jacó, Tamarindo is one of the country's most popular surfer hangouts, and thanks to boards for rent and manageable waves, they are good spots for people who have been away from the sport for a while. More consistent and less populated breaks are found nearby those two towns, such as Hermosa, a short drive south of Jacó. There are about a dozen surf spots scattered along the coast to the south of Tamarindo, among them Langosta, Avellanas, and Negra, and two isolated breaks hidden within Parque Nacional Santa Rosa, to the north. Polluted, but mightily long, are the waves at Boca Barranca, just south of Puntarenas. Manuel Antonio often has surf, but the waves are usually bigger at Dominical, farther to the south. And those willing to make the long journey to Pavones and Matapalo, in the extreme southwest, will get to ride some of the longest waves in the world. Though Costa Rica's short Atlantic coast has few surf spots, Puerto Viejo's Salsa Brava is one of the best breaks in the country, and the islands of Bocas del Toro, just over the border in Panama, offer similar waves.

Volcanoes

Volcanic activity was one of the principal forces in the geological process that created Costa Rica and Panama, and volcanoes remain a predominant part of the landscape in those countries. They range from sleeping giants, such as Panama's extinct Volcán Barú, to hyperactive Arenal, whose perfectly conical form towers over the lake of the same name. The easiest ones to visit are Irazú and Poás, both of which have paved roads leading up to the edges of their craters, each just a 90-minute drive from San José. Irazú's crater bears the scars of an active period that ended three decades ago, whereas the active crater of Poás regularly emits a plume of sulfuric smoke. Volcanoes that can only be ascended on foot or horseback include nearby Barva and Turrialba, Rincón de la Vieja, in Guanacaste Province, and Panama's Barú. Only lunatics try to scale Arenal, Costa Rica's most active volcano, which regularly spews lava and incandescent boulders into the air—an incendiary performance most spectacular when viewed by night.

White-Water Rafting

Costa Rica and western Panama together constitute a rafter's paradise. It is no coincidence that several Olympic kayaking teams include Costa Rican rivers as part of their winter training schedule. Nevertheless, the warm weather (water temperatures average about 70°F), spectacular river scenery, and the wide variety of runs make these countries worthy destinations for neophytes and experts. Costa Rica's most popular rafting river is the Reventazón, on the country's Atlantic side, which has an excellent first-time run and intense class IV and V sections that are fit for experts only. The Pacuare, which runs parallel to it, is one of the most beautiful rafting rivers in the world, with a breathtaking mix of rain forest, waterfalls, rocky gorges, and lively class III and IV rapids. It is usually run in one day, but two- and three-day trips, with camp-out or lodge overnights by the riverbank, are highly recommended. Less navigated rivers include the Parrita, near Manuel Antonio; the more beautiful Sarapiquí, near La Fortuna; the Penas Blancas, with class II and III trips available out of the La Fortuna area; and the Corobicí, in Guanacaste, which is a mellow river enlivened with an abundance of very visible animal life. Panama's western province of Chiriquí has two rafting rivers, both of which carry the name

of the province and offer exciting whitewater action year-round.

Windsurfing

Although there are a limited number of spots to practice the sport, windsurfing has reached legendary proportions in Costa Rica. A combination of natural and manmade events have conspired to produce one of the best freshwater windsurfing sites in the Western Hemisphere at Laguna de Arenal. It was ICE, Costa Rica's national electric institute, that in the 1970s created Laguna de Arenal—a large, electricity-producing reservoir—and it is nature, in the form of trade winds passing through a conveniently located gap in the mountains, that produces the 32- to 80-kph (20- to 50-mph) winds that rip across the lake's northwest end. This northern end of Laguna de Arenal has been compared with such windsurfing meccas as the Columbia River Gorge and Italy's Lago di Garda. (The wind is so consistent that wind generators run by windmills have been placed on the hills above the north end of the lake.) If the timing is right, you can watch distant Volcán Arenal erupt while you're tacking across the lake. You'll find serious windsurfers here from December to April, when the winds are too strong for beginners, whereas it becomes a good spot to learn the sport during the rest of the year. There's a well-supplied rental shop run by the Hotel Tilawa on the shore, by a convenient launch site. Although fanatics head straight for Laguna de Arenal, a less demanding windsurfing area is Playa Hermosa, where rental equipment and windsurfing tours are available.

FODOR'S CHOICE

Archaeological Sites and Museums

★ **Monumento Nacional Guayabo.** This ancient city, once home to 20,000 inhabitants, was abandoned in the 1400s and wasn't rediscovered until 1968.

Dining

★ **Ambrosia, San José.** Fifteen minutes from downtown San José, this eclectic restaurant has long been popular among local epicureans, thanks to its menu of delicious culinary inventions such as *sopa Neptuna*. $$$

⭐ **The Garden, Puerto Viejo de Limón.** Chef and owner Vera Mabon's Indian-Canadian-Trinidadian background provides inspiration for Tican fusion cooking at its most inventive. This charming restaurant, tucked in a garden a few blocks from the waterfront, offers the most sophisticated menu on Costa Rica's east coast. Don't miss it if you're in the area. $$–$$$

⭐ **Nogui's (Sunrise Cafe), Tamarindo.** Most of the expatriate restaurateurs and hoteliers who call Tamarindo home swear by Nogui's, a scruffy little restaurant located just off the circle near the south end of Tamarindo. They say Nogui's *langostino* (lobster) is the best in Guanacaste. Hearty American-style breakfasts are also served. $$–$$$

⭐ **Cafe Mundo, San José.** Set in a lovely old wooden house in historic Barrio Amón, this popular spot offers an inventive selection of pastas, salads, meat, and seafood dishes at very reasonable prices. Save room for dessert—the pastries are to die for. $$

⭐ **Chubascos Restaurant, Poás Volcano.** Whether you prefer the brisk mountain air, the delicious refrescos, the green surroundings, or the platters packed with traditional Costa Rican taste treats, this spot on the road to Volcán Poás offers a winning combination. $$

⭐ **Edith Soda y Restaurant, Cahuita.** Ticos and outsiders alike flock to this restaurant for the outrageous Caribbean menu, which includes a variety of vegetarian dishes and herbal teas that owner Miss Edith claims will remedy whatever ails you. $$

Lodging

⭐ **Hotel La Mariposa, Manuel Antonio.** This elegant, white Spanish-style villa and series of private bungalows set high on a promontory offer luxury and tranquility complemented by the best view in Manuel Antonio. $$$$

⭐ **Hotel Punta Islita, Guanacaste.** This isolated luxury resort spread over a hill overlooking the Pacific features comfortable rooms, splendid views, good food, and an abundance of peace and quiet. $$$$

⭐ **Lapa Rios, Cabo Matapalo.** Perched on a ridge in a private rain-forest reserve, with views of the surrounding jungle and ocean beyond, Lapa Rios is a small luxury hotel that provides close contact with tropical nature without ever skimping on the amenities. $$$$

⭐ **Villa Caletas, Tárcoles.** Each of these exquisite bungalows scattered over a forested promontory seems to enjoy a better view than the rest. Though isolation and natural beauty would seem to be this hotel's strongest points, the architecture, interior decorating, and cuisine are equally impressive. $$$$

⭐ **Grano de Oro, San José.** Built at the turn of the century, this pink, wooden house has been transformed into one of the capital's finest hotels, with interior gardens, a sundeck, and a first-class restaurant. $$$–$$$$

⭐ **Hotel Capitán Suizo, Tamarindo.** Many visitors consider this Swiss-run gem to be the finest beachfront hotel in Guanacaste, since its lush gardens provide a wonderful sense of seclusion, yet Tamarindo's resort town amusements and gorgeous beach are close at hand. Birds, monkeys, and flowers adorn the lovely landscaped grounds surrounding the pool. $$$–$$$$

⭐ **Sueño del Mar, Playa Langosta.** Susan Money's sweet little Mexican-style B&B has Balinese outdoor showers, fantastic breakfasts, lovely gardens, and a perfect beach for a front yard. With just three rooms and a casita, the level of intimacy is high, but you won't mind—Susan's a high-energy charmer. Rent the whole place for a family reunion or a gathering of friends. You will not regret it. $$$–$$$$

⭐ **Fonda Vela, Monteverde.** Spacious rooms crafted using local hardwoods have plenty of windows for enjoying the surrounding forest and distant Gulf of Nicoya, and the restaurant features great food to match the view. $$$

⭐ **Le Bergerac, San José.** The deluxe rooms and extensive gardens have long kept this friendly hotel in a quiet neighborhood a notch above the competition, and the recent addition of L'Ile de France, one of the city's best restaurants for the past two decades, simply makes Le Bergerac that much more attractive. $$$

★ **Pacific Edge, Dominical.** These four simple cabins perched on a ridge high in the hills south of town feature great views and close contact with nature. $$

Natural Wonders

★ **Arenal Volcano erupting at night.** If you have never seen an active volcano, then this will be a spectacular first—the perfect conical profile dominates the southern end of Laguna de Arenal, where it thrills visitors with regular incendiary performances.

★ **Jungle rivers.** Many Costa Rican and Panamanian rivers are actually excellent routes into the rain forest, and the river trips available range from an invigorating, heart-stopping paddle down the somewhat hair-raising rapids of the Pacuare to the lazy navigation of Costa Rica's Caribbean Canals or Pacific coast estuaries. With any luck, in the estuaries like the Tamarindo you'll spot the regal roseate spoonbill, the quirky purple gallinule, and hundreds of other birds, howler monkeys, and possibly an American crocodile or caiman.

★ **Pacific sunsets.** The suggestion that sunsets are more beautiful on the Pacific coasts of Costa Rica than in other parts of the world may seem ridiculous, but there is something about the cloud formations, colors, and venues that make them exemplary crepuscular productions. Frequently, flocks of frolicking, diving pelicans, scarfing up sardines and other treats, add a layer of foreground action to the dramatic backdrops.

Wildlife Encounters

★ **Quetzal spotting in the cloud forest.** One of the New World's most beautiful creatures, the quetzal—with metallic green feathers, a bright crimson stomach, and long tail streamers—is best observed in the forests of San Gerardo de Dota, in the southwest, and Monteverde, in the northwest, and in Panama's Chiriquí highlands.

★ **A simian encounter.** Whether you listen to the roar of a howler monkey reverberating through the forest canopy, or come face to face with a playful troop of spider monkeys, it's hard not to be fascinated by the local monkey business.

★ **Turtle-watching on the beach.** Several different types of turtles lay eggs on a number of different beaches throughout Costa Rica and Panama during the year, but one of the most amazing sights is that of a leatherback, the size of a small sofa, dragging herself up the beach (the trail she leaves looks like a bulldozer's). After delicately digging a hole with her hind flippers, and dropping her eggs in, she will painstakingly bury the eggs, and then rough up the sandy surface to camouflage their exact location. Finally she lumbers back down the beach and out to sea. Watching the emergence of the hatchlings on the beach is equally as moving.

2 San José

Most visits to Costa Rica begin and end in San José, the capital, home to excellent museums and cultural attractions, and some of the country's best hotels, restaurants, and nightlife. You can use San José as a base for exploring the Central Valley and points beyond: drive to the top of one of the nearby volcanoes, raft white-water rapids, or take a day tour to a Pacific island.

DOWNTOWN SAN JOSÉ IS A BUSY grid-plan city—
population estimates range from 300,000 to more
than a million, depending on how many suburbs
you include—with a rather untidy pastiche of buildings ranging from
mirrored-glass high-rises to elegant stuccoed bungalows. On one block
you'll find dull, prefabricated office blocks and then, only a street away,
brightly colored terraces of one- and two-story wood and adobe houses.
In the affluent suburbs at the eastern and western ends of the city, mid-
dle-class Ticos (as Costa Ricans call themselves) tend their tidy gardens behind high-security metal fencing, but the sprawling barrios
that stretch out to the north and south contain neighborhoods that you'll
definitely want to steer clear of.

Updated by
David
Dudenhoefer

San José's best assets are its location and climate. The city stands in a
broad fertile bowl at an altitude of more than 3,000 ft, bordered to
the southwest by the jagged Cerros de Escazú, to the north by Volcán
Barva, and to the east by lofty Volcán Irazú. In the dry season, these
green uplands are almost never out of sight, and during rainy season
afternoons, they are usually enveloped in cloudy mantles. Cool nights
and pleasant days welcome temperatures ranging from 15°C to 26°C
(59°F–79°F). The rainy season lasts from May to December, although
mornings during this time are often sunny and brilliantly clear.

The city was founded in 1737, and replaced nearby Cartago as the country's capital in 1823, shortly after independence from Spain. San José
grew relatively slowly during the following century, as revenues from
the coffee and banana industries financed the construction of stately
homes, theaters, and a trolley system that was later abandoned. The
city mushroomed after World War II, when scads of older buildings
were razed to make room for cement monstrosities and an ever-grow-
ing urban sprawl eventually connecting it with nearby cities. Today,
San José truly dominates national life, and nearly one-third of the country's population lives within its metropolitan area. The national government, diplomats, industry, and agribusiness have their headquarters
here, and all the institutions required of a capital city—good hospitals, schools, the main university, theaters, restaurants, and night-
clubs—flourish within its limits.

Pleasures and Pastimes

Day Tripping

San José's central position in the Central Valley and relative proximity to both the Pacific coast and the mountains allow you to make easy
day trips—and refuge from the city can be found in just 20 to 30 minutes. The Central Valley is a boon for quick outdoor adventures,
among them horseback tours on private ranches, mountain hikes, and
white-knuckle rafting excursions down the Reventazón and Pacuare
rivers. Most tours—several of which head out to the Central Valley—
will pick you up and return you to your San José hotel the same day
(☞ Guided Tours *in* San José A to Z, *below*).

Dining

Costa Rican specialties include *arroz con pollo* (chicken with rice), *en-
salada de palmito* (heart of palm salad), *sopa negra* (black bean soup),
gallo pinto (rice and black beans), and *casados* (plates of rice, beans,
fried plantains, salad, cheese, and fish or meat). Take advantage of the
cheap lunch special *plato del día,* ("plate of the day") which includes
a main course, *fresco natural* (fresh fruit drink), and often soup and
dessert. Tico food, however, is often bland, so luckily, the capital is home

to a smorgasbord of international restaurants. To complement San José's selection, you can also choose from restaurants in Escazú (☞ Chapter 3), a town dotted with coffee crops just 5 km (3 mi) southeast.

Festivals

Two weeks in late March an arts festival, Festival Internacional de las Artes, brings performances by dancers, theater groups, and musicians from Costa Rica and other nations to a dozen venues in San José. There's a December dance festival, Festival de Coreógrafos, and the International Music Festival is held annually in July and August. A carnival parade heads down Avenida 2 every December 26, and a horse parade gets underway December 27. During *Semana Universitaria* (University Week), usually held in April, students at the Universidad de Costa Rica put their studies on hold to spend the week drinking and dancing. The Día de la Virgen de Los Angeles honors Costa Rica's patron saint every August 2 with processions and a well-attended mass. On the night before, nuns, athletes, families, and friends walk *la romaría,* a 22-km (14-mi) trek along the highway from San José to Cartago.

Lodging

San José offers every type of accommodation, from luxury to bare necessity. You'll find massive hotels with all the modern conveniences and amenities, historic buildings with more atmosphere but fewer creature comforts, and smaller establishments with the kind of atmosphere appreciated by backpackers. Dozens of former residences in the city's older neighborhoods, such as Barrio Amón and Barrio Otoya, have been converted to bed-and-breakfasts (B&Bs), most in the middle price range.

EXPLORING SAN JOSÉ

The Costa Rican capital is laid out on a grid: *avenidas* (avenues) run east and west; *calles* (streets), north and south. Avenidas north of the Avenida Central have odd numbers, and those to the south have even ones. On the western end of the city, Avenida Central becomes Paseo Colón; on the eastern end, it's an equally busy, though nameless, four-lane boulevard. Calles to the east of Calle Central have odd numbers; those to the west are even. Sounds straightforward, doesn't it? It would be, but Costa Ricans do not use street addresses. Instead, Ticos use an archaic system of directions that makes perfect sense to them, but tends to confuse foreigners. A typical Tico address could be 200 m north and 50 m east of the *Correos* (Post Office). The key to interpreting such directions is to keep track of east and west, and remember that a city block is 100 m (330 ft) long.

Beyond the block and street level, downtown San José is divided into numerous *barrios* (neighborhoods), which are also commonly used in directions. Some of those barrios are worth exploring, others you'll want to avoid. Northeast of the town center, Barrio Amón and Barrio Otoya are two of the oldest parts of the city, and are consequently home to plenty of historic buildings, many being transformed into charming hotels. Los Yoses and Barrio Escalante, east of downtown, are basically residential neighborhoods that include some nice restaurants and a few B&Bs. San Pedro, another pleasant area even farther east, is the home of the University of Costa Rica and numerous bars and restaurants catering to students.

The northwest quarter of the city is a much different story; called the Zona Roja, it is frequented by hard-luck whores, drunks, and other delinquents. It's an area that is best avoided, unless you're headed to one of the bus companies there, in which case you should take a taxi. Much of the city's southern half is equally undesirable. If you follow

Avenida Central west to where it becomes Paseo Colón, you'll enter a nice area, with plenty of restaurants, cinemas, and hotels. The farther west you head, the more exclusive the neighborhoods become. Escazú, in the hills west of San José, is a traditional town with relaxed ambience and numerous small inns and good restaurants.

Numbers in the text correspond to numbers in the margin and on the San José map.

Great Itineraries

San José is home to several interesting museums and theaters, more shops than you can shake a credit card at, and such urban amenities as newsstands and ice-cream vendors, which makes it a comfortable base for day trips (☞ Day Tripping, *above* and Chapter 3) into the surrounding countryside. If you are visiting San José during the rainy months, head into the countryside in the morning and return to the city to shop and visit museums during the afternoon.

IF YOU HAVE 3 DAYS

On day one you'll definitely want to explore San José and visit at least one or two of its many museums. In the morning of day two, you may want to horseback ride in the mountains above town, visit a butterfly farm, or tour the Café Britt coffee plantation (☞ Chapter 3) in Heredia, saving the afternoon for another museum. On day three you'll no doubt want to head up a volcano, or, if it's cloudy, explore the Orosí Valley southeast of San José.

IF YOU HAVE 5 DAYS

San José really deserves two days' exploration, since it has excellent museums, plentiful shopping, and an enticing enough nightlife to make you want to sleep in. On day three you'll definitely want to climb either the Poás or Irazú volcanoes, stopping in at the nearby towns of Alajuela and Cartago. Head to the Orosí Valley on day four, spending the morning in Refugio Nacional de Fauna Silvestre Tapantí and the afternoon touring the valley. On day five, take a white-water rafting trip down the Río Pacuare on the class III and IV rapids (thrilling but not heart attack inducing); swimmable warm water and spectacular scenery make this a must for the moderately adventurous traveler.

IF YOU HAVE 7 DAYS

Spend day one getting acquainted with the city and visit at least one museum. On day two, hit one or two museums and either the Serpentarium, Parque Zoológico Simón Bolívar, or Jardín de Mariposas Spyrogyra, the butterfly garden. On day three, try a horseback riding trip or coffee-plantation tour in the morning and return to San José in the afternoon for a museum or another sight. On day four, visit the Orosí Valley. By day five, you'll be ready to head to the top of either Poás or Irazú. Though only hikers can reach the summit of Volcán Barva, anyone can drive along its green slopes and visit historic Heredia. Dedicate day six to a far-flung excursion, either white-water rafting or the cruise to Isla Tortuga. The Guápiles Highway enters Parque Nacional Braulio Carrillo (☞ Chapters 8 and 10), a short drive north from San José, which makes an excellent day trip for day seven that can easily be combined with the Rain Forest Aerial Tram (☞ Chapter 8).

Downtown and Environs

A Good Walk

Start at the eastern end of the **Plaza de la Cultura** ①, where wide stairs lead down to the **Museo de Oro** ② with a gold collection that deserves an hour or two of perusing. After wandering around the bustling plaza, slip into the **Teatro Nacional** ③ for a look at the elegant interior and maybe a cup of coffee in the lobby café. When you leave the theater, you will be facing west; the city's main eastbound corridor, Avenida 2, will be to your left. Walk 1½ blocks west along Avenida 2 and cross the street to the **Parque Central** ④ and the **Catedral Metropolitana** ⑤. Cross Avenida 2 and head north one block on Calle Central to Avenida Central, where you should turn left and follow the pedestrian zone to the small plaza next to the **Banco Central** ⑥. Continue west along the pedestrian zone to the **Mercado Central** ⑦, where you can do a bit of shopping or browsing. After exploring the market, head back east two blocks on the Avenida Central pedestrian zone, then turn left on Calle 2 and walk one block north to the green-and-gray stuccoed **Correos** ⑧. From there, return to the Avenida Central and walk east along the mall back to the Plaza de la Cultura.

From the eastern end of the Plaza de la Cultura, near the Museo de Oro, walk two blocks east on Avenida Central, turn left, walk one block north, turn right, and slither halfway down the block to the **Serpentario** ⑨, home to an interesting collection of creepy crawlers. Turn left when you leave and head 1½ blocks west on Avenida 1 and one block north to **Parque Morazán** ⑩. Walk across the park—be careful crossing busy Avenida 3—and walk along the yellow metal school building to shady **Parque España** ⑪. On the north side of the park, on Avenida 7, is the modern Instituto Nacional de Seguros (INS) building and its 11th-floor **Museo de Jade** ⑫, with an extensive American jade collection and great city vistas.

From the INS building, continue east on Avenida 7 two blocks, passing the Cancilleria, or Foreign Ministry, and the Embajada de México, the Mexican Embassy, on your left, then turn right Calle 15 and walk a block south to the corner of **Parque Nacional** ⑬. Take a look at the **Monumento Nacional** at the center of the park, then head two blocks south to the entrance of the **Museo Nacional** ⑭, housed in the old Bellavista Fortress, on the west side of which lies the terraced **Plaza de la Democracia** ⑮. From here you can walk west down Avenida Central to return to the Plaza de la Cultura, five blocks away.

TIMING

It could take an entire day to walk this tour, if you spend a little time exploring each museum and monument, and stop to shop here and there. You could, however, easily split the tour in half: see all the sights west of Plaza de la Cultura (bullets ①–⑧) one day, and the remaining places (bullets ⑨–⑮) on another. Every stop on this tour is open Tuesday to Friday; if you're visiting on Monday or a weekend, check the hours listed below to make sure the sights you want to see will be open.

Sights to See

⑥ **Banco Central** (Central Bank). Outside of the western end of the country's unattractive, modern federal reserve bank are 10 sculpted figures of bedraggled *campesinos* (peasants). The small, shady plaza south of the bank is popular with hawkers, money changers, and retired men, and can be a good spot to get a shoe shine and listen to street musicians. Beware: the money changers here are notorious for circulating counterfeit bills and using doctored calculators to shortchange customers. ✉ *Between Avdas. Central and 1 and Cs. 2 and 4.*

⑤ **Catedral Metropolitana.** To the east of the park stands this mostly uninteresting 1871 neoclassical exterior and corrugated tin dome; inside, however, the cathedral interior has patterned floor tiles and framed polychrome bas-reliefs. The interior of the small chapel on the north side of the cathedral is much more ornate than the main building, but it is usually closed. The cathedral recently underwent an ambitious restora-

San José

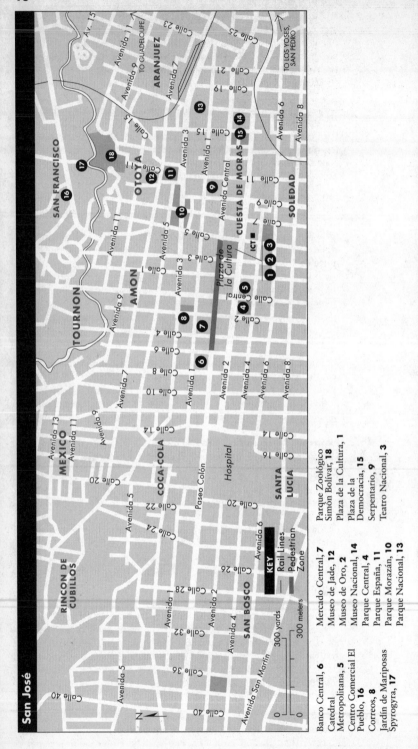

KEY

— Rail Lines

Pedestrian Zone

Banco Central, **6**
Catedral Metropolitana, **5**
Centro Comercial El Pueblo, **16**
Correos, **8**
Jardín de Mariposas Spyrogyra, **17**

Mercado Central, **7**
Museo de Jade, **12**
Museo de Oro, **2**
Museo Nacional, **14**
Parque Central, **4**
Parque España, **11**
Parque Morazán, **10**
Parque Nacional, **13**

Parque Zoológico Simón Bolívar, **18**
Plaza de la Cultura, **1**
Plaza de la Democracia, **15**
Serpentario, **9**
Teatro Nacional, **3**

tion project to repair damage from several earthquakes. ⊠ *Between Avdas. 4 and 2 and Cs. Central and 1.* ☉ *Daily 8–8.*

❽ Correos. The ornate, handsome exterior of the central post office circa 1917 is hard to miss amid the insipid architecture surrounding it. Upstairs is a display of first-day stamp issues. Also, here's your opportunity to watch the loading of *apartado* (post office boxes) going on below: Ticos covet having one of these hard-to-come-by boxes, since the city's lack of street addresses makes mail delivery quite a challenge. Opposite the post office is a small park shaded by massive fig trees, behind which stands the marble facade of the exclusive, members-only Club Unión. The large building behind the Correos is the Banco Nacional, one of the country's state-run banks. ⊠ *C. 2 between Avdas. 1 and 3.* ☉ *Weekdays 8–6:30, Sat. 8–noon.*

Instituto Costarricense de Turism (ICT). Got some questions? Head for the country's main tourist office, catercorner from the back of the **Teatro Nacional** (☞ *below*). The people who work here are usually friendly and informative, and have maps, bus schedules, and other information. ⊠ *Avda. 4 between Cs. 5 and 7, 11th floor,* ☎ *223–1733.* ☉ *Weekdays 9–3:30.*

❼ Mercado Central (Central Market). San José's block-long melting pot is a warren of dark, narrow passages flanked by stalls peddling exotic spices (some purported to have medicinal value), fish, fruit, flowers, pets, and wood and leather crafts. You'll also find dozens of cheap restaurants and food stalls, including the country's first ice-cream vendor. Be warned: the concentration of shoppers here makes this a hot spot for pickpockets, purse snatchers, and backpack slitters. ⊠ *Block bounded by Avdas. Central and 1, Cs. 6 and 8.* ☉ *Mon.–Sat. 6–6.*

★ ⑫ Museo de Jade (Jade Museum). Nearly all the items exhibited at this museum—the world's largest collection of American jade—were produced in pre-Columbian times, and most of the jade dates from between 300 BC to AD 700, before the local Indians learned goldsmithing. In the spectacular **Jade Room**, pieces are illuminated from behind so you can appreciate the jade's translucency. A series of drawings explains how this extremely hard stone was cut using string saws with quartz and sand abrasive. Although jade was used to create a variety of jewelry, it was most often carved into oblong pendants, evidently to represent ears of corn, that also doubled as knives. The museum also contains other pre-Columbian artifacts, such as polychrome vases and three-legged *metates* (low tables for grinding corn). The final room on the tour displays a startling array of ceramic fertility symbols. ⊠ *11th floor of INS building, Avda. 7 between Cs. 9 and 11,* ☎ *223–5800, ext. 2584.* ☜ *$2.* ☉ *Weekdays 8:30–4:30.*

★ ❷ Museo de Oro (Gold Museum). The dazzling, modern museum of gold, in a three-story underground building, contains the largest collection of pre-Columbian gold jewelry in Central America—20,000 troy ounces in more than 1,600 individual pieces—all owned by the Banco Central. Many pieces are in the form of frogs and eagles, two animals perceived by the region's pre-Columbian cultures to have great spiritual significance. Most spectacular are the varied shamans, representing man's connection to animal deities in that period. ⊠ *Eastern end of Plaza de la Cultura,* ☎ *223–0528.* ☜ *$5.* ☉ *Tues.–Sun. 10–4:30.*

⑭ Museo Nacional (National Museum). In the whitewashed colonial interior of the **Bellavista Fortress,** the National Museum gives you a quick and insightful lesson in Costa Rican culture from pre-Columbian times to the present. Rooms display pre-Columbian artifacts, period dress, colonial furniture, and photos of Costa Rican life through the ages. Outside is a veranda and a pleasant manicured courtyard garden. A former army headquarters, this now-tranquil building saw fierce fighting during the 1948 revolution, as the bullet holes pocking its turrets attest. ⊠ *C. 17 between Avdas. Central and 2,* ☎ *257–1433.* 🎫 *$2.* ☉ *Tues.–Sun. 8:30–4:30.*

❹ Parque Central (Central Park). Technically the city's nucleus, this simple tree-planted square has a gurgling fountain and cement benches. In the center of the park is a spiderlike, avocado-color gazebo donated by former Nicaraguan dictator Anastasio Somoza. Several years ago, a referendum was held to decide whether to demolish the despot's gift, and the citizens voted to preserve the bandstand for posterity. Across Avenida 2, to the north, stands the **Melico Salazar Theater,** San José's second leading venue, after the Teatro Nacional. The venerable **Soda Palace,** a restaurant and black-market exchange, is on the western end of that block. The fast-food outlet sitting between the two was once one of the city's main movie theaters, the Cinema Palace. ⊠ *Between Avdas. 2 and 4 and Cs. 2 and Central.*

⓫ Parque España. This shady little park is one of the capital's most pleasant spots. A bronze statue of a conquistador overlooks an elevated fountain on its southwest corner; the opposite corner has a lovely tiled guardhouse. A bust of Queen Isabella of Castille stares at the yellow compound to the east of the park, a government liquor factory until 1994, then converted into the **Centro Nacional de Cultura.** Covering a double block, the complex includes two theaters, an extensive modern art museum, and the Ministerio de Cultura. To the west of the park is a two-story, metal-sided school made in Belgium and shipped to Costa Rica in pieces more than a century ago. The yellow colonial-style building to the east of the INS building is called the **Casa Amarilla;** it houses the country's Cancilleria, the Foreign Ministry. The massive kapok tree in front, planted by the presidents of all the Central American nations in 1963, gives you an idea of how quickly things grow in the tropics. A few doors to the east is the elegant Mexican Embassy, a former private home. ⊠ *Between Avdas. 7 and 3 and Cs. 11 and 17.*

❿ Parque Morazán. Centered around a neoclassical bandstand, downtown San José's largest park is slightly barren and dull—though the tabebuia trees on its northwest corner brighten things up when they bloom during the dry months. Avoid it late at night, when prostitutes, drunks, and occasional muggers hang out. Along the park's southern edge are a public school and two lovely old mansions, both with beautiful facades (one is a private residence, the other is a prostitute pickup bar). The park also has an annex with a large fountain to the northeast, across busy Avenida 3, in front of the metal school building. ⊠ *Between Cs. 5 and 9 at Avda. 3.*

★ ⓭ Parque Nacional (National Park). A large and leafy downtown park, the Nacional is centered around a monument commemorating the nation's battle against American invader William Walker (1824–60) in 1856. It's a pleasant block of downtown greenery, dominated by tall trees that often have colorful parakeets high in their branches. An enjoyable spot to relax in by day, it gets very dark at night, when it becomes a haven for young couples, gay men, and muggers. The massive red building to the west of the park houses the Registro Nacional (National Registry) and the Tribunal Electoral (Electoral Tribunal). The modern building to the north is the **Biblioteca Nacional** (National Library). Across from the southwest end is the Moorish **Asamblea Legislativa** (Leglislative Assembly), home to Costa Rica's congress. Next door is the **Casa Rosada,** a colonial-era residence now home to bureaucrats, and behind it is a more modern onetime home used by the government for parties and special events. One block to the northeast of the park is the old train station for the Atlantic coast. ⊠ *Between Avdas. 1 and 3 and Cs. 15 and 19.*

★ ❶ **Plaza de la Cultura.** This large cement square surrounded by shops and fast-food restaurants is somewhat sterile, but it is a pleasant spot to feed the pigeons and buy some souvenirs. It is also a favored performance spot for local marimba bands, clowns, jugglers, and colorfully dressed South Americans playing Andean music. The stately **Teatro Nacional** (☞ *below*) dominates the Plaza's southern half, and its western edge is defined by the venerable **Gran Hotel Costa Rica,** with a 24-hour Parisienne café. ⊠ *Between Avdas. Central and 2 and Cs. 3 and 5.*

⓯ **Plaza de la Democracia.** President Oscar Arias built this terraced open space, to the west of the Museo Nacional, to mark 100 years of democracy and to receive visiting dignitaries during the 1989 hemispheric summit. The view west toward the jagged Cerros de Escazú is nice, and it's a great spot from which to enjoy a sunset. Along the western edge of the plaza are a number of stalls where vendors sell jewelry, T-shirts, and varied crafts from Costa Rica, Guatemala, and South America. ⊠ *Between Avdas. 1 and 2 and Cs. 13 and 15.*

☜ ❾ **Serpentario** (Serpentarium). Don't be alarmed by the absence of motion within the display cases here—all the snakes and lizards are very much alive. Most notorious is the terciopelo, responsible for more than half the poisonous snakebites in Costa Rica. The menagerie also features boa constrictors, Jesus Christ lizards, poison dart frogs, iguanas, and an aquarium full of deadly sea snakes. There are also such exotic creatures as king cobras and Burmese pythons. ⊠ *Avda. 1 between Cs. 9 and 11,* ☎ *255–4210.* ⊡ *$5.* ✆ *Weekdays 9–6, weekends 10–5.*

★ ❸ **Teatro Nacional** (National Theater). Easily Costa Rica's most enchanting building, the National Theater stands at the southwest corner of the Plaza de la Cultura. Chagrined that touring prima donna Adelina Patti bypassed San José in 1890, wealthy coffee merchants raised export taxes to pay for the Belgian architects, cast iron, Italian marble, and decorators to construct the theater. The sandstone exterior is decorated with Italianate arched windows, marble columns with bronze capitals, and statues of odd bedfellows Ludvig van Beethoven (1770–1827) and 17th-century Spanish Golden Age playwright Calderón de la Barca. The Muses of Dance, Music, and Fame are silhouetted in front of a maroon iron cupola. Given the provenance of the building funds, it's not surprising that frescoes on the stairway inside depict coffee and banana production. The theater was inaugurated in 1894 with a performance of Gounod's *Faust,* starring an international cast. The sumptuous baroque interior sparkles owing to an extensive restoration project undertaken after the theater was damaged in a 1991 earthquake. Tickets are remarkably inexpensive. The theater closes occasionally for rehearsals. The stunning belle-epoque **Café Teatro Nacional** serves exotic coffees, good sandwiches, and exquisite pastries. ⊠ *On the Plaza de la Cultura,* ☎ *221–1329.* ⊡ *$2.50 entry fee, performance tickets $4–$40, $10 average.* ✆ *Mon.–Sat. 9–5, Sun. 10–5.*

North of Downtown

A Good Tour

The first two of these destinations are north of the city center, and best visited individually. Take a taxi to the **Centro Comercial El Pueblo** ⓰, in the northern neighborhood of Barrio Tournón. One block east and half a block south of El Pueblo is the **Jardín de Mariposas Spyrogy-**

ra ⑰, a butterfly garden, which overlooks the greenery of the country's zoo, the **Parque Zoológico Simón Bolívar** ⑱. The best way to reach the zoo, however, is to walk north from the bandstand in **Parque Morazán.** along Calle 7 to the bottom of the hill, then turn right.

TIMING

You can visit all three sites in one day. Allow a half hour to see the Centro Comercial El Pueblo, an hour or two for the Jardín de Mariposas Spyrogyra, and an hour to see the Parque Zoológico Simón Bolívar. All sites are open daily.

Sights to See

⑯ **Centro Comercial El Pueblo** (El Pueblo Shopping Center). This shopping center was built to resemble the kind of colonial village that Costa Rica lacks. "Pueblo" is the Spanish term for town, and the cobbled passages, adobe walls, and tiny plazas are surprisingly convincing. Most of the locales are occupied by bars, restaurants, and discotheques—El Pueblo gets very busy at night, especially on weekends—but there are also a few shops worth checking out. ⊠ *Barrio Tournón, north of downtown, no street address, but a local landmark.* ☉ *Daily 24 hrs.*

★ ☙ ⑰ **Jardín de Mariposas Spyrogyra** (Butterfly Garden). An hour or two spent at this magical garden will prove entertaining and educational for travelers of all ages. Self-guided tours provide information about butterfly ecology and a chance to observe the winged jewels close up. Visitors watch a 15-minute video, then guide themselves through screened-in gardens following a numbered trail. Some 30 species of colorful butterflies flutter around the gardens, together with several types of hummingbirds. Visit when it's sunny, since that's when butterflies are most active. Though the garden abuts the northern edge of the Parque Zoológico Simón Bolívar (☞ *below*), its entrance is on the outskirts of the Barrio Tournón, near the El Pueblo shopping center. ⊠ *55 yds west and 164 yds south of brick church of San Francisco, Guadelupe,* ☎ *222–2937.* ⊡ *$6.* ☉ *Daily 8–3.*

☙ ⑱ **Parque Zoológico Simón Bolívar.** Bearing in mind the country's mind-boggling diversity of wildlife, San José's zoo is rather modest in scope. It does, however, provide an introduction to some of the animals that you may or may not see in the jungle. The park is set in a forested ravine in historical Barrio Amón, and provides soothing green space in the heart of the city. ⊠ *Avda. 11 and C. 11, Barrio Amón,* ☎ *233–6701.* ⊡ *$1.50.* ☉ *Weekdays 8–3:30, weekends 9–4:30.*

DINING

Wherever you eat—whether it be a small *soda* (café) or a sophisticated city restaurant—in San José, dress is casual. Meals tend to be taken earlier here than in many Latin American countries—few restaurants serve past 10 PM. Also note that 23% is added to all the prices on the menu—13% for tax and 10% for the service. Because the gratuity is included, there is no need to tip, but if service is good, it's nice to add a little money to the obligatory 10%. In Panama, on the other hand, only 5% tax is added to the check, and you are expected to leave a 10% tip over and above the tax charge. Caveat: except for those in hotels, most restaurants close during Holy Week (Palm Sunday to Easter Sunday), and those that do stay open aren't allowed to sell alcohol from Thursday to Easter Sunday.

Central San José

CHINESE

$–$$ ✕ **Fulusu.** Some like it hot: this Chinese place around the corner from the pink Hotel Presidente is one of the very few restaurants in the country where you can get a spicy food fix. The decor is mundane, with red-and-white tablecloths and Chinese prints, but the food is authentic and delicious. Start off with some *empanadas chinas* (dumplings similar to pot stickers), then head on to something like *vainicas con cerdo* (green beans with pork) or *pollo estilo sichuan* (Szechuan chicken). Note that one entrée and two orders of rice is usually enough food to satisfy two people. ⊠ *C. 7 between Avdas. Central and 2,* ☎ *223–7568. Reservations not accepted. MC, V. Closed Sun.*

COSTA RICAN

$$–$$$ ✕ **La Cocina de Leña.** In the charming Centro Comercial El Pueblo,
★ La Cocina serves up traditional Costa Rican fare surrounded by white walls hung with old tools and straw bags to make you feel like you're down on the farm. Popular Tico dishes such as black bean soup, seviche, tamales, oxtail with yucca, and plantains cost more here than in the Mercado Central, but the quality and hygiene are more in keeping with the standards of the North American palate and stomach. The restaurant presents folk dancing and music several nights a week during the high season. This is one of the few places that doesn't close during Holy Week. ⊠ *Centro Comercial El Pueblo, Barrio Tournón,* ☎ *223–3704. AE, MC, V.*

$–$$ ✕ **Mama's Place.** Mama's is a Costa Rican restaurant with a difference; the difference being that the owners are Italian, so in addition to such Tico standards as arroz con pollo and *carne en salsa* (beef in a tomato sauce), they serve homemade pastas and fish or meat dishes with delicate wine sauces. The brightly decorated coffee shop opens onto busy Avenida 1; the more subdued restaurant is upstairs. At lunch time, it is usually packed with business types drawn by the delicious and inexpensive daily specials. ⊠ *Avda. 1 between Cs. Central and 2,* ☎ *223–2270. Reservations not accepted. AE, MC, V. Closed Sun., around Easter, and last wk in Dec.*

$ ✕ **Pipos.** This is a narrow establishment—two floors packed with small tables and chairs—and during weekday lunch hours it's usually full of businesspeople drawn by the inexpensive lunch special, the plato del día. Snapshots of local scenery decorate the walls, and there's usually rock on the radio and sports on TV. You can fill up on such Tico standards as arroz con pollo and *olla de carne* (tropical beef stew with cassava and plantains). The *plato vegetariano* (vegetarian plate) pairs an ample salad and a fried fish fillet. Breakfast is also served. ⊠ *Avda. Central between Cs. 9 and 11,* ☎ *233–4623. Reservations not accepted. DC, AE, MC, V. Closed around Easter and last wk in Dec.*

ECLECTIC

$$$ ✕ **Ambrosia.** A navy-blue canopy of an open-air shopping mall her-
★ alds this chic restaurant serving innovative international dishes in San Pedro. From among the choices of inventive salads, soups, pasta, and fish dishes, start with the *sopa Neptuna* (a mixed fish soup with tomato, onion, bacon, and cream); follow with either the light fettuccine *ambrosia* (with white sauce, cheese, ham, and oregano) or *corvina troyana* (steamed sea bass, covered with a sauce of mushrooms, shrimp, and tarragon). The atmosphere is relaxed and informal, and the decor matches the adventurous cooking: watercolors, wood and cane chairs, and plants. ⊠ *Centro Comercial de la Calle Real, San Pedro,* ☎ *253–8012. AE, DC, MC, V. No dinner Sun.*

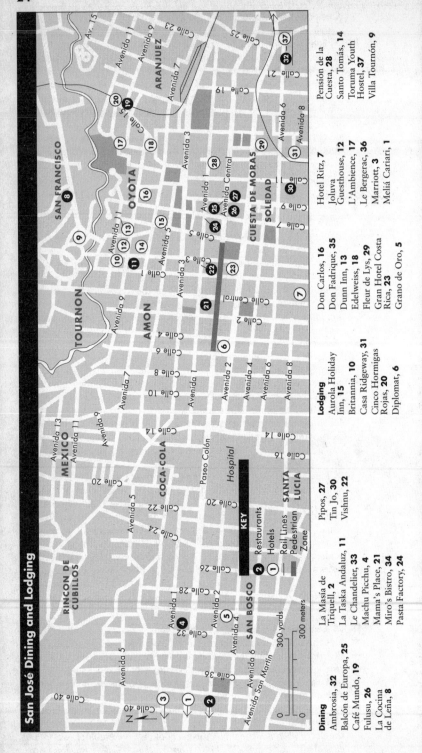

San José Dining and Lodging

24

KEY

- **2** Restaurants
- **1** Hotels
- Rail Lines
- Pedestrian Zone

Dining

Ambrosia, **32**
Balcón de Europa, **25**
Café Mundo, **19**
Fulusu, **26**
La Cocina de Leña, **8**
La Masía de Triquell, **2**
La Taska Andaluz, **11**
Le Chandelier, **33**
Machu Picchu, **4**
Mama's Place, **21**
Miro's Bistro, **34**
Pasta Factory, **24**
Pipos, **27**
Tin Jo, **30**
Vishnu, **22**

Lodging

Aurola Holiday Inn, **15**
Britannia, **10**
Casa Ridgeway, **31**
Cinco Hormigas Rojas, **20**
Diplomat, **6**
Don Carlos, **16**
Don Fadrique, **35**
Dunn Inn, **13**
Edelweiss, **18**
Fleur de Lys, **29**
Gran Hotel Costa Rica, **23**
Grano de Oro, **5**
Hotel Ritz, **7**
Joluva Guesthouse, **12**
L'Ambience, **17**
Le Bergerac, **36**
Marriott, **3**
Meliá Cariari, **1**
Pensión de la Cuesta, **28**
Santo Tomás, **14**
Toruma Youth Hostel, **37**
Villa Tournón, **9**

$$ ✕ **Café Mundo.** You could easily walk by this corner restaurant with-
★ out noticing it behind the foliage or seeing its small sign. Step through
the entrance and up the stairs, however, and you'll discover an elegant
little restaurant. Seating is available on the porch and in the garden
out front. The menu includes an inventive array of homemade soups,
salads, pastas, pizzas, hot and cold sandwiches at lunch, and grill
dishes at dinner. Start off with a half plate of pasta with shrimp and
grilled vegetables, then sink your teeth into a New York steak *en salsa
de vino tinto* (in a red-wine sauce). Save room for dessert—the pas-
tries are to die for. ⊠ *Barrio Otoya, C. 15 and Avda. 9,* ☎ *222–6190.
AE, MC, V. Closed Sun.*

$$ ✕ **Miro's Bistro.** Hidden in a little brick building by the railroad tracks,
★ Miro's has long been popular with locals. Croatian-born Miro spent
most of his life in Italy, and the menu reflects the mix: goulash, egg-
plant Parmesan, and various types of tortellini. You might see Miro
greeting guests, taking orders, and cooking. The decor is very red, with
a few watercolors on the walls and simple pine tables and chairs. It's
a bit cramped, especially at the three-stool bar tucked away in the corner, but the terrific food and reasonable prices make it well worth your
while. ⊠ *Barrio Escalante, 333 yds north of Pulpería de la Luz, around
the corner of brick building,* ☎ *253–4242. Reservations not accepted.
MC, V. Closed Sun.*

FRENCH

$$$$ ✕ **Le Chandelier.** In terms of decor, ambience, and cooking, this is San
★ José's classiest restaurant, with wicker chairs, tile floor, original paintings, and formal service. The Swiss chef, Claude Dubuis, creates such
unique dishes as *corvina* (sea bass) in a *pejibaye* (peach palm) sauce
or the more familiar *pato a la naranja* (duck with orange sauce). ⊠
San Pedro, from ICE, 1 block west and 109 yds south, ☎ *225–3980.
AE, MC, V. Closed Sun. and last wk in Dec. No lunch Sat.*

ITALIAN

$$–$$$ ✕ **Balcón de Europa.** In existence since 1909, this restaurant was long
owned and managed by chef Franco Piatti, who died in 1996. His widow
now runs it, and maintains the good food and service that has kept the
Balcón popular with residents and visitors alike. The ambience has
always been half the attraction, with hardwood floor and walls, old
sepia photos of Costa Rica, and a strolling guitarist. Pasta dishes like
the *plato mixto* (mixed plate with lasagna, tortellini, and ravioli) are
the house specialty, but some quality Costa Rican fare is also available. ⊠ *Avda. Central and C. 9,* ☎ *221–4841. AE, MC, V. Closed
Sat.*

$$–$$$ ✕ **Pasta Factory.** The Italian food at this place is so authentic, it's hard
to believe the owners are French. The homemade gnocchi, ravioli, and
fettuccine will have you swearing there's an Italian in the kitchen. The
pizza is equally convincing—they offer a dozen different combinations—
and weekday lunch specials are a great deal. The restaurant is on a busy
corner, with lots of windows, two seating levels, green table cloths, and
a few prints on the walls. Start off with some focaccia and perhaps some
mushrooms *al ajillo* (sautéed with garlic), then move on to fresh pasta,
a meat dish, or pizza (try the vegetarian pie). ⊠ *C. 7 and Avda. 1,* ☎
222–4642. AE, MC, V. Closed Sun. and Dec. 25–Jan. 2.

PAN-ASIAN

$$ ✕ **Tin Jo.** There are two other Chinese restaurants on this block, but
★ thanks to its food, Tin Jo stands apart from them and from the vast
majority of the city's other Asian eateries. Set in a former home, the
restaurant achieves an elegant ambience with hardwoods, pastel table-
cloths, and flowers on every table. The menu includes Cantonese,

Szechuan, Thai, and Indian dishes, among which are such treats as *kaeng* (Thai shrimp and pineapple curry in coconut milk), *mu shu* (a beef, chicken, or veggie stir-fry with crepes), and *samosas* (stuffed Indian pastries). ✉ *C. 11 between Avdas. 6 and 8,* ☏ *221–7605. AE, MC, V.*

PERUVIAN

$$–$$$ ✕ **Machu Picchu.** On a quiet street just north of Paseo Colón, this small
★ restaurant set in a converted house is *the* place for excellent Peruvian cuisine or just a good pisco sour, a cocktail made with lime juice, egg whites, and pisco brandy. A few travel posters and a fishnet clutching crab and lobster shells are about the only concessions the management makes to decor—but no matter: the food is anything but plain and the seafood is excellent. The *pique especial de mariscos* (special seafood platter), big enough for two people, has shrimp, conch, and squid cooked four ways. The seviche here is quite different, and better, than that served in the rest of the country. A blazing Peruvian hot sauce served on the side adds zip to any dish. ✉ *C. 32, 136 yds north of Kentucky Fried Chicken, Paseo Colón,* ☏ *222–7384. AE, MC, V. No dinner Sun.*

SPANISH

$$$–$$$$ ✕ **La Masía de Triquell.** San José's most authentic Spanish restaurant is appropriately housed in the Casa España, a Spanish cultural center. The dining room follows the theme with a tile floor; wood beams; red, green, and yellow walls; white tablecloths; and leather-and-wood Castilian-style chairs. Start with *champiñones al ajillo* (mushrooms sautéed with garlic and parsley), and, as a main course, try the *camarones Catalana* (shrimp in a tomato, onion, and garlic cream sauce). The wine list is long and strongest in the Spanish and French departments. ✉ *Sabana Norte, 53 yds west and 190 yds north of Burger King,* ☏ *296– 3528. AE, DC, MC, V. Closed Sun. and last wk in Dec.*

$$–$$$ ✕ **La Taska Andaluz.** From the flamenco music usually playing on the tape deck to the mantillas hung on the wall, this place is unmistakably Spanish. In this former home in Barrio Amón, you'll dine in one of the several eclectic rooms, or during the dry season on a small terrace out front. Iberian favorites include paella, *conejo a la parrilla* (grilled rabbit), and *corvina a la andaluza* (sea bass sautéed in olive oil with garlic and parsley). If you're not too hungry, or as an appetizer, you may opt for a drink and something from the *tapa* menu, with small portions of Spanish standards such as *tortilla española* (egg and potato pie). ✉ *C. 3 near Avda. 9,* ☏ *257–6556. Reservations not accepted. AE, MC, V. Closed daily 2:30 to 5, and Sun. off-season.*

VEGETARIAN

$ ✕ **Vishnu.** Though a restaurant named after a Hindu god may seem a bit out of place, Vishnu has become a bit of an institution in San José. Even the ambience is institutional—sterile Formica booths and posters of fruit hanging on the wall—but the attraction is the inexpensive vegetarian food. The best bet is usually the plato del día, which includes soup, beverage, and dessert, but they also serve soy burgers, salads, fresh fruit juices, and a yogurt smoothie called *morir soñando* (literally, die dreaming). Vishnu is open long hours. ✉ *Avda. 1, just west of C. 3,* ☏ *222–2549. Reservations not accepted. No credit cards.*

LODGING

Central San José

$$$$ 🏨 **Aurola Holiday Inn.** The upper floors of this 17-story mirrored-glass building, three blocks north of Plaza de la Cultura, have the best views in town. Rooms are decorated with cream-stripe wallpaper, pale burgundy carpets, patterned bedspreads, and attractive native prints. The

wide beds are a real treat. Ask for a room facing south or, better still, for one on the southwest corner from which you can see the city and the Cerros de Escazú beyond. The Aurola's public areas are high-ceilinged, modern, and airy. ✉ *Avda. 5 and C. 5, Apdo. 7802–1000,* ☎ *233–7233; 800/465–4329 in the U.S.,* FAX *255–1036. 188 rooms with bath, 12 suites. Restaurant, bar, cafeteria, indoor pool, hot tub, sauna, exercise room, casino. AE, DC, MC, V.*

$$$–$$$$ 🏨 **Britannia.** On a busy corner in Barrio Amón, this pink house with a tiled porch has changed very little since its construction in 1910, except for a row of newer rooms; the old cellar, too, has been converted into an intimate restaurant. Rooms in the newer wing are slightly small, with carpeting and hardwood furniture. Deluxe rooms and junior suites in the old house are spacious, with high ceilings and windows on the street side—they're worth the extra money, but are close enough to the street that it could be a problem if you're a light sleeper. The cellar restaurant has brick walls and arches and overlooks the interior gardens that separate the old and new wings. It's only open for breakfast and dinner, serving dishes such as cream of pejibaye soup and tenderloin with béarnaise sauce. ✉ *C. 3 and Avda. 11, Apdo. 3742–1000,* ☎ *223–6667,* FAX *223–6411. 19 rooms with bath, 5 junior suites. Restaurant. AE, DC, MC, V.*

$$$–$$$$ 🏨 **Grano de Oro.** This turn-of-the-century wooden house, on a quiet
★ side street on the western edge of San José, is one of the city's most charming inns. The former home underwent extensive remodeling, which included the addition of new rooms, a restaurant, and indoor gardens. The older rooms are the nicest, especially the Garden Suite, with its hardwood floors, high ceilings, and private garden. The standard rooms are a bit small, but tasteful. The restaurant overlooks an interior patio, and the kitchen is run by a French chef. The hotel's sundeck has a spiffy view of both the city and the far-off volcanoes. ✉ *C. 30 between Avdas. 2 and 4,* ☎ *255–3322,* FAX *221–2782;* ✉ *Box 025216, SJO 36, Miami, FL 33102-5216. 31 rooms with bath, 3 suites. Restaurant, fans, hot tub. MC, V.*

$$$–$$$$ 🏨 **L'Ambience.** In a quiet, upscale residential neighborhood five blocks
★ from the city center, L'Ambience inhabits an elegant, restored, colonial manor house. Each of this hotel's rooms overlooks the central courtyard, where potted tropical plants spill onto multicolor glazed tiles. The antique furniture, gilt mirrors, and old prints in the rooms are from the owner's personal collection. The Presidential Suite has a large drawing room attached to it. ✉ *C. 13 between Avdas. 9 and 11,* ☎ *222–6702,* FAX *223–0481;* ✉ *Interlink 179, Box 526770, Miami, FL 33152. 6 rooms with bath, 1 suite. No credit cards.*

$$$ 🏨 **Don Carlos.** A rambling gray villa houses this eclectic hotel-cum-
★ crafts shop. Public areas are a split-level maze of polished hardwood floors, greenery-draped courtyards, and tile patios, some adorned with colorful crafts sold in the on-site shop. Room sizes vary greatly: those in the Colonial Wing cost $10 extra per night and have polished wood floors, high white ceilings, and heavy furniture. Another $10 buys even more space. Breakfast is included. ✉ *C. 9 at Avda. 9,* ☎ *221–6707,* FAX *255–0828;* ✉ *Box 025216, Dept. 1686, Miami, FL 33102-5216. 25 rooms with bath, 11 suites. Restaurant, bar, breakfast room. AE, MC, V.*

$$$ 🏨 **Don Fadrique.** This tranquil, family-run B&B on the outskirts of San José was named after Fadrique Gutierrez, an illustrious great uncle of the owners. It is set in a former home in the upscale residential neighborhood of Los Yoses, behind a wall that encloses an extensive garden patio. A collection of original Costa Rican art decorates the lobby and rooms, most of which have hardwood floors, peach walls, and pastel bedspreads. Several carpeted rooms downstairs open onto the garden, while the best room upstairs is number 20. Complimentary breakfast and dinner à la carte are served in a dining room off the lobby or at tables in the garden. ⊠ *C. 37, Avda. 8, Los Yoses,* ☎ *225–8186,* ☏ *224–9746. 20 rooms with bath. Restaurant. AE, DC, MC, V.*

$$$ ⊞ **Fleur de Lys.** Although it's run by Swiss International Hotels, you would never guess that this elegant hotel is part of a chain. Guest rooms in this lavender-color restored mansion are small but bright, with big closets, floral bedspreads, Tiffany-style lamps, and paintings by Costa Rican artists. The Fleur de Lys has a prime location on a quiet street between the Museo Nacional and the Plaza de la Cultura. A buffet breakfast is included in the price. ⊠ *C. 13 between Avdas. 2 and 6, Apdo. 10736–1000,* ☎ *223–1206,* ☏ *257–3637. 18 rooms with bath, 1 suite. Restaurant, bar, free parking. AE, DC, MC, V.*

$$$ ⊞ **Gran Hotel Costa Rica.** Opened in 1930, the dowager of San José hotels remains a focal point of the city. All bedrooms have beige walls, pastel patterned bedspreads, subdued carpets, and individual abstract watercolors. Rooms that overlook the Plaza de la Cultura are noisy but have the best views. The bathrooms have old-fashioned taps and modern comfort. There are two drawbacks here: there have been complaints of no air-conditioning and the hotel's size, combined with the flow of nonguests who frequent the ground-floor 24-hour casino and bars, reduces the intimacy quotient to zero. ⊠ *Avda. 2 at C. 3, Apdo. 527–1000,* ☎ *221–4000,* ☏ *221–3501. 106 rooms with bath, 4 suites. Restaurant, bar, cafeteria, casino. AE, DC, MC, V.*

$$$ ⊞ **Le Bergerac.** Set in the quiet, residential, eastern neighborhood of
★ Los Yoses, Le Bergerac is the cream of a growing crop of small upscale San José hotels. French owned and managed, it occupies two former private homes furnished with antiques and surrounded by extensive green areas. Guest rooms have custom-made stone-and-wood dressers and writing tables. Deluxe rooms, an extra $10, have private garden terraces, or balconies, and larger bathrooms. The open-air restaurant, overlooking a luxuriant garden patio, was taken over by French chef Jean-Claude Fromont, whose L'Ile de France has been one of San José's most popular restaurants for the past two decades. Dinner reservations are necessary, even for guests, especially on weekends. Breakfast is included. ⊠ *C. 35, first entrance to Los Yoses, Apdo. 1107–1002,* ☎ *234–7850,* ☏ *225–9103. 18 rooms with bath. Restaurant, meeting room. AE, MC, V.*

$$$ ⊞ **Santo Tomás.** Step back to the days of the coffee barons at this restored, turn-of-the-century plantation house elegantly decorated with mahogany floors and handmade tile. Select an upstairs room for a view north toward Heredia, although tall people may find the eaved ceilings hazardous. The downstairs rooms have white walls and elegant fittings. Request a room with a window, because those that open onto the corridor are gloomy. If you want peace and quiet, ask for a room in the back. Complimentary breakfast is included. ⊠ *Avda. 7 between Cs. 3 and 5,* ☎ *255–0448,* ☏ *222–3950;* ⊠ *Box 025216, SJO 1314, Miami, FL 33102-5216. 20 rooms with bath. Bar. MC, V.*

$$$ ⊞ **Villa Tournón.** Just a few minutes' walk north of downtown and a
★ two-block jaunt from El Pueblo shopping center, the Tournón is a modern businessperson's hotel, noted for its true-value accommodations. Sloping wooden ceilings and bare, redbrick walls recall a ski chalet. Landings lead to snug rooms painted in pastel shades and adorned with prints. The restaurant serves a wide variety of meat and fish dishes, brought to the tables by white-jacketed waiters. The small garden is attractively laid out with lawns, shrubs, and a kidney-shape pool. ⊠ *Barrio Tournón, Apdo. 6606–1000,* ☎ *233–6622,* ☏ *222–5211. 80 rooms with bath. Restaurant, pool. AE, MC, V.*

$$ ⊞ **Cinco Hormigas Rojas.** The name of this colorful little lodge trans-
★ lates as "Five Red Ants." The interior is full of original art and is wildly
decorated—from the bright colors on the walls and the fruit she puts
in the garden to attract birds, right down to the toilet seats. What can
we say—the owner's an artist. Mayra Güell, who lives here, turned the
house she inherited from her grandmother into San José's most origi-
nal B&B-turned-art gallery. It's in historic Barrio Otoya, one of San
José's few pleasant neighborhoods. A hearty breakfast is included in
the room rate. ⊠ *C. 15 between Avdas. 9 and 11,* ☎ ℻ *257–8581.
6 rooms, 1 with bath. Free parking. AE, MC, V.*

$$ ⊞ **Dunn Inn.** Despite the morbid-sounding name, most guests actually
survive their stay at the Dunn Inn. Pat Dunn opened one of the first
B&Bs in historic Barrio Amón. A former home—built in 1926—this
handsome wooden building has tile floors, a little reading room with
a beautiful wall of stained glass, and a garden restaurant. Rooms all
have indigenous names, and the nicest ones are in the original building, especially *Durika,* which has a small balcony. Rooms on the
ground floor of the annex have old brick walls, and airy rooms upstairs are more modern. A light breakfast is included. ⊠ *C. 5 and Avda.
11, Apdo. 6241–1000,* ☎ *222–3232,* ℻ *221–4596. 24 rooms with
bath, 1 suite. Restaurant, minibars, barbershop, travel services. V.*

$$ ⊞ **Edelweiss.** The name may seem out of place—one of the owners is
★ Austrian—and the interior may look more European than Latin Amer-
ican, but this elegant little hotel offers comfortable accommodations
in a charming corner of the city, and at very reasonable prices. Rooms
have carved doors, custom-made furniture, small baths, and ceiling fans.
Most have hardwood floors and windows; several have bathtubs.
Complimentary breakfast is served in a garden courtyard, which dou-
bles as a bar. ⊠ *Barrio Otoya, Avda. 9 at C. 15,* ☎ *221–9702,* ℻
222–1241. 16 rooms with bath. Bar. AE, MC, V.

$$ ⊞ **Joluva Guesthouse.** This small B&B caters primarily to a gay clientele, but the accommodations and price make it appealing to every-
one. It would be easy to pass by this white cement building, on one of
the quieter streets of Barrio Amón, since it is marked by only a small
sign. A narrow entrance, flanked by white columns detailed in gold,
leads to a high-ceiling common area with a lovely tile floor, couches
and armchairs. Rooms have hardwood floors, rugs, and small baths;
the two cheapest rooms share a bath. Complimentary Continental
breakfast is served. ⊠ *C. 3B between Avdas. 9 and 11, Apdo. 1998–
1002,* ☎ *223–7961; 619/224–2418 in the U.S.,* ℻ *257–7668. 8
rooms, 6 with bath. Breakfast room. AE, MC, V.*

$$ ⊞ **Pensión de la Cuesta.** The rooms of this laid-back, central wooden
villa on Cuesta de Nuñez have hardwood floors, brightly painted
walls, and original art. Rooms in back are quieter, but those in front
are brighter. You can lounge and read in the sunken sitting area (also
used as the breakfast room), which has a high ceiling, a wall of win-
dows, and cable TV. Breakfast is included in the price, and you are wel-
come to use the kitchen. The nine rooms share three baths. ⊠ *Avda.
1 between C. 11 and 15, Apdo. 1332,* ☎ ℻ *255–2896. 9 rooms with-
out bath. Breakfast room. AE, DC, MC, V.*

$–$$ ⊞ **Diplomat.** This colorless place on a commercial street half a block
from the busy Avenida 2 is popular among bargain hunters. With tan
walls, worn carpets, twin beds, and tiny bedside tables, the boxlike rooms
have all the warmth of an army barracks, but they're quiet and im-
peccably clean. The sitting areas on each floor have more flair owing
to their huge tropical murals. ⊠ *C. 6 between Avdas. Central and 2,
Apdo. 6606–1000,* ☎ *221–8133,* ℻ *233–7474. 30 rooms with bath.
Restaurant, bar. AE, MC, V.*

$ ⚕ **Casa Ridgeway.** Affiliated with the Quaker Peace Center next door,
★ Casa Ridgeway is the budget option for itinerants concerned with peace, the environment, and social issues in general. In an old villa on a quiet street, the bright, clean premises include a planted terrace, lending reference library, and kitchen where you can cook your own food. There are rooms for couples and bunk dormitories for larger groups and individuals. Two baths serve six rooms. ⊠ *Avda. 6B and C. 15, Apdo. 1507–1000,* ☎ FAX *233–6168. 6 rooms without baths. Kitchenettes, library, meeting room. No credit cards.*

$ ⚕ **Hotel Ritz.** Inexpensive accommodations and a safe neighborhood are the selling points of this Swiss-owned hotel a couple of blocks south of the Parque Central. You get what you pay for: the rooms are clean but very basic, with wood floors and soft beds; rooms in back are quiet but gloomy. The hotel's ground floor is actually the "Pensión Centro Continental," which has even cheaper rooms, all of which share a bath. Breakfast is served in a common area upstairs. ⊠ *C. Central between Avdas. 8 and 10, Apdo. 6783–1000,* ☎ *222–4103,* FAX *222–8849. 25 rooms, 7 with bath. Travel services. AE, DC, MC, V.*

$ ⚕ **Toruma Youth Hostel.** The headquarters of Costa Rica's expanding hostel network is housed in an elegant colonial bungalow in the suburb of Los Yoses, east of downtown. The tiled lobby and veranda are ideal spots for backpackers to hang out and exchange travel tips. Beds on the ground floor are in little compartments with doors, whereas the second-floor rooms have standard bunks. There are also two private rooms available for couples. An on-site information center offers discounts on tours. ⊠ *Avda. Central between Cs. 29 and 31, Apdo. 1355–1002,* ☎ FAX *224–4085. 2 rooms and 80 beds with shared baths. Dining room. MC, V.*

Metro San José

$$$$ ⚕ **Marriott.** Towering over a coffee plantation west of San José, the
★ stately building evokes an unusual colonial splendor. The thick columns, wide arches, and central courtyard are straight out of the 17th century, and hand-painted tiles and abundant antiques complete the historic ambience. Guest rooms have a more contemporary decor, though they're elegant enough, with hardwood furniture—including a cabinet that holds the TV set—and sliding glass doors that open onto tiny "Juliet" balconies. ⊠ *San Antonio de Belén,* ☎ *298–0000; 800/228–9290 in the U.S.,* FAX *298–0044. 245 rooms with bath, 7 suites. 2 restaurants, café, lobby lounge, 2 pools, beauty salon, driving range, putting green, 3 tennis courts, health club, shops, business services, meeting rooms, travel services, car rental. AE, DC, MC, V.*

$$$$ ⚕ **Meliá Cariari.** The low-rise Meliá Cariari was San José's original luxury hotel, and it remains popular because of a wide range of facilities and its out-of-town location. Set down from the busy General Cañas Highway, about halfway between San José and the international airport, the Cariari is surrounded by thick vegetation that buffers it from traffic noise. Spacious, carpeted guest rooms in back overlook the pool area. The relaxed poolside bar, with cane chairs and mustard tablecloths, and nearby casino are popular spots. ⊠ *Autopista General Cañas, just east of intersection for San Antonio de Belén, Apdo. 737–1007,* ☎ *239–0022; 800/227–4274 in the U.S.,* FAX *239–2803. 220 rooms with bath. 2 restaurants, bar, cafeteria, pool, hot tub, golf privileges, 4 tennis courts, casino. AE, DC, MC, V.*

NIGHTLIFE AND THE ARTS

The Arts

Film

Dubbing is rare in Costa Rica, so moviegoers can see films in their original language, usually English, and brush up on their Spanish by reading the subtitles. The film scene is dominated by U.S. movies, which reach San José about a month after their release in the United States. Check the local paper *La Nación* for current listings. **Sala Garbo and Laurence Olivier** (⊠ Avda. 2 and C. 28, ☎ 222–1034) shows art and independent films. **Cine Variedades** (⊠ C. 5 between Avdas. Central and 1, ☎ 222–6108) is San José's other art cinema.

Theater and Music

The baroque **Teatro Nacional** (⊠ Plaza de la Cultura, ☎ 221–1329 for tickets and info) hosts performances of the excellent National Symphony Orchestra, whose season runs from April to December, with concerts on Friday evening and Sunday morning. The Teatro Nacional also stages performances from visiting musical groups and dance troupes. San José's second main theater is the **Teatro Melico Salazar** (⊠ Avda. 2 between Cs. Central and 2, ☎ 221–4952 for tickets and info). Dozens of theater groups, including one that performs in English, put on shows at smaller theaters around town; check the English-language *Tico Times* for play and concert information.

Nightlife

Bars and Discos

Blending white walls, bare brickwork, and timber, **La Esmeralda** (⊠ Avda. 2 between Cs. 5 and 7) is a late-night mariachi bar where visitors are serenaded and can check out at paintings depicting old scenes of San José. The food here isn't bad either. A trendy place to see and be seen is **El Cuartel de la Boca del Monte** (⊠ Avda. 1 between Cs. 21 and 23), a large, low-ceiling bar, where young artists and professionals gather to sip San José's fanciest cocktails, and share plates of tasty *bocas* (appetizers or snacks). They have live music on Monday and Wednesday nights. **Río** in the Los Yoses suburb is always rocking and crowded with young Ticos on weekends. **La Maga** in the back of the Cocorí shopping center, in Los Yoses, has live jazz Tuesday night. In San Pedro, lively bars line the streets around the university. The Spanish village–themed shopping arcade **Centro Comercial El Pueblo** (☞ Exploring San José, *above*) hosts a range of bars, restaurants, and discos. Recommended are **Cocoloco**, which often has a live salsa band, and **La Plaza**, across the street, with its huge dance floor.

Déja Vù (⊠ C. 2 between Avdas. 14 and 16A) is a mostly gay, techno-heavy disco with two dance floors. Gay and lesbian travelers can also hit the following bars and dance clubs: **Buenas Vibraciones** (⊠ Paseo de los Estudiantes). **El Churro Español** (⊠ Avda. 8 and C. 11). **La Avispa** (⊠ C. 1 between Avdas. 8 and 10).

Casinos

The 24-hour **Casino Colonial** (⊠ Avda. 1 between Cs. 9 and 11, ☎ 258–2827) has a complete casino, cable TV, bar, restaurant, and a betting service for major U.S. sporting events. Most of the country's larger hotels also have casinos, including the Aurola Holiday Inn (the view from the casino is breathtaking), Meliá Cariari, and Gran Hotel Costa Rica (☞ Lodging, *above*).

Nightclub

La Benny (⊠ Avda. 7 at C. Central) hosts an authentic Cuban floor show—a miniature Copacabana—Friday nights at 11.

OUTDOOR ACTIVITIES AND SPORTS

Participant Sports

Gyms

Luxury hotels like the Aurola Holiday Inn, Marriott, and the Meliá Cariari (☞ Lodging, *above*) have modern gyms attached, available to guests only. **Gimnasio Perfect Line** (⊠ C. 1 at Avda. Central, 6th floor) is a full gym offering inexpensive one-month memberships. For a complete listing, look under "Gimnasios" in the *Páginas Amarillas* (Yellow Pages).

Horseback Riding

Most of the city's travel agencies can arrange one-day horseback tours, which take you to farms in the surrounding Central Valley. Several Central Valley hotels also run their own horseback tours, one of the best of which is offered by La Providencia, near the top of Volcán Poás. The **Sacramento Lodge** (⊠ Just above Sacramento, ☎ 237–2116, ℻ 237–2976), on the upper slopes of Volcán Barva, has a horseback tour that includes round-trip transportation, breakfast, lunch, and great views.

Running

Once the airport but now a eucalyptus-shaded park, **Parque La Sabana,** at the end of the Paseo Colón, is the best place to run in San José, with 5-km (3-mi) routes along cement paths.

White-Water Rafting

White-water trips down the Reventazón, Pacuare, and General rivers all leave from San José (☞ Guided Tours *in* San José A to Z, *below*), but the action takes place in other parts of the country. At least six licensed tour companies out of San José operate similar rafting and kayaking trips of varying length and grade on the Pacuare and other rivers with their headwaters in the Turrialba area. The Reventazón's class III and IV–V runs are both day trips, the General is descended in a three-day camping trip, and the Pacuare can be run in one, two, or three days. Accommodations are in a tent or a rustic lodge, depending on the outfitter. A couple of the companies have built lodges halfway down the run, making it possible to overnight in great comfort on the riverbank.

Try **Costa Rica Whitewater** (☎ 257–0766, ℻ 255–4354), **Ríos Tropicales** (☎ 233–6455, ℻ 255–4354), **Aventuras Naturales** (⊠ Behind Banco Nacional, San Pedro, ☎ 225–3939 and 224–0505, ℻ 253–6934), and **Pioneer Raft** (☎ 225–8117 and 225–4735, ℻ 253–4687). The cost is around $70 to $90 for one day. Call around to price two- and three-day packages with overnight stays.

SHOPPING

Specialty Items

Antiques

Antigüedades El Museo (⊠ C. 5 between Avdas. 3 and 3B, ☎ 223–9552) sells antique paintings, ceramics, and other smaller items.

Arts and Crafts

The **Mercado Central** (☞ Exploring San José, *above*) has the best range and prices for hammocks and leather bags, belts, and shoes, but shop around and haggle before digging out your wallet. The best place for bags and belts at the market is near the northwestern entrance. The **Centro Comercial El Pueblo** (☞ Exploring San José, *above*), on the northern edge of Barrio Tournón, is an open-air shopping center designed to look like a colonial village, and most of its shops cater to tourists. You'll find dozens of stalls on the western end of the **Plaza de la Democracia** (☞ Exploring San José, *above*), where vendors sell inexpensive handicrafts, T-shirts, and other items.

Atmósfera (⊠ C. 5 between Avdas. 1 and 3, ☎ 222–4322) is good for jewelry, masks, wall hangings, and dishes with bright, primitive designs. **Boutique Annemarie** (⊠ C. 9 at Avda. 9, in the lobby of the Don Carlos hotel, ☎ 221–6707, ☞ Lodging, *above*), is particularly strong in small wooden objects and imitation pre-Columbian stoneware. **La Casona** (⊠ C. Central between Avdas. Central and 1, ☎ no phone) is an indoor market selling almost every craft typical of Central America. **Magia** (⊠ C. 5 between Avdas. 1 and 3, in the lobby of the Don Carlos hotel, ☎ 233–2630), a few doors north of Atmósfera, specializes in fine woodwork. **Suráska** (⊠ C. 5 and Avda. 3, ☎ 222–0129) has an interesting selection of wooden crafts, ceramics, and paintings.

Books and Maps
Chispas Books (⊠ C. 7 between Avdas. Central and 1, ☎ 256–8251) has an excellent selection of books in English, especially those concerning Latin America and tropical ecology. **Lehmann** (⊠ Avda. Central between Cs. 1 and 3, ☎ 223–1212) has some books in English, as well as a stock of large-scale topographical maps.

Coffee and Liquor
Coffee can be purchased in souvenir shops and supermarkets; the best brand is Café Rey Tarrazú; the second best is Café Britt. You can also buy good, fresh-roasted coffee at **La Esquina del Café** (⊠ Avda. 9 at C. 3 Bis., ☎ 257–9868). The country's best rum is the aged Centenario, and you can pick up a bottle for about $5. There are also several brands of coffee liqueurs, which are all good. **Yamuni** (⊠ Avda. 2 and C. 7, ☎ 222–3132) is one of San José's largest liquor stores.

SAN JOSÉ A TO Z

Arriving and Departing

By Bus
San José has no central bus station. For bus stops for the city's suburbs, *see* Chapter 3.

By Car
San José is the hub of the national road system. Paved roads fan out from Paseo Colón south to Escazú, or north to the airport and Heredia. For the Pacific coast, Guanacaste, and Nicaragua, take the Inter-American Highway (CA1). Calle 3 runs east into the highway to Guápiles, Limón, and the Atlantic coast. If you follow Avenidas Central or 2 east through San Pedro, you'll enter the Inter-American Highway (CA2) south, which has a turnoff for Cartago, Volcán Irazú, and Turrialba, before heading over the mountains to the Southwest and Panama.

By Plane
AIRPORTS
All international and some domestic flights arrive at **Aeropuerto Internacional Juan Santamaría** (☎ 441–0744), 16 km (10 mi) north-

west of downtown San José. Some domestic flights depart from **Aerop-uerto Internacional Tobías Bolaños** in the suburb of Pavas, 3 km (2 mi) west of downtown San José.

BETWEEN THE AIRPORT AND DOWNTOWN

Taxis from the airport to downtown cost around $10. Beware of taxi drivers eager to take you to a hotel they know, which no doubt pays them a hefty commission. Far cheaper, and almost as quick, is the bus marked RUTA 200 SAN JOSÉ, which will drop you at the west end of Avenida 2, close to the city's heart. The other option is to rent a vehicle from one of the car-rental offices (☞ Car Rentals, *below*). Driving time is about 20 minutes, but allow 40 to be safe. Note that some hotels provide a free shuttle service—inquire when you book.

Getting Around

By Bus

Bus service within San José is absurdly cheap and easy to use. For Paseo Colón and La Sabana take buses marked SABANA-CEMENTERIO from the stop on Avenida 3 and Calle 2. For the university-vicinity suburbs of Los Yoses and San Pedro take those marked SAN PEDRO, CURRIDABAT, or LOURDES from Avenida 2, between Calles 5 and 7.

By Car

Almost all the streets in downtown San José are one-way. Traffic gets surprisingly congested at peak hours, when it's ill-advised to drive.

By Taxi

Taxis are a good deal in the capital. You can hail them—all taxis are red—in the street or call a taxi company directly. A 3-km (2-mi) ride costs around $1; tipping is not usually done here. Taxis parked in front of expensive hotels charge about twice the normal rate. By law, all cabbies must use their meters; if one refuses, negotiate a price before going anywhere. Cab companies include: **San Jorge** (☎ 221–3434), **Coopetaxi** (☎ 235–9966), and if you need to go to the airport, **Taxis Unidos** (☎ 221–6865).

Contacts and Resources

Car Rentals

ADA (⊠ Avda. 18 between Cs. 11 and 13, ☎ 233–7733). **Budget** (⊠ Paseo Colón at C. 30, ☎ 223–3284). Note: it is practically impossible to rent a car in Costa Rica from December 20 to January 3; try to book far in advance.

Doctors and Dentists

Your embassy can provide you with a list of recommended doctors and dentists. Hospitals open to foreigners include: **Clínica Bíblica** (⊠ Avda. 14 between Cs. Central and 1, ☎ 257–0466 emergencies; 221–3922 appointments), and **Clínica Católica** (⊠ Guadalupe, attached to San Antonio Church on C. Esquivel Bonilla St., ☎ 283–6616).

Embassies

Canada (⊠ Sabana Sur, next to tennis club, ☎ 296–4146). **U.K.** (⊠ Centro Colón, Paseo Colón between Cs. 38 and 40, ☎ 221–5566). **U.S.** (⊠ Pavas, ☎ 220–3939).

Emergencies

In just about any emergency you can dial ☎ 911, but here are some additional useful numbers: **Fire** (☎ 118). **Ambulance** (☎ 128). **Police** (☎ 117; 127 outside cities). **Traffic Police** (☎ 222–9330).

English-Language Bookstores
See Shopping, *above,* for English-language bookstores.

Guided Tours

ADVENTURE

Aventuras Naturales (✉ Behind Banco Nacional, San Pedro, ☎ 225–3939, FAX 253–6934) leads rafting and mountain-biking tours. **Costa Rica Expeditions** (✉ Avda. 3 at Calle Central, San José, ☎ 222–0333, FAX 257–1665) is one of the country's most experienced rafting outfitters. **Ríos Tropicales** (✉ 50 m south of Centro Colón, San José, ☎ 233–6455, FAX 255–4354) offers rafting, sea-kayaking, and mountain-biking tours. **Rain Forest Aerial Tram** (✉ Avda. 7, between Calles 5 and 7, ☎ 257–5961) takes visitors floating through the treetops on a modified ski lift. **Tropical Bungee** (✉ Sabana Sur, 100 m west and 200 m south of Controlaría, Sabana, ☎ 232–3956) runs bungee jumps near San José on weekends.

DAY TRIPS

Bay Island Cruises (✉ 125 m north of Toyota Paseo Colón,, ☎ 258–3536, FAX 258–1189) and **Calypso** (✉ Arcadas building, 3rd fl., next to Gran Hotel Costa Rica, Apdo. 6941–1000, ☎ 256–2727, FAX 256–6767) run cruises to Isla Tortuga. Hail coffee lovers: the popular coffee tour run by **Café Britt** (✉ 900 m north and 400 m west of the Comandancia, Heredia, ☎ 260–2748, FAX 238–1848), in Heredia, presents the history of coffee via skits, a tour of a coffee farm, and coffee tasting. **Cruceros del Sur** (✉ Across from Colegio Los Angeles, Sabana Norte, San José, ☎ 232–6672, FAX 220–2103).

NATURAL HISTORY

Although everyone is setting up ecological tours, there are a few companies that have more experience than the majority, among them the following: **Cosmos Tours** (✉ 50 m north and 50 m east of Centro Cultural Norteamericano Costarricense, ☎ 234–0607, FAX 253–4707). **Costa Rica Expeditions** (✉ Avda. 3 at Calle Central, San José, ☎ 222–0333, FAX 257–1665). **Horizontes** (✉ 150 m north of Pizza Hut Paseo Colón, ☎ 222–2022, FAX 255–4513). **Costa Rica Sun Tours** (✉ 200 m south of Toyota Paseo Colón, ☎ 255–2011, FAX 255–4410). **Tikal Ecoadventures** (✉ Avda. 2 between Calles 7 and 9, ☎ 223–2811, FAX 223–1916).

WHITE-WATER RAFTING

See Outdoor Activities and Sports, *above.*

Late-Night Pharmacies
The Clínica Bíblica (☞ Doctors and Dentists, *above*) operates a 24-hour pharmacy.

Travel Agencies
Galaxy (✉ C. 3 between Avdas. 5 and 7, ☎ 233–3240). **Aviatica** (✉ Avda. 1 at C. 1, ☎ 222–5630). **Intertur** (✉ Avda. Central between C. 31 and 33, ☎ 253–7503).

Visitor Information
The main tourist office for the entire country is on the 11th floor of the **Instituto Costarricense de Turism** (ICT) building, 1 block southeast of the Teatro Nacional. The helpful staff can provide maps, bus schedules, and information. ✉ *Avda. 4 between Cs. 5 and 7, 11th floor,* ☎ *223–1733.* ☉ *Weekdays 9–3:30.*

3 Central Valley: Around San José

A ring of spectacular volcanoes defines the boundaries of the Central Valley. This densely populated agricultural area is heavily planted with neat rows of coffee bushes and dotted with colorful farm towns and small cities. Set in its center is San José, a convenient base for exciting day excursions. Peer into the crater of a volcano, wander amidst flowering orchids and other tropical plants, or visit colonial-era towns that have prospered thanks to the grano de oro (golden bean).

THE MESETA CENTRAL, OR CENTRAL VALLEY, is Costa Rica's approximate geographic center. The valley's southern edge is defined by the foothills of the

By David
Dudenhoefer
and Justin
Henderson

Cordillera de Talamanca, its northern side dominated by three sentinel-like volcanoes, the summits of which are protected within national parks. Volcán Irazú, Costa Rica's highest, towers to the east of San José; Poás, whose active crater often spews a plume of sulfuric smoke, stands to the northwest; the older Volcán Barva looms between the two. Dramatic craters and thick cloud forests envelop these conical giants, while the slopes in their shadows host a variety of farms and charming agricultural hamlets.

The plateau is the nation's cultural cradle, with San José and other important historical cities among its inhabitants—not to mention a population of 1.5 million. Though most of the region's colonial architecture was destroyed by earthquakes and the ravages of time, several smaller cities preserve a bit more history than does San José. The central squares of Alajuela, Escazú, and Heredia, for example, are surrounded by an architectural mixture of old and new. Cartago, the country's first capital, has scattered historical structures and the impressive Basílica de Los Angeles. Beyond those small cities lie dozens of tiny agricultural communities, where you can discover lovely churches and adobe farmhouses with coffee growing in the backyard.

The Central Valley's varied attractions can easily be experienced on a series of half- or full-day excursions from San José, and the abundance of excellent accommodations and restaurants in the valley's other cities and towns means lodging in San José is by no means obligatory.

Pleasures and Pastimes

Dining

This region's dining options run the gamut, from the rustic mountain lodges, where hearty meals are enhanced by the beauty of the natural surroundings, to the gourmet restaurants in the hills above Escazú—fine dining with a backdrop of San José's city lights. Since Escazú lies so close to San José, consider venturing to this bedroom community for a meal or two.

Festivals

The Día de la Virgen de Los Angeles, which honors Costa Rica's patron saint, is celebrated in Cartago on August 2, with processions and a well-attended mass. On the night before, tens of thousands of the faithful walk *la romaría*, a 22-km (14-mi) trek down the highway from San José to Cartago. April 11 is Juan Santamaría Day, celebrated in Alajuela with a loud parade and other fun. The Festival of Mangoes, also in Alajuela, involves nine days of music, parades, markets, and general merrymaking in July. The second Sunday in March marks the Día del Boyero (Oxcart Driver Day), when a colorful procession of carts parades through San Antonio de Escazú.

Lodging

The accommodations scattered across this area range from the rustic *cabinas* (cottages) to elegant suites. Most travelers tend to stay in San José, since its convenient position makes it possible to visit all the Central Valley's attractions on day trips. The city has an ample selection of hotels and restaurants, but it also has the crime, noise, and pollution that accompany crowds and traffic, which can make lodging in one of the surrounding communities a more attractive option.

Volcanoes

Some of Costa Rica's most accessible volcanoes stand along the northern edge of the Central Valley, two of which, Poás and Irazú, have paved roads right to their summits. Volcán Poás is very popular, since it packs in an extensive visitor's center, impressive active crater, luxuriant forest, and a jewel-like, blue-green lake. Volcán Irazú, the country's highest, is topped by a desolate but impressive landscape—the result of violent eruptions in the early 1960s—but on a clear day the view is unparalleled. Barva in the southern section of Parque Nacional Braulio Carrillo, is cloaked in an extensive cloud forest resounding with the chittering of colorful birds such as the emerald toucanet and multicolored quetzal. All three volcanoes can be visited on day trips from San José; Poás and Irazú require only a morning, whereas you'll need a full day to hike the summit of Barva.

Exploring the Central Valley: Around San José

Numbers in the text correspond to numbers in the margin and on the Central Valley: Around San José map.

Great Itineraries

Most of the Central Valley's towns stand in the shadows of volcanoes, so include stops at one or two of those towns. To reach Volcán Poás, for example, you have to drive through Alajuela. Heredia lies on the road to Volcán Barva, and Cartago sits at the foot of Irazú. From Irazú, you can take the serpentine roads eastward to Volcán Turrialba, Turrialba, and the Monumento Nacional Guayabo, the country's most important archaeological site. Paraíso, just southeast of Cartago, is the gateway to the Valle de Orosí (Orosí Valley) southeast of San José.

IF YOU HAVE 2 DAYS

Start by ascending 🖬 **Volcán Poás** ⑤, where you can settle in for a night near the summit, or simply enjoy a good lunch before returning to warmer 🖬 **Alajuela** ④, or San José. Next day, explore the Orosí Valley, stopping at the fascinating **Jardín Lankester** ⑩ on the way.

IF YOU HAVE 4 DAYS

On day one, head north to 🖬 **Heredia** ② and the adjacent coffee communities, continuing up the slopes of **Volcán Barva** ③ for a picnic or gourmet lunch in the cool mountain air. Energetic travelers may want to dedicate a day to hiking up to the crater lakes atop the volcano. Head northeast and spend the next day exploring **Cartago** ⑧ and the **Orosí Valley** ⑪– ⑬, starting with a morning in **Refugio Nacional de Fauna Silvestre Tapantí** ⑬. Early the next morning, head up to the summit of **Volcán Irazú** ⑨, then wind your way down its slopes to 🖬 **Turrialba** ⑭, stopping at **Monumento Nacional Guayabo** ⑮ on the way. If you spend that night in Turrialba, you could go rafting on the fourth day, or you can return to western Central Valley and spend your fourth day at 🖬 **Volcán Poás** ⑤, visiting the towns of 🖬 **Grecia** ⑥ and **Sarchí** ⑦ in the afternoon.

IF YOU HAVE 6 DAYS

Start by exploring the community of 🖬 **Escazú** ①, then spend the afternoon in **Sarchí** ⑦ and 🖬 **Grecia** ⑥. On day two, visit the summit of 🖬 **Volcán Poás** ⑤, stopping at 🖬 **Alajuela** ④ and Zoo Ave, the bird zoo, afterwards. Dedicate day three to horseback riding or hiking in the mountains above 🖬 **Heredia** ②, or exploration of that historic city and surrounding towns. Head for the 🖬 **Orosí Valley** ⑪–⑬ on the following day, where you should start by visiting **Refugio Nacional de Fauna Silvestre Tapantí** ⑬. The fifth day should begin with a trip up **Volcán Irazú** ⑨, after which you can wander through **Cartago** ⑧ and **Jardín Lankester** ⑩, continuing east to 🖬 **Turrialba** ⑭. Dedicate day six to ex-

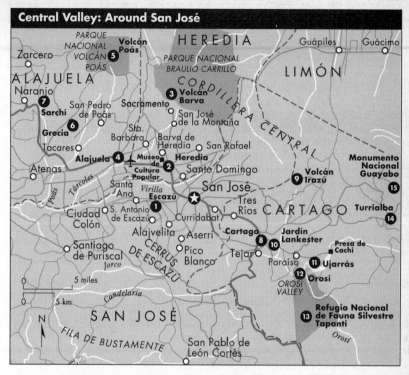

Central Valley: Around San José

ploring **Monumento Nacional Guayabo** ⑮ and the CATIE, or white-water rafting on either the Río Reventazón or Río Pacuare.

When to Tour The Central Valley: Around San José

From January to May it tends to be sunny and breezy on an almost daily basis. Nights in January and February can get quite cold. After mid-May, skies begin to cloud up and rain almost every afternoon. Regular afternoon downpours are consistent during May and June, dropping off a bit between mid-July and mid-September. The precipitation becomes more copious from September to December. There are many dry days scattered throughout the rainy season, and normally it only storms a few hours every afternoon. The area is swathed in green during the rainy months, but come January the sun begins to beat down, and by April the countryside is parched. Despite rain the wet months can be a pleasant time to explore the region. Few tourists visit during this period, so you probably won't need reservations.

Though it rains very little in December, it is very difficult to rent a car during the last two weeks of the year, when Costa Ricans reserve them for the holidays. Since it can also be very difficult to get a room anywhere outside San José during the week preceding Easter, you'll want to make your reservations well in advance.

WESTERN CENTRAL VALLEY

Escazú, Heredia, Barva Volcano, Alajuela, Poás Volcano, Grecia, and Sarchí

As you drive north or west out of San José, the bungalowed, grid-plan suburbs of the city quickly give way to arable land, most of which is dedicated to vast coffee plantations. Coffee has come to symbolize the prosperity of both the Central Valley and the nation as a whole; as such, this all-important cash crop has developed a certain amount of cultural mystique and folklore. Costa Rican artists, for example, have long venerated coffee workers, and the painted oxcart, once used to transport coffee to the coast, has become a national symbol.

Within Costa Rica's coffee heartland, you'll find plenty of tranquil agricultural towns and two provincial capitals, Alajuela and Heredia, with a few rare architectural treasures. Those two cities owe their relative prosperity to coffee beans cultivated on the fertile lower slopes of Poás and Barva volcanoes, which tower to the north. The upper slopes of both these volcanoes are too cold for coffee and have thus been dedicated to dairy cattle, strawberries, ferns, and flowers.

This area deserves at least two days: one for Alajuela, Volcán Poás, Grecia, and Sarchí, and one for Heredia and Volcán Barva. Escazú lies close enough to San José to be visited in a matter of hours, or it can serve as your base in the Central Valley. Since there are some pleasant lodges in the hills above these towns, rural overnights can be a wonderful way to stretch out your exploration of this compact area.

Escazú

① *5 km (3 mi) southwest of San José.*

A quick drive to the west of San José takes you to Escazú, a traditional coffee-farming town, now a bedroom community of the capital, at the foot of a small mountain range. Local lore has coined it "the city of witches," as it is known as a popular spot among those spell-casting women. An ancient church faces a small plaza here, and plenty of adobe homes have been erected nearby. Scattered amidst the coffee fields that cover the steep slopes above town are well-tended farmhouses, often painted blue and white, with tidy gardens and the occasional oxcart parked in the yard. There are also plenty of fancy homes between those humble farmhouses, since Escazú has long been popular among wealthy foreigners and Ticos.

High in those hills above Escazú stands the tiny community of **San Antonio de Escazú,** famous for its annual oxcart festival, held on the second Sunday of March. The view of the Central Valley—nearby San José and distant volcanoes—is impressive from San Antonio, both by day and night, but for even greater drama, head higher: practically vertical roads wind up into the mountains, toward **Pico Blanco,** the highest point in the Escazú Cordillera.

Dining and Lodging

$$$$ ✕ **Le Monastere.** The view from this place is one of Escazú's best—a 270-degree panorama featuring those pensive, ominous volcanoes. The interior is equally impressive, a former chapel dressed up with antiques. But Le Monastere would probably be popular regardless. The Belgian owner has stayed true to his homeland's outstanding culinary tradition, offering the classic French dishes and some interestingly original Costa Rican items, such as iguana sautéed with vegetables. They only serve dinner, from 7 PM to 11 PM. Reservations are recommended. ✉ *San Rafael de Escazú, take old road to Santa Ana, turn left 4 streets after U.S. ambassador's residence, follow signs,* ☎ *289–4404. AE, DC, MC, V. Closed Sun. No lunch.*

$$$ ✕ **Hostaria Cerutti.** This little Italian restaurant on a busy intersection in Escazú is the diva of San José's Italian eateries. It occupies a lovely adobe house more than 100 years old, its whitewashed walls adorned with antique prints. The seafood-friendly menu is extensive: start off with octopus and asparagus in pesto, or ravioli with mushrooms in a truffle sauce, then sink your teeth into some grilled tuna or a *sirloin hostaria*, in a tomato sauce with mushrooms, artichoke hearts, and olives. Reservations are recommended. ⊠ *Cruce de San Rafael de Escazú,* ☎ *228–4511. AE, DC, MC, V. Closed Tues.*

$$$$ ⊞ **Alta.** This is lofty in both location, appearance, *and* prices. Its design evokes colonial Spain through such details as barrel-tile roofs, ocher mixed into the stucco on the walls, and hand-painted bathroom tiles. A high-ceilinged foyer leads into a sloping stairway lined with tall columns and palm trees, recalling a narrow street in some ancient Iberian city. Rooms on floors two through five have small balconies, and ground-floor rooms have garden terraces and direct pool access. The culinary creations of the Californian chef have made the restaurant popular among residents. ⊠ *Old road to Santa Ana, Escazú,* ☎ *282–4160,* ᴀ̃ᴄ *282–4162;* ⊠ *Interlink 964, Box 02–5635, Miami, FL 33102,* ☎ *U.S. toll free 888/388–ALTA. 19 rooms with bath, 4 suites. Restaurant, pool, sauna. AE, DC, MC, V.*

$$$$ ⊞ **Tara Resort Hotel.** Scarlett never had it so good. Modeled after the
★ house of the same name in *Gone With the Wind* and decorated in antebellum style, this hotel near the top of Pico Blanco is a luxurious little inn. Hardwood floors throughout the three-story, white-and-green building are covered with patterned area rugs. Guest rooms are decorated with floral spreads and lace curtains; French doors open onto the veranda. At the Atlanta Dining Gallery, try the beef tenderloin in green-pepper sauce and chicken Tara in a mango-avocado sauce. ⊠ *Apdo. 1459–1250, Escazú, from central church head south and follow signs,* ☎ *228–6992,* ᴀ̃ᴄ *228–9651. 12 rooms with bath, 1 suite, 1 bungalow. Restaurant, pool, hot tub, massage, spa. AE, DC, MC, V.*

$$$ ⊞ **Posada El Quijote.** At this friendly, family-run bed-and-breakfast— perched on a hill in the neighborhood of Bello Horizonte on the San José side of Escazú—you'll find the best vantage point from the sundeck. The living room has big windows, a couch, a fireplace, and lots of modern art. Deluxe rooms also have city views, and superior rooms overlook the gardens. All rooms have queen-size beds, ceiling fans, and cable TV; complimentary breakfast is served on a covered, interior patio. ⊠ *Bello Horizonte de Escazú,* ☎ *289–8401,* ᴀ̃ᴄ *289–8729;* ⊠ *Dept. 239–SJO, Box 025216, Miami, FL 33102-5216 . 8 rooms with bath. Breakfast room, travel services. AE, MC, V.*

$$–$$$ ⊞ **Costa Verde Inn.** Rooms at this B&B on the outskirts of Escazú make nice use of local hardwoods. South American art adorns the main building, where a large sitting area has comfortable chairs and a fireplace. The inn is surrounded by gardens, and at night you can see the lights of San José twinkling to the east. Complimentary breakfast is served on the shady patio. ⊠ *From the southeast corner of the Parque Central, 654 yds west and 109 yds north,* ☎ *228–4080,* ᴀ̃ᴄ *289–8591;* ⊠ *SJO 1313, Box 025216, Miami, FL 33102-5216. 15 rooms with bath. Pool, hot tub, tennis court. AE, DC, MC, V.*

Heredia

➋ *9 km (6 mi) north of San José.*

With a population of around 30,000, Heredia is the capital of one of the country's most important coffee-producing provinces. Perhaps Costa Rica's best-preserved colonial town, Heredia bears witness to just how little that means in an earthquake-prone country: it has lost nearly all its colonial structures. Nevertheless, a fair amount of old adobe buildings are still scattered through Heredia, and even more can be seen in nearby Barva de Heredia, Santo Domingo, and San Rafael.

The **Parque Central** does retain a bit of its colonial charm. At its eastern end stands an impressive **stone church**, dating back to 1797, whose thick walls, small windows, and squat buttresses have kept it standing through countless quakes and tremors. Unfortunately, the church's stained-glass work has not fared as well as the walls. The park itself is sparsely landscaped with a simple kiosk and a cast-iron fountain imported from England in 1897. Surrounding the park are some interesting buildings, such as the barrel-tile roofed **Casa de la Cultura,** which often houses art exhibits, and the brick **Municipalidad,** behind which stands a strange, decorative tower called the *fortín,* or small fort.

The small community of **Barva de Heredia,** just to the north of Heredia proper (about 2 km/1 mi), has a wonderful **central plaza** surrounded by old Spanish-tiled adobe houses on three sides, and a white stucco **church** to the east. That squat, handsome church is flanked by royal palms dates from the late 18th century; behind the rather simple interior is a lovely little garden shrine to the Virgin Mary. On a clear day, you can see verdant Volcán Barva towering to the north, and if you follow the road that runs in front of the church, veering to the right, you'll reach Sacramento, where it turns into a steep, dirt track leading to the Barva sector of Parque Nacional Braulio Carrillo.

A worthwhile stop between Heredia and Barva is the **Museo de Cultura Popular** (Museum of Popular Culture), run by the Universidad Nacional. A turn-of-the-century farmhouse constructed with an adobe-like technique called *bahareque* has been furnished with antiques and is surrounded by a small garden and coffee fields. An inexpensive, open-air, lunch-only restaurant serves authentic Costa Rican cuisine; it can be a lively spot on weekends, when a more extensive menu is sometimes paired with marimba music and folk dancing. ⊠ *Between Heredia and Barva, follow signs for right turn,* ☎ *260–1619.* ☞ *$1.50.* ☺ *Daily 9–5; restaurant 11–2:30. No credit cards.*

Costa Rica's most popular export-quality coffee, **Café Britt,** offers tours at its working coffee plantation. The tour highlights the history of coffee cultivation in Costa Rica, and includes a theatrical presentation, a short walk through the coffee farm and processing plant, and a coffee-tasting session. ⊠ *900 m north and 400 m west of the Comandancia, Heredia,* ☎ *260–2748,* ﬁﬂ *238–1848.* ☞ *$15, $20 with transport from San José.* ☺ *Daily 9 and 11, Dec.–May also 3.*

Just to the northeast (about 2 km/1 mi) of Heredia lies **San Rafael,** another quiet, mildly affluent coffee town with a large church notable for its stained-glass windows and bright interior. The road north from the church winds its way up the slopes of Volcán Barva to the Hotel Chalet Tirol (☞ Lodging *in* Volcán Barva, *below*), and the Monte de la Cruz. **Santo Domingo,** to the southeast of Heredia, is another attractive agricultural community with two churches, an abundance of adobe houses, and some traditional coffee farms on its outskirts.

Lodging

$$$$ ▥ **Finca Rosa Blanca Country Inn.** There's nothing common about
 ★   this bed-and-breakfast overlooking the coffee farms west of Barva de Heredia; you need merely step through the front door of the Gaudiesque main building and marvel at the soaring ceiling, white stucco arches, columns, and polished wood. Each guest room is different, all with original art, local hardwoods, colorful fabrics, and paintings. The spacious, two-story suite is out of a fairy tale, with its spiral staircase

COSTA RICA'S GOLDEN BEAN

WHEN COSTA RICA'S first elected president, Juan Mora Fernandez, in about 1830 began encouraging his compatriots to cultivate coffee, he could hardly have imagined how profound an impact the crop would have on his country. During the last century, coffee transformed Costa Rica from a colonial backwater into a relatively affluent and cosmopolitan republic.

The "golden bean" financed the construction of most of the nation's landmarks. Founding families owned the biggest plantations, creating a coffee oligarchy from which the majority of Costa Rican presidents have come. The bean also provided an economic incentive for tens of thousands of immigrant families, who, in the 1960s and 70s, were given land if they would cut down the forest and plant coffee. These farmers formed the backbone of a middle class majority that has long distinguished Costa Rica from most of Latin America.

Thanks to its altitude and mineral-rich volcanic soil, the Central Valley is ideal for growing coffee. The crop covers nearly every arable acre of that region. Whether you credit the power of the caffeine, or the socioeconomic factors surrounding the crop, the tidy homes, colorful gardens, and orderly farms of the Central Valley make Costa Ricans look like the world's original coffee achievers.

Considering its domination of the Central Valley's physical and cultural landscape, it may come as a surprise that coffee isn't native to Costa Rica; biologists claim the plant evolved in the mountains of Ethiopia. Arab nations were sipping the aromatic beverage as early as the 7th century—its scientific name is *Coffea arabica*—but it didn't gain popularity in Europe until the 1600s. Coffee plants first arrived in Costa Rica from the Caribbean, probably in the early 1800s.

The coffee growing cycle begins in May, when the arrival of annual rains makes the dark green bushes explode into a flurry of white blossoms—as close as it comes to snowing in Costa Rica. By November, the fruit starts to ripen, turning from green to red, and the busy harvest begins, as farmers race to get picked "cherries" to *beneficios,* processing plants where the beans—two per fruit—are removed, washed, dried, and packed in burlap sacks for export. Costa Rica's crop is consistently among the world's best, and most of the high-grade exports wind up in Europe and the United States.

Coffee bushes are grown in the shade of trees, such as citrus, or nitrogen-fixing members of the bean family. Recently, however, many farmers have switched to sun-resistant varieties, cutting down shade trees to pack more coffee bushes into every acre. Shade farms provide habitats for migratory birds and other animals, and the new shadeless farms are practically biological deserts. Environmentalists are promoting a return to the old system, labeling shade coffee "ECO-OK."

TICOS ARE FUELED BY AN inordinate amount of coffee, which they filter through cloth bags— a method that makes for a stronger cup of José than your average American brew. The mean bean is even employed in cooking: a favorite local dish is chicken roasted with coffee wood. Ticos drink the low-grade stuff, often mixed with molasses, peanuts, or corn, and burned while roasting. You are thus best off buying such reliable brands as Café Rey's Tarrazú, Café Britt, Volio, or Montaña.

leading up to a window-lined tower bedroom. On the grounds—nicely planted with tropical flowers, and shaded by massive fig trees—are two villas, each with two bedrooms. Four-course dinners are optional. ⊠ *Barrio Jesus, 6 km (4 mi) west of Barva de Heredia,* ☎ *269–9392,* FAX *269–9555.* ⊠ *SJO 120, Box 025216, Miami, FL 33102-5216. 6 rooms with bath, 2 villas. Dining room, pool. AE, MC, V.*

$$$ ⊞ **Hotel Bougainvillea.** Here you'll easily forget that you're just 15 min-
★ utes from San José. Set amidst the coffee farms of Santo Domingo de Heredia, the hotel has extensive areas dominated by tall trees and decorated with plentiful flowers. Spacious, carpeted rooms feature local hardwoods; tiled baths come with tub and hair dryer. Decorating the lobby and excellent restaurant are paintings by local artists and pre-Columbian pieces. ⊠ *Apdo. 69–2120, San José, from San José take Guápiles Hwy. to Tibas exit then take road to Santo Domingo; follow signs,* ☎ *244–1414,* FAX *244–1313. 80 rooms with bath, 4 suites. Restaurant, bar, pool, sauna, tennis court. AE, MC, V.*

Volcán Barva

❸ *20 km (12 mi) north of Heredia.*

North of the community Barva de Heredia, the road becomes narrow and steep, as it winds its way up the verdant slopes of Volcán Barva, the 9,500-ft summit which is the highest point in **Parque Nacional Braulio Carrillo** (☞ Chapter 8). Long extinct, Barva is massive in size: its lower slopes are almost completely covered with coffee fields, interspersed among about a dozen small towns. The upper slopes consist of pastures divided by exotic pines, and the occasional native oak and cedar, which give way to the botanical diversity of the cloud forest near the top. The air is usually cool at the top; coupled with the pines and pastures, the atmosphere here will surprise if you expect only rain forest, bananas, and coffee beans to grow in Costa Rica.

Any vehicle can make the trip above San Rafael to the **Monte de la Cruz**, and even buses follow the loop above Barva via **San José de la Montaña**, but it's rough going if you want to get much higher than that. Expect a four-hour hike from San José de la Montaña to the crater; but a four-wheel-drive vehicle will get you to the park entrance during the dry months.

The misty, luxuriant summit is the only part of the park where camping is allowed and is a good place to see the rare resplendent quetzal, if you camp or arrive in the early morning. Because of its difficult access, Barva receives a mere fraction of the visitors that flock to the summits of Poás and Irazú. A 30-minute hike in from the ranger station takes you to the main crater, which is about 200 yds across. Its almost vertical sides are covered in poor man's umbrellas, a plant that thrives in the highlands, and oak trees laden with epiphytes. At the bottom of the crater is a dark lake; farther down the track into the forest lies another crater lake. Bring rain gear, boots, and a warm shirt, and stay on the trails—even experienced hikers who know the area have lost their way up here. ☎ *192 or 290–8202 National Parks Service information office.* 🎫 *$6.* ⊙ *Tues.–Sun. 7–4.*

Lodging

$$$ ⊞ **Hotel Chalet Tirol.** Amazingly enough, this place's Austrian archi-
★ tectural styles don't seem out of place amidst the pines, pastures, and cool air of Volcán Barva's upper slopes (it's 5,900 ft above sea level). The replica of a cobbled Tirolean town square—complete with fountain and church—may be a bit too much, but the cozy, bright two-story wooden chalets are quite charming, as is the restaurant, with its ivy,

wooden ceiling, and elegant murals. Quality French cuisine makes it a popular weekend destination for Costa Ricans, and the hotel hosts occasional classical music concerts. The newer suites offer more privacy and fireplaces. Breakfast is complimentary. ⊠ *San Rafael de Heredia, 10 km (6 mi) north of Heredia,* ☎ *267–7371,* FAX *267–6229. 10 chalets, 23 suites. Restaurant, bar, 2 tennis courts. AE, DC, MC, V.*

Outdoor Activities and Sports

HORSEBACK RIDING

Horseback riding tours along the upper slopes of Volcán Barva, near the Parque Nacional Braulio Carrillo, combine views of the Central Valley with close exposure to the cloud forest and resident bird life. They can be booked through the **Hotel Chalet Tirol** (☞ *above*), the **Sacramento Lodge** (⊠ Just above Sacramento, in the mountains due north of Barva de Heredia, ☎ 237–2116, FAX 237–2976), or most San José travel agents (☞ Contacts and Resources *in* San José A to Z, *in* Chapter 2).

HIKING

The upper slopes of Volcán Barva provide excellent hiking conditions, thanks to cool air, vistas, and an abundance of birds. The crater lakes that top the volcano can only be reached by hikers, and if you haven't got a four-wheel-drive vehicle, you'll have to hike from Sacramento up to the entrance of Parque Nacional Braulio Carrillo. Hotel Chalet Tirol runs an early morning walking tour down a 4-km (2½-mi) trail through the cloud forest—an excellent trip for bird-watchers.

Alajuela

❹ *20 km (13 mi) northwest of San José.*

Although it is Costa Rica's second-largest city (population 50,000), and only a 30-minute bus ride from the capital, Alajuela has a decidedly provincial feel. Architecturally it differs little from the bulk of Costa Rican towns: a low-rise grid plan with structures painted in primary colors. Alajuela's picturesque **Parque Central** is well worth a look. Dominated by royal palms and mango trees, the plaza has cement benches where the locals gather to chat, and a lovely fountain imported from Glasgow. Surrounding the plaza is an odd mix of charming old buildings and insipid cement boxes. The large, neoclassical **cathedral** to the east of the park, badly damaged by a 1990 earthquake, has interesting capitals decorated with local agricultural motifs and a striking red dome. Although spacious, the interior is rather plain, except for the ornate dome over the altar. To the north of the park stands the **old jail,** which now houses the local offices of the Ministry of Education—an appropriate metaphor for a country that claims to have more teachers than police.

Alajuela was the birthplace of Juan Santamaría, the national hero who lost his life in a battle against the mercenary army of U.S. adventurer William Walker (1824–60), who invaded Costa Rica in 1856 (☞ Parque Nacional Santa Rosa *in* Chapter 4). A statue of Santamaría has been erected in the Parque Juan Santamaría, one block south of the Parque Central, and his deeds are celebrated in the **Museo Juan Santamaría,** one block north of the Parque Central. The museum contains maps, compasses, weapons, and paintings, including one of Walker's men filing past to lay down their weapons. The colonial building that houses it is more interesting than the displays, however. ⊠ *Corner of C. 2 and Avda. 3,* ☎ *441–4775.* 🎫 *Free.* ☉ *Tues.–Sun. 10–6.*

☺ Spread over the lush grounds **Zoo Ave** (bird zoo) is a collection of large cages holding macaws, toucans, hawks, and parrots, as well as crocodiles, monkeys, and other interesting critters. The zoo is running a breeding project for rare and endangered birds, which are eventually destined for release. Head west from the center of Alajuela past the cemetery, then turn left after the stone church in Barrio San José. ⊠ *La Garita de Alajuela,* ☎ *433–8989.* ☞ *$8.* ☉ *Daily 9–5.*

☺ The **Finca de Mariposas** (Butterfly Farm) in La Guácima, Alajuela, features a presentation about the ecology of those delicate insects, as well as a chance to observe and photograph them up close. The farm contains a variety of habitats holding 40 rare species of butterfly and an apiary exhibit; you'll also find a restaurant. It's best to visit the farm when it is sunny, since that's when butterflies are most active. ⊠ *Turn south at the intersection just past Cariari Hotel, then right at church of San Antonio de Belén, then left, and then follow the signs with butterflies on them,* ☎ *438–0115.* ☞ *$14.* ☉ *Daily 9–4.*

Lodging

$$$$ ⊞ **Xandari.** Along a ridge about 5 km (3 mi) north of Alajuela, in the
★ middle of a coffee plantation and well-tended gardens, the tranquil Xandari is a strikingly original inn. The brainchild of a talented couple—he's an architect, she's an artist—exhibits aesthetic sensibility in everything from the design of the villas to the furniture and artwork that fill them. They are all spacious, with plenty of windows, large terraces, and secluded lanai sunbathing patios. Ultra villas are independent; two prima villas share one building. The attractive restaurant serves low-fat food, many ingredients grown on the grounds. A trail through the hotel's forest reserve winds past five waterfalls. ⊠ *Apdo 1485–4050 Alajuela,* ☎ *443–2020 ,* ℻ *442–4847. 16 villas. Restaurant, bar, 2 pools, hot tub, horseback riding. MC, V.*

$$$ ⊞ **Orquídeas Inn.** Shaded by tall trees, and surrounded by colorful tropical blossoms, the Orquídeas Inn was once the home of a coffee farmer. The Spanish-style residence, complete with arches and barrel-tile roof, now houses a couple of suites; a third suite sits under a geodesic dome. Pastel-color standard rooms have red tile floors, Guatemalan bedspreads, and paintings by Central American artists. The Marilyn Monroe bar displays an impressive collection of posters and photos of old Norma Jean, and is a popular watering hole for American expatriates. Pet toucans, parrots, and macaws inhabit the wooded grounds, which means there's lots of squawking by the light of day. ⊠ *Apdo. 394, Alajuela, 5 km (3 mi) west of the cemetery,* ☎ *433–9346,* ℻ *433–9740. 20 rooms with bath, 3 suites. Restaurant, bar, pool. AE, MC, V.*

Volcán Poás

❺ *37 km (23 mi) north of Alajuela (to the summit).*

The massive active crater, idyllic lake, and highland forests atop Volcán Poás are worth trekking up a mountain to see, but one of the reasons so many people visit this park is that a paved road leads all the way to the top of the 8,800-ft summit. The road up from Alajuela winds past coffee fields, pastures, screened-in fern plantations, and, near the summit, thick cloud forest. The volcano's main crater, at nearly 1½ km (1 mi) across and 1,000 ft deep, is one of the largest active craters in the world. The sight of this vast, multicolored pit, gurgling with smoking fumaroles and a greenish-turquoise sulfurous lake at its bottom, is simply breathtaking. All sense of scale is absent here because of the lack of vegetation within the crater. The summit is frequently en-shrouded in mist, and many who come up see little beyond the lip of the crater. But wait a while, especially if there is some wind, because the clouds can disappear quickly. If you're lucky, you will see the fa-mous geyser in action, spewing a column of gray mud high into the air. Poás last had a major eruption in 1953, and is thought to be ap-proaching another active phase; at any sign of danger, the park is closed to visitors. The earlier in the day you go, the better. And since it can be very cold and wet at the summit, dress accordingly; if you come ill-equipped, you can duck under the poor man's umbrella plant. It is forbidden to venture down the side of the crater.

The 22–sq mi **Parque Nacional Volcán Poás** protects epiphyte-laden cloud forest on the volcano's slopes and dwarf shrubs near the sum-mit. One trail, which leads some 15 minutes off to the right of the main crater trail, winds through shrubs and dwarfed trees toward the large and eerie **Laguna Botos** which occupies an extinct crater. Another leads from the parking lot through a taller stretch of cloud forest; boards along the way feature sentimental eco-poetry. Mammals are rare in the area, but you should see various birds, including insect-size hum-mingbirds and larger sooty robins. On occasion, quetzals have also been spotted in the park. A last note of warning: this is a popular site, and because of the crowds, especially on Sunday, it is not a good choice if you seek solitude. ⊠ *From San José, take Inter-American Hwy. to Ala-juela, Rte. 130 to Poás, and follow signs.* ☎ *192 National Parks in-formation; or 290–8202.* ◷ *Daily 7–4.*

Dining and Lodging

$$ ✕ **Chubascos Restaurant.** Set amidst tall pines and colorful flowers on
★ the upper slopes of Poás Volcano, this popular restaurant has a lim-ited menu of traditional Tico dishes and delicious daily specials. Pick from the full selection of *casados* (plates of white rice, beans, fried plan-tains, salad, cheese, and meat) and platters of *gallos* (a variety of fill-ings served on homemade tortillas). The *refrescos* (fresh fruit drinks) are top-drawer, especially the locally grown *fresas* (strawberries) and *moras* (blackberries) in milk. Reservations are recommended. ⊠ *West side of road to Parque Nacional Volcán Poás, between Fraijanes and Poasito,* ☎ *482–2069. AE, MC, V.*

$$ ⌂ **La Providencia Lodge.** If you're looking for outdoor adventure,
★ tranquility, and close contact with nature, this rustic lodge perched on the northern edge of Parque Nacional Volcán Poás is just the place. It's well off the beaten path—the road requires four-wheel drive. The restaurant's walls are mostly glass. Cabins scattered along the hillside have red cement floors, colorful quilts, and hot water. Hiking trails wind through the lodge's 500-acre forest reserve, where you may spot quet-zals and dozens of other birds. The three horseback tours are among the country's best. It can get very cold at night, so bring warm clothes and rain gear. ⊠ *Apdo. 10240–1000, San José, on left after entering Parque Nacional Volcán Poás,* ☎ *380–6315,* ☏ *290–0289. 6 cabins with bath. Restaurant, hiking, horseback riding. No credit cards.*

Outdoor Activities and Sports

HIKING

Although the footpaths in Parque Nacional Volcán Poás are rather short, the nearby **La Providencia Lodge** (☞ *above*) has more extensive trails for exploring the cloud forest. Xandari has a small forests reserve with 3 km (2 mi) of footpaths.

HORSEBACK RIDING

La Providencia Lodge offers three different horseback tours, one of which heads to the back side of Volcán Poás to view waterfalls and charred forests. You don't need to be a guest to take the tours, but you'll have to call the day before to reserve one.

Shopping

There are a number of **roadside stands** on the way up Poás that sell strawberry jam, *cajeta* (a pale fudge), and corn crackers called *biscoche*. The **Neotrópica Foundation** has a store in the visitor's center of Parque Nacional Volcán Poás, which sells a variety of T-shirts, cards, and posters with natural themes—a portion of the profits is spent on conservation projects.

Grecia

❻ *26 km (16 mi) northwest of Alajuela, 7 km (4½ mi) southeast of Sarchí.*

This town's claim to fame is its brick-red, prefabricated iron **Gothic church,** overlooking a small central park, where you might spot one of the resident sloths in the trees. The church was one of two buildings in the country imported from Belgium in the 1890s—the second is the metal schoolhouse next to San José's Parque Morazán—when some prominent Costa Ricans became convinced that metal structures would better withstand the periodic earthquakes that have taken their toll on the country's architecture. The pieces of metal were shipped from Antwerp to Limón, then transported by train to Alajuela—from there, the church was carried, appropriately, by oxcarts.

An interesting collection of mounted insects from Costa Rica and other tropical countries is on display half a block from the park. The **Joyas del Bosque Húmedo** (Jewels of the Rainforest) exhibit was donated to a local foundation by biologist Richard Whitten, who traveled the world collecting and mounting those colorful creepy crawlers. ⊠ *Half a block north of the central park's western end,* ☎ *494–5620.* ⊡ *$5.* ☉ *Daily 9–5.*

The **Mundo de las Serpientas** (World of Snakes) serpents are kept in large cages outside—and they'll sometimes take snakes out for you to handle or photograph. ⊠ *3 km (2 mi) east of Grecia, on road to Alajuela,* ☎ *494–3700.* ⊡ *$11.* ☉ *Daily 8–4.*

Lodging

$$$$ ⊞ **Posada las Palomas.** This lovely little B&B on an orange and cof-
★   fee plantation outside Grecia overlooks the Río Grande canyon. Optional three-course dinners—the menu changes daily—are served in the main house, where guests can relax in the spacious living room. Guest rooms in the house are comfortable, but the cottages are much nicer—well worth the extra money—with lots of windows and porches; the Tea House is the biggest, but El Nido has the best view. The hotel has a forest reserve in the canyon, with a trail leading down into it for a look at a waterfall. Complimentary breakfast is served by the pool. ⊠ *Apdo 1485–4050 Alajuela, on highway 1 km (½ mi) west of Grecia, first right after bridge, follow signs,* ☎ *450–0800,* 𝔽𝔸𝕏 *451–1165. 2 rooms with bath, 3 cottages. Dining room, pool. No credit cards.*

Sarchí

❼ *53 km (33 mi) northwest of San José.*

Tranquil little Sarchí is spread over a collection of hills surrounded by coffee plantations. Though plenty of its inhabitants are farmers, it is also one of the country's principal carpentry and crafts centers. People from other Central Valley communities drive here to shop for furniture, and caravans of tour buses regularly descend on the souvenir shops outside of town. Local artisans work native hardwoods into bowls, boxes, toys, platters, and even jewelry, but the area's most famous products are its brightly colored oxcarts—replicas of the carts traditionally used to transport coffee. Trucks and tractors have replaced oxcarts on the farm, but the little wagons retain their place in the local folklore, and can be spotted everywhere from small-town parades to postcards.

The vast majority of people who visit Sarchí spend all their time wandering down the aisles of one of the craft bazaars, but this traditional community is well worth poking around. The **church** dates only from the 1950s and is much less elaborate than some of the region's other temples, but it is a colorful structure with several statues of angels alighted on its facade and a simple interior revealing some nice woodwork. It is flanked by small gardens and faces a multilevel park with a brightly decorated oxcart displayed beneath a roof. If you turn right when you leave the church, walk two blocks north, turn right again and walk another block and a half, you'll come upon the town's only real oxcart factory on your left. **Taller Eloy Alfaro e Hijos** (Alfaro and Sons) was founded in 1923, and their carpentry methods have changed little since then. The two-story wooden building housing the wood shop is surrounded by trees and flowers—there are usually orchids on display—and all the machinery on the ground floor is powered by a waterwheel at the back of the shop. Carts are painted in back, and though the factory's main product is a genuine oxcart—which sells for about $2,000—they make some smaller things to sell to visitors. There is also a donation box by the stairs. The street behind the shop comes alive on Fridays, when the local **farmers' market** is held there.

Shopping

Sarchí is the best place in the country to purchase miniature oxcarts, the larger of which are designed to serve as patio bars and can be broken down for easy transport. Another popular item is a locally produced rocking chair with leather seat and back. All the big stores can ship oxcarts and furniture home for you. One store is just north of town, and several larger complexes to the south, the nicest of which is the **Chaverri Factory,** a couple of kilometers south of town on the main road, which has workshops in back that you can wander through and watch people work. These shops are good places to buy wood crafts, but coffee, T-shirts, and most other nonwood products are cheaper in San José.

EASTERN CENTRAL VALLEY

East of San José you'll find Costa Rica's highest volcano and the remains of both the country's most important archaeological site and its oldest church. There are actually several interesting churches in the area, two of which are in the scenic Orosí Valley (☞ *below*), as well as the ecological attractions of a botanical garden and a protected cloud forest. Cartago, the country's first capital, has scattered historical structures and the impressive Basílica de Los Angeles. You could explore this area in one day but only if you want to be on the road from dawn until well past dusk. For a more leisurely pace, dedicate two days to this end of the valley, visiting Volcán Irazú and Cartago one day, and tackling the Orosí Valley on another. Jardín Lankester could be easily included in either trip.

Cartago

8   *22 km (14 mi) southeast of San José.*

The country's original capital is much older than San José, but earth-quakes have destroyed most of its colonial structures, leaving very few examples of its traditional architecture. The country's capital for al-most three centuries, Cartago became Costa Rica's second city in 1923, when the seat of government was switched to San José. A major quake in 1910 was one of the reasons the capital was moved. The quake also prevented completion of the central Romanesque cathedral; **Las Ruinas** (the ruins) now stand in a pleasant central park planted with tall pines and bright bougainvillea. You'll spot some attractive old build-ings as you head through town, most of which were erected after the 1910 quake. The majority of the city's architecture, however, is bland. Exception: Cartago's most impressive landmark, the gaudy Basílica, on the eastern edge of town.

The spectacular **Basílica de Nuestra Señora de Los Angeles** (Basilica of Our Lady of the Angels) at the edge of Cartago, 10 blocks east of the central square, is a hodgepodge of architectural styles from baroque to Byzantine, with a dash of Gothic. The church's interior is even more impressive, with a colorful tile floor, intricately decorated wood columns, and lots of stained glass. It is also the focus of an amazing annual pilgrimage: During the night of August 1 and well into the early morning hours of the 2nd, the road from San José clogs with people on their way to celebrate the 1635 appearance of La Negrita (Black Virgin), Costa Rica's patron saint. The faithful come here to fill bot-tles at a spring behind the church believed to have curative waters. Mirac-ulous healing powers are attributed to the saint, and the devoted have placed thousands of symbolic crutches, ears, eyes, and legs next to her diminutive statue in recognition of her gifts. The constant arrival of tour buses and school groups, along with shops selling candles and bot-tles of holy water in the shape of the saint, add a bit of a circus atmo-sphere to the scene. La Negrita has twice been stolen, most recently in 1950 by José León Sánchez, now one of Costa Rica's best known nov-elists, who spent 20 years on the prison island of San Lucas for the purloined Madonna. ⊠ *C. 16 between Avdas. 2 and 4.*

En Route   Bear left where Irazú is signposted, 4 km (2½ mi) short of Cartago, to bypass the city. Driving time from San José to the summit is just short of 1½ hours.

Volcán Irazú

9   *31 km (19 mi) northeast of Cartago, and 50 km (31 mi) east of San José, to the summit.*

Volcán Irazú is Costa Rica's highest volcano at 11,260 ft, and its sum-mit has long been protected as a national park (☞ Central Valley Na-tional Parks *in* Chapter 10). The mountain looms to the north of Cartago, and its eruptions have dumped a considerable amount of ash on the city over the centuries. The most recent eruptive period lasted from 1963 to 1965, beginning on the day that John F. Kennedy arrived in Costa Rica for a presidential visit. Boulders and mud rained down on the countryside, damming rivers and causing serious flooding. Al-though farmers who cultivate Irazú's slopes live in fear of the next erup-tion, they are also grateful for the soil's richness, a direct result of the volcanic deposits.

The road up to the summit climbs past vegetable fields, pastures, and native oak forests. You'll pass through the villages of Potrero Cerrado and San Juan de Chicoá, both with lookout points, before reaching the bleak, gaping **crater** at the summit. Although Irazú is currently dormant, the gases and steam that billow out from fumaroles on the northwestern slope are sometimes visible from the peak above the crater lookouts. The gray, moonscape summit of Irazú is one of the few places from which both the Pacific Ocean and the Caribbean Sea can be seen, although clouds frequently obscure both from view. The **Area Recreativa de Prusia,** halfway down, has hiking trails through oak and pine forest. Picnic areas are available if you want to bring your own supplies; warm, waterproof clothing is advisable for the summit. Leave San José very early in the day so as not to be thwarted by low clouds. ☎ 192 *National Parks information line, or 290–8202.* ☒ *$6.* ⊙ *Daily 8–3:30.*

Jardín Lankester

⑩ *7 km (4½ mi) east of Cartago on the road to Paraíso.*

If you are interested in plants, especially orchids, you should visit Jardín Lankester (Lankester Botanical Gardens). Created in the 1950s by the English naturalist Charles Lankester to help preserve the local flora, it is now under the auspices of the University of Costa Rica. The lush garden and greenhouses contain one of the world's largest orchid collections, more than 800 native and introduced species. Orchids, by the way, are mostly epiphytes, meaning they use other plants for support without damaging them in the process. Bromeliads and aroids also abound, along with 80 species of trees, including rare palms, bamboo, heliconias, torch ginger, and other ornamentals; the diversity of plants attracts a wide variety of birds. The best time to visit is January through April, when the widest variety of orchids are in bloom. To reach the gardens, drive through the center of Cartago, turn right at the Basílica, then left on the busy road to Paraíso and Orosí. After 6 km (4 mi), an orange sign on the right marks the short dirt road that leads to Jardín Lankester. ☒ *Dulce Nombre, Cartago,* ☎ *552–3151.* ☒ *$2.50.* ⊙ *Daily 9–3:30.*

Shopping

The gift shop in Jardín Lankester is one of the few places in Costa Rica where you can buy orchids that you can bring home legally. Along with the endangered plants comes CITES papers—a sort of orchid passport—that permits you to take them across international borders without any customs problems.

OROSÍ VALLEY

The Orosí Valley, an area of breathtaking views and verdant landscapes 30 km (19 mi) south of San José, contains remnants of the colonial era and of the tropical forest that covered the country when the Spanish first arrived. The valley was one of the earliest parts of Costa Rica to be settled by Spanish colonists, as ruins and a colonial church attest. The rich soil and proximity to San José have combined to make it an important agricultural area, with extensive plantations of coffee, chayote, and other vegetables. The valley is fed in the west by the confluence of the Navarro and Orosí rivers and drained in the east by the ferocious Reventazón; a dam built in the 1970s to create one of the country's first hydroelectric projects formed the Lago de Cachí, or Cachí Reservoir.

Two roads descend into the valley from Paraíso, an unattractive town 8 km (5 mi) east of Cartago, both of which lead to a loop around the reservoir, past the tidy patchworks of cultivated crops, small towns, and the Presa di Cachí (Cachí Dam). The roads are reached by turning right just before Paraíso's shady central park. If you turn left at the *bomberos* (fire station), which houses some splendid old-style fire engines, you'll be on your way to Ujarrás. If you go straight, the road will lead you toward the town of Orosí and the Refugio Nacional de Fauna Silvestre Tapantí. Whichever route you choose, you'll eventually end up back at the same intersection, since both roads lead into a loop around the valley floor. As you snake down into the valley, past coffee plantations, pastures, and patches of forest, keep your eyes open for the *mirador* (vantage point).

Ujarrás

⓫   *10 km (6 mi) southeast of Paraíso, 18 km (11 mi) southeast of Cartago.*

The ruins of the **country's oldest church** stand in a small park at the site of the former town of Ujarrás, on the floor of the Orosí Valley, just down the hill from Paraíso. Built between 1681 and 1693 in honor of the Virgin of Ujarrás, the church, together with the surrounding village, was abandoned in 1833 after a series of earthquakes and floods. An unlikely victory by the Spaniards over a superior force of invading British pirates was attributed to a prayer stop here. Today it is a pleasant monument surrounded by well-kept gardens and large trees that often attract flocks of parakeets and parrots. ☉ *Daily 8–5.*

Dining

$$$ ✕ **La Casona del Cafetal.** Set in a coffee plantation overlooking the Cachí
★   Reservoir, this restaurant is the best lunch stop when exploring the valley. It's housed in a spacious brick building with a high, barrel-tile roof, and has seating both inside and on a tiled portico on the lake side. Inventive twists on the local fare include *arroz tucurrique* (baked rice with palm heart and cheese) and *corvina jacaranda* (sea bass fillet stuffed with shrimp), as well as a variety of casados. If you're a coffee aficionado, definitely have a cup—the beans are grown in the valley, and brewed Tico style using a cloth filter. ✉ *2 km (1 mi) southwest of Cachí Dam,* ☎ *533–3280. Reservations essential. AE, DC, MC, V.*

Shopping

In the Orosí Valley, just south of the Cachí Dam, stands the unique **Casa del Soñador** (House of the Dreamer), which was built by local wood sculptor Macedonio Quesada. Though Macedonio died several years ago, his son and a former apprentice are still there, carving interesting little statues out of coffee wood.

Orosí

⓬   *7 km (4 mi) south of Paraíso.*

The town of Orosiac:, in the heart of the valley, has but one tourist attraction: a beautifully restored **colonial church.** Built in 1743, the structure has a squat, whitewashed facade; the roof is made of cane overlaid with terra-cotta barrel tiles. Inside are an antique wooden altar and ancient paintings of the Stations of the Cross and the Virgin of Guadelupe, all brought to Costa Rica from Mexico. The **museum** in the cloister annex houses a small collection of old religious regalia, multicolored wood carvings, and colonial furniture. Opening times fluctuate, but should you find it closed, ask around and somebody will open it up for you. South of town there are some **thermal pools** fed by a hot spring, which are open to the public for a nominal fee.

En Route   From Orosí, veer right at the fork in the road for Tapantí. The road becomes rougher as you near the park, but is in decent shape once you enter it.

Refugio Nacional de Fauna Silvestre Tapantí

⓭   *12 km (7 mi) south of Orosí, 28 km (17 mi) southeast of Cartago.*

Tucked into a steep valley to the south of Orosí you'll find Refugio Nacional de Fauna Silvestre Tapantí (Tapantí Wildlife Refuge, ☞ Chapter 2), an 18-sq-mi cloud forest preserve teeming with birds. This extremely lush forest, drained by countless streams, provides refuge for 211 bird species, including the graceful, shy, and endangered quetzal. Quetzals are most visible during the dry season, when they mate; ask the park rangers where to look for them. The 10-km (6-mi) track to Tapantí follows the course of the Río Orosí past coffee plantations, elegant *fincas* (farmhouses), and seasonal barracks for coffee pickers before being hemmed in by the steep slopes of thick jungle. However, the track was in rough shape at press time. The green rangers' office, on the right upon entering the park, is where you stop to pay the entry fee. The road continues through the reserve; you can leave your vehicle at the start of the various trails, one of which leads to some small swimming holes in the chilly Rió Orosí. Since the park tends to cloud up in the afternoon, it's best to get an early start. Taxis carrying up to six people will make trips to the reserve from the soccer field in Orosí. ☎ *192 National Parks, 758–3996 Amistad Atlántico branch of the National Parks Service.* ☒ *$6.* ☼ *Daily 7–4.*

TURRIALBA AND THE GUAYABO NATIONAL MONUMENT

The tranquil town of Turrialba, and nearby Guayabo ruins, lie considerably lower than the rest of the Central Valley, and consequently enjoy more tropical climates. There are two ways to reach this area, both of which will take you past spectacular scenery. The more direct route, which is reached by heading straight through both Cartago and Paraíso, winds through coffee and sugar plantations before abruptly descending into Turrialba. For the second route, turn off the road between Cartago and the summit of Irazú near the town of Cot. That narrow route twists its way along the slopes of Irazú and Turrialba volcanoes, passing some stunning scenery—pollarded jaul trees line the road to form formal avenues, and white girdered bridges cross crashing streams. From Santa Cruz a track leads up to within hiking distance of the 10,900-ft summit of Volcán Turrialba. As you begin the descent to Turrialba, the temperature rises and neatly farmed coffee crops blanket the slopes.

Turrialba

⓮   *58 km (36 mi) east of San José.*

The relatively well-to-do grid-plan agricultural center of Turrialba, population 30,000, suffered when the main San José–Limón route was diverted through Guápiles. The demise of the famous Jungle Train that connected San José and Puerto Limón was an additional blow to the town. Although lively enough, Turrialba itself doesn't have much to offer, but there are still interesting places to investigate. Kayakers and white-water rafters, for instance, flock here to ride the Reventazón and Pacuare rivers (☞ Outdoor Activities and Sports, *below*). Serious enthusiasts, including the white-water Olympic kayaking teams from a handful of countries, stay all winter.

OFF THE BEATEN PATH

CATIE – Just outside of Turrialba, on the road to Siquirres, is the Centro Agronómico Tropical de Investigación y Enseñanza (Center for Tropical Agricultural Research and Instruction or CATIE), one of the world's leading tropical research centers. The 3-sq-mi property includes modern labs and offices, landscaped grounds, seed conservation chambers, greenhouses, orchards, experimental agricultural projects, lodging for students and teachers, and a large swath of rain forest. A muddy trail leads down into the forest behind the administration building, where there is a view of some of the biggest rapids on the Reventazón River, well worth the trek. CATIE is also a good bird-watching spot; in fact, you might catch sight of the brilliant, yellow-winged jacana spinosa in the lagoon near the main building. ☎ 556–6431 or 556–0169, ℻ 556–1533. ☉ Daily 7–4.

Dining and Lodging

$$ ✕🏨 **Turrialtico.** Eight kilometers (5 mi) out of Turrialba on the Limón road, a hedged drive winds its way up to this dramatically positioned, open-sided hotel. The second-floor rooms, handsomely designed with wooden floors and Guatemalan spreads on the firm beds, could be the country's best bargain. Try to get a room on the west side for a dazzling view toward Turrialba and, if you're in luck, Volcán Irazú. The restaurant's menu isn't extensive, but the cooking is tasty. A possible minus is that the place is a stopover for tour-rafting buses: about three per week come here to eat. ✉ *Apdo. 121, Turrialba take Carretera to Limón 8 km/5 mi)*, ☎ *556–1111. 12 rooms with bath. Restaurant, bar. AE, MC, DC, V.*

$$$$ 🏨 **Rancho Naturalista.** This 125-acre private reserve specializes in guided horseback and bird-watching tours. Three hundred species of birds and thousands of different types of moths and butterflies live on the reserve, and a resident naturalist guide helps visitors see and learn as much as they want. The two-story lodge is rustically decorated throughout, as are two separate cabins. Good home cooking is served in both the indoor and outdoor dining rooms. The hotel provides free transportation from San José. The management requires a two-day minimum stay. ✉ *Southeast of Turrialba, 2½ km (1½ mi) up a dirt track from village of Tuís*, ☎ *267–7138;* ✉ *Dept. 1425, Box 025216, Miami, FL 33102-5216. 11 rooms with bath, 2 without bath. Dining room. No credit cards.*

$$–$$$ 🏨 **Albergue Volcán Turrialba.** In the foothills of the volcano and reachable only by four-wheel drive (the lodge will arrange transport for a fee), the Volcán has comfortable rooms with hot-water baths. You'll eat well, too: the proprietors serve healthy, Costa Rican–style meals cooked up on a wood-burning stove (all meals are included in the room price). More compelling are the tours they offer: one goes deep into the Turrialba crater; a second visits the fumaroles and thermal waters of Volcán Irazú; mountain biking, horseback riding, and a 10-hour trek from the Volcán Turrialba to Guápiles via Parque Nacional Braulio Carrillo can also be arranged. ✉ *Apdo. 1632–2050, San José, 5 km (3 mi) from Irazú crater up posted access road*, ☎ *273–4335. 9 rooms with bath. Bar, dining room, library. AE, MC, V.*

Outdoor Activities and Sports
RAFTING AND KAYAKING

It's no coincidence that half a dozen Olympic kayaking teams use Turrialba as their winter training ground; it lies conveniently close to two excellent white-water rivers: the Reventazón and the Pacuare. But despite their appeal among the experts, these rivers offer the perfect conditions for neophytes, which is why thousands of people have experienced the thrill of white-water rafting for the first time in Costa Rica.

The **Río Reventazón** flows right by Turrialba, and has several navigable stretches, below and above the city. The most popular stretch of the Reventazón is the Tucurrique section (class III), which offers an easy enough but exciting excursion perfect for a first-time rafting trip. That 20-km (12-mi) section of river winds past farms and scattered patches of forest above Turrialba. The Pascua section (class IV–V), below Turrialba, is one of the country's wildest stretches of white water—a liquid roller coaster requiring previous rafting experience. The Peralta section (class V), between the two, is Costa Rica's toughest rafting route, open to experts only.

Just to the south is the **Río Pacuare,** Costa Rica's most spectacular white-water route, which provides rafters with an unforgettable experience—exhilarating, beautiful, and great fun. Currently, however, the river's rapids are threatened with the possibility of sinking forever behind a new hydroelectric dam. If you make it to the river before the dam does, you're in for a treat: the Pacuare's 32-km (20-mi) of white-water runs include a series of class III and IV rapids with evocative nicknames such as Double Drop, Upper Huacas, Lower Huacas, Toucan, Magnetic Rock, and Dos Montañas (where two mountains nearly meet—the potential site of the dreaded dam). If you know about these things, the gradient averages 48 ft per mi, and the volume of water ranges from 1,400 up to 4,000 cubic ft per second. The runs terminate near Siquirres, and from there it is a lovely drive back to San José through Braulio Carrillo.

A good guide—and there are many—will teach you not only how to ride the rapids but also about the natural history, the geography, and the geology of the area, which is astoundingly beautiful (stretches of the Pacuare stood in for Africa in the otherwise eminently forgettable 1995 film *Congo*). You'll see numerous exotic birds—toucans, assorted kingfishers, aracaris, and *oropéndolas* (golden orioles) among them—along with blue Morpho butterflies, and maybe the odd river otter, sloth, or coati as well, especially if you're first down the river. The rafting outfitters Aventuras Naturales and Ríos Tropicales have their own lodges on the river, which make them the best options for highly recommended two- and three-day trips.

Costa Rica Whitewater (☎ 257–0766, FAX 255–4354), **Rios Tropicales** (☎ 233–6455, FAX 255–4354), **Aventuras Naturales** (☎ 225–3939 and 224–0505, FAX 253–6934), and **Pioneer Raft** (☎ 225–8117 and 225–4735, FAX 253–4687). **Serendipity Tours** (✉ Next to Servicio Super, ☎ 566–2592) has hot-air balloon flights, white-water rafting, mountain biking, and other outdoor adventures.

Monumento Nacional Guayabo

⑮ *19 km (12 mi) north of Turrialba.*

Nestled on the slopes of the Volcán Turrialba is the Monumento Nacional Guayabo, Costa Rica's most significant archaeological site. In

1968 a local landowner was out walking her dogs when she discovered what she thought was a tomb. A friend, archaeologist Carlos Piedra, began excavating the site and unearthed the base wall of the chief's house in what eventually turned out to be a large city (around 20,000 inhabitants) covering 49 acres. The city was abandoned in AD 1400, probably due to disease or starvation. A guided tour (in Spanish only) takes you through the rain forest to a mirador (lookout) from where you can see the layout of the excavated circular buildings. Only the raised foundations survive, since the conical houses themselves were built of wood. As you descend into the city ruins, observe the well-engineered surface and covered aqueducts leading to a drinking-water trough still functioning today; next you'll pass the end of an 8-km (5-mi) paved walkway used to transport the massive building stones. Carved abstract patterns on the stones continue to baffle archaeologists, although some clearly depict jaguars, which were revered by the Indians as deities. The hillside jungle setting is captivating, and the trip is further enhanced by the bird-watching possibilities; sacklike nests of oropéndolas hang from many of the trees. ☏ 192 National Parks Service information, or 290–8202. ✉ $6. ☉ Tues.–Sun. 8–4.

CENTRAL VALLEY: AROUND SAN JOSÉ A TO Z

Arriving and Departing

By Bus

WESTERN CENTRAL VALLEY

Departures for Escazú from San José, from Avenida 6 between Calles 12 and 14, are every 20 minutes. Departures for Heredia, from Calle 1 between Avenidas 7 and 9, are every 10 minutes (25-min ride). For Volcán Barva, take Paso Llano bus from Heredia (first bus 6:30 AM), get off at Sacramento crossroads (note: some go only as far as San José de la Montaña, adding an hour to the hike; check first). Departures for Alajuela are from Avenida 2 between Calles 12 and 14 (TUASA, ☏ 222–5325) daily every 10 minutes 6 AM–7 PM, every 40 minutes 7 PM–midnight, every hour midnight–6 AM (20-min ride). An excursion bus for Volcán Poás departs San José daily at 8:30 AM from Calle 12 between Avenidas 2 and 4 (90-min ride) and returns at 2:30 PM.

EASTERN CENTRAL VALLEY

Departures to Cartago from Calle 5 and Avenida 18 (SACSA, ☏ 233–5350) are daily every 10 minutes (45-min ride); however, it is more convenient to catch it on Calle 9 at Avenida Central. An excursion bus departs San José for Irazú every Saturday and Sunday at 8 AM from Avenida 2, between Calles 1 and 3, outside the Gran Hotel Costa Rica (Metropoli, ☏ 272–0651) and returns at 1 PM (90-min ride).

TURRIALBA AND THE MONUMENTO NACIONAL GUAYABO

Departures to Turrialba from Calle 13 between Avenidas 6 and 8 (TRANSTUASA, ☏ 556–0073) every hour 8–8 (two-hr ride).

By Car

WESTERN CENTRAL VALLEY

To reach Escazú from San José, turn left at the western end of Paseo Colón, take the first right, get off the highway at the first exit, and turn right at the traffic light. Turn right at the bottom of the hill for San Rafael and the old road to Santa Ana The Paseo Colón ends at La Sabana park, on the west end of San José; turn right there for Alajuela and Heredia. For Heredia, turn right off the highway just before it heads up an overpass, where the Hotel Irazú stands on the right; turn left when you reach the Universidad Nacional to reach the center of Heredia, or continue straight for the town and volcano of Barva. The route to Volcán Barva heads north out of Heredia through the communities of Barva, San José de la Montaña, Paso Llano, and Sacramento. At Sacramento the paved road turns to dirt, growing worse as it nears the ranger station. A four-wheel-drive vehicle can make it all the way to the ranger station during the dry season. For Alajuela, take the highway all the way out to the airport, where you turn right. Grecia can be reached by continuing west on the highway past the airport—the turnoff is on the right—or by turning left just before the Alajuela cemetery. For Sarchí, take the highway well past the airport to the turnoff for Naranjo, then veer right just as you enter Naranjo.

EASTERN CENTRAL VALLEY

All the eastern Central Valley's attractions are reached from San José by first driving east on Avenida 2 through San Pedro; a traffic light shortly before Cartago marks the beginning of the road up Irazú, with traffic to Cartago veering right. For the Jardín Lankester head straight through Cartago (entrance on right).

OROSÍ VALLEY

For the Orosí Valley head straight through Cartago, turning right at Paraíso's central plaza.

TURRIALBA AND THE MONUMENTO NACIONAL GUAYABO

The road east through Cartago continues on to Turrialba, where you pick up the road that leads to the monument.

By Plane

The **Aeropuerto Internacional Juan Santamaría** (☏ 441–0744) is 16 km (10 mi) northwest of downtown San José.

BETWEEN THE AIRPORT AND CENTRAL VALLEY

There is taxi service to and from the airport to anywhere in the Central Valley. Buses travel between the airport and Alajuela from every five minutes to on the half hour, according to the time. There is less frequent service (every 20 minutes to one hour) to Heredia. For trips from the airport and either Escazú or Cartago, you must change buses in San José.

Getting Around

By Bus

WESTERN CENTRAL VALLEY

Buses travel between Alajuela and Heredia's main bus stations every half hour. To reach Zoo Ave take the bus to La Garita, which departs every hour from the main bus station in Alajuela. For Sarchí, first take the bus to Naranjo, which departs from San José's Coca-Cola station (Calle 16 between Avdas. 1 and 3) every 40 minutes 6 AM–6 PM; buses to Sarchí leave from Naranjo every half hour. Departures for Grecia leave from Naranjo hourly 6 AM–7 PM.

EASTERN CENTRAL VALLEY

To visit Jardín Lankester, take the Paraíso bus, which departs from the south side of the Parque Central in Cartago daily every 30 minutes.

OROSÍ VALLEY

Buses from Cartago (one block east and three blocks south of Las Ruinas, Mata, ☏ 551–6810) do a loop around the Orosí Valley, stopping at Orosí, Ujarrás, and Tapantí. Buses leave Cartago weekdays every 90 minutes, and every hour on weekends.

TURRIALBA AND THE MONUMENTO NACIONAL GUAYABO

The bus to Monumento Nacional Guayabo departs once a day from one block south of the bus station in Turrialba, Monday to Saturday at 11 AM, Sunday at 9:30 AM (50-min ride).

By Taxi

Taxis parked near the central plazas of Alajuela, Cartago, and Heredia can take you to up Poás, Irazú, and Barva volcanoes, but the trips will be quite expensive, unless you can get a small group together.

Contacts and Resources

Car Rentals
See Car Rentals *in* San José A to Z , *in* Chapter 2.

Emergencies
In just about any emergency you can dial ☎ 911, but the following are some additional useful numbers: **Fire** (☎ 118), **Police** (☎ 117), and **Traffic Police** (☎ 222–9330).

Guided Tours

CRUISES

Cruceros del Sur (✉ Across from Colegio Los Angeles, Sabana Norte, San José, ☎ 232–6672, FAX 220–2103).

FROM SAN JOSÉ

Most San José tour offices can set you up with guided tours to such spots as Poás and Irazú volcanoes, or the Orosí Valley. **Swiss Travel** (✉ Melia Corobici Hotel lobby, San José, ☎ 231–4055) is one of oldest operators in the country. For information about white-water rafting tours, *see* Outdoor Activities and Sports *in* Turrialba, *above*.

Visitor Information
See Visitor Information *in* San José A to Z, *in* Chapter 2.

4 Northern Guanacaste and Alajuela

From Caño Negro's remote, bird-filled waters to the windsurfing mecca of Laguna de Arenal, Costa Rica's northernmost reaches contain wonders to endlessly beguile: astonishingly verdant Monteverde cloud forests; sparkling Pacific coast beaches; dusty, deforested uplands with cowboys and grazing cattle; exotic jungles alive with birds, monkeys, and butterflies; a ragged row of fiercely beautiful volcanoes.

Updated by
Justin
Henderson

WITH ABOUT 65 INCHES OF RAINFALL per year, Costa Rica's northwest is the country's driest region. The northwest is also home to countless natural wonders: large expanses of wet and dry forest, river deltas and estuaries overflowing with animal life, and miles of sun-kissed beaches. The northwest offers travelers far more than the myriad ecosystems of the dry coastal plain; the territory contains cloud and rain forests of Monteverde and other mountain preserves as well as the volcanoes and peaks of the Cordillera de Guanacaste, Cordillera de Tilarán, and sections of the Cordillera Central. East of Guanacaste are northern uplands and lowland plains of Alajuela, from the wildlife-filled wetlands of Caño Negro Wildlife Refuge in the far north, down to the green farmlands and foothills east of Volcán Arenal.

Costa Rica's northwesternmost province, Guanacaste is bordered by Nicaragua and the Pacific Ocean. The province derives its name from the broad ear-pod trees that shade the lounging white Brahman cattle so prevalent in the region. An independent province of Spain's colonial empire until 1787 when it was ceded to Nicaragua, Guanacaste became part of Costa Rica in 1814. After independence in 1821, both Nicaragua and Costa Rica claimed Guanacaste for their own. The Guanacastecos themselves were divided: The provincial capital, Liberia, wanted to return to Nicaragua, the rival city Nicoya favored Costa Rica. Nicoya got its way, helped by the fact that at the time the vote was taken, Nicaragua was embroiled in a civil war.

Guanacaste's far northwestern coastline, still unblemished for the most part, offers everything Nicoya has to offer and more: the dry forests and pristine sands of Parque Nacional Santa Rosa, the bird sanctuary of Isla Bolaños, the endless beaches of the Golfo de Santa Elena, and breezy Bahia Salinas. But tourist-driven development is not limited to the Nicoya: a pair of new beachfront resort hotels have opened in Bahia Salinas, and others were in the works. Time will tell if this relatively untraveled stretch of Costa Rican turf near the town of La Cruz and the Nicaraguan border finds itself home to the unnatural green of fairways and the artificial swimming pool–aqua blue.

East of the Carretera Interamericana (Inter-American Highway), Guanacaste's dry plains and forests slope upward into volcano country. Marching northwest to southeast in a rough but formidable line, the volcanoes of the Cordillera de Guanacaste include Orosí, Rincón de la Vieja, and its nearby sister, Santa Maria, Miravalles, Tenorio (newly anointed as a national park), and Arenal, a perfect cone looming over the southeast end of Laguna de Arenal. The most northerly peak in the Cordillera de Tilarán, Arenal ranks as one of the most active volcanoes in the world. Below and between these active and not-so-active craters and calderas, the terrain ranges from dry forest to impassable jungle; from agricultural plain to roadless swamp.

A few of the parks and destinations in this region are relatively accessible from San José, even for day trips. Others require grueling hours of driving over pothole-scarred roads. As you contemplate spending time in this region—or anywhere in Costa Rica, for that matter—be sure to plan well, allowing plenty of time for excruciatingly slow driving when and where necessary. That brief hop from the smooth pavement of the Inter-American Highway up to the famously lush cloud forests of Monteverde, for example, looks like 30 minutes behind the wheel when measured on the map. In reality, it's two hours of bone-jarring road, barely passable without high clearance or a four-wheel drive.

Pleasures and Pastimes

Dining

Although you won't find them served in many of the restaurants frequented by travelers, Guanacaste's traditional foods derive from dishes prepared by pre-Columbian Chorotegan Indians. Typical dishes include *frito guanacasteco* (similar to the traditional *gallo pinto* dish of beans, rice, vegetables, and meat), *pedre* (a mixture of carob beans, pork, chicken, onions, sweet peppers, salt, and mint), *sopa de albóndigas* (meatball soup with chopped eggs and spices), and *arroz de maíz* (a kind of corn stew made with chicken). More prevalent at breakfast is gallo pinto ("spotted rooster," a mix of beans and rice) and eggs; at lunch and dinner you can always depend on a *casado*, the *tipico* Costa Rican meal of rice and beans served with meat, chicken, or fish. Seafood here is plentiful: *camarones* (shrimp in garlic and butter served with fries and salad), *langostinos* (a kind of lobster), and a fine variety of fish are available in most restaurants at reasonable prices, although langostino dinners can get costly. Meat lovers rejoice: the northwest, whose plains are covered with cattle ranches, produces the country's best steak. Most of the places in this area serve international and local dishes, so you can take your pick.

Lodging

Both east and west of the mountains, Costa Rica's far north zone offers a good mix of quality hotels, nature lodges, and more basic *cabinas* (cottages). In the areas of Monteverde and La Fortuna, a range of low- and mid-priced hotels, cabinas, and resorts appear to be filling the demand generated by visitors to the Volcán Arenal and the cloud forest. If you're headed to the coast it is wise to book ahead during the dry season (December–April), especially for weekends, when Ticos flock to the beach. Note that at press time many hotels were due to receive quality phone connections for the first time, so many properties listed might now accept major credit cards; call ahead.

Volcanoes

If you have never seen an active volcano, the perfect conical profile of Volcán Arenal makes a spectacular first. Night is the best time for observing it, when you can clearly see rocks spewing skyward and red-hot molten lava enveloping the top of the cone. Arenal can be easily reached from the Inter-American Highway—watch for the turnoff at the town of Cañas—or from the east through La Fortuna. You may have to spend more than one day there, as the cone can be covered by clouds. Farther northwest, experienced hikers can trek to the lip of the steaming Rincón de la Vieja crater on trails through the national park of the same name, while less active travelers can check out Las Pailas, a cluster of miniature volcanoes, fumaroles, and mud pots encircled by a relatively easy-to-walk trail lower down on the mountain slope. Among the other (inactive) volcanoes, Orosí lies within the borders of Parque Nacional Guanacaste, and Tenorio now boasts of its own national park. Parque Nacional Guanacaste is minimally developed for tourism, and Tenorio as yet has no infrastructure whatsoever.

Exploring Northern Guanacaste and Alajuela

An exploration of Northern Guanacaste and Alajuela encompasses the volcanic mountains of the Cordillera de Guancaste as well as the plains stretching west from the mountains to the sea, and north to the Nicaraguan border, about an hour by car north on the Inter-American

Highway from Liberia. Most of the destinations on the west side of the mountains, including the coastal beaches, national parks, and the northwestern end of Laguna de Arenal, lie within easy reach of the Inter-American Highway. To reach the areas to the east, including Caño Negro, Upala, La Fortuna, and the Volcán Arenal and the east end of Laguna de Arenal, the easiest drive is by way of Zarcero and Ciudad Quesada. You will find several roads that pass through the mountains, linking these two distinct zones.

Though they are paved for the most part, these roads—one follows the northern bank of Laguna de Arenal, the other skirts the volcanoes along the northern edge of the country—still have unpaved stretches and can be subject to washouts and other difficulties. Always try to get a report on road conditions before setting out on any long trips.

Numbers in the text correspond to numbers in the margin and on the Northern Guanacaste and Alajuela map.

Great Itineraries

As you consider these assorted itineraries, know in advance that a fair amount of your time—more, perhaps, than you had realized or hoped as you planned this trip—will be spent on the road. That is simply the reality of travel in Costa Rica and this spread-out region.

IF YOU HAVE 3 DAYS AND CAN DO WITHOUT THE BEACH

Head northeast out of San José and through the mountains around **Zarcero** ①, en route to ⊡ **Ciudad Quesada** ② or ⊡ **La Fortuna** ③. The next day, drive to ⊡ **Volcán Arenal** ④, check out the Tabacón Resort's hot springs, hike to the La Fortuna waterfall, or take a rafting trip on the Río Peñas Blancas. Stay the night or continue north by northwest around ⊡ **Laguna de Arenal** ⑤, with a stop at ⊡ **Tilarán** ⑥ or one of the lake-view hotels for a day or two of windsurfing, hiking, mountain biking, or volcano viewing.

IF YOU HAVE 3 DAYS

Note: like most Costa Rican trips, this itinerary requires a lot of driving; realistically, it could be done, but would work better, and would be less exhausting, with five days.

Start from San José with a predawn drive to the ⊡ **Reserva Biológica Bosque Nuboso Monteverde** ⑦ and spend a day hiking in the cloud forest. If Monteverde is too crowded, the compelling but smaller **Santa Elena** reserve is just down the road (north). After overnighting in the area, another crack-of-dawn drive will take you either to ⊡ **Tilarán** ⑥ by way of the mountain track, for an active day at ⊡ **Laguna de Arenal** ⑤; or return to the highway and drive north and then inland again for a day hike in ⊡ **Parque Nacional Rincón de la Vieja** ⑧; alternatively, head farther north for a day and night at Hacienda Los Inocentes, the wonderful, 100-year-old hacienda lodge on the northern border of ⊡ **Parque Nacional Guanacaste** ⑪. On day three, head down to the beaches of ⊡ **La Cruz's** ⑫ Bahia Salinas to swim, windsurf, or snorkel; or visit **Parque Nacional Santa Rosa** ⑨. After touring La Casona, your four-wheel-drive vehicle will safely deliver you to Playa Naranjo for a day at the beach.

IF YOU HAVE 5 DAYS

After a pass through **Zarcero** ①, spend a day and night in the ⊡ **Laguna de Arenal** ⑤ to ⊡ **La Fortuna** ③ area, and see the volcano, lake, Tabacón Resort, and/or the La Fortuna waterfall. From La Fortuna, head north to spend a day touring Caño Negro Wildlife Refuge. Then drive northwest on the road that leads through the San Rafael de Guatuso area and continues around the Volcán Orosí. Stop for a

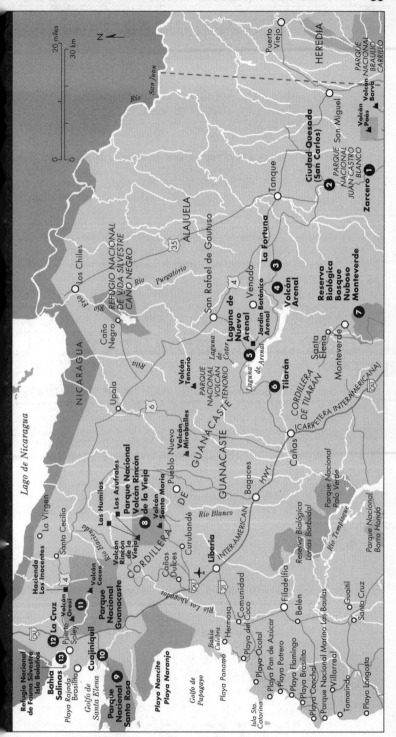

mind-expanding look at Lago de Nicaragua from the *mirador* (lookout) at La Virgen, near Santa Cecilia, then continue down the west slope of the mountains. Spend a night at **Hacienda Los Inocentes,** near the ⊞ **Parque Nacional Guanacaste** ⑪, then a day hiking or horseback riding before continuing on to ⊞ **La Cruz** ⑫ and the new resorts on ⊞ **Bahia Salinas** ⑬. After a night there, work your way down with a day on the beach in **Parque Nacional Santa Rosa** ⑨ or in the mixed environments of **Parque Nacional Rincón de la Vieja** ⑧ with overnights either camping in the park or, more comfortably, tucked into one of the nearby lodges or hotels.

When To Tour Northern Guanacaste and Alajuela

The areas in Guanacaste west of the Cordillera de Guanacaste are best toured in the dry season from December to March. However, during the rainy season, rain generally falls on this coastal plain for just an hour or two each day, and it's not too much of a problem beyond its effect on the roads. Farther inland, the northern uplands and lowlands offer a mixed climactic bag—the more easterly lowlands share the humid Caribbean weather of the east coast, while the uplands partake of the drier, cooler mountain clime. Given the larger numbers of tourists that visit places like the Volcán Arenal and especially Monteverde, if you are lucky enough to have a flexible schedule it might be wise to try an off-season, or edge-of-season, trip, simply to avoid the high-season crowds at Monteverde and popular destinations.

ARENAL AND THE CORDILLERA DE TILARÁN

Dense green cloud forests cloak the rugged mountains and rolling hills of the Cordillera de Tilarán, extending northwest from San José. On the east side of the hills and on the plains below, logging and farming contend with tourism for dominance of the local economy. Still, there are great swaths of primary forest and jungle to be experienced, including the marvelous cluster of forest reserves that straddle the continental divide at Monteverde. Farther north and west, Laguna de Arenal and the rolling green hills around the lake pay homage to the dark heart of this region—fiery, magnificent Volcán Arenal.

Zarcero

❶ *70 km (43 mi) northwest of San José.*

Ninety minutes from San José, the small town of Zarcero looks like it was designed by Dr. Seuss. For a fan of topiaries, this place is a must: cypress shrubs in fanciful animal shapes—motorcycle-riding monkeys, a light-bulb-eyed elephant—decorate the park in front of the church, the work of Evangelisto Blanco. The church interior is covered with elaborate pastel stencils and detailed religious paintings by Misael Solis, a local old-timer.

Shopping

Zarcero is renowned for its peach preserves and white cheese, both of which are sold in stores around town and along the highway.

SOUVENIRS

Stop at **El Tiesto Souvenir Shop** (☎ 463–3196) across from the park and talk politics with owner Rafael, a native Tico who lived in New Jersey for a while. He knows everything about the area and can arrange day trips to nearby waterfalls. At the tiny café-store **Super Dos,** on the main road opposite the church in Zarcero, you can get a coffee and empanada *de piña* (of pineapple) while you mull over buying some of the excellent local peach preserves.

En Route Passing through Sarchi, Naranjo, and Zarcero, you'll wind upward through miles of coffee plantations, with spectacular views of the mountains, and come down the other side to the city of Ciudad Quesada. There are some hair-raising roadside chasms, particularly on the east slope of the mountains, but the road is paved all the way. The drive should take roughly 2½ to three hours.

Ciudad Quesada

➋ *115 km (71 mi) northwest of San José.*

This lively, if not particularly picturesque, mountain market town (also known as San Carlos) is worth a stop for a soak in the soothing thermal waters of the El Tucano Resort and Spa. The new **Parque Nacional Juan Castro Blanco** (☞ Chapter 10) can also be found nearby, although as of mid-1998 there were no facilities in the park.

Lodging

$$$$ ⊞ **Hotel El Tucano Resort and Spa.** You come to El Tucano for the wa-
★   ters—hot, healing, marvelously refreshing and invigorating natural springs. The hotel sits atop rocks with hot springs bubbling forth out of fissures. Two large outdoor hot tubs, the Olympic-size swimming pool, freestanding natural steam room, cool plunge, and in-room shower-tubs are all fed by the aptly named Río Aguas Caliente, the rocky, cascading river that flows through the property. The spa center offers facials, massages, and other indulgent treatments. The hotel itself is somewhat overscale, and its public spaces suffer from the impersonality that affects any hotel subject to tour-group bookings. Still, the complex is surrounded by primary-growth forest, and the guest-room interiors are a study in understated luxury: simple, elegant, and comfortable. ⊠ *8 km (5 mi) east of Ciudad Quesada, Apdo. 114–1017, San José,* ☎ *460–3141, 460–3142 or 233–8936,* 𝔽𝔸𝕏 *460–1692 or 221–9095 reservations office in San José. 81 rooms with bath, 9 suites. Restaurant, bar, pool, spa, steam room, 2 tennis courts, horseback riding, bicycles. AE, MC, V.*

La Fortuna and Vicinity

➌ *40 km (27 mi) east of Volcán Arenal; 125 km (80 mi), or 3 hours, from San José by car, via Ciudad Quesada and Zarcero.*

At the foot of towering, overpowering Volcán Arenal, the small farming community of La Fortuna de San Carlos (commonly called La Fortuna) attracts volcano watchers from around the world. The town overflows with restaurants, hotels, and tour operators. La Fortuna is also the number-one place to arrange tours to the Caño Negro refuge (☞ *below*). Tours vary in price and quality, so ask around, but whoever you choose will provide an easier alternative than busing up north to Los Chiles and hiring a boat on your own to take you down through the rain forest on Río Frío.

Besides access to a multitude of outdoor adventures, La Fortuna also provides one the opportunity for some serious pampering. Kick back at the **Tabacón Resort,** 12 km (7 mi) northwest of La Fortuna on the highway toward Nuevo Arenal. This heavily touristed day spa and new-fangled 42-room hotel ($$$$) is a highly recommended stop in spite of the crowds and the slightly tacky design. An inspired medley of spacious gardens, waterfalls, swimming pools, swim-up bars, and dining facilities mingles in a florid Latin interpretation of grand European baths—except that you won't see this lavish array of flowers, palm trees, and exotic flora anywhere in Europe. Where else can you lounge in a natural hot-springs waterfall with a volcano spitting fireballs overhead? ☎ 222–1072 or 233–0780, 𝖥𝖠𝖷 221–3075. ✉ *$14, $13 after 6 PM, $26 for a 45-min massage, $9 for a mud-pack facial.* ☉ *Daily 10–10.*

In 1945 a farmer in the northern mountain hamlet of Venado fell in a hole, and thus were discovered the **Venado Caves.** The limestone caves, 45 minutes (about 35 km/21 mi) north of La Fortuna and 15 km (9 mi) southeast of San Rafael, include a series of eight rooms with an assortment of stalactites, stalagmites, underground streams, and other unusual subterranean formations.

OFF THE
BEATEN PATH

REFUGIO NACIONAL DE VIDA SILVESTRE CAÑO NEGRO – The 38½-sq-mi Caño Negro Wildlife Refuge (☎ 460–1301) in the far northern reaches of the province is miles off most people's itineraries, but the vast Lago di Caño Negro is an excellent place for watching such waterfowl as the roseate spoonbill, jabiru stork, and anhinga, as well as for observing a host of resident exotic animals (also ☞ Chapter 10). In the dry season you can rent horses; in the rainy season you are better off renting a boat. Camp or stay in basic lodging for around $8, including meals. Approach via Upala—a bus from there takes 45 minutes. You can take the popular tour down the Río Frío run by Esteban Cruz (☎ 471–1032). The tour starts in Los Chiles, about a 90-minute drive on local roads east to Highway 35 north from La Fortuna (100 km/62 mi), near Volcán Arenal. Sunset Tours (☎ 479–9415) is one of the best of the many operators in La Fortuna running day-long tours down the Río Frío to Caño Negro. Bring your jungle juice: the mosquitoes are voracious.

FAR NORTHERN LA FORTUNA–LA CRUZ ROUTE – A newly paved road leads northwest (Highway 4) from Tanque, 10 km (6 mi) east of La Fortuna, passing through the towns of San Rafael de Guatuso and Upala as well as several hamlets tucked in among forest preserves, farmland, and reserves belonging to the indigenous Guatuso peoples. The road winds west, roughly paralleling Costa Rica's northern border, and offers smooth, pothole-free driving except for one short, nasty stretch just east of Santa Cecilia. As you head through remote rural territory, you'll see the eastern slopes of Guanacaste's volcanoes on the left and rolling farmland to the right. The dwellings here and there along the road and visible in the distance are small and ramshackle, and many lack electricity in this beautiful but economically deprived region of Costa Rica. From Santa Cecilia, a short trip north on a dirt track leads to La Virgen, a hamlet noteworthy for a nearby mirador, or lookout, with a spectacular view north across Lago de Nicaragua and the volcanoes beyond. From Santa Cecilia, the road descends westerly toward the coast, skirting the northern edge of Parque Nacional Guanacaste. After passing citrus groves and the splendid hacienda lodge at Hacienda Los Inocentes (☞ Parque Nacional Guanacaste, *below*), the road terminates at the Inter-American Highway a few miles south of La Cruz. An alternative route south from Upala traverses the saddle between volcanoes Tenorio and Miravalles, arriving at the Inter-American Highway just north of Cañas.

Dining and Lodging

$–$$ ✕ **La Vaca Muca.** It isn't a posh place, but the food is good (the cook, Emilce Vargas, used to be chef at the Arenal Lodge) and the servings generous. Try the casado heaped with chicken or fish, rice, beans, fried egg, fried banana, cabbage salad, and your meat course—easily enough for two! This restaurant is draped with foliage outside and, inside, has turquoise paneling and bamboo aplenty. ⊠ *1 km (½ mi) west of town,* ☎ *479–9186. Reservations not accepted. MC, V.*

$ ✕ **El Jardín.** This friendly diner serves respectable fish dishes. Try *guapote* (rainbow bass) if it's on the menu, but it's very bony, so ask if they'll fillet it. The extensive menu also includes chicken legs, pork chops, liver, tongue, and more. The *refrescos naturales* (fruit juices) are especially good. ⊠ *Opposite the gas station,* ☎ *479–9072. Reservations not accepted. MC, V.*

$$$ ▥ **Chachagua Rain Forest Lodge.** At this working ranch intersected by a sweetly babbling brook, you can see the caballeros at work, ride into the rain-forested mountains, and watch toucans feed off fruit plates in the open-air restaurant, which serves beef, milk, and cheese produced on the premises. The large, reflective windows enclosing each cabina's shower serve a marvelous purpose: birds are drawn to their own reflections, so the birds—more than 125 different types have been identified in the area—gather outside your window to watch themselves while you bathe and watch them. Downstream from the Children's Eternal Rainforest, San Ramon, and Monteverde reserves, the lodge is 3 km (2 mi) up a rough dirt and rock track—four-wheel drive recommended in rainy season—on the road headed south from La Fortuna to La Tigra. ⊠ *Apdo. 476–4005, Ciudad Cariari, San José,* ☎ *239–1164, 239–1049, or 239–0328,* ℻ *239–4206. 23 cabinas. Restaurant, fans, pool, horseback riding, meeting room. AE, MC, V.*

$$$ ▥ **Las Cabañitas Resort.** This group of red-roof cabinas set on landscaped grounds has terraces that face the volcano and rocking chairs from which to enjoy the view. The wood-panel cabins with bath have solid wood furnishings and quilted bedspreads. ⊠ *1 km (½ mi) east of La Fortuna, Apdo. 5–4417, La Fortuna, San Carlos,* ☎ *479–9000,* ℻ *479–9408. 30 cabins. Restaurant, bar, room service, pool, car rental. AE, MC, V.*

$$$ ▥ **Tilajari Hotel Resort.** As a comfortable, upscale base from which to tour the attractions of the northern lowlands and Volcán Arenal area, the Tilajari can't be beat. This 40-acre, elegantly landscaped resort has a broad array of amenities. "Papaya on a stick" bird feeders hang from trees just outside the open-air dining room, attracting a raucous array of toucans, parrots, and other winged beauties while you sip your morning coffee. Bear in mind, however, that it is relatively isolated and very popular with tour groups: you may see crocodiles on the Río San Carlo riverbank, but rest assured you'll see white loafers aplenty in the dining room (rather cheesy and overlit). But let's not be uncivil: the comfortable guest quarters have river-view balconies, satellite TV, and excellent bedside reading lights—a surprisingly infrequent amenity in Costa Rica. The hotel offers horseback or tractor tours through its own 1½-sq-mi rain-forest preserve and organizes tours to nearby sites. ⊠ *San Carlos Valley just outside Muelle, about 25 km (15 mi) from La Fortuna; follow signs for Muelle, Apdo. 81, Ciudad Quesada, San Carlos,* ☎ *469–9091,* ℻ *469–9095. 56 rooms with bath, 4 suites. Restaurant, bar, air-conditioning, 2 pools, saunas, 4 tennis courts, basketball, horseback riding, racquetball, meeting room. AE, MC, V.*

$$–$$$ ▥ **Arenal Lodge.** This modern white bungalow is surrounded by macadamia trees and rain forest, high above Laguna de Arenal Dam and midway between Nuevo Arenal and La Fortuna. Four-wheel drive is needed to negotiate the steep 2-km (1-mi) drive, but the hotel will ferry you from the bottom for a small fee. The bedroom suites, some in a newer annex, are all pleasantly furnished, and there are also cheaper, smaller, and darker rooms that don't look out at the volcano. The lodge's perks include an extensive library, a small snooker table, breakfast with the price of a room, and manicured gardens. ⊠ *Posada Arenal, Apdo. 1139–1250, Escazú 1250 San José,* ☎ *383–3957,* ℻

289–6798 reservations office in San José. 6 rooms with bath, 9 suites. Dining room, hiking, fishing, library. AE, MC, V.

$$–$$$ 🏨 **Hotel San Bosco.** The owners have added a two-story hotel covered
★   in blue-tile mosaics to complement the string of small, inexpensive cabinas. Two kitchen-equipped cabinas (which sleep 8 or 12) are a good deal for families. The spotlessly clean, white rooms have polished wood furniture and firm beds and are linked by a long veranda lined with benches and potted plants. You pay a little more for air-conditioning. ⊠ *La Fortuna de San Carlos, 220 yds north of La Fortuna's gas station,* ☎ *479–9050,* 𝙵𝙰𝚇 *479–9109. 18 rooms with bath, 11 cabinas. Restaurant, hot tub, laundry service. AE, MC, V.*

$$ 🏨 **La Pradera.** A building containing 10 comfortable cabinas has been put up next to La Pradera, a moderate-priced roadside restaurant beneath a high *rancho* on the route from La Fortuna to Arenal. Five rooms have air-conditioning, two have hot tubs, and all have verandas. Beef lovers should try the restaurant's steak with jalapeño sauce—a fine, spicy dish. ⊠ *About 5 km (3 mi) west of La Fortuna de San Carlos towards Arenal, Alajuela,* ☎ 𝙵𝙰𝚇 *479–9167. 10 rooms with bath. Restaurant. AE, MC, V.*

$$ 🏨 **Montana de Fuego Inn.** A few miles west of La Fortuna, these cabinas with hot-water bath are set on a grassy roadside knoll with utterly spectacular views of Volcán Arenal to the west. The spacious, well-made hardwood structures are notable for their large porches. Plans are afoot for a restaurant, but meanwhile a host of good, low-priced eateries are to be found in nearby La Fortuna. The management can arrange all the area tours. ⊠ *Just outside La Fortuna on the road to Arenal,* ☎ *382–0759,* 𝙵𝙰𝚇 *479–9579. 18 cabinas. MC, V.*

Outdoor Activities and Sports

HIKING

A pleasant day hike from La Fortuna takes you to the 164-ft-high **La Fortuna Waterfall.** The 6-km (4-mi) walk begins off the main road toward the volcano; look for the yellow sign marking the entrance. After walking 1½ km (1 mi) and passing two bridges, turn right and continue hiking straight until you reach the river turnoff. If you don't feel like walking, several operators in La Fortuna will take you on horseback or in a four-wheel-drive vehicle. If you've got your own wheels, use them: non–four-wheel-drive cars can also navigate the rocky road, but take it very slow—and double-check passability in the rainy season. A man at a desk under a large tent collects a $1.50 entrance fee at the head of the trail. From the top to the falls is 10 or 15 minutes down a steep but very well-constructed step trail, with a few vertiginous spots along the way. Swimming in the pool under the waterfall is fairly safe, and the water is refreshingly cool. You can work your way around into the cavelike area behind the cataract for an unusual rear view, if you don't mind swimming in turbulent waters and/or hiking over slippery rocks.

HORSEBACK RIDING

If you are interested in getting up to Monteverde from the Arenal–La Fortuna area without taking the grinding four-hour drive, there's an alternative: the ever-ingenious Suresh Krishnan, a transplant from Huntington Beach, California, is offering a new adventure out of his tour agency, **Desafio** (⊠ Apdo. 37–4417, La Fortuna SC,, ☎ 479–9464, 𝙵𝙰𝚇 479–9178)—a 4½-hour guided horseback trip around Volcán Arenal and up to Monteverde. They'll take your luggage and drive your car up there if need be, meaning you arrive in Monteverde by horse and all your stuff arrives separately, eliminating at least half of the backbreaking drive there. Plus you've horse-trekked a trail unseen by 99.9% of the tourists in Costa Rica. Suresh claims there are spots along the route that allow you to look down into Volcán Arenal. We haven't actually tried this route, but it sounds inspiring. You leave La Fortuna at 7 AM, arrive in Monteverde at 1 PM. It's $65 per person, plus $20 for a pack horse and car shuttle.

RAFTING

Desafio (☞ *above*) and several other La Fortuna operators offer class III and IV white-water trips on the Río Sarapiquí and the Río Peñas Blancas (literally, white stones river), whose headwaters in the Monteverde–Santa Elena region assure the pristine quality of the waters. The Peñas Blancas' narrow shape requires the use of special, streamlined U.S.-made boats that seat just four and go very fast. Fees range from $37 per person for half-day Peñas Blancas trips to $65–$80 for longer trips on the Sarapiquí.

SPELUNKING

Sunset Tours (✉ La Fortuna de San Carlos, across from Desafio, ☎ 479–9415, FAX 479–9099) will take you to the Venado Caves for $25, including guide, entrance fee, boots, and a lantern. Prepare to get wet and muddy.

Volcán Arenal

❹ *17 km (11 mi) west of La Fortuna, 128 km (80 mi) northwest of San José; 2½–3 hours north of Santa Elena.*

For those who have never seen an active volcano, Arenal makes a spectacular first—its perfect conical profile dominates the southern end of Laguna de Arenal. Arenal lay dormant until 1968; on July 29 of that year an earthquake shook the area, and 12 hours later Arenal blew. The town of Pueblo Nuevo to the west bore the brunt of the shock waves, poisonous gases, and falling rocks; 80 people perished in all. Since then, Arenal has been in a constant state of activity—eruptions, accompanied by thunderous grumbling sounds, are sometimes as frequent as one per hour. Night is the best time for observing it, when you can clearly see rocks spewing skyward and red-hot molten lava enveloping the top of the cone. Phases of inactivity do occur, however, so it is wise to check just before you go to judge whether your trip will be worthwhile. The volcano is also frequently hidden in cloud cover, so you may have to stay more than one day to get in a good volcano-viewing session.

Hiking is possible on the volcano's lower slopes, but definitely not higher up; in 1988 two people were killed when they attempted to climb it. Ask at the **Smithsonian Institution's Observatory,** near the base of the volcano, or at any one of the dozens of tour operators, such as Desafio, working out of La Fortuna. They'll let you know how close you can safely approach. Beyond that, you should attempt exploration only with a guide.

Laguna de Arenal, Nuevo Arenal, and Tilarán

❺ ❻ *Nuevo Arenal: 40 km (25 mi) west of La Fortuna; Tilarán: 22 km (14 mi) southwest of Nuevo Arenal, 62 km (38 mi) west of La Fortuna.*

Laguna de Arenal (Lake Arenal) has two distinct personalities: the northwest end is windsurf central; a row of recently installed power-generating windmills, with blades awhirl on the ridge above the Hotel Tilawa, signals another use for the relentless, powerful wind. The more sheltered southeast end, closer to the dam, is popular for other water sports, especially fishing for guapote. The southeast is also a marvelous place from which to view the volcano. If you took away the volcanoes, you might mistake the surrounding countryside of green, rolling hills for the English Lake District.

If you're staying overnight in the area make sure you find a hotel with a view of the volcano. Shortly before the dam at the southern end of the lake is the turn to Arenal Lodge (☞ Dining and Lodging *in* La Fortuna and Vicinity, *above*). On the north shore, between the dam and the town of Nuevo Arenal there is one short stretch of road still unpaved, adding a bone-jarring hour to an otherwise lovely drive (but beware of deep, tire-wrecking potholes and washouts at all times) with spectacular lake and volcano views all the way. Heading west around the lake, you'll pass a couple of small villages and several charming hotels ranging from the Cretan-inspired fantasy Hotel Tilawa to the rustic Rock River Lodge (☞ Lodging, *below*). The quiet whitewashed town of Tilarán, on the southwest side of Laguna de Arenal, is used as a base by bronzed windsurfers.

Five kilometers (3 mi) east of Nuevo Arenal, the **Jardín Botánico Arenal** (Arenal Botanical Gardens, ☎ 694-4273) offers visitors the opportunity to see more than 2,000 plant species from around the world gathered in a single, elegantly organized site. Countless orchids, bromeliads, heliconias, and roses, myriad ferns, and a Japanese garden with a waterfall are among the many floral splendors laid out along well-marked trails. An accompanying brochure describes everything in delightful detail; well-placed benches and a fruit and juice stand provide resting places along the paths.

Lodging

$$$$ 🏨 **Hotel Joya Surena.** In the midst of a working coffee plantation about 1½ km (1 mi) down a rocky road that leads north out of Nuevo Arenal, this property's variously sized suites occupy a rather imposing three-story hacienda-style building surrounded by tropical gardens. The style is fairly luxurious for up-country Costa Rica. There are extensive trails in and around the property, with a rich diversity of plant, animal, and bird life to view. ⊠ *Nuevo Arenal, Guanacaste*, ☎ 694–4057, ℻ 694–4059. *28 rooms with bath. Restaurant, pool, hot tub, massage, sauna, health club, hiking, horseback riding, boating, fishing. AE, MC, V.*

$$$–$$$$ 🏨 **Hotel Tilawa.** Eight kilometers (5 mi) north of Tilarán, this unique-
★   looking hotel sits on a bluff overlooking the windy western end of Laguna de Arenal. It's a knockoff of the Palace of Knossos on Crete—and with its neoclassical murals, columns, and arches draped with flowering plants—scarily enough, it works. Owned and operated by serious windsurfers, Tilawa started out servicing the needs of the windsurfing set, but now offers a host of activities such as sailing tours in a 36-ft catamaran and motorboat tours to the east end of the lake for volcano viewing. The hotel runs a windsurfing school and shop on the shore of the lake below; packages include the use of windsurfing gear. ⊠ *Apdo. 92–5710, Tilarán*, ☎ 695–5050, ℻ 695–5766. *28 rooms with bath. Restaurant, bar, pool, hiking, horseback riding, windsurfing, boating, mountain bikes. AE, MC, V.*

$$$ 🏨 **Lake Coter Eco-Lodge.** This ruggedly handsome mountain hideaway is tucked into cloud forest, 3 km (2 mi) up a rough rock-and-dirt track off the highway on the north shore of Laguna de Arenal. Among UFO cognoscenti, an as-yet-unexplained aerial photograph of a saucer (a replica hangs in the lodge) over this lake is well known. The lodge is associated with a tour company and tends to fill up with oversized groups, but hit it on a nontour day and you'll have a choice of comfortable ridge-top cabinas. Additional basic rooms are attached to the main brick-and-hardwood reception building, with a friendly

bar, dining facilities, fireplace, and pool table. The lodge offers canopy tours; hikes on 29 km (18 mi) of trails; kayaking, sailing, and beginning windsurfing on Laguna de Coter; and an extensive stable for trail rides through the cloud forest. ✉ *Apdo. 85570–1000, San José,* ☎ *257–5075,* ⅆ *257–7065. 23 rooms with bath, 14 cabinas. Restaurant, bar, hiking, horseback riding, boating. AE, MC, V.*

$$–$$$ ▦ **Rock River Lodge.** This handsome hotel perches on a grassy hill above the road leading from Tilarán to Nuevo Arenal. A long building houses half a dozen rustic wooden cabinas sharing a shaded front porch. Eight Santa Fe–style cabinas are farther up the hill. The restaurant, bar, and lobby occupy another rustic wooden building a bit closer to the road, with plenty of porch space and lounging sofas, an open kitchen, a welcoming fireplace, and cafeteria-style dining tables. The owner, Norman List, is a dedicated windsurfer and rents gear; his is the launching site across the lake from the Hotel Tilawa's. He also organizes tours for inner tubing on the Sarapiquí and bird-watching. The restaurant serves well-made food at reasonable prices. ✉ *Apdo. 95, Tilarán,* ☎ ⅆ *695–5644. 6 rooms with bath, 8 cabinas. Restaurant, bar, horseback riding, fishing, mountain bikes. No credit cards.*

$$–$$$ ▦ **Xiloe Lodge and Equus Bar/Full Moon Disco.** On the road between Tilarán and Nuevo Arenal, the Xiloe stands out among the plethora of low-budget cabinas, hotels, and inns for its lovely setting, sheltered from the wind on a rise in the trees not far from the northwesternmost end of the lake. Xiloe offers three spacious wooden cabinas with three bedrooms, and kitchenettes, plus two smaller two-bedroom cabinas that sleep up to four; all have hot-water bath. The barbecue at Equus restaurant fires up excellent carnivorous fare—grilled beef, smoked chicken, and the like—every night but Monday. And on Friday and Saturday night, nights when the moon is full, or just about any night that calls for a party, the Full Moon disco, a multilevel, stone-floored, open-air extravaganza behind the restaurant, is one of the hottest dance floors in Costa Rica. ✉ *Apdo. 35, Tilarán,* ☎ *259–9806,* ⅆ *259–9882. 5 cabinas. Restaurant, dance club. No credit cards.*

$$ ▦ **Arenal Observatory Lodge.** On your way to the observatory, the closest lodge to Arenal's base, you cross three large rivers whose bridges are regularly washed away, restricting access to those with four-wheel drive. Built in 1987 for researchers, the lodge is rustic but comfortable; some bedrooms are dorms, and some are doubles. The dining room has great views in both directions and serves hearty food included in the price of the room. ✉ *3 km (2 mi) east of dam on Laguna de Arenal, at intersection turn right and continue for 9 km (5½ mi),* ☎ ⅆ *695–5033;* ☎ *257–9489,* ⅆ *257–4220 reservations office in San José;* ✉ *John Aspinall, Arenal Observatory Lodge, Box 025216–1660, Miami, FL 33102-5216. 23 rooms with bath, 5 rooms and 1 cabina without bath. Restaurant, bar. AE, MC, V.*

$ ▦ **Cabinas El Sueño.** Upstairs on a street just off Tilarán's central plaza, "The Dream" is probably the best low-priced deal in town—and for you budget-minded wind riders, it's a few scant km from the pricier Hotel Tilawa's waterfront windsurf center. The quiet rooms with hot-water bath surround a serene central courtyard with a fountain and a hammock for lounging. Downstairs, the hotel's Restaurant El Parque specializes in seafood dishes. ✉ *Off the central plaza,* ☎ *695–5347. 12 rooms with bath. Restaurant. No credit cards.*

Outdoor Activities and Sports

FISHING

Laguna de Arenal has the best freshwater fishing in Costa Rica, with guapote aplenty, although it is difficult to fish from the shore. Arenal Lodge (☞ Dining and Lodging *in* La Fortuna and Vicinity, *above*) is one of many hotels and tour companies in the area offering boats and guides.

Hotel Tilawa (☞ Lodging, *above*) and nearly every reputable hotel in the area offer access to guided and unguided horseback rentals. The Lake Coter Eco-Lodge (☞ Lodging, *above*) has 25 horses in its own stable. There are uncounted kilometers of good trails for horses and/or bikes in the region, covering a marvelous mix of terrain.

For those days when the windsurfers get "skunked" (the wind fails to blow), the Hotel Tilawa (☞ Lodging, *above*) rents mountain bikes for riding a network of roads and trails in the area at the north end of Laguna de Arenal.

When winter settles in up north, serious American windsurfers look south. These days many of them look to Arenal, which many world-champion windsurfers have called "one of the world's top five wind-surfing spots." Trade winds from the Caribbean sneak through a pass in the Cordillera Central, crank up to 80 kph (50 mph) or more from December through April, and blow from the east toward the north-west end of the lake, creating perfect conditions for high-wind fresh-water sailing. The scenery here, too, is unmatched: watch the frequent volcanic eruptions while you glide across the lake. The lake is some-what choppy due to its narrow shape, but strong winds, freshwater, and hassle-free rigging and launch sites on both shores make it worth-while. Several hotels, including the Rock River Lodge (☞ Lodging, *above*) have equipment for rent, but the best selection, fully updated in late 1997, can be found at **Tilawa Viento Surf** (☎ 695–5008), the lakefront shop associated with the Hotel Tilawa (☞ Lodging, *above*).

Shopping

Toad Hall, along the road between Nuevo Arenal and La Fortuna (☎ 470–9178), an eclectic store-café, is open daily from 8:30 to 5 and sells everything from indigenous art to maps to recycled paper. The store is also a terrific information center—the owners can give you the low-down on every tour and tour operator in the area. There's also a deli-café with tables on a veranda featuring stunning views of the lake and volcano.

Reserva Biológica Bosque Nuboso Monteverde and Environs

❼ *35 km (22 mi) southeast of Tilarán, 167 km (104 mi) northwest of San José.*

If your bones can take it, a very rough track leads from Tilarán, via Cabeceras, to Santa Elena, near Monteverde, doing away with the need to cut across to the Inter-American Highway. You may well need four-wheel drive—inquire as to the present condition of the road—but the views of Nicoya Peninsula, Laguna de Arenal, and Volcán Arenal reward those willing to bump around a bit. Consider also the fact that you don't really save much time—it takes about 2½ hours as opposed to the three required via Cañas and Lagarto on the highway.

To reach Monteverde from San José, travel north approximately 125 km (78 mi) on the Inter-American Highway to the Río Lagarto turnoff. From here, an unpaved 30-km (19-mi) track to the reserve snakes dra-matically up through hilly farming country; it takes 1½ to two hours to negotiate it, faster by four-wheel drive. (If you aren't renting four-wheel drive, at least get a car with high clearance—you'll be glad you did.) Those inclined to complain about the road should contemplate how busy the already-crowded Monteverde area would be if the road was smooth. At the junction for Santa Elena, bear right for the reserve. The Monteverde settlement has no real nucleus; houses and hotels flank a 5-km (3-mi) road at intervals until you arrive at the reserve's entrance.

In close proximity to several fine hotels, Reserva Biológica Bosque Nuboso Monteverde (Monteverde Cloud Forest Biological Reserve) is one of the country's best-kept reserves, with well-marked trails, lush vegetation, and a cool climate. The area's first residents were a handful of Costa Rican families, fleeing the rough-and-ready life of nearby goldmining fields during the 1940s. They were joined in the 1950s by Quakers from Alabama who came in search of peace, tranquility, and good grazing, but the cloud forest that lay above their dairy farms was soon to attract the attention of ecologists.

The collision of moist winds with the continental divide here creates a constant mist whose particles provide nutrients for plants growing at the upper layers of the forest. Giant trees are enshrouded in a cascade of orchids, bromeliads, mosses, and ferns, and, in those patches where sunlight penetrates, brilliantly colored flowers flourish. The sheer size of everything, especially the leaves of the trees, is striking. No less astounding is the variety: 2,500 plant species, 400 species of birds, 500 types of butterflies, and more than 100 different mammals have so far been cataloged at Monteverde. A damp and exotic mixture of shades, smells, and sounds, the cloud forest is also famous for its population of resplendent quetzals, which can be spotted feeding on the *aguacatillo* (like an avocado) trees; best viewing times are early mornings from January until September, especially in April and May, during mating season. Other forest-dwelling inhabitants include hummingbirds and multicolored frogs. For those who don't have a lucky eye, a **short-stay aquarium** is in the field station; captives here stay only a week before being released back into the wild. Although the reserve limits visitors to 100 people at a time, Monteverde is one of the country's most popular destinations and gets very busy, so get there early and allow a generous slice of time for leisurely hiking to see the forest's flora and fauna; longer hikes are made possible by some strategically placed overnight refuges along the way. At the entrance to the reserve you can buy self-guide pamphlets and rent gum boots, and a map is provided when you pay the entrance fee. ☎ 645–5122. ✉ $8 reserve; $15 guides. ☉ Daily 7–4.

The Monteverde cloud forest can be visited from high in the air courtesy of **Canopy Tours,** which has three platforms up in the trees that you arrive at using a cable-and-harness traversing system, and another which you climb 40 ft inside a strangler fig to reach. The tours last 2½ hours. Tours leave from the Canopy Tour Basecamp in Santa Elena at 7:30 and 10:30 AM and 2:30 PM. ✉ Apdo. 80–5655, Santa Elena de Monteverde ☎ 645–5243, FAX 645–5022; San José ☎ 226–1315, FAX 255–3573. ✉ $40.

Introducing a new twist on the canopy tour, **Valverde's Puentes Colgantes** lets visitors hike between treetops, up to a height of 126 ft, by way of five hanging bridges connected from tree to tree. ☎ 645–5238. ✉ $5.

At the **Serpentario Monteverde,** you can check out an exhibition of live Costa Rican reptiles. ☎ 645–5238. ✉ $3.

Several conservation areas that have sprung up near Monteverde make attractive day trips for reserve visitors, particularly if the Monteverde reserve is too busy. The **Santa Elena Reserve,** an almost 1½-sq-mi forest 5 km (3 mi) north of the town of Santa Elena, just west of Monteverde, has a series of trails that can be walked alone or with a guide. ☎ *645–5014.* 🎟 *$5.*

Operating out of the **El Sapo Dorado Hotel** (☞ Dining and Lodging, *below*), the **Reserva Sendero Tranquilo** offers you a chance to hike 200 acres containing four different stages of cloud forest, including one area illustrating the results of cloud forest devastation. ☎ *645–5010.* 🎟 *$20, 2-person minimum.*

🐾 The **Jardin Mariposa** (Butterfly Garden), near the Pensión Monteverde Inn, displays tropical butterflies in three enclosed botanical gardens from which there are stunning views of the Golfo de Nicoya. A guided tour helps you understand the stages of a butterfly's life. The private **bird farm** next door has several trails through secondary forest. More than 90 bird species have been sighted here, from the crowned motmot to the spectacular quetzal. 🎟 *$6.* ☯ *Daily 9:30–4.*

Dining and Lodging

$ ✕ **Stella's Bakery.** This shop serves everything from chocolate brownies to hearty breakfasts in a warm, wood-panel room decorated with Stella's oil paintings and her daughter Meg's stained-glass windows. You can also sip coffee on the backyard patio. ⊠ *Halfway between Santa Elena and Monteverde,* ☎ *645–5560. No credit cards. No lunch or dinner.*

$$$ ✕🏨 **El Sapo Dorado.** Having started its life as a nightclub, El Sapo Do-
★   rado (The Golden Toad) became a popular restaurant and graduated into a very pleasant hotel. Geovanny Arguedas' family arrived here to farm 10 years before the Quakers did, and he and his wife, Hannah Lowther, have built secluded hillside cabins with polished paneling, tables, open fires, and rocking chairs. The restaurant is renowned for its pasta, pizza, vegetarian dishes, and fresh sailfish from Puntarenas; the dance floor is still put to use with live music on weekends. The 6-km (4-mi) distance from the park entrance isn't a problem if you enjoy hiking or have a car. ⊠ *Apdo. 09–5655, Monteverde,* ☎ 📠 *645–5010 or 645–5181,* 📠 *645–5180. 20 rooms with bath. Restaurant, bar, massage, bicycles. No credit cards.*

$–$$ ✕🏨 **El Bosque.** Convenient to the Bajo Tigre nature trail and Meg's riding stable (☞ Outdoor Activities and Sports, *below*), El Bosque is a popular shady diner with a veranda; the paneled dining room has a tile floor and wood tables. A bridge from the veranda crosses a stream, and a track from there leads to the hotel. Across the creek and a short walk away from the restaurant, the hotel features quiet, simple rooms with private baths grouped around a central camping area with a volleyball court. For $60 the hotel will deliver two people to the Monteverde reserve entrance, and pay entry fees. ⊠ *Apdo. 5655, Santa Elena,* ☎ *645–5221 or 645–5158,* 📠 *645–5129. 21 rooms with bath. Restaurant. AE, MC, V. Closed Oct.*

$$$ 🏨 **Fonda Vela.** The most innovatively designed of Monteverde's ho-
★   tels is also one of the closest to the reserve entrance. Owned by the Smith brothers, whose family were among the first American arrivals in the 1950s, these steep-roofed chalets have large bedrooms with white stucco walls, wooden floors, and huge windows. Some have markedly better views of the wooded grounds, so specify when booking. Local and international recipes, prepared with flair, are served in the dining room or on the veranda. ⊠ *Apdo. 70060–1000, San José, 1½ km (1 mi) northwest of Monteverde entrance,* ☎ *645–5125,* 📠

645–5119, ☎ FAX 257–1413 *in San José. 28 rooms with bath. Restaurant, bar, horseback riding. AE, DC, MC, V.*

$$$ 🏨 **Hotel Belmar.** Built into the hillside, Hotel Belmar resembles two
★ tall Swiss chalets and commands extensive views of the Golfo de
Nicoya and the hilly peninsula. The amiable Chilean owners have designed both elegant and rustic rooms, paneled with polished wood; duvets cover the beds and most rooms have balconies. In the dining
room, you can count on adventurous and delicious *platos del día*
(daily specials). ✉ *4 km (2½ mi) north of Monteverde, Puntarenas,* ☎
645–5201, FAX *645–5135. 34 rooms with bath. Restaurant, bar, basketball. No credit cards.*

$ 🏨 **Pensión Monteverde Inn.** Situated on a 28-acre private preserve, the
cheapest inn in Monteverde is quite far—about 5 km (3 mi)—from the
park entrance. The bedrooms are basic, but they have stunning views
of the Golfo de Nicoya and contain hardwood floors, firm beds, and
powerful, hot showers. Home cooking is served by the chatty David
Savage and family. Their dog, Bambi, warms up to guests soon enough.
✉ *Monteverde, next to Butterfly Garden, Puntarenas,* ☎ *645–5156.
10 rooms, 8 with bath. Dining room. No credit cards.*

Outdoor Activities and Sports

HIKING

The Monteverde Conservation League's **Bajo del Tigre trail** (follow signs
along the highway on the way to Monteverde) makes for a pleasant,
1½-km (1-mi) hike through secondary forest.

HORSEBACK RIDING

Next door to Stella's Bakery (☞ Dining and Lodging, *above*), **Meg's
Stables** (☎ 645–5052) offers horseback riding for everyone from toddlers to seasoned experts. Guided rides through the Monteverde area
cost around $10 an hour, with prices dropping for longer rides. Reservations are a good idea in high season.

Shopping

In Monteverde, the **Cooperative de Artesanas Santa Elena y Monteverde**
(CASEM, ☎ 645–5190), an artisans' cooperative open next door to
the El Bosque hotel-restaurant (☞ Dining and Lodging, *above*), sells
locally made crafts. The **Hummingbird Gallery,** near the reserve entrance,
sells prints, slides, books, gifts, T-shirts, and great Costa Rican coffee.
Farther down on the right is the **Cheese Factory** (☎ 645–5029), established by the Quakers in the 1950s and now one of the largest dairy
producers in Costa Rica. Admission is free, and it's open Monday–
Saturday 7:30–4 and Sunday 7:30–12:30. Watch the art of cheese making through a window in the sales room—you'll surely be lured into
buying some.

FAR NORTHERN GUANACASTE

This area encompasses the mountains, plains, and Pacific coastline north
of Liberia up to the border of Nicaragua. The primary town in the area,
Liberia (☞ Chapter 5), serves as the capital of Guanacaste and home
to Costa Rica's second-largest airport. You will most likely pass through
Liberia on your way to the beaches west of the city and on the Nicoya
Peninsula (☞ Chapter 5), or up north to the national parks of Rincón
de la Vieja, Guanacaste, or Santa Rosa. Rincón, an active volcano that
last erupted in 1991, is pocked with eerie wonders such as boiling creeks,
bubbling mud pools, and vapor-emitting streams—look, but don't
touch!

West of Rincón de la Vieja, on the coast, Parque Nacional Santa Rosa
is a former cattle ranch, where Costa Ricans defeated the invading mer-

cenary army of American William Walker in 1857. Santa Rosa is also home to Playas Naranjo and Nancite, where hundreds of thousands of olive ridley turtles lay their eggs between June and November. And, closer still to the Nicaraguan border, are Parque Nacional Guanacaste and the town of La Cruz, overlooking the pristine beaches and new resorts of the lovely Golfo de Santa Elena and Bahia Salinas.

En Route   From Liberia, access to the Parque Nacional Rincón de la Vieja is via 27 km (17 mi) of unpaved road. The road begins 6 km (4 mi) north of Liberia off the Inter-American Highway (for Albergue Guachipelín) or 25 km (15 mi) along the Colonia Blanca route northeast from Liberia, which follows the course of the Río Liberia to the Santa María park headquarters. A four-wheel-drive vehicle is recommended, though not essential, for either of these bone-rattling 1- to 1½-hour rides.

Parque Nacional Rincón de la Vieja

8   *27 km (17 mi) north of Liberia..*

Some compare the geysers, mud pots, and hot springs of Parque Nacional Rincón de la Vieja (Rincón de la Vieja National Park) to those of Yellowstone National Park in the United States. The park's more than 54 sq mi of protected land is primarily dry forest, much of which has been regenerated since the park's inception in 1973. The wildlife here is tremendously diverse: 200 species of birds, including keel-billed toucans and blue-crowned motmots, plus mammals such as brocket deer, tapirs, coatis, jaguars, sloths, armadillos, and raccoons. Needless to say, hiking here is fantastic, but it's wise to do some planning to know where to head. Trail maps and hiking information are available at the park headquarters by the entrance gate; alternatively, head to Rincón de la Vieja Mountain Lodge (☞ Lodging, *below*), which has guides for foot or horseback hiking available; call ahead to check availability. ☎ 695–5598. ✆ *$6.* ☉ *Daily 8–4.*

The composite mass of **Volcán Rincón de la Vieja,** often enveloped in a mixture of sulfurous gases and cloud, dominates the scenery to the right of the Inter-American Highway as you head north. The volcano complex has two peaks: **Santa María** (6,284 ft) and **Rincón de la Vieja** (6,225 ft) to the northeast. The latter is vegetationless and has two craters. Rincón de la Vieja is thought unlikely to erupt violently due to the profusion of fumaroles through which it can constantly let off steam. The last violent eruptions were between 1966 and 1970. If you want to explore the slopes of the volcano, it is advisable to go with a guide; the abundant hot springs and geysers have given unsuspecting visitors some very nasty burns in the past. **Las Hornillas** ("the kitchen stoves"), on the southern slope of the Rincón de la Vieja crater, is a 124-acre medley of mud cones, hot-water pools, bubbling mud pots, and vent holes most active during the rainy season. To the east, **Los Azufrales** are hot sulfur springs in which you can bathe; be careful not to get sulfur in your eyes.

Lodging

$$ ☒ **Rincón de la Vieja Mountain Lodge.** Resting on the slopes of Rincón
★   de la Vieja, this lodge has paneled cabins, small doubles, or comfy bunk dormitory-style rooms. The sitting room has a terra-cotta floor, local maps, and cases of butterflies and some intimidatingly oversize insects. The food is good: meat, fish, and vegetarian entrées, and much of the produce is homegrown. The owner Alvaro's affable staff can take you to explore the park and volcano on foot or on horseback through the woods. Trails lead to a hot-water, sulfur bathing pool and a "blue lake" and waterfall. Four- and seven-hour canopy tours are run by Treetop

Trails (☞ Outdoor Activities and Sports, *below*). ✉ *Apdo. 114–5000, Liberia,* ☎ *695–5553, 666–0473, 284–3023, or 256–8206,* 𝖥𝖠𝖷 *695–5553, 256–7290. 27 rooms without bath. Dining room, pool. AE, MC, V.*

Outdoor Activities and Sports

From the Rincón de la Vieja Mountain Lodge (☞ Lodging, *above*), **Treetop Trails** runs four-hour canopy tours (☎ $49.50) that include a forest floor hike and canopy observation from 16 cable-linked treetop platforms. A more elaborate seven-hour tour (☎ $77) also includes horseback riding to the park's blue lake and waterfall.

Parque Nacional Santa Rosa

9 *48 km (30 mi) south of the Nicaraguan border, west of the Inter-American Highway at Km 269.*

Campers enjoy the rugged terrain and isolated feel of Parque Nacional Santa Rosa (Santa Rosa National Park). The sparseness of vegetation in this arid zone makes it easier for you to spy animals in the wild. From the entrance gate 7 km (4½ mi) of paved road leads to the park headquarters. The campsite, overhung by giant strangler figs, provides washing facilities and picnic tables. Be careful of snakes. Between Playas Naranjo and Nancite, another campground at Estero Real is available with tables only.

Santa Rosa was established in 1971 to protect **La Casona Hacienda,** scene of the famous 1856 battle in which a ragged force of ill-equipped Costa Ricans routed the superior army of William Walker. A U.S. filibuster from Tennessee, Walker had established himself as chief of staff of the Nicaraguan army as part of his Manifest Destiny–influenced scheme to create a slave empire in the region. In 1857, the hostilities having continued onto Nicaraguan soil, Juan Santamaría, a drummer boy from Alajuela, threw burning wood into the building where Walker and his henchmen were gathered, so ending the war, and thereby winning undying national fame for himself (Walker was later turned over to Honduras and shot by a firing squad). The rambling colonial-style farmstead of La Casona stands as a monument to this national triumph and contains an interesting museum, with maps, weapons, uniforms, and furniture. The start of a short explanatory nature trail is visible just out front. Keep an eye out for the numbers of large green parrots inhabiting the trees around the farmstead. ☉ *Museum daily 8–4:30.*

For ecologists, Santa Rosa has a more important role—protecting and regenerating 191 sq mi of forest land, both moist, basal belt transition and deciduous tropical dry forests. The central administrative area is a hive of scientific activity. Much of the research here has been into forest propagation, the fruits of which are evident in former cattle pastures where windblown seeds have been allowed to establish themselves. Bush fires are a constant hazard in the dry season, making firebreaks a necessity. Typical dry forest vegetation includes oak, wild cherry, mahogany, calabash, bullhorn acacia, hibiscus, and gumbo-limbo, with its distinctive reddish-brown bark. Because of its less luxuriant foliage, the park is a good one for viewing wildlife, especially if you station yourself next to water holes during the dry season. Inhabitants include spider, white-faced, and howler monkeys, deer, armadillos, coyotes, tapirs, coatis, and ocelots. Ocelots, commonly known as *manigordos* (fat paws) on account of their large feet, are striped wildcats that have been brought back from the brink of extinction by the park's conservation methods. These wildlands also define the southernmost distribution of many North American species such as the Virginia opossum and the *cantil* moccasin. Throughout the park it is wise to carry your own water since water holes are none too clean. ☎ 695–5598. 🖃 $6 *park.* ☉ *Daily 7–5.*

Thirteen kilometers (8 mi) west of the administrative area—a two- to three-hour hike or one hour by four-wheel drive—is the white-sand **Playa Naranjo,** popular for beachcombing thanks to its pretty shells and for surfing because of its near-perfect break. The campsite here has washing facilities, but bring your own drinking water. Make sure to catch the lookout at the northern tip of the beach with views over the entire park.

Turtle *arribadas*—the phenomenon of turtles arriving on a beach to nest—do take place on Naranjo, but the big ones occur at a point reached via a two-hour walk north to **Playa Nancite,** also accessible by four-wheel drive. It is estimated that 200,000 of the 500,000 turtles that nest each year in Costa Rica choose Nancite. Backed by dense hibiscus and button mangroves, the gray-sand beach is penned in by steep, tawny, brush-covered hills. Previously a difficult point to get to, it is now the only totally protected olive ridley turtle arribada in the world. The busy time is August to December, peaking in September and October. Olive ridleys are the smallest of the sea turtles (average carapace, or hardback shell, is 21–29 inches) and the least shy. The majority arrive at night, plowing the sand as they move up the beach and sniffing for the high-tide line, beyond which they use their hind flippers to dig holes into which they will lay their eggs. They spend an average of one hour on the beach before scurrying back to the sea. Hatching also takes place at night. The phototropic baby turtles naturally know to head for the sea, which is vital for their continued survival, since the brightest light is that of the shimmering ocean. Many of the nests are churned up during subsequent arribadas, and predators such as *pizotes* (coatis), ghost crabs, raccoons, and coyotes lie in wait; hence just 0.2% of eggs reach the sea as young turtles. Permits are needed to stay at Nancite; ask at the headquarters.

Cuajiniquil

🔟 *10 km (6 mi) north of Santa Rosa National Park.*

North from Santa Rosa on the Inter-American Highway is the left turn to Cuajiniquil, famous for its waterfalls. If you have time and a four-wheel-drive vehicle, Cuajiniquil has lovely views. The **Golfo de Santa Elena** is renowned for its calm waters, which is why it is now threatened by tourist development. **Playa Blanca** in the extreme west has smooth white sand, as its name implies. The rough track there passes through a valley of uneven width caused, according to geologists, by the diverse granulation of the sediments formerly deposited here. To the south rise the rocky **Santa Elena hills** (2,332 ft), bare except for a few chigua and nancite shrubs.

Parque Nacional Guanacaste

⑪ *32 km (20 mi) north of Liberia.*

To the east of the Inter-American Highway is Parque Nacional Guanacaste (Guanacaste National Park, ☎ 695–5598 at Santa Rosa for information and reservations), created in 1989 to preserve rain forests around **Volcán Cacao** (5,443 ft) and **Volcán Orosí** (4,877 ft), which are seasonally inhabited by migrants from Santa Rosa. Much of the park's territory is cattle pasture, which it is hoped will regenerate into forest. Three biological stations within the park have places for visitors to stay. **Mengo Biological Station** lies on the slopes of Volcán

Cacao at an altitude of 3,609 ft; accommodation is in rustic wooden dormitories with bedding provided, but bring a towel. From Mengo one trail leads up Volcán Cacao, and another heads north to the modern **Maritza Station,** a three-hour hike away at the base of Orosí, with more lodging available. You can also reach Maritza by four-wheel drive. From Maritza you can trek two hours to **Llano de los Indios,** a cattle pasture dotted with volcanic petroglyphs. Farther north and a little east is rustic **Pitilla Station** and, despite its lower elevation, it has views of the coast and Lago de Nicaragua.

Lodging

$$–$$$ ☷ **Hacienda Los Inocentes.** Constructed more than 100 years ago by the great-grandfather of Violeta Chamorra, the president of Nicaragua, this handsome, exquisitely maintained hardwood hacienda is in a private reserve along the northern border of Guanacaste National Park. A 14-km (8½-mi) drive on a smoothly paved road east from the Inter-American Highway takes you to the entrance of the working ranch, with its various horses, herds of cattle, and numerous birds—a pair of scarlet macaws and an outgoing bread-eating toucan are but the closest of an astonishing array that makes this one of the best bird-watching perches in all of Costa Rica. The hardwood-finished rooms are rustic but comfortable, with heat-on-demand showers in bathrooms (some shared by two rooms) across the halls. Meals are included in most packages. Experienced ranch-hand guides, docile, friendly horses, and miles of fantastic trails get you into the forests. If you'd rather not ride or walk, the lodge offers a tractor tour. ⊠ *Apdo. 228–3000, Heredia,* ☎ FAX *679–9190;* ☎ *265–5484 reservations office in San José; 888/613–2532 in U.S.,* FAX *265–4385. 11 rooms without bath. Dining room, pool. AE, MC, V.*

La Cruz and Vicinity

⑫ *56 km (35 mi) north of Liberia, 20 km (12 mi) south of the Nicaraguan border.*

Farther north on the west side of the highway is a turnoff to La Cruz, noteworthy for the stunning views of Bahía Salinas (☞ *below*) from the restaurants and hotels along the bluff. It also serves as a gateway to the new resorts on Bahia Salinas, as well as the hamlet of Puerto Soley and the beaches of Bahia Salinas and the Golfo de Santa Elena.

Dining and Lodging

$$ ✕ **El Mirador Ehecatl.** You don't want to pass up a chance to have a drink at this two-story restaurant and bar with a cliffside promenade overlooking Bahia Salinas, Isla Bolaños, and the Nicaraguan coastline. Even better, the Mirador's food is delicious: try anything with seafood—the seviche is especially well prepared—or one of the many cheap, rice-based combination plates. The chef has a surprisingly refined hand. Ehecatl, by the way, means "god of the wind" in the old Chorotegan language, and the name suits, for Bahia Salinas is a very windy place. To find the restaurant turn left and go around the La Cruz town square; at the "end" of the road veer slightly left rather than taking the steep downhill road that leads to Bahia Salinas, and you're there. ☎ *No phone. V.*

$$ ☷ **Amalia's Inn.** The late Lester Bounds, American artist, and his Tican wife Amalia created this breezy little inn on the cliff overlooking Bahia Salinas. Amalia now runs the inn with help from her brother. Bounds is also survived by his art, colorful modern paintings and prints that decorate the property. On the left or south side of the road as you head into town, the inn features spacious rooms with private baths, balconies, and awesome views of Bahia Salinas. The surrounding forest preserve was given to the town of La Cruz by Amalia's sister, who lives in and owns the magnificent Hacienda Quebrada de Agua, visible in the valley below La Cruz. If you'd rather look down on the bay than immerse yourself in it, Amalia's is a fine budget alternative to the pricier new resorts on the bay's south shore. ✉ *La Cruz, Guanacaste,* ☎ FAX *679–9181. 8 rooms with bath. Pool. No credit cards.*

$$ 🏨 **Colinas del Norte.** Nicaragua-bound adventurers will appreciate this outpost. On the Inter-American Highway halfway between La Cruz and the Nicaraguan border 20 km (12 mi) north at Peñas Blancas, this rugged two-story hardwood hotel bills itself as a touring base for the surrounding dry tropical forest, but its most appealing feature appears to be its large pool, surrounded by shady palms. At the outdoor disco you can dance till you drop, then hop into the pool. The indoor-outdoor restaurant specializes in pizza and Italian food. Modest but comfortable upstairs rooms come with private hot water baths and view terraces. ✉ *Inter-American Highway, about 10 km/6 mi north of La Cruz, Box 10493–1000, San José,* ☎ FAX *679–9132, 284–3972, 289–7318 in San José. 24 rooms. Restaurant, pool. AE, MC, V.*

Bahia Salinas

⓭ *7 km (4½ mi) west of La Cruz.*

Several dirt and rock roads dead end on different beaches along Bahia Salinas, the pretty little half-moon bay that lies at the very top of Costa Rica's Pacific coast—just try a turn right off the "main" road to the resorts. You'll probably end up on or near the beach, or in the hamlet of Puerto Soley, a tiny town tucked in off the bay—look for the salt flats to find the town, which is roughly 5 or 6 very slow-going km (3–4 mi) from La Cruz. There is public beach access along the bay, so if you have your own windsurfing equipment there's no need to utilize the resorts, which have inevitably crept up on the bay.

The wind usually blows year-round except in September and October, the height of the rainy season, so windsurfing here is supreme. Winds here are generally not as powerful as at Laguna de Arenal, but there is enough to make this a viable alternative (stay on the south side for stronger winds), or accompaniment, to the Arenal experience. Ranking among the most beautiful beaches in all of Costa Rica are a couple of secluded, wind-sheltered strands, including the gorgeous, pristine **Playa Rajada,** with fine swimming and snorkeling. Just offshore is **Isla Bolaños,** a bird refuge and nesting site for thousands of endangered frigate birds as well as brown pelicans. The Bolaños Bay Resort (☞ Lodging, *below*) has a motor launch for Isla Bolaños tours, but don't try to land—it is against the law.

Lodging

$$$–$$$$ 🏨 **Ecoplaya Beach Resort.** On the same stretch of Bahia Salinas as the Bolaños Bay Resort (☞ *below*), the Ecoplaya emphasizes upscale luxury amenities; eventually it will be transformed into a timeshare resort with 89 villas and suites. This means that every well-made room has a small but fully equipped kitchen, satellite TV, air-conditioning, phones, plentiful hot water, and custom hardwood furniture. Little recreational equipment was evident in late 1998, but management plans to have it all, from windsurfing gear to (unfortunately) Jet Skis, which may wreak havoc on peace, quiet, and possibly the bird refuge. The nearly 1 km- (½ mi-) long beach fronting the hotel is flanked by bird- and wildlife-filled estuaries at both ends. Be warned, nonsailors: the wind blows hard here, much of the time. ✉ *Plaza Colonial Escazú Local #4, San José,* ☎ *679–9380; 289–8920 reservations office in San José,*

FAX 679–9460, 289–4536 *in San José. 16 villas and suites. Restaurant, bar, pool. AE, MC, V.*

$$$ ☷ **Bolaños Bay Resort.** Take the dirt road down the steep hill from La Cruz, follow the signs for about 15 km (9 mi), and you'll soon spot the high double *rancho* that shelters the resort's reception, bar, and restaurant areas. Given the fairly relentless winds that rocket across the bay, the resort's emphasis on windsurfing—there's a well-stocked rental shop with European-made equipment and lessons—comes as no surprise. For windsurfing widows and nonsailors, a sheltered pool with a swim-up bar provides a diversion. The Belgian-based Three Corners Company run their hotels European style, with high quality meals—especially hearty breakfasts—and modest rooms tucked into multiunit low-rise cabinas neatly arrayed across grassy lawns. A total of 72 rooms are in the planning. Three Corners currently plans for two more resorts in the same area. ✉ *325 oeste de la Rodonda de la Bandera Oficentro Holland House, #4, San José,* ☎ *679–9444; 283–8901 reservations office in San José,* FAX *679–9654, 283–8870 in San José. 36 rooms with bath. Restaurant, bar, pool, hot tub, windsurfing. AE, MC, V.*

Outdoor Activities and Sports

WATER SPORTS

The windsurfing **Pro Center** (☎ 679–9444) at Bolaños Bay Resort (☞ Lodging, *above*) is run by friendly, knowledgeable Bjorn Voigt. Charlie at La Cruz–based **Iyok Trips** (☎ 679–9444 at Bolaños Bay Resort) offers boat trips around Isla Bolaños, and snorkeling, fishing, and waterskiing trips to Playa Cuajiniquil and other spots in the Golfo de Santa Elena. Charlie promises sightings of nurse sharks, manta rays, and lots of large fish. Iyok's guides also lead horseback riding and mountain biking tours of the area, and know where the monkeys hang out in the woods. At press time, Iyok (and the resort) were planning tours to Nicaragua's beautiful colonial city of Granada, and—even better for the wave-hungry set—trips by boat to "secret" surf spots up the Nicaraguan coast.

NORTHERN GUANACASTE AND ALAJUELA A TO Z

Arriving and Departing

By Bus

ARENAL AND THE CORDILLERA DE TILARÁN

Buses (☎ 255–4318) for Ciudad Quesada leave San José from Calle 16 between Avenidas 1 and 3 daily, every hour 5 AM–7:30 PM (3-hr trip). You can continue from Ciudad Quesada to Arenal and Tilarán. Buses (☎ 222–3854) for Tilarán leave from Calle 14 between Avenidas 9 and 11 daily at 7:30 AM, 9:30 AM, 12:45 PM, 3:45 PM, and 6:30 PM (4-hr trip). You can continue to Nuevo Arenal and Volcán Arenal from Tilarán. Buses (☎ 222–3854) for Monteverde depart from Calle 14 between Avenidas 9 and 11 weekdays at 6:30 AM and 2:30 PM (4-hr trip).

Buses (☎ 460–5032) for Los Chiles (Caño Negro) depart from Calle 12, Avenida 9, daily 5:30 AM and 3:30 PM. Buses (☎ 221–0953, 222–3006, 669–0145, or 284–1923) for Cañas, and the turnoff for Tilarán and Arenal, run daily at 8:30 AM, 10:30 AM, 12:30 PM, 1:20 PM, 2:30 PM, and 4:30 PM, Calle 16, between Avenidas 3 and 5.

FAR NORTHERN GUANACASTE

Buses (☎ 222–1650) to Liberia (4-hr ride) leave from Calle 14, Avenidas 3 and 4 daily at 6 AM, 7 AM, 9 AM, 11:30 AM, 1 PM, 4 PM, 6

PM, and 8 PM, with direct buses at 3 PM and 5 PM. Friday they leave every hour from 1 PM to 8 PM, and Saturday they leave at 6 AM, 7 AM, 9 AM, 10 AM, and 11:30 AM. Buses (☎ 222–3006, 669–0145, or 284–1923) to La Cruz and Peñas Blancas (6-hr trip, passing through Liberia) leave daily at 5 AM, 7:45 AM, 10 AM, 1:10 PM, and 4:10 PM. Express buses (4½-hr trip) leave from Calle 16, Avenidas 3 and 5 at 4:30 AM and 7 AM. Buses for the Santa Rosa National Park leave San José at 5 AM, 7:45 AM, and 4:15 PM for Peñas Blancas, reaching the park entrance about five hours later.

By Car

ARENAL AND THE CORDILLERA DE TILARÁN

Road access to the northwest is by way of the paved two-lane Inter-American Highway (Carretera Interamericana, CA1), which starts from the top of Paseo Colón in San José, and runs northwest through Cañas and Liberia, and to Peñas Blancas (Nicaraguan Border). The drive to Liberia takes about three to four hours. Turnoffs to Monteverde, Arenal, and other destinations are often poorly marked—drivers must keep their eyes open. The Monteverde turnoff is at Lagarto, about 125 km (78 mi) northwest of San José. The turnoff for Tilarán and the northwestern end of Laguna de Arenal lies in the town of Cañas. At Liberia, Highway 21 west leads to the beaches of the northern Nicoya Peninsula (☞ Chapter 5). To reach Ciudad Quesada, La Fortuna, and Caño Negro, a picturesque drive (Highway 35) takes you up through the coffee plantations and over the Cordillera Central by way of Sarchí and Zarcero.

FAR NORTHERN GUANACASTE

On the Inter-American Highway (CA1) north of Liberia, the first turn for Rincón de la Vieja is easy to miss. Look for the Guardia Rural station on the right around 5 km (3 mi) north of town, turn inland and head for Curubande. Turnoffs for the Parque Nacional Santa Rosa and La Cruz on CA1 are well marked.

By Plane

At press time, various charter companies were flying in to Liberia on changing schedules, and several commercial airlines were finally about to schedule regular flights to Liberia from Europe, Canada, and the United States. If your destination lies in Guanacaste, make sure your travel agent investigates the possibility of flying into Liberia instead of San José—you'll save some serious hours on the road. Locally, **Sansa** (⊠ C. 24, between Avda. Central and Avda. 1, San José, ☎ 506/221–9414 or 506/441–8035, FAX 506/255–2176) and **Travelair** (⊠ Aeropuerto Internacional Tobías Bolaños, Apdo. 8–4920, ☎ 506/220–3054 or 506/232–7883, FAX 506/220–0413) fly to Liberia from San José daily.

Getting Around

By Bus

ARENAL AND THE CORDILLERA DE TILARÁN

Buses to Ciudad Quesada continue to Tilarán and Arenal (☞ Arriving and Departing, *above*).

FAR NORTHERN GUANACASTE

Buses do not serve Rincón de la Vieja and Guanacaste National Parks.

By Car

Once you get off the main highways, the pavement holds out only so far, and then dirt, dust, mud, potholes, and other impediments interfere with driving conditions and hours spent behind the wheel. Take a four-wheel drive if possible. Most minor roads are unpaved, and either muddy in rainy season or dusty in dry season. Four-wheel-drive vehicles are recommended, but not essential, for most roads. The most important thing to know is that short drives can take a long time when the road is potholed or torn up. Plan accordingly.

ARENAL AND THE CORDILLERA DE TILARÁN

From this easterly zone (La Fortuna), you can head west by way of the road around Laguna de Arenal. For the newly paved road (Highway 4) that parallels the Nicaraguan border and loops west all the way to La Cruz, follow the signs out of Tanque (east of La Fortuna) northwest to San Rafael de Guatuso, Upala, and Santa Cecilia.

FAR NORTHERN GUANACASTE

The Inter-American Highway (CA1) and other paved roads run to the Nicaraguan border; paved roads run west to the small towns like Filadelfia and La Cruz.

The roads into Rincón de la Vieja are unpaved and very slow; figure on an hour from the highway, and be prepared to walk the last half mile to the Las Pailas entrance. The road into Santa Rosa National Park is smooth going as far as La Casona. Beyond that, it gets dicey and very steep in places. The national park service encourages you to walk, rather than drive, to the beach. A couple of dirt roads lead into various sections of Guanacaste National Park. A four-wheel-drive vehicle is recommended for all of them.

Contacts and Resources

Car Rentals

A few of the high-end resorts on the beach will arrange car rentals. Otherwise, *see* Contacts and Resources *in* San José A to Z, *in* Chapters 2 and 5.

Emergencies

In just about any emergency you can dial ☎ 911. **Ambulance** (☎ 221–5818). **Fire** (☎ 118). **Police** (☎ 117 in towns; 127 in rural areas). **Traffic Police** (☎ 227–8030).

Guided Tours

DAY TRIPS

Guanacaste Tours (☎ 666–0306) is recommended for day trips from within the northwest to Santa Rosa and Arenal; you can get transportation from large hotels in the area.

SPECIAL-INTEREST TOURS

Tikal Ecoadventures (✉ Avdas. 2, between Cs. 7 and 9, Apdo. 6398–1000, San José, ☎ 223–2811) runs highly informative weeklong tours that take in Carara, Manuel Antonio, the Lomas Barbudal reserve, Playa Grande (☞ Chapter 5), Santa Rosa, and Arenal. The excellent **Horizontes** (✉ 150 m north of Pizza Hut Paseo Colón, San José, ☎ 222–2022) specializes in more independent tours with as few as eight people, including transport by four-wheel drive, naturalist guides, and guest lectures. **Geotur** (☎ 234–1867) operates a three-day horseback exploratory tour of the dry forests around Los Inocentes Lodge, near Parque Nacional Guanacaste.

Visitor Information

The tourist office in San José (☞ Visitor Information *in* San José A to Z, *in* Chapter 2) has information covering the northwest.

In Liberia, the **Casa de la Cultura** (✉ 3 blocks from Central Plaza, ☎ 666–1606) has local tourist information. It is open Monday–Saturday 8–4.

5 Nicoya Peninsula

On the sun-drenched Nicoya Peninsula, expatriate California surfers wander endless golden beaches, coatimundis caper, monkeys howl in the dry tropical forests, and turtles ride in on the night high tide to lay their eggs on the beaches. All these natural wonders, coupled with a burgeoning number of high-end resorts with golf courses and convention centers, make the Nicoya Peninsula a microcosm of Costa Rica.

SEPARATED FROM THE MAINLAND BY THE GOLFO DE NICOYA, the Peninsula de Nicoya, or Nicoya Peninsula, is a roughly thumb-shape protrusion comprising the southwestern section of Guanacaste, Costa Rica's northwesternmost province. (The south end of the Nicoya Peninsula lies within Puntarenas province.) Averaging just 65 inches of rain per year, the Nicoya Peninsula and much of Guanacaste constitute the country's driest region. Nevertheless the Peninsula contains myriad natural wonders: large areas of wet and dry forest, limestone caverns, bird-filled river deltas, and miles of palm-flanked beaches.

Updated by
Justin
Henderson

The Guanacastecos, descendants of the Chorotegan Indians and early Spanish settlers, started many of the traditions that are now referred to as typically Costa Rican, and a strong folkloric character pervades the region. As you travel through the region, watch for traditional costumes, folk dancing, music, and recipes handed down from colonial times.

As a travel destination, the Nicoya Peninsula—especially the coastal areas—feels somewhat confused at present: on one hand, politically correct ecotourists and their backpack- and surfboard-toting younger brethren still come in search of environmental enlightenment or good waves; on the other hand, sun- and golf-seekers, content to admire caged toucans in plush hotel lobbies, are lured by azure pools and putting greens bathed in tropical sun. As a result, the area has been targeted for huge amounts of investment, and at a cost to the environment. Large luxury resort and condominium projects are under way in Tambor, Flamingo, and Nosara. A new project on the Río San Francisco estuary at Playa Langosta will place a large hotel, condominium complex, and casino at the mouth of that sensitive delta. Thousands of homes, hotel rooms, and tourism facilities are planned for the Golfo de Papagayo as well, although the fervor at Papagayo has abated of late, with environmentalists gaining the upper hand thanks to the discovery of a pre-Columbian archaeological site.

A golf course with luxury housing for sale is now open adjacent to the Parque Nacional Marino Las Baulas, and there are several hotels open directly behind the park's Playa Grande turtle preserve. The future for nesting turtles and wild birds remains uncertain, as it is doubtful they will be able to exist in ecological harmony with golf courses and luxury hotels, despite the assurances of the developers, most of whom appear more concerned by the greenness of their dollars than that of the environment.

Most, but not all. It would be incorrect to accuse every developer along the Nicoya's lovely shores of craven, insensitive behavior, when so many of them are doing their best to keep the turtles and the monkeys happy along with the investors and the tourists. And don't be fooled into thinking the Nicoya Peninsula has been spoiled: in spite of the land rush, the many new resorts, and the ugly concrete skeletons of a few failed hotel and condo projects that mar several otherwise pristine shorelines, there remain endless miles of untracked beaches, and thousands of acres of unexplored territory, in the Nicoya.

Pleasures and Pastimes

Beaches

Although you'll find graceful palms and elegant tamarindo trees lining most beaches, the shrubby dry forest vegetation of the northwest coast contrasts sharply with the tropical beach backdrops you'll encounter farther south. The great advantage here is the climate, which is far drier during the rainy season. Swimmers, however, should be careful of riptides, which are quite prevalent.

Near Coco, which is rather dirty, both the beaches **Playa Ocotal**, in a very pretty cove with snorkeling potential and good views, and **Playa Hermosa**—a curving gray-sand beach hemmed in by rocky outcrops—are recommended strands. **Playa Pan de Azúcar** offers good snorkeling and is deserted, but it's rather stony in the rainy season. Despite a few half-built condos and the Flamingo Beach Hotel, **Playa Flamingo** is still relatively low-key, and the beach is white and handsome. **Playa Brasilito** allows you to observe the goings-on of fishing-village life. **Playa Conchal** is famous for its tiny shells, though an enormous new hotel behind it will forever change its isolated character. **Playa Grande**, a restricted-access (at night) turtle-nesting beach stretching north from Tamarindo for 5 km (3 mi), is safest for swimming, except in the surfing area near the Hotel Las Tortugas, and **Tamarindo** itself has a long white strand, interrupted by the occasional rock formation and sheltering a small fleet of fishing and sailing boats on the lee side of an island a few hundred yards offshore. There are several good local beachfront bars in Tamarindo.

Playa Langosta, adjacent to a bird sanctuary, has good surfing waves, nesting turtles at night, and few people. **Playa Avellanes** offers a half mile of pristine sand, eight good surfing spots, and both a river estuary and a mangrove swamp close at hand for bird-watching. **Playa Negra** is a mix of short sandy stretches and rocky outcroppings and has one of the best surfing waves in Costa Rica. **Playa Junquillal** features an uninterrupted 3-km (2-mi) stretch of grayish white sand with small shorebreak waves and very few buildings. **Playa Pelada** is a perfect little jewel of a beach hemmed in by rocks on both sides, great for snorkeling. **Nosara** has a long beach backed by dense jungle where you might see wildlife. The long, clean, and smooth **Playa Guiones** has a good beachbreak surfing wave, and a coral reef suitable for snorkeling. Pretty **Playa Sámara** offers some lively stretches near the Sámara community, and quieter stretches farther down the beach. **Playa Carrillo** is on a very picturesque and deserted half-moon bay. **Playa Cabo Blanco**, on the southwestern tip of the Nicoya Peninsula, is a pristine jewel reached only by hiking through the Reserva Natural Absoluta Cabo Blanco. **Montezuma** has several colorful, shell-strewn beaches, some of them long and some short. **Tambor,** in Bahía Ballena, edges up to calm swimming waters.

Dining

Seafood is plentiful on the peninsula: *camarones* (shrimp), *langostinos* (a kind of lobster), and a fine variety of fish are available in most restaurants at reasonable prices, although langostino dinners can get costly. Most of the places serve international as well as local dishes including the ubiquitous, moderate-priced *casados* (plates of white rice, beans, fried plantains, salad, cheese, and meat), so you can take your pick.

Festivals

Santa Cruz celebrates its patron-saint day on January 15 with marimba music, folk dances, and Tico-style bullfights. On July 16 you can see a colorful regatta and carnival in Puntarenas in honor of its patron saint. The annexation of Guanacaste is celebrated July 17–25 with folk dances, bullfights, and rodeos in Liberia. The festival of La Yeguita in Nicoya on December 12 features a solemn procession, dancing, fireworks, and bullfights. Almost every small town in Guanacaste has a rodeo fiesta once a year, complete with carnival rides, gaming, and the Costa Rican rodeo version of bullfighting. It's wild! Guanacasteco cowboys ride the bulls, American rodeo style, while troupes of young men race about in the ring, distracting the bulls after they throw the riders, and a couple of cowboys with lariats stand by on horseback to lasso the beasts should they get too ornery. If you're in Guanacaste and you're not too squeamish (they do torment the bulls to get them riled up, and the riders get thrown really hard, and occasionally are stomped or gored by the bulls) be sure to take one in. Ask around, or check posters, and you'll probably find one to attend.

Lodging

A good mix of quality hotels, nature lodges, and more basic *cabinas* (cottages) can be found on the Nicoya Peninsula. It is wise to book ahead during the dry season (December–April), especially for weekends, when Ticos can fill beach hotels, especially, to bursting. A number of luxury hotels, both large and small, have opened along the coast, catering to a more upscale clientele. Note that many hotels in area—Nosara, for instance—are recently receiving quality phone connections for the first time, so many of the properties listed have probably started to take major credit cards since press time; call ahead.

Spelunking

For the modern-day troglodyte, the caves in Parque Nacional Barra Honda offer the opportunity to make a serious plunge into the underworld. The 60-ft Terciopelo Cave, in particular, contains a vast assortment of oddly shaped rock formations; some stretches of the cave system are reputedly unexplored to this day.

Surfing

Costa Rica was "discovered" in the 1960s surf film classic, *The Endless Summer,* and revisited in the sequel. But with its miles of coastline indented with innumerable points, rock reefs, river-mouth sandbars, and other wave-shaping geological configurations, it comes as no surprise that the Nicoya Peninsula is a surfer's paradise—warm water, beautiful beaches, cheap beer, and relatively uncrowded waves. What more could an aging California boy or girl ask for?

Boca Barranca near Puntarenas—a somewhat dingy mainland town you might encounter while waiting for the ferry to the Nicoya Peninsula's south end—has one of the world's longest lefts, but the water is dangerously polluted with sewage runoff from the nearby river. Tamarindo is a good base for a couple of decent sandbar and rock-reef breaks, a superb low-tide river-mouth break, and the consistently high quality, if at times overcrowded, Playa Grande beach break 5 km (3 mi) up the beach. The best waves at Playa Grande can be found just south of the Hotel Las Tortugas. Inquire at Iguana Surf, the surfboard shop in Tamarindo, to find out where the waves are breaking. Sámara, Giuones, and Nosara have decent beach breaks. Avellanes features a total of eight different surf spots, ranging from beach breaks to rock-reef breaks to river-mouth sandbar breaks. Roca Bruja (Witches Rock), in the Parque Nacional Santa Rosa (☞ Chapters 4 and 10), accessible by car only in summer (you can also get there by a 1½-hour boat trip, informally chartered at Playa Coco or other beaches along the Guanacaste coast), has a right river-mouth, and Ollie's Point, a bit farther north and also reachable primarily by boat, offers excellent right point-break waves. For well-heeled wave riders, there's a good break directly in front of the Hotel Tango Mar. Playa Negra, about a 45-minute dirt road drive south from Tamarindo, is also gnarly—in surferspeak—its excellent right rock-reef break having been featured in *The Endless Summer II.* Playa Langosta, just south of Tamarindo, has a good river-mouth wave. Malpais, just above Cabo Blanco, is home to some of the largest waves in Costa Rica. At all these spots you should be careful of riptides.

Turtle-Watching

The Nicoya Peninsula provides wonderful opportunities for viewing the nesting rituals of several varieties of sea turtles. The nesting season of the olive ridley turtle runs year-round, but peaks from July to October. Leatherbacks arrive from October through April, though nesting is largely over by mid-February. Small numbers of Pacific green turtles are also occasionally seen.

Difficult to reach but worth it are Playa Nancite in Parque Nacional Santa Rosa (☞ Chapters 4 and 10, and Close Up: Tican Turtles *in* Chapter 8) and the Refugio Nacional de Fauna Silvestre de Ostional near Nosara. Both are prime for watching the mass nestings, or *arribadas,* of thousands of olive ridley turtles. More accessible are Playa Langosta and Playa Grande—they book-end the resort town of Tamarindo to the south and north, respectively—which provide wonderful opportunities for viewing the nesting rituals of the enormous, ponderous, and yet exquisitely dignified leatherback turtles, who arrive with high tide to dig holes and deposit their eggs. They also show up in smaller numbers at Junquillal and other beaches.

Word of mouth has it that locals at Junquillal and possibly Langosta are still poaching the eggs like there's an endless supply. You can go on your own to find the Langosta turtles at night from Tamarindo, but you've got to get across the Río San Francisco estuary—not something one wants to attempt in the middle of the night. On the other hand, Playa Grande's turtle tours, now run by officially sanctioned guides drawn from the local populace, have become very well organized. If you don't mind the rather strict approach taken by the guides at Playa Grande, go for it!

It can get crowded (though the guides at the Playa Grande park entrance take people out in small groups), and you have to stay up very late, but many find the arrival and egg-laying ritual of the leatherback mothers a singularly moving event. Others find the appearance of the babies, or hatchlings, even more interesting, and you can see them during the day! Just walk down Playa Grande at dawn, two to three months after the commencement of the egg-laying season, and you'll have a good chance of watching the amazing emergence of the hatchlings from the sand. If you're like most ecotourists, you'll want to spend some time with them, shepherding the tiny creatures on their arduous, dangerous journey from the nest to the sea. If you don't perform this protective function, chances are you'll be watching a less pleasant slice of life in the natural world, as a predatory frigate bird scoops your hatchling from the sand and eats it for breakfast.

If you do want to watch the turtles, do it with a legitimate guide, and follow the rules. You'd be better off not trying it during the Christmas–New Year's week, when the crowds get very heavy. It may be frustrating to experience this natural phenomenon while governed by such unnatural rules, but it is critical for the health of the turtles.

Exploring the Nicoya Peninsula

Bear in mind that aside from the Inter-American Highway (CA1), many of the roads in the region are of the pitted, pocked, and rock-and-dirt variety, with the occasional river rushing over, rather than under, the pavement. As a result, covering seemingly short distances can require long hours behind the wheel, and a four-wheel-drive vehicle is often essential. For this reason, we highly recommend flying, when pos-

Restaurante y Marisquería Paso Real

Chango y Chango, S. A.
Céd. Jur. 3-101-234998
Tel: **666-3455**

COSTADO OESTE DE LA GOBERNACIÓN
LIBERIA, GUANACASTE

DIA	MES	AÑO
6	9	99

Señor:

CANT.	DESCRIPCION	VALOR
	Servicio Rest	8545

SALONERO		
	SUB-TOTAL ¢	8545
MESA	PROPINA ¢	750
	I.V.I. TOTAL ¢	9295.

utorizado mediante Oficio Nº 05-0003-97. De
fecha 01-10-97 de la Administración Tributaria
de Guanacaste. Del 0001 al 5000.

Nº 3124

LITO - IMP. LIBERIA □ TEL. - FAX: 666-0156 □ 100 x 50/2 • pasoreal

sible and affordable, if any of the beach resorts you plan to visit have nearby airstrips, such as Tamarindo, Carrillo, and Tambor. Many northern beach resorts can be most easily reached from Liberia, where an international airport has been operational for a couple of years.

Numbers in the text correspond to numbers in the margin and on the Nicoya Peninsula map.

Great Itineraries

The ideal Nicoya Peninsula itinerary can be comfortably divided between lazy days on the beach, swimming in the surf, and hiking and visiting a number of appealing or unusual sites—caverns, forests, rivers, and estuaries—exploring at leisure the most interesting.

The beach towns and resorts can be clustered into three loose geographical groups based, in part, on location and, in part, on the routes you must take to reach them: those on the south end of the Nicoya Peninsula, accessible by ferry from Puntarenas or by plane to Tambor; areas in the central Nicoya Peninsula, reachable by plane to Punta Islita, Carrillo, and Nosara, or by car via the Tempisque Ferry and the roads through Carmona, Curime, and Nicoya; and towns in the northern Nicoya Peninsula, accessible by plane to Tamarindo or Liberia, or by car through Liberia and Comunidad. These three loose clusters of beaches have a lot in common, but there are distinct differences as well: if your time is limited and you have to make a choice, consider whether you want, for example, lively surf or calm waters; turtle-watching options at night; an isolated resort or a more active beach town.

IF YOU HAVE 3 TO 5 DAYS

Fly to ☷ **Tambor** ④, ☷ **Punta Islita** ⑫, ☷ **Playa Carrillo** ⑬, ☷ **Nosara** ⑯, or ☷ **Tamarindo** ㉘ for a three-night stay at one of the dozens of beach resorts on the Nicoya Peninsula. From Tambor or ☷ **Montezuma** ⑤, a short drive takes you to Cabo Blanco, where you can hike the trail through the **Reserva Natural Absoluta Cabo Blanco** ⑥ to deserted Playa Cabo Blanco, where hundreds of pelicans dive and frolic. You can also visit the ☷ **Refugio Nacional de Vida Silvestre Curú** ③, or surf at Tango Mar Hotel, if you are a hotel guest, or at **Malpais**, just north of Cabo Blanco, which reputedly has the largest surfing waves in Costa Rica.

From any of the central Nicoya beaches, those around Nosara, spend a day hiking, birding, or spelunking at **Parque Nacional Palo Verde** ⑦ or **Parque Nacional Barra Honda** ⑧, or visit **Guaitil** ⑩ and **Santa Cruz** ⑪ for pottery shopping. If lounging on the sand isn't enough, if it's the right season you can stay up late to watch the arribada of the olive ridley turtles at **Refugio Nacional de Fauna Silvestre de Ostional** ⑰.

To extend this itinerary to five days, consider driving back to Santa Cruz and heading south on Highway 21, which is now smoothly paved almost all the way to ☷ **Playa Naranjo** ②; near Naranjo, book a two- or three-day sea-kayaking adventure with guide JeriLin Ruhlow at the Hotel Oasis del Pacific. You can also go southwest from Liberia, and spend anywhere from three to five nights at one or more of the beaches between ☷ **Tamarindo** ㉘ and ☷ **Hermosa** ⑳. Just south at Playa Langosta; in season, you can also watch the leatherback turtles come in at night at **Parque Nacional Marino Las Baulas** ㉗. For dedicated surfers, ☷ **Playa Negra** ㉚ and ☷ **Playa Avellanes** ㉚ offer great access to excellent surfing waves, and myriad other recreational activities—just pick your spots.

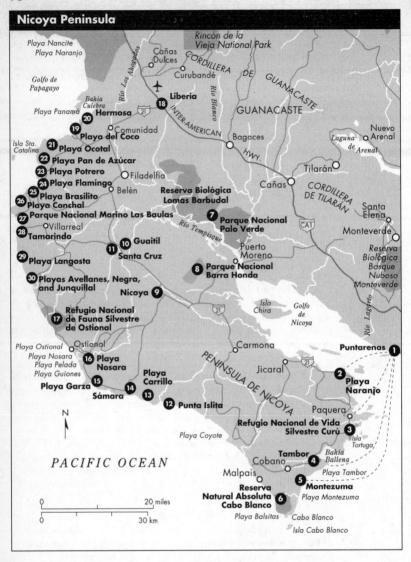

Nicoya Peninsula

IF YOU HAVE 7 DAYS

Take the ferry from ▥ **Puntarenas** ①, and drive from ▥ **Playa Naranjo** ②, spending nights at ▥ **Refugio Nacional de Vida Silvestre Curú** ③, ▥ **Tambor** ④, or ▥ **Montezuma** ⑤ and bird- and animal-watching, people-watching, and swimming in the lazy, sheltered waters of the southern Nicoya by day. Alternatively, stay in ▥ **Playa Naranjo** ②, and spend a day or even two sea kayaking among the many ruggedly beautiful islands in the Golfo de Nicoya. Then take a ferry back to Puntarenas, head north on the Inter-American Highway, and follow signs to the Río Tempisque. Catch the ferry across and do some bird-watching on the river or in **Parque Nacional Palo Verde** ⑦; then spend a day hiking and spelunking in **Parque Nacional Barra Honda** ⑧. Continue on through **Nicoya** ⑨ and **Santa Cruz** ⑪ and overnight in ▥ **Tamarindo** ㉘ or at one of the beach resorts north. Spend several days on the beach or exploring the Tamarindo and Río San Francisco estuaries north and south of Tamarindo, with nights watching turtles at **Parque Nacional**

BONUS MILES MAKE GREAT SOUVENIRS.

Earn Miles With Your MCI Card.

Take the MCI Card along on this trip and start earning miles for the next one. You'll earn frequent flyer miles on all your calls and save with the low rates you've come to expect from MCI. Before you know it, you'll be on your way to some other international destination.

Sign up for MCI by calling 1-800-FLY-FREE

Earn Frequent Flyer Miles.

Is this a great time, or what? :-)

Easy To Call Home.

1. To use your MCI Card, just dial the WorldPhone access number of the country you're calling from.
2. Dial or give the operator your MCI Card number.
3. Dial or give the number you're calling.

American Samoa	633-2MCI (633-2624)
# Antigua	1-800-888-8000
(Available from public card phones only)	#2
# Argentina (CC)	0-800-5-1002
# Aruba ÷	800-888-8
# Bahamas	1-800-888-8000
# Barbados	1-800-888-8000
# Belize	557 from hotels
	815 from pay phones
# Bermuda ÷	1-800-888-8000
# Bolivia ♦ (CC)	0-800-2222
# Brazil (CC)	000-8012
# British Virgin Islands ÷	1-800-888-8000
# Cayman Islands	1-800-888-8000
# Chile (CC)	
To call using CTC ■	800-207-300
To call using ENTEL ■	800-360-180
# Colombia (CC) ♦	980-16-0001
Collect Access in Spanish	980-16-1000
# Costa Rica ♦	0800-012-2222
# Dominica	1-800-888-8000
# Dominican Republic (CC) ÷	1-800-888-8000
Collect Access in Spanish	1121
# Ecuador (CC) ÷	999-170
El Salvador	800-1767
# Grenada ÷	1-800-888-8000
Guatemala (CC) ♦	9999-189
Guyana	177
# Haiti ÷ Collect Access	193
Collect Access in French/Creole	190
Honduras ÷	8000-122
# Jamaica ÷ Collect Access	1-800-888-8000
(From Special Hotels only)	873
From payphones	★2
# Mexico (CC)	
Avantel	01-800-021-8000
Telmex ▲	001-800-674-7000
Mexico Access in Spanish	01-800-021-1000
# Netherlands Antilles (CC) ÷	001-800-888-8000
Nicaragua (CC)	166
(Outside of Managua, dial 02 first)	
Collect Access in Spanish from any public payphone	★2
# Panama	108
Military Bases	2810-108
# Paraguay ÷	00-812-800
# Peru	0-800-500-10
# Puerto Rico (CC)	1-800-888-8000
# St. Lucia ÷	1-800-888-8000
# Trinidad & Tobago ÷	1-800-888-8000
# Turks & Caicos ÷	1-800-888-8000
# Uruguay	000-412
# U.S. Virgin Islands (CC)	1-800-888-8000
# Venezuela (CC) ÷ ♦	800-1114-0

You've read the book. Now book the trip.

For all the best deals on flights, hotels, rental cars, and vacation packages, book them online at www.previewtravel.com. Then click on our Destination Guides featuring content from Fodor's and more. You'll find hotels, restaurants, attractions, and things to do around the globe. There are even interactive maps, videos, and weather forecasts. You'll have everything you need to make your vacation exactly what you want it to be. All it takes is a trip online.

preview
travel SM

Travel on Your Terms™
www.previewtravel.com
aol keyword: previewtravel

Marino Las Baulas ㉗ (in season only), then head back to the highway via 🍴 **Liberia** ⑱.

When to Tour the Nicoya Peninsula

Although the dry season from December to April is considered the best time to visit Costa Rica, if there is one part of the country that is most appealing during the rainy season (except for the *really* wet months of September and October) it is the northwest, especially the Nicoya Peninsula. The Guanacastecos have renamed the rainy season the "green" season, and that it is: the rain falls for a couple of hours each day, and the countryside—tending toward brown and arid in the dry season—remains lush and green, yet warm and sunny before and after the rain. The roads are muddy, but there are far fewer people, and the prices go down everywhere. For the seasonal activity of turtle-watching, you have to go during dry season, but for most other activities in the northwest, you can go at almost any time of year. A good bet would be traveling in November or April–May, around the edges of the dry season.

PUNTARENAS TO CABO BLANCO

Catch a ferry from Puntarenas to the southern Nicoya Peninsula, home to spectacular beaches like Montezuma and Tambor. The peninsula also offers well-preserved and undervisited national parks: come here to explore caves, waterfalls, and pristine forests, or travel by boat or sea kayak to remote islands and wildlife preserves for bird-watching, snorkeling, diving, and camping. Not too remote, and thus at times somewhat overcrowded, is Isla Tortuga, accessible by day boat from Puntarenas, Montezuma, and other beach towns. Tortuga offers some of the most beautiful beaches in all of Costa Rica. But why stop there? From a base near the ferry dock at Playa Naranjo, paddle a sea kayak to the less-visited islands: San Lucas, with its fascinating history as a penal island; Negritos, Guayabo, Venado, and Chira islands, home to isolated, unchanged fishing villages or wildlife refuges. Or ride some waves: Near Puntarenas itself is the spectacularly long surfing wave of Boca Barranca; some have reported single rides up to 15 minutes in length! (But beware, surfers, the water is dirty.) If you like to mix nightlife with your outdoor experiences, the little town of Montezuma and its nearby beaches are frequently jammed with an international cast of hippies, mystics, musicians, and misfits of all sorts, from German boys in leather pants to Swedish girls in nothing at all. (One wise guy has called it a gathering place for the "toxic youth of Europe.") The beaches east of Montezuma, including Cocal, Cocalito, and Quizales, are gorgeous, with waterfalls and tide pools galore. The Reserva Natural Absoluta Cabo Blanco at the tip of the Nicoya Peninsula is one of the more undervisited parks in Costa Rica; it's also worth noting that when founded, in 1963, it was the first protected nature area in the country.

Puntarenas

❶ *95 km (59 mi) west of San José.*

Five kilometers (3 mi) beyond Esparza, a popular truck stop about 90 km (56 mi) northwest of San José on the Inter-American Highway, is the turn to Puntarenas. As its name implies, this erstwhile coffee-shipping port is on a narrow spit of sand protruding into the Gulf of Nicoya, with splendid views across to the peninsula. Most tourists stop here only on the way by ferry to the Nicoya Peninsula. The boardwalk is pleasant in a honky-tonk kind of way, but this downtrodden town suffers from rising crime and polluted water and is not worth a special trip. Its grid-plan streets abound in restaurants and markets, and the southern palm-lined promenade is popular with day-trippers from San José, although the Ministry of Health warns against swimming here. On Saturday nights the massive influx of weekenders from San José presents a golden opportunity to watch the middle class at play. In summer the series of theater, music, and dance shows at the **Casa de la Cultura** (⊠ 3 blocks from Central Plaza, ☎ 666–1606) can be fun.

The murky estuary to the north is fringed with mangroves; at its western end pelicans cast a watchful eye from the treetops over the Nicoya ferries, whose departures provide the only sound reason to stay overnight. A modern harbor has been built at **Caldera,** 10 km (6 mi) southeast.

The Puntarenas ferries connect with Playa Naranjo, Paquera, and, for pedestrians only, with Montezuma (☞ Getting Around by Boat *in* Nicoya Peninsula A to Z, *below*). If you're driving, be prepared to spend some hours at the wheel: the road to the southern tip of the peninsula is partly paved, partly gravel, and it winds up and down and around various bays. Much of the countryside is still wild and wooded, although some has been turned into fruit farms or cattle pasture. Paquera, 45 minutes southeast of Playa Naranjo, is the next place with shops and bars, also linked to Puntarenas by ferry. Heading north toward Nicoya, the road from Playa Naranjo (Highway 21) is paved almost all the way.

Dining and Lodging

$$–$$$ ✕ **La Caravelle.** The red-pattern tablecloths and dark-blue walls adorned with antique musical instruments create a chic ambience in this unexpectedly classy French restaurant opposite the sea. The cooking concentrates on sauces: try the corvina *al gratin con hongos* (with a white wine sauce and mushrooms) or fillet *con salsa Oporto y hongos* (with port and mushroom sauce). If you want to accompany this with claret, prepare to dig deep into your pocket. ⊠ *Paseo de los Turistas,* ☎ 661–2262. MC, V. Closed Mon.–Tues.

$$–$$$ ▥ **Hotel Las Brisas.** A white, two-story, motel-style building wraps around the swimming pool of this hotel out near the west end of town, where the views of the sun setting over the Nicoya Peninsula are terrific. The beach is across the street, it's not far from the ferry docks, and the restaurant serves fine Greek-influenced seafood and meats. The fluorescent lighting in the open-air dining room could be improved. ⊠ *Puntarenas, Paseo de los Turistas,* ☎ 661–4040, FAX 661–2120. 19 *rooms with bath. Restaurant, pool. MC, V.*

$$ ▥ **Hotel Porto Bello.** Porto Bello's main asset is its thickly planted garden next to the wide estuary. Bedrooms are housed in white stucco bungalow units with tile floors, zanily patterned bedspreads, air-conditioning, TVs, and verandas. ⊠ *Apdo. 108, Puntarenas, 2 km (1½ mi) from downtown, 1 block north of main road,* ☎ 661–1322, FAX 661–0036. 35 *rooms with bath. Restaurant, bar, pool. AE, MC, V.*

$$ ▥ **Hotel Tioga.** The blue-and-white courtyard in this central hotel has
★ the look of an ocean liner. Bedrooms, the best are upstairs overlooking the gulf, have air-conditioning, tile floors, quilted pink bedspreads, floral pastel curtains, and functional 1970s furniture. There is a tiny pool in the courtyard with a palm tree growing from the islet in its center. ⊠ *Apdo. 96, Puntarenas, Paseo de los Turistas,* ☎ 661–0271, FAX 661–0127. 46 *rooms with bath. Bar, cafeteria, pool. AE, MC, V.*

Playa Naranjo

❷ *1½–2 hrs by ferry southwest of Puntarenas.*

Accessible by ferry from Puntarenas or by car from Nicoya (the road is smoothly paved almost all the way as of early 1998), Playa Naranjo's reputation as a kind of nowheresville en route from Puntarenas to Montezuma and points west is undeserved. This is the best access point to the islands in the Golfo de Nicoya; there is also wonderful hiking, mountain biking, and sea kayaking in the area.

Dining and Lodging

$$–$$$ ✕▥ **Hotel Oasis del Pacific.** The enticing pier and coconut palms of the Oasis del Pacific's 12 roomy acres of waterfront terrain lie invitingly in the last cove on the left before the Playa Naranjo ferry dock. Run by former ship captain Lucky Wilhelm and his wife Aggie, the hotel itself is a tad run-down and frayed around the edges, but no matter when you're lazing in your hammock, catching the afternoon breeze off the gulf. The indoor-outdoor restaurant-bar does a fine job with all three meals. Fishing charters, sailing, horseback riding, and hiking trips can be arranged, and perhaps best of all, JeriLin Ruhlow uses the hotel as a base for her fantastic sea-kayaking trips along the coast and among the islands of the Golfo de Nicoya (☞ Outdoor Activities and Sports, *below*). ✉ *Apdo. 200–5400, Puntarenas,* ☎ 🖷 *661–1555;* ✉ *P.l. Wilhelm 1552, Box 025216, Miami, FL 33102-5216. 36 rooms with bath. Restaurant, bar, pool, beach, dock. AE, MC, V.*

Outdoor Activities and Sports

Ranging in length from one day up to seven or more, JeriLin Ruhlow's sea-kayaking trips along the coast and among the islands of the Golfo de Nicoya offer kayakers of every level of experience a chance to visit wild islands, remote fishing villages, wildlife reserves, national parks, and more. You can reach Ms. Ruhlow and book kayak trips through the Hotel Oasis del Pacific (☞ *above*). She claims the area offers the best kayaking in Costa Rica, and she's paddled everywhere.

Refugio Nacional de Vida Silvestre Curú

❸ *7 km (4½ mi) south of Paquera.*

South of the ferry dock at Paquera is the private Refugio Nacional de Vida Silvestre Curú (Curú Wildlife Refuge), where you'll find hordes of phantom crabs on the beach, howler and white-faced monkeys readily visible in the banana trees, and plenty of bird-watching opportunities. Some very basic accommodations, originally designed for students and researchers, are available by the beach; call ahead if you're interested. ☎ *661–2392.* ✇ *$10; lodging $25 per person, including 3 meals per day and admission.*

Tambor

❹ *20 km (14 mi) south of Refugio Nacional de Vida Silvestre Curú.*

The next village you reach after Curú is Tambor, nestled in the back of the large half-moon Bahía Ballena. Thanks to the massive and controversy-plagued Hotel Playa Tambor, this area is undergoing a land-sale frenzy similar to that at Tamarindo. You can hike from here around the Piedra Amarilla point to Tango Mar resort; it's about an 8-km (5-mi) trek. The trees nearby resound with the throaty utterings of male howler monkeys. Tambor can also be reached by plane from San José.

Lodging

$$$$ ⚄ **Tambor Tropical.** This collection of five cabinas, with two units per
★ building, surrounding a pool in the palm trees off Playa Tambor in Bahía
Ballena is remarkable for the buildings themselves. Using local hardwoods, the builders have outdone themselves: the details are exquisitely
wrought. Each comfortable and spacious 1,000-sq-ft cabina contains
a living room, bedroom, hot-water bathroom, and a fully equipped
kitchen. ⊠ *Follow main street of Tambor toward water, hotel fronts
beach,* ☎ *683–0011,* 𝔽𝔸𝕏 *683–0013;* ⊠ *867 Liberty St. NE, P.O. Box
12945, Salem, OR 97301,* ☎ *503/365–2872,* 𝔽𝔸𝕏 *503/371–2471. 10
cabinas. Restaurant, bar, kitchenettes, pool, hot tub. AE, MC, V.*

$$$$ ⚄ **Tango Mar.** At this fine resort choose between rustic palm-thatch
★ cabins on stilts or rooms in the main hotel. The former are much more
interesting; some have fully equipped kitchens and all are paneled and
come with fans, air-conditioning, and hot showers. Those in the main
hotel are luxurious by conventional standards but largely uninspired,
and all have balconies and excellent sea views. The restaurant serves
international cuisine. On the grounds are a small spring-fed pool
sculpted from rock and an immaculate nine-hole golf course. There is
a good surfing wave in front of the hotel. ⊠ *Apdo. 3877–1000, San
José, 2 km (1 mi) west of Tambor,* ☎ *683–0002, 222–3503 reservations office in San José,* 𝔽𝔸𝕏 *683–0003. 6 villas with bath, 20 rooms
with bath, 12 suites. Restaurant, 2 bars, pool, 9-hole golf course, 2
tennis courts, hiking, horseback riding, surfing, boating, waterskiing,
fishing. AE, DC, MC, V.*

En Route As you continue past the turn to Tango Mar resort, **Cobano** is the next
real village, a motley collection of wooden bungalows straddling a dusty
crossroads. Turn left to Montezuma and Cabo Blanco, and bear in mind
that the final hill down to Montezuma is extremely steep and should-
n't be attempted in a non–four-wheel-drive vehicle if the hill is wet.

Montezuma

❺ *7 km (4½ mi) southeast of Cobano.*

Montezuma is beautifully positioned next to a sandy bay, hemmed in
by a precipitous wooded bank. Postpunk hipsters and other wannabe
bohemians seem to make this their first destination after touching
down in San José, and if you don't mind entering the odd conversation on such Mother Jones–related subjects as yogurt and cheap deals,
it is an entertaining place to be. But Montezuma is on the international
vagabond circuit these days, and its hippie aura has taken on a distinctly seedy quality, although the beaches remain gorgeous. In 1995,
hotel owners in Montezuma banded together to form the **Cámara de
Turismo de Montezuma (CATUMA),** an organization dedicated to clean-
ing up and improving the area. Meanwhile, the atmosphere feels ripe
for intrigue, and the bars are full and resound with out-of-date music
from the 1960s to the early '80s. Just over a bridge 900 ft south, a path
leads upstream to a 100-ft waterfall, a good swimming spot but overcrowded at times.

Lodging

$$$ ⚄ **Cabinas El Sano Banano.** This bungalow colony serves creative
★ dishes and is a good place to acquaint yourself with the town's vaguely
hippie atmosphere. The owners have built several cabinas and some
funky domed bungalows (sleeping four) in the woods near the beach,
about a 10-minute walk from town. Some bungalows have kitchen fa-
cilities. If you don't care to cook, stop by the unpretentious vegetar-
ian restaurant for the eggplant Parmesan with mashed potatoes. ⊠

Montezuma, on right of road, ☎ ☒ *642–0068. 3 rooms with bath, 8 bungalows. Restaurant. AE, MC, V.*

$$ ☒ **Cabinas Mar y Cielo.** The advantage of this property is its quiet location—still on the beach, but far from the boisterous bars. Decor and prices are much like those in the Hotel Moctezuma. Book ahead. ☒ *Puntarenas, 43 yds from town center,* ☎ ☒ *642–0036. 6 rooms with bath. Restaurant, bar. AE, MC, V.*

$ ☒ **Hotel Moctezuma.** The large rooms in this beachside hotel have var-
★ nished paneling, firm beds, large fans, and clean bathrooms. The best ones open onto a wide veranda overlooking the beach. ☒ *Cobano de Puntarenas, center of Montezuma,* ☎ *642–0258. 21 rooms, 15 with bath. Restaurant, bar. V.*

En Route The 40- to 60-minute drive from Montezuma to Cabo Blanco is on a rough track that fords two streams on the way. If traveling in the rainy season, take a four-wheel-drive.

Reserva Natural Absoluta Cabo Blanco

❻ *10 km (6 mi) southwest of Montezuma.*

Conquistadors named Cabo Blanco on account of the area's white earth and cliffs, but it was a more benevolent pair of foreigners who bestowed the other half of Cabo Blanco's name. The Reserva Natural Absoluta Cabo Blanco (Cabo Blanco Strict Nature Reserve) covers 4½ sq mi in all and was created by the pioneering efforts of Nils Olof Wessberg and his wife Karen, who arrived here from Sweden in 1950. Appalled by the first clear-cut in the Cabo Blanco area in 1960, they launched an international appeal to save the forest. In time their efforts and those of their supporters not only led to the creation of the reserve in 1963, but also to the founding of Costa Rica's national parks service. Olof Wessberg was murdered in the Osa Peninsula in 1975 while researching that area's potential as a national park.

As a strict reserve, no tourist facilities exist in Cabo Blanco, although rangers will act as guides to visitors who turn up. A 4-km (2½-mi) trail leads from the entrance to Playa Cabo Blanco. It's a fairly strenuous two-hour hike in each direction. The reserve receives more rainfall than other parts of the peninsula, and hence the vegetation is properly described as tropical moist forest; there are more evergreen species here than in Santa Rosa (☞ Chapters 4 and 10), and it is generally lusher. The most abundant trees are strawberry, *apamate*, brazilwood, cow tree, *capulen, pochote,* and sapodilla. Sapodillas produce a white latex used to make gum; you will often see V-shape scars where they have been cut to allow the latex to run into containers placed at the base. The wildlife is quite diverse, notwithstanding the comparatively diminutive size of the reserve. Olof Wessberg cataloged a full array of animals here: porcupine, hog-nosed skunk, spotted skunk, gray fox, anteater, cougar, and jaguar. Resident birds include coastal pelicans, white-throated magpies, toucans, cattle egrets, green herons, parrots, and turquoise-browed motmots. **Playa Cabo Blanco**, at the end of the hike, is magnificent, with hundreds of pelicans flying in formation, dive-bombing for fish, and paddling in the calm waters offshore. You can wade right in and join them. Trickling down a small cliff behind the beach is a small stream of potable water. Off the tip of the cape is the 7,511-sq-ft **Isla Cabo Blanco**, with pelicans, frigate birds, brown boobies, and an abandoned lighthouse. ☒ $6. ☉ *Daily 8–4.*

NICOYA AND THE TEMPISQUE RIVER DELTA REGION

This area encompasses the parks in and around the Río Tempisque basin—prime spots for viewing birds and other wildlife—and Nicoya, the commercial and political hub of the northern Nicoya Peninsula. Besides providing the best access to the central Nicoya beach towns, Nicoya is also linked by a smooth, well-paved road to the artisan communities of Santa Cruz and Guaitil, to the northern Nicoya beach towns, and to Playa Naranjo and the southern Nicoya Peninsula by way of Carmona.

Parque Nacional Palo Verde and Reserva Biológica Lomas Barbudal

❼ *Palo Verde 28 km (17 mi) southwest of Bagaces, Lomas Barbudal 20 km (12 mi) southwest of Bagaces via Inter-American Highway (CA1).*

Bordered in the west by the meandering Río Tempisque, the territories in Parque Nacional Palo Verde (Palo Verde National Park) and Reserva Biológica Lomas Barbudal (Lomas Barbudal Biological Reserve) extend over 36½ sq mi of mainly flat terrain (also ☞ Chapter 10). Migrant herons, egrets, ducks, and grebes pause here to rest up on the Tempisque's abandoned oxbow lakes and lagoons. ☎ 671–1062 *both parks.* ⊠ $6 each park. ☉ Daily 8–4.

You can camp in the park, and sometimes lodging and meals are available on request (Palo Verde only). Lodging is also available at the **Organization for Tropical Research** station (☎ 240–6696, ℻ 240–6783 reservations office in San José).

If you come via Puerto Moreno (☞ *below*) you'll get a closer look at **Isla Pajaros** (Bird Island) home to thousands of birds from January to March. Boats are available on the west bank of the Río Tempisque, to the right of the ferry dock as you disembark. The trip takes roughly 45–60 minutes. The price is negotiable but will probably be high, in the range of $50. However, along with spotting the birds on the island, you may see alligators, howler monkeys, and other wildlife on the way. Bring something soft to put on your plank seat and something waterproof to wear—these are small fishing boats, not tour boats, and the river ride can be windy, bumpy, and wet.

There are two ways to reach the parks near the Río Tempisque: by car and boat via the Río Tempisque ferry or by car from farther north. Heading north from San José on the Inter-American Highway, you turn left about 48 km (30 mi) north of the Puntarenas turnoff, and drive 25 km (16 mi) to the ferry, which takes you across to the riverside hamlet of Puerto Moreno; remember, the ferry gets extremely crowded during high season and a wait of several hours is possible. From here it is possible to leave your car and hire a motorboat to take you north up the river into the Parque Nacional Palo Verde and Bird Island.

The second option is to continue north another 42 km (26 mi) on the Inter-American Highway and make a left at the gas station in Bagaces, 15 km (9 mi) north of Cañas, which will lead you after 15 km (9 mi) to the Reserva Biológica Lomas Barbudal and after 35 km (22 mi) to the adjacent Parque Nacional Palo Verde.

Outdoor Activities and Sports

CATA Tours (☎ 221–5455 or 690–1203) offers wildlife and birdwatching boating adventures down the Río Bebedero into Palo Verde

from a starting point on the Inter-American Highway north of Cañas.
Safaris Corobicí's (☎ FAX 669–1091) low-level white-water adventures
on the Río Corobicí cover some of the same wildlife-rich territory not
far from Palo Verde and Lomas Barbudal.

En Route   In summer the series of theater, music, and dance shows at the **Casa
de la Cultura**

Parque Nacional Barra Honda

8   *6 km (4 mi) west of Puerto Moreno and the Río Tempisque ferry.*

Parque Nacional Barra Honda (Barra Honda National Park, (also ☞
Chapter 10) covers almost 9 sq mi north of the road that runs between
the Nicoya–Carmona highway and Tempisque ferry. The limestone ridge
that rises from the surrounding savanna was once thought to be a volcano but was later found to contain an intricate **network of caves**, formed
as a result of erosion once the ridge had emerged from beneath the sea.
Some remain unexplored, and surprisingly abundant animal life exists
in the caves, including bats, birds, blindfish, salamanders, snails, and
rats. In the dry season, with a week's notice, rangers will take you down
a 60-ft steel ladder to the **Terciopelo Cave**, which shelters unusual formations shaped like fried eggs, popcorn, shark's teeth, and sonorous
columns collectively known as the organ. Travel companies no longer
take tourists or speleologists deeper underground, but local groups reportedly have organized tours into the caves. Check with park guards
to verify safety standards before taking a trip, and don't attempt to
visit the caves on your own unless accompanied by a park guard.
Those with vertigo, asthma, or claustrophobia are advised not to attempt these explorations.

Barra Honda peak (1,082 ft) can be climbed from the northwest (the
southern wall is almost vertical): follow in sequence the Ojoche, Trampa,
and Terciopelo trails. From the summit plateau there are fantastic views
over the islet-studded Golfo de Nicoya; the plateau surface is dotted with
small orifices and whimsically eroded white rocks, and some of the ground
feels dangerously hollow. Surface wildlife includes howler monkeys,
skunks, coatis, parakeets, and iguanas. The relatively open, deciduous-
forest vegetation makes viewing the fauna easy. The park has camping
facilities. ☎ 671–1062 or 233–5284. ☞ $6. ☾ Daily 8–4.

Nicoya

9   *30 km (19 mi) west of Puerto Moreno and the Río Tempisque ferry.*

Nicoya, although often referred to as Guanacaste's colonial capital, is
a typical small town, not really worth visiting unless you want a taste
of everyday life. The Chorotegan chief Nicoya greeted the Spanish con-
quistadors upon their arrival here in 1523, and many of his people were
converted to Catholicism. Great emphasis is being placed on reviving
the culture and traditions of the Chorotegans. A small Chinese population, descendants of 19th-century railroad workers, gives the place
a certain cosmopolitan feel, as evidenced by the numerous Chinese restaurants in town. Its only colonial landmark is the whitewashed 16th-cen-
tury **San Blas** church in the central square; its museum displays silver,
bronze, and copper objects dating from pre-Columbian times.

Lodging

$ **⊞ Hotel Jenny.** If you do need to stay in Nicoya, choose this hotel—
it's a bit sterile, but adequate. The rooms have white walls, wooden
beds, tile floors, and reasonable rates. ⊠ *South of main square,* ☎ *685–
5050. 24 rooms with bath. No credit cards.*

Guaitil

⑩ *12 km (7 mi) east of Santa Cruz.*

Near the town of Santa Bárbara (look for the left just south of Santa Cruz) is the charming, sleepy little country village of Guaitil. Artists here, most of them women in this matriarchal indigenous culture, have rescued a vanishing tradition by producing clay pottery handmade in the manner of pre-Columbian Chorotegans. The town square is a soccer field, and almost every house facing the square has a pottery shop in the front and a round, wood-fired kiln in the back. The designs range from imitation Mexican to inspired Picasso-like abstractions. Every artisan's style is different, so take the time to wander from shop to shop until you find a designer whose work you like. The prices are very reasonable, and though the pieces are rumored to crack rather too easily, if you get one home in one piece it'll be a wonderful keepsake or gift.

Santa Cruz

⑪ *22 km (13 mi) north of Nicoya, 16 km (10 mi) south of the Belén junction.*

The National Folklore City of Santa Cruz is dedicated to preserving Guanacaste's rich traditions and customs. Music and dance programs are still held in town despite a fire, which destroyed much of the town's center and the popular Casa de la Cultura. From a resort-oriented point of view, Santa Cruz isn't very exciting, but it's a lively little town with a bustling commercial center. Hang out here for an hour and shop in the *supermercados* (supermarkets) and the meat and vegetable stores, and while stocking up on necessities at much better than resort-town prices, you'll also get a feeling for the daily life of the Guanacastecans.

Dining

$–$$ ✕ **Coope-Tortillas.** Founded to help create jobs for local women, Coope-Tortillas has enjoyed resounding success as a country restaurant and tortilla bakery. Watch tortillas baked the old-fashioned way—on thick, round plates on an open fire by chatty, bustling women in pink uniforms—and have a hearty, family-style meal at a picnic table in a long, high-ceilinged corrugated metal building that once served as an electricity-generating plant. This is one of the few places around still serving traditional Guanacasteco foods: try the arroz de maíz—it's absolutely delicious! It isn't that easy to find; go straight through the town business district, past the plaza, and look for the peaked-roof metal structure. ⊠ *Near the central plaza,* ☎ *no phone.* ⊘ *Daily 5 AM–7 PM. No credit cards.*

CENTRAL NICOYA BEACHES: PUNTA ISLITA TO NOSARA

Strung along the coast of the Nicoya Peninsula are sparkling sand beaches lined with laid-back fishing communities along with hotels and resorts in every price category. Don't be in a rush to get anywhere; take life one day at a time, and you'll soon be as mellow as the locals.

Bus service connects the larger cities to each other and to the more popular beaches, but forget about catching a bus from beach to beach; you'll have to backtrack to the inland hubs of Nicoya, Carmona, or Santa Cruz. The road that leads southwest from Nicoya via Curime continues to Sámara, Nosara, Carrillo, Guiones, Punta Islita, and Ostional.

As of early 1998 the road was smoothly paved all the way to the beach at Sámara except for a 100-yd stretch near Curime. However, the dirt roads between the beach towns are subject to washouts, and are often passable only by four-wheel drive. You literally have to drive through two rivers, for example, to get from Sámara north to Garza and Nosara (consider renting a Jeep, especially for Nosara). There are airstrips at Carrillo and Nosara, so flying in from San José is worth considering.

Punta Islita

⑫ *8 km (5 mi) south of Carrillo.*

Hidden in a small cove, Islita beach is rather rocky, but there is good snorkeling around the point, and the only hotel in the area, the small, luxurious Hotel Punta Islita, has a private dry-forest nature preserve laced with well-made trails.

Lodging

$$$$ **🏨 Hotel Punta Islita.** This secluded inn overlooking the Pacific south
★ of Carrillo and Sámara may be Guanacaste's best. Adobe-style bungalows with barrel tiles and clay-color walls surround the main building, where a massive thatched dome rises over the open-air restaurant. The hotel's French chef turns fresh seafood into inventive daily specials, and both bar and restaurant open onto a blue-tile pool. Rustic rooms have private porches and are complete with hammock, big windows, red-tile floors, and rough-hewn wooden bedposts (plus TVs and hair dryers). Suites have private hot tubs and interior gardens. Boat tours to nearby beaches are available. Since the "road" to the hotel is passable only by a four-wheel-drive, most guests fly in and are picked up at the airstrip by the hotel staff. *Just below Playa Camaronal, a few km south of Playa Carrillo; San José office:* ☎ *296–5787,* FAX *296–5773 or 231–0715;* ✉ *SJO 2505, Box 0255216, Miami, FL 33131-5216. 22 rooms with bath, 2 suites. Restaurant, bar, minibars, pool, driving range, tennis court, exercise room, horseback riding, boating, fishing, mountain bikes, laundry service. AE, DC, MC, V.*

Playa Carrillo

⑬ *6 km (4 mi) south of Sámara.*

A long, reef-protected beach backed by an elegant line of swaying palms and sheltering cliffs, Carrillo is good for swimming, snorkeling, walking, and lounging. Camping is allowed here, too. This is one of the most beautiful and undeveloped beaches in Costa Rica—fly in and land at the airstrip, or head south on the dirt road from Sámara.

Lodging

$$$$ **🏨 Hotel La Guanamar.** Beautifully positioned above the southern end
★ of Playa Carrillo, this used to be a private fishing club, and as a hotel it continues its tradition as a sportfishing mecca, with two boats of its own for use by guests. It occupies several levels, connected by wooden terraces and steps, thus bringing to mind a luxury cruiser. The white bedrooms have elaborate headboards, patterned bedcovers, olive-green carpets, and amazing views. ☎ *680–0054,* FAX *686–6501;* ✉ *Costa Sol International, 2490 Coral Way, Suite 301, Miami, FL 33145,* ☎ *800/245–8420. 41 rooms with bath. Restaurant, bar, pool, horseback riding. AE, MC, V.*

Sámara

⑭   *29 km (18 mi) south of Nicoya.*

When you reach Sámara, you'll see a sign proclaiming it the BEST BEACH IN AMERICA. Maybe this is a slight overstatement, but not much. Two forest-covered hills jut out on either side of a clean, white-sand beach, forming one giant cove ideal for swimming. The coral reef 1½ km (1 mi) from shore is a snorkeler's nirvana. With a smooth road paved all the way from Nicoya, Sámara is flourishing these days, and the numerous hotels springing up around town cater to both Ticos and foreigners—and thankfully Tico spirit, not tourist spirit, still dominates.

Lodging

$$$$ 🏨 **Hotel Villas Playa Sámara.** This lovely and secluded hotel well down the beach from the bustling little town of Sámara has rooms set up in 57 freestanding, Spanish-style white bungalows with red-tile roofs. The bungalows range in size from one bedroom to three, and they are nicely dispersed among gardens, a pool, and the beachfront. Each unit has a kitchen along with living room, bedroom, and bathroom, so you can cook your own meals if desired. The hotel runs tours to most destinations, and equipment for every water sport from snorkeling (there's a little reef-surrounded island a few hundred yds offshore) to waterskiing can be rented or booked. Windsurfing equipment is free of charge. ✉ *No street address,* ☎ *233–0223 or 223–7587; 256–8228, 656–0100 reservations office in San José. 88 rooms with bath. Restaurant, bar, kitchenettes, pool, hot tub, horseback riding, snorkeling, windsurfing, waterskiing. AE, MC, V.*

Playa Garza

⑮   *16 km (10 mi) north of Playa Sámara.*

Playa Garza occupies a small and serene horseshoe-shape bay 16 km (10 mi) north of Playa Sámara. The rustic fishing village of Garza is front and center, its small fleet of fishing boats anchored offshore. Driving here is tough at times, as coming from either direction you'll be driving on badly maintained dirt roads, and your car will have to ford a river or two. These rivers are manageable in the dry season with two-wheel drive, but don't try it without four-wheel drive in the rainy season.

Lodging

$$$–$$$$ 🏨 **Hotel Villagio La Guaria Morada.** Don't be confused by the rustic thatch: this is a luxury complex whose elegant white freestanding guest rooms—slightly shabby after 15 years of wear and tear but nearing a renovation at press time—form an arc around a landscaped tropical garden. Kitchenettes are to be installed in the cabinas, as plans are afoot to transform the property into a time-share resort. Meanwhile, the restaurant serves inspired pasta and seafood dishes in a new open-air dining area. They've closed the casino, and the disco by the sea was washed away in a 1997 storm. Nonetheless, poolside lounging is topnotch, and there's a wide-screen satellite TV for sports-starved gringos. ✉ *Apdo. 860–1007, Centro Colón, San José,* ☎ *680–0784 or 233–2476,* FAX *222–4073 reservations office in San José. 30 rooms with bath. Restaurant, bar, pool, horseback riding, volleyball, snorkeling, waterskiing, fishing. MC, V.*

Nosara

16 *10 km (6 mi) northeast of Garza.*

Set a bit inland, the small and not very exciting town of Nosara is a good base from which to explore Playa Nosara and neighboring beaches as well as the nearby Refugio Nacional de Fauna Silvestre de Ostional, a haven for nesting turtles. This whole area of Guanacaste is currently being subdivided and settled by Europeans and Americans at a fairly rapid pace. If you're looking to buy a little piece of Costa Rica and you want the security of other expatriates nearby, try Nosara. To approach from the north, you'll need to ford the Río Nosara; from the south, you're coming from Garza and should have already done your river crossings.

Dining and Lodging

$–$$ ✕ **Olga's Bar.** Directly behind Playa Pelada, Olga's serves local food at local prices. The social hall next door looks promising as a Saturday-night dance floor. This is a great place to eat fresh seafood after a day on one of the area's prettiest little beaches. ⊠ *Playa Pelada,* ☎ *no phone. No credit cards.*

$$$ ▦ **Hotel Rancho Suizo Lodge.** The proximity to lovely little Playa Pelada, just 300 yds away by forest trail, makes this one of the most attractive small hotels in the Nosara area. The Swiss operators are renowned for their hearty breakfasts, included with the price of a room; they also do the occasional beach barbecue, and turtle tours during the arribadas. Monkeys are partial to the property's shady ambience. ⊠ *Apdo. 14 Bocas de Nosara 5233,* ☎ *682–0057,* ℻ *682–0055. 10 bungalows. Restaurant, 2 bars, hot tub. No credit cards (may change by 1999).*

$$$ ✕▦ **Hotel Villas Taype.** Roughly 100 yds back from the long, lovely Playa Guiones, the Villas Taype's low-rise building forms a U shape around a pair of pools set in a garden; five freestanding bungalows with refrigerators complement the main building's 18 cabinas. A breakfast buffet comes with the price of a room. Dinner is offered in a separate restaurant with its own street entrance. Air-conditioning and laundry service ease the way, and the German owners rent surfboards, boogie boards, and snorkeling gear as well as bicycles and tennis racquets for the night-lit tennis court. They can also arrange all the local tours. ⊠ *Apdo. 8–5233, Nosara,* ☎ *682–0188,* ℻ *682–0187. 18 cabinas, 5 bungalows. Restaurant, 2 bars, breakfast room, 2 pools, tennis court, Ping-Pong, beach, laundry service. AE, MC, V.*

$$$ ▦ **Lagarta Lodge.** Named for the alligators that live in the river delta (where the Ríos Nosara and Montaña meet and enter the sea), which is visible from the hotel's bird- and beach-watching lobby area, this property is graced with a magnificent promontory setting offering inspired views of the Refugio Nacional de Fauna Silvestre de Ostional. The rooms are in a separate building with hot showers and private balconies. The hotel property includes a 125-acre private nature reserve on the banks of the Río Nosara; stairs lead to boats and riverside trails. Tours to neighboring Ostional can be arranged, and a 10-minute walk through a monkey-filled forest takes you out onto beautiful Playa Guiones. ⊠ *Apdo. 18, Nosara,* ☎ *682–0035,* ℻ *682–0135. 7 rooms with bath. Restaurant, pool. V.*

Refugio Nacional de Fauna Silvestre de Ostional

⑰ *7 km (4½ mi) north of Nosara.*

Apart from sun and sand, the main reason to travel to the central Nicoya is to visit the Refugio Nacional de Fauna Silvestre de Ostional (Ostional Wildlife Refuge), with its wonderful opportunities for turtle-watching. During the rainy season you will probably need four-wheel drive to ford the river just north of Nosara. A track then leads through shrubs to the reserve, which protects one of Costa Rica's major breeding grounds for olive ridley turtles. Local people run the reserve on a cooperative basis. During the first 36 hours of the arribadas, they harvest the eggs—eggs laid during this time would as likely as not be destroyed by subsequent waves of mother turtles. These eggs, believed by some to be powerful aphrodisiacs, are sold to be eaten raw in bars! Members of the cooperative take turns guarding the beach from poachers, but they are happy to let visitors view the turtles.

Turtle arrivals at this and most other nesting sites are dependent on the moon and tides as well as the time of year. Wherever you go to watch the turtles, be sure to consult with local people to get a feel for the conditions and a sense of when, if ever, the turtles will arrive. (For further information, *see box* Tican Turtles *in* Chapter 8, and Parque Nacional Santa Rosa *in* Chapters 4 and 10.)

LIBERIA AND THE NORTHERN NICOYA BEACHES

Highway 21, from Liberia south toward Nicoya, starts opposite Liberia's Hotel Bramadero on the Inter-American Highway. It runs in straight sweeps through cattle country sporadically shaded by guanacaste and tabebuia trees. Just past the village of Comunidad is the turn to Playas Hermosa, Coco, and Ocotal. Continue on toward Belén, and 5 km (3 mi) past Filadelfia you'll hit the Belén junction, where you turn right to the surfing hot spots of Tamarindo and Playa Grande, and the ritzier Meliá Playa Conchal and Hotel Sugar Beach. This road is intermittently paved, depending on which beach you head for. As you work your way toward the coast, pay close attention to the assorted hotel signs at intersections—they may be the only indicators of which road to take. At the Huacas junction, for example, you turn right for Playas Flamingo, Brasilito, Grande, Conchal, and Sugar, but turn left for Tamarindo, Avellanes, Negra, and Junquillal. If you head toward Tamarindo, at Villarreal you turn right for Tamarindo and Langosta but continue farther south for Playas Avellanes, Negra, and Junquillal.

Liberia

⑱ *234 km (145 mi) northwest of San José.*

North of San José on the Inter-American Highway, Liberia is a low-rise, grid-plan, cattle-market town, with a huge central square dominated by a hideous modern church. It is the capital of Guanacaste province, and acts as the gateway to a northern route that encompasses Volcán Rincón de la Vieja (☞ Chapters 4 and 10), several spectacular and biologically important national parks, and a turtle-nesting site on the Pacific coast (☞ Chapter 4). Liberia's Daniel Oduber International Airport jet runway is now open; if and when San José and Liberia sort out their differences on the economically volatile issue of air traffic, the city's proximity to the resort-oriented beaches of Guanacaste will make it the arrival point of choice for even more travelers. Though it's a pleasant and prosperous small city, Liberia doesn't pack in much to see or do. If you do have the time, visit the museum and get tourist information at the **Casa de Cultura.** ⊠ *3 blocks south of Parque Central,* ☎ *666–1606.* ⊘ *Mon.–Sat. 8–4.*

Dining and Lodging

$$ ✗ **Pókopí.** In Costa Rica's cattle capital, Pókopí eclipses rival steak houses. Try the delicious chateaubriand with *salsa Barnesa* (béarnaise sauce, fresh vegetables, and a stuffed tomato). And it ain't all beef: dig into the *dorado* (sea bass) in white sauce with mushrooms, onions, green pepper, and white wine. ⊠ *500 yds down road to Nicoya, on the right, 75 yds west of gas station,* ☎ *666–1036. AE, MC, V.*

$$$ 🏨 **Hotel El Sitio.** If you're overnighting in Liberia, El Sitio is worth considering for its spacious, modern rooms with TVs, as well as for the on-premises Italian restaurant, casino, volleyball court, swimming pools, car rental agency, tour planning, and walking trails. ⊠ *Apdo. 134–5000,* ☎ *280–0211or 280–0226,* ☎ *280–5704. 52 rooms with bath. Restaurant, air-conditioning, 2 pools, spa, horseback riding, mountain bikes, meeting rooms. AE, MC, V.*

$$ 🏨 **Hotel La Siesta.** The advantage of this modern hotel is its quiet location three blocks south of the central plaza. The rooms surround a landscaped patio with a small pool. Narrow, firm beds; white walls; and functional bathrooms beginning to show signs of age sum up the pickings. The upstairs rooms are slightly larger and quieter. ⊠ *Apdo. 15–5000,* ☎ *666–0678,* ☎ *666–2532. 24 rooms with bath. Restaurant, bar, air-conditioning, pool. AE, MC, V.*

Nightlife and the Arts

In late July, Liberia hosts an annexation-secession from Nicaragua celebration with folk dances, bullfights, and rodeos. Semana Cultural, or Cultural Week, heralds arts events in Liberia in the first week of September.

Year-round, the Fiestas Bravas at the **Hacienda la Cueva Liberia** (☎ 666–0450) will appeal to the John Wayne—or the kitschy tourist—in you. Hollering, whooping cowboys accompany visitors on the last stretch as they arrive at the working ranch and 1824 adobe farmhouse. Music, lasso shows, bull-riding, dancing, and a Guanacaste specialty dinner all follow.

Playa del Coco

⑲ *35 km (22 mi) southwest of Liberia.*

Playa del Coco is a slightly seedy beachfront town for those who want noise, discos, and bustle in the height of the season. As perhaps the most accessible beach in Guanacaste, Playa del Coco serves as a playground for Costa Rica's college kids, who are unfortunately not all possessed of a high level of environmental awareness. The beaches can get quite trashy, and the holiday season is impossibly crowded. But Coco's scruffy little pier, slightly down-at-the-heels ambience, and open-air trinket and souvenir stands are actually rather appealing, especially if you like your resorts with a little color.

Dining and Lodging

$–$$ ✗ **Mariscos La Guajira.** Try seviche for starters at this informal open-sided, beachfront restaurant with wooden tables, a cement floor, and potted plants. As main courses, dorado served with salad and fried bananas, camarones, and *langosta al ajillo* (lobster in garlic) are all recommended. ⊠ *West along beach, look for round, palm-thatch shades,* ☎ *670–0107. Reservations not accepted. AE, MC, V.*

$–$$ ✕ **San Francisco Treats.** The friendly, long-haired former San Francisco corporate lawyer who, with his wife, started this wonderful little open-air eatery on the main road into Coco has put it on the market—but along with the business, they're selling the recipes, so the great American-style sandwiches, home-baked bread, lasagnas—both vegetarian and *con carne* (with meat)—and especially, the fantastic desserts should still be available if someone does buy them out. Want to buy a successful biz by the beach in Guanacaste? It's only $125,000. ☎ *670–0484. No credit cards.*

$$–$$$ ✕▥ **Villa Flores.** Weight-lifting, scuba-diving Italians run the Villa Flores, on the same street—paralleling the beach—as Cabinas Chale (☞ *below*; turn right at San Francisco Treats). Their bed-and-breakfast/dive center specializes in scuba trips. The hotel features a well-equipped gym and a large swimming pool. The beach is a minute away; the three-meal restaurant tends towards the Italian. The handsome two-story hardwood building has fan-cooled downstairs rooms, two upstairs rooms with air-conditioning, and one—Room 9—that contains an amazingly commodious bathtub. ⊠ *Apdo. 2,* ☎ ℻ *670–0269. 10 rooms with bath. Restaurant, pool, exercise room. AE, MC, V.*

$$ ▥ **Cabinas Chale.** To find Chale, turn right at San Francisco Treats and head down the road. Bedrooms are bright and large, containing up to five beds, a refrigerator, table and chairs, tile floor, and overhead fans. They are spotlessly clean and have modern bathrooms. Take a 50-yd stroll to the beach straight ahead, and walk west 500 yds to town. ☎ *670–0036,* ℻ *670–0303. 25 rooms with bath. Pool, badminton, basketball. V.*

$$ ▥ **Villa del Sol.** The French-Canadian operators of the Villa del Sol offer seven quiet, spacious, light-filled rooms in a small contemporary B&B with a pool out front. Well away from Coco's main drag (turn right at San Francisco Treats), the Villa del Sol lies just 100 yds from the quieter part of Playa del Coco, visible from the upstairs balconies. They will organize the usual area tours and activities. ☎ ℻ *670–0085. 7 rooms, 2 without bath. Breakfast room, pool. AE, MC, V.*

Hermosa

㉕ *13 km (8 mi) east of Playa del Coco.*

Hermosa has a relaxed village atmosphere, reminiscent of a Mexican beach town. Although several large hotels have opened here in recent years, the full length of the village beach is occupied by small buildings—hotels, restaurants, and private houses—and so the newer, larger hotels and other developments have been forced to set up shop off the beach, or on other beaches in the area. Hermosa's crescent of grayish sand fronts a line of trees that provide a welcome respite from the heat of the sun. At the north end of the beach, low tide reveals great rock-lined tide pools for exploring.

Dining and Lodging

$–$$ ✕▥ **Aqua Sport.** This beachfront complex has a gift shop, minimarket, and water-sports equipment rentals, but the main draw is a casual open-air restaurant decorated with tree trunks. The seafood platter of lobster, shrimp, calamari, and oysters is highly recommended. ⊠ *Apdo. 100–5019, Playa del Coco,* ☎ ℻ *672–0050. 6 rooms with bath, 1 suite. Restaurant. AE, MC, V.*

$$$$ 🏨 **Blue Bay Village Papagayo.** Encompassing 78 hilly beachfront acres, the resort is on the south shore of Bahía Culebra, a bit north of Hermosa. (A grim reminder of a luxury housing development is well under way next door, marring the views.) Freestanding villas house two guest rooms with private baths, marble floors, in-room satellite TV, and direct-dial phones. The Blue Bay package is all-inclusive, with meals and use of all facilities included in the per-couple price. All water sports and tours can be arranged through the concierge desk. ⊠ *Playa Arenilla, Golfo de Papagayo,* ☎ *670–0033,* FAX *670–0300;* ☎ *233– 8566, 256–4623 in San José,* FAX *221–0739 in San José. 80 bungalows. 2 restaurants, 3 bars, 2 snack bars, pools, hot tub, tennis court, health club, theater, meeting rooms. AE, DC, MC, V.*

$$$$ 🏨 **Costa Smeralda.** The grand scale of the Costa Smeralda—the all-inclusive resort contains air-conditioned, satellite-TV-equipped guest rooms—is evident from the size of the Mediterranean-style lobby-reception building, with its large entry, enormous, open-air buffet dining area, casino, and upstairs conference rooms. But the guest rooms counterpoint the overscale quality, as they are carefully distributed down a long, gently sloping site from the main building to a pretty little beach, with gardens, lawns, and an appealing, amoeba-shape pool. The restaurant's dishes reflect the resort's Italian ownership. Guests can pick and choose from a wide range of extracurricular activities. ⊠ *Playa Panamá,* ☎ *672–0042, 672–0070, or 672–0041,* FAX *672–0079. 120 rooms with bath. Restaurant, snack bar, pool, beach, casino, meeting rooms. AE, MC, V.*

$$$–$$$$ 🏨 **Sula Sula.** Pleasingly set in a shady forest behind quiet Playa Panamá, just north of Hermosa, Sula Sula's yellow cabinas with red-tile roofs have telephones, air-conditioning, minibars, satellite TV, hair dryers, good reading lights, and comfortable furnishings. A rather formal-looking restaurant serves international cuisine; three bars and a large pool enhance the cool provided by the shade trees. A stone wall encloses the entire property, and separates it from a popular campground at the south end of the beach. ⊠ *Playa Panamá,* ☎ *670–0000,* FAX *670–0492. 24 cabinas. Restaurant, 3 bars, pool. AE, MC, V.*

$$$ 🏨 **El Velero Hotel.** The elegant, two-story Velero has large, white rooms with arched doorways. The new Canadian owners have added a boutique, a satellite-equipped TV room upstairs, and resident toucans, unfortunately caged in. Along with Jet Skis and sea kayaks, the hotel has a sailboat and offers sunset cruises and all-day snorkeling trips. The sailboat also serves as a spare guest room on occasion—don't be afraid to ask if you like sleeping on board. By late 1998, David and Jessica Anne Trogler, from Baltimore, will be anchoring their 44-ft sailing yacht, the *Jessica Anne,* and offering three-day sailing charters. At the restaurant, sample the jumbo shrimp with rice and vegetables, or anything with mashed potatoes—a rare treat in Costa Rica! ⊠ *Playa Hermosa,* ☎ *672–0016,* ☎ FAX *672–0036. 13 rooms with bath. Restaurant, bar, pool, boating, snorkeling, jet skiing. AE, MC, V.*

$$ 🏨 **Hotel Cabinas Playa Hermosa.** Monkeys, coatis, and birds once frolicked outside these peaceful white cabinas (sleeping five with bath) on the quiet south end of the beach. Now two miserable coatis reside in a very small cage—it's an ugly sight, and an unfortunate choice. Nevertheless, this hotel is still a good deal. The restaurant serves pasta, steak, and seafood. ⊠ *Apdo. 112, Liberia,* ☎ FAX *672–0046. 22 cabinas. Restaurant. V.*

Outdoor Activities and Sports

SCUBA DIVING

Just off the beach at the Hotel Sol Playa Hermosa (at the north end of Playa Hermosa), **Bill Beard's Diving Safaris** (☎ FAX 672–0012 or 670–

0495; 800/779–0055 in the U.S., FAX 954/351–9740 U.S.) offers a complete range of scuba activities from beginner training through open-water certification courses to multitank dives at more than 20 tantalizing sites off the coast of Guanacaste. A quick read through Beard's literature reveals that his guides and trainers know Guanacaste underwater as well as anyone: for every dive site they visit, their brochures provide a thorough description of the underwater geography as well as the myriad types of rays, sharks, fish, and turtles that frequent the area. Prices range from $40 for a one-tank afternoon dive to $375 for a PADI (Professional Association of Diving Instructors) open-water certification course. On the beach below the dive shop, a small, independent **kiosk** rents boogie boards, plastic kayaks, Jet Skis, and other water toys.

Playa Ocotal

㉑   *3 km (2 mi) west of Playa del Coco.*

Ocotal is isolated, in spite of its proximity to Coco, and though very small in size, the beach is a quiet, rock-sheltered gem. At the entrance to the Golfo de Papagayo, it's a good spot for sportfishing enthusiasts to hole up between excursions. Good diving can be found at Las Corridas, just 1 km (½ mi) away.

Lodging

$$$–$$$$ ⊞ **El Ocotal Beach Resort.** Three kilometers (2 mi) west of Playa del
★   Coco down a paved road, this luxury hotel with a sportfishing fleet and dive shop is situated above secluded Ocotal Bay. From the upper rooms you look north to the Peninsula Santa Elena and northwest to Rincón de la Vieja. Air-conditioned rooms have blue carpets, patterned bedspreads, white walls, watercolors, overhead fans, TVs, and huge French windows. Units down the hill are bigger and triangular in shape with polished wood floors. ⊠ *Apdo. 1, Playa del Coco,* ☎ *670–0321,* FAX *670–0083. 40 rooms with bath, 3 suites, 6 bungalows. Restaurant, bar, pool, tennis court, horseback riding, boating. AE, DC, MC, V.*

$$$ ⊞ **Villa Casa Blanca.** Surely one of the finest B&Bs in Costa Rica, the Casa Blanca offers guests Victorian-influenced room decor. In a hillside Mediterranean-style building buried in a bower of tropical plantings, the charming rooms have air-conditioning, lovely wood details and artwork, spacious showers, and canopy beds. Secluded, romantic, and with a fine little pool, the Casa Blanca also provides guests with Guanacaste's heartiest breakfasts, included in the price of a room. They will also deliver dinner from one of the area's many restaurant's if guests so desire. The intimate, junglelike setting attracts numerous colorful, talkative birds. ⊠ *Box 176–5019, Playa Ocotal,* ☎ FAX *670–0448. 13 rooms with bath. Breakfast room, pool. AE, MC, V.*

Playa Pan de Azúcar

㉒   *8 km (5 mi) north of Playa Flamingo.*

Pan de Azúcar's lovely beach, at the end of a hilly dirt road, lends its only hotel one quality that is not always easy to come by in this area—privacy. There are good islands for snorkeling just offshore.

Lodging

$$$$ ⊞ **Hotel Sugar Beach.** Reached via a dirt track 8 km (5 mi) north of
★   Flamingo, this hotel overlooks a small, curving white-sand beach. The nicely varied, air-conditioned rooms and suites feature inspired views. A beach house with two or three bedrooms can be rented by the day or week. Wildlife abounds, most noticeably howler monkeys and iguanas, and excellent snorkeling is done at either edge of the bay. The hotel

charges a lot extra for use of snorkeling and other gear, and has virtually no competition. The open-sided rotunda restaurant should not disappoint, especially if you choose seafood. Management offers a full complement of activities and area tours, from boat trips to surfing at Witches Rock to golf, horseback riding, and volcano tours. ⊠ *Apdo. 90, Santa Cruz,* ☎ *654–4242,* ℻ *654–4239. 29 rooms with bath, 1 beach house. Restaurant, bar, pool, snorkeling. AE, MC, V.*

$$ ★ **Casa Sunset.** Just north of the village of Potrero up high on the inland side of the dirt road to Hotel Sugar Beach, the American-run Casa Sunset offers wonderful views of the sunset from cabinas stacked up the steep hillside above the road. Each cabina contains four single beds, ceiling fans, and a bath with warm, not hot, showers. A sunbathing patio surrounds a small pool near the top of the property, and a community kitchen allows some on-site cooking. The village of Potrero is five minutes away on foot, and has a couple of restaurants to choose from. Secluded Playas Penca and Prieta are also within walking distance, as is the hustle and bustle of Flamingo Beach, about a half-hour walk. ⊠ *5111 Playa Potrero, Santa Cruz,* ☎ ℻ *654–4265. 7 cabinas. Pool, horseback riding, surfing, boating, fishing. No credit cards.*

Playa Potrero

㉓ *1 km (½ mi) north of Flamingo.*

Although lovely Potrero previously has been known mostly for its views of nearby Flamingo, it is possessed of its own charm, primarily due to the presence of a wide, white-sand beach. There's excellent swimming to a small offshore island, and the bird refuge **Isla Santa Catalina** is 10 km (6 mi) offshore.

Lodging

$$$$ **Bahía Potrero Beach and Fishing Resort.** At this squat, white bungalow, fishing and water sports are the major activities. The beach is ideal for young children because the sea is shallow and safe, and the long, practically deserted strand is relaxing for all. ⊠ *Apdo. 45, Santa Cruz,* ☎ *654–4183,* ℻ *654–4093. 14 rooms with bath. Restaurant, bar, pool, fishing. AE, MC, V.*

$$$ **Hotel El Sitio Cielomar.** Sister to the well-run El Sitio in Liberia, the simple and secluded (but slightly overpriced) Cielomar sits just a few feet back from the pretty little beach just north of Potrero called Playa Penca. This is a charming hideaway: the white-sand beach and green lawn behind it are well-shaded, and little islets a few hundred yds offshore offer great opportunities for snorkeling. If you want action, the Flamingo resorts are 5 minutes away by car, 20 on foot. The three-meal restaurant is for guests only. Breakfast is included with the price of a room. ⊠ *No street address,* ☎ *666–1211 or 654–4194,* ℻ *666–2059. 11 rooms with bath. Restaurant. MC, V.*

Playa Flamingo

㉔ *39 km (24 mi) west of Filadelfia.*

Flamingo was one of the first of the northern Nicoya beaches to experience the wonders of overscale resort development. Although the huge Hotel Flamingo Beach dominates the landscape, the beach is still lovely. If you like large, characterless hotels with your beach—and some do, strictly for their impersonality—this is a good place for you. A half-finished condo project adds an unfortunate sour note to the south end of an otherwise beautiful stretch of sand.

Dining and Lodging

$$ ✕ **Marie's Restaurant.** Friendly Marie and her fresh food make this
★ place well worth a visit. Shortly after the road bends to the north end
of Flamingo, look for Marie's small veranda furnished with sliced
tree-trunk tables, and settle back for a rewarding meal of generous help-
ings of fresh seafood at very reasonable rates. The seviche is delight-
ful, as is the house specialty, *plato de mariscos* (shrimp, lobster, and
oysters served with garlic butter, potatoes, and salad), but be sure to
save room for pudding—the *tres leches,* topped with the cream of three
different milks, is superb. ✉ *No street address,* ☎ *654–4136. Reser-
vations not accepted. V.*

$$$–$$$$ 🏨 **Aurola Flamingo Beach Resort.** Major renovations in the last few
years have turned this overscale beachfront property into a five-star
hotel. Reality check: stay here and you could easily forget that you are
in Costa Rica; you might, instead, think yourself to be in Miami, Can-
cún, or Palm Springs. ✉ *Apdo. 692–4050, Alajuela,* ☎ *654–4011,*
FAX *654–4060. 136 rooms with bath, 36 condominiums. 2 restau-
rants, 4 bars, 3 pools, tennis court, health club, casino, travel services.
AE, DC, MC, V.*

$$$ 🏨 **Mariner Inn.** Near the marina, this white, two-story building is the
least expensive hotel in Flamingo. Rooms are tiny, but they do have
ceiling fans, air-conditioning, and firm beds. ✉ *Apdo. 65, Santa Cruz,*
☎ *654–4081,* FAX *654–4024. 11 rooms with bath, 1 suite. Restaurant,
bar, pool. AE, MC, V.*

Brasilito

㉕ *35 km (22 mi) west of Filadelfia.*

Brasilito is a pretty little fishing village with boats lined up just offshore of a white-sand beach that is the equal of Flamingo, but without the megahotels. This little town still has some charming local color
and character in spite of the nearby boom.

Dining and Lodging

$–$$ ✕ **El Camerón Dorado.** This bar-restaurant derives much of its appeal
from the shady setting on Brasilito's beautiful beach, and no less from
the small-vessel fishing fleet anchored offshore that assures you of the
freshness of seafood available. The westernmost tables are literally on
the beach, and the surf crashes just yds away as you dine beneath the
stars. Due to the spectacular sunsets, it's a popular place for an early
evening drink. ✉ *220 yds north of Brasilito Plaza,* ☎ *654–4244. AE,
DC, MC, V.*

$$ 🏨 **Hotel Brasilito.** This appealing, intimately scaled German-run es-
tablishment has a high-ceiling dining room just off the beach. Two rooms
feature great sea views. ✉ *Next to square and soccer field,* ☎ *654–
4237,* FAX *654–4247. 17 rooms with bath. Restaurant. V.*

Playa Conchal

㉖ *Immediately south of Playa Brasilito. .*

Playa Conchal, one of Guanacaste's prettiest little beaches, remains ac-
cessible to the public despite the huge resort now perched behind it.
The beach is aptly named, as it is literally made out of shells that offer
themselves up for easy collecting.

Lodging

$$$$ ⊞ **Meliá Playa Conchal Beach & Golf Resort.** When you stand in the enormous, open-air, marble-floored reception lobby of this massive resort and look out over the almost 1½ sq mi of manicured grounds, golf courses, bungalows, tennis courts, and distant beach, it's a toss-up whether the appropriate emotion is awe or resignation: for the golfing traveler in search of luxury in a remote destination, this resort is ideal. The buildings are low-rise, and as small-hotel neighbors have pointed out, by putting in a single large project, Meliá has prevented the subdivision of lovely Playa Conchal. The rooms (four per bungalow) are large and luxurious, air-conditioned, and satellite-TV equipped; the restaurants serve a range of international fare. ⊠ *No street address, entrance less than 1 km (½ mi) south of Brasilito,* ☎ *654–4123; 800/ 336–3542 in the U.S.;* ℻ *654–4181; 308 bungalows. 5 restaurants, 2 bars, pool, 2 golf courses, 4 tennis courts, meeting rooms. AE, MC, V.*

En Route   To get to the Parque Nacional Marino Las Baulas, take the Inter-American Highway north to Liberia and from there head south to Santa Cruz, then west to the coast.

Parque Nacional Marino Las Baulas

㉗   *37 km (23 mi) west of Filadelfia, 3 km (2 mi) north of Tamarindo.*

Just north of Tamarindo, on the other side of an estuary, the Parque Nacional Marino Las Baulas (Las Baulas Marine National Park) protects the long and lovely **Playa Grande**, an important nesting site of the leatherback sea turtle (☞ Chapter 10). It's a great surf spot as well. Unfortunately, the Guanacaste resort boom is beginning to encroach on this bucolic spot—a couple of small hotels have opened not far from Hotel Las Tortugas (☞ Lodging, *below*), and a golf and country club is offering property for sale behind the adjacent estuary.

Lodging

$$$ ⊞ **Hotel Las Tortugas.** This hotel stands at the edge of Parque Nacional Marino Las Baulas, right on the edge of the turtle-nesting beach. Owners Louis Wilson and Marianela Pastor—he American, she Costa Rican—struggled for a decade to get the national park established and have a real understanding of the importance of balancing the oft-conflicting needs of locals, tourists, and turtles. An evening spent discussing ecotourism, ecopolitics, and related matters with them is a real education. Although the rooms don't have great views, they are comfortable, with good beds and air-conditioning, as well as stone floors and stucco walls. Louis and Marianela also offer a number of long-term rentals; the apartments they call Greek 1, 2, and 3 are very atmospheric. The restaurant serves healthy, high-quality food. Las Tortugas stands in front of the surf break but sometimes has dangerous rip currents; there's also a turtle-shape swimming pool. Local guides escort visitors along the beach at night, and the hotel also offers canoe trips in the nearby Refugio Vida Silvestre de Tamarindo (Tamarindo Wildlife Refuge). ⊠ *Apdo. 164, Santa Cruz de Guanacaste,* ☎ *653–0423,* ☎ ℻ *653–0458. 11 rooms with bath. Restaurant, pool, boating. V.*

Tamarindo

㉘   *37 km (23 mi) west of Filadelfia.*

Tamarindo is a lively little town with a great variety of restaurants, cabins, bars, and hotels at all price levels. Developmental hustle is everywhere evident in the presence of condo projects, mini–strip malls, and other resort-town evils. Still, Tamarindo remains appealing because it's a virtually complete self-contained Costa Rican destination: its beaches are great for snorkeling, boating, kayaking, diving, surfing, and just plain swimming; there are estuaries north and south of town for bird- and animal-watching; and two turtle-nesting beaches—Langosta to the south and Grande to the north—are nearby. With an airstrip just outside town, Tamarindo's also a convenient base from which to explore all of Guanacaste. But there are some downsides: the town is in dire need of a paved road (sections were being paved in early 1998), better sewage systems, and a coherent lighting plan that reflects the needs of the Playa Grande turtles. A fund has been set up to deal with these issues, which bear directly on the future of the town as an attractive destination for tourism. Many businesses contribute, others, unfortunately, do not.

Dining and Lodging

$$–$$$ ✕ **Nogui's.** Local gringos swear by this scruffy little near-beachfront
★ restaurant. Also known as the Sunrise Café, Nogui's is considered by aficionados to have the freshest, best, and most reasonably priced seafood in all of Tamarindo. A dirt road separates Nogui's alfresco plastic tables and chairs from the beach. When it gets crowded, some stand in the parking area eating on their feet rather than wait for a table. The langostino is highly recommended, as is the swimsuit selection in the adjacent Nogui's shop. ⊠ *Just south of Zullymar on the Tamarindo circle,* ☎ 653–0029. V.

$–$$ ✕ **Bakery de Paris/Restaurant Cocodril.** The new owners of this bak-
★ ery, formerly Johann's, on the right side of the road near the entrance to town have also purchased the adjacent Cocodril Restaurant and Disco 24. At dining tables nicely distributed on a shady, off-road patio you can enjoy three meals, especially the great morning European pastries. Have a closer (not too close) look at the pond behind the adjacent tire-repair shop: you may be rewarded with a sighting of the rather fat crocodile that lives there, feeding, they say, on roast chickens from the Cocodril. ⊠ *On right side of the main road just as you enter town,* ☎ 653–0255. AE, MC, V.

$–$$ ✕ **Fruitas Tropicales.** They hose down the road to dampen the dust that
★ would otherwise smother this busy street-side eatery. The white plastic tables and chairs stay full for a reason—they do a great job, dishing out Costa Rican food at Costa Rican prices to tourists of every shape and description. The food is nothing fancy, but the casados and other dishes are tasty and substantial. There are plenty of American-style items on the menu as well and great *fruitas tropicales* (tropical fruit drinks). ⊠ *On off-beach-side of main dirt drag through Tamarindo, toward north end of town,* ☎ 653–0041. AE, MC, V.

$–$$ ✕ **Iguana Grill.** Beneath the Iguana Surf's high Rancho, Nancy Money's Iguana Grill (her mother owns the Sueño del Mar in nearby Playa Langosta, ☞ *below*) offers hearty, nuevo Mexican-American breakfasts—burritos, *huevos rancheros* (egg tortillas), and other less ethnic delights—and lunches. Don't miss the great coffee drinks from the best espresso machine in Tamarindo, and the tropical smoothies. This is a good place for a break from the casado routine. ⊠ *Below Iguana Surf,* ☎ FAX 653–0148. MC, V.

$ ✕🖭 **Arco Iris Restaurant & Cabinas.** A pair of spirited Italian sisters,
★ Laura and Simona Fillipini, run a wonderful Italian vegetarian restaurant and hotel set up on the hill behind the Tamarindo circle (follow the signs). There's nothing on the menu more than about $5, and the food is healthful and lovingly prepared. The four cabinas the sisters built are each a different primary color and decorated with a distinct theme, and one comes with two bedrooms and a kitchen. ⊠ *Follow*

signs past Hotel Pasatiempo and up the hill to the right, ☎ 653–0330.
4 cabinas. Restaurant. No credit cards.

$$$$ 🏨 **El Jardín del Eden.** The only disadvantage suffered by the "Jardín"
★   is that it is not located directly on the beach (and that's not really much
of a disadvantage in the dust of the dry season). The three-tiered,
mauve hotel, set among lush gardens (hence the name) on a hill, has
rooms with green interiors and elegantly styled bathrooms. All rooms
have ocean views, air-conditioning, refrigerators, and fans. A thatched-
roof restaurant prepares French and Italian food and outstanding
steaks. Fishing packages are available. ⊠ *Apdo. 1094–2050, San
Pedro,* ☎ *653–0137,* 🖷 *653–0111. 18 rooms with bath, 2 apartments.
Restaurant, 2 bars, 2 pools, hot tub. AE, MC, V.*

$$$$ 🏨 **Hotel Capitán Suiz.** The "Swiss Captain" is Ruedi Schmid, and he
and his partner Ursula Schmid have created an elegant accommodation at the south end of Tamarindo, near a lineup of high-priced beachfront houses. The bungalows are set in a lushly landscaped garden
surrounding a swimming pool, and a relatively quiet stretch of
Tamarindo's gorgeous beach is just a few steps away. The rather pricey
restaurant serves international cuisine. They will arrange horseback riding, kayaking, sportfishing, and diving trips. A lot of monkeys hang
around the Swiss Captain's place as well, so you get your "wildlife"
with the price of a room. ⊠ *Veer left at the right turn to the circle and
head toward Playa Langosta, Swiss Captain is on the right,* ☎ *653–
0075,* 🖷 *653–0292. 22 rooms with bath, 8 bungalows. Restaurant,
pool. AE, MC, V.*

$$$$ 🏨 **Hotel Tamarindo Diriá.** A shady tropical garden next to the beach
does away with the need to stray far from the bounds of Tamarindo's
first high-end hotel, still a very posh spot. The modern three-story building has striking white-painted furnishings with aqua trim and match-
ing ceilings. It's a bit much, but each has a spacious balcony looking
onto treetops. The thatched rotunda bar and restaurant overlook a large
rectangular pool. ⊠ *Apdo. 676–1000, San José,* ☎ *653–0031; 293–
4340 reservations office in San José,* 🖷 *289–8727 in San José. 80 rooms
with bath. Restaurant, bar, pool. AE, DC, MC, V.*

$$$–$$$$ 🏨 **Casa Cook.** These comfortable beachfront villa and cabinas are
★   owned by a retired American couple, Chuck and Ruthann Cook. Two
one-bedroom, hardwood-detailed cabinas positioned just off Tamarindo's
lovely beach contain full kitchens, ceiling fans, screened doors and win-
dows, individual hot-water heaters, plus a queen-size bed in the bed-
room and a queen-size sofa bed in the living room. The second story
of the main house is the "villa," a 1,500-sq-ft apartment with two bed-
rooms with private baths, a kitchen, dining area, living room, and a
large deck. There is no restaurant on premises, but fully equipped kitchens
and a number of quality restaurants nearby more than cover dining
requirements. ⊠ *South of the circle and north of the Swiss Captain
Hotel,* ☎ 🖷 *653–0125;* ⊠ *4269 Chapman Way, Pleasanton, CA
94588,* ☎ *500/675–0421 or 510/846–0784,* 🖷 *500/677–1781 or 510/
426–1141. 2 cabinas, 1 villa. Pool. AE, MC, V.*

$$–$$$ 🏨 **Cabinas Marielos.** In high season there are few decent bargain
rooms to be had in Tamarindo. Among the best of the relatively less
expensive places is Cabinas Marielos, across the main dirt road from
the beach, in what is more or less town center. The cabinas are housed
in two wings, flanking a courtyard set well back from the noise and
dust of the road. The atmosphere is surprisingly serene. Note the water
doesn't get too, too hot. ⊠ *Near the north of town, follow signs,* ☎
🖷 *653–0141. 16 cabinas. V.*

$$ \quad $$ **Hotel Pasatiempo.** Some 656 ft from the beach just off the dirt road to Playa Langosta, the Pasatiempo is one of the better bargains in Tamarindo. The cabinas, each named after a Guanacaste beach, are placed amidst nicely landscaped grounds and around a small swimming pool; each has a hand-painted mural over the bed, hot water, and ceiling fans (two have air-conditioning). The bar frequently hires live music—"grown up rock and roll," according to owner Ron Stewart—and a wide-screen satellite TV provides American sports fans with their necessary fix (an important consideration since high season coincides with NFL play-offs). ✉ *200 yds from the beach behind the Tamarindo circle,* ☎ *653–0096,* FAX *653–0275. 10 cabinas. Restaurant, bar. AE, MC, V.*

Outdoor Activities and Sports

BOATING, SURFING, AND KAYAKING

Iguana Surf (☎ FAX 653–0148, http://www.tamarindo.com/iguana) rents surfboards and also offers guided kayak tours into the bird-watching paradises of the nearby Ríos San Francisco and Tamarindo estuaries. The San Francisco seems to have more birds, and a nature walk upriver on a recent trip provided a wonderful encounter with a troop of howler monkeys. The larger Tamarindo is a more exotic, over-grown, junglelike estuary, with *African Queen*–like ambience deep in the mangrove jungle.

SPORTFISHING

For saltwater anglers, a number of fishing charter operations operate in Tamarindo. Probably the best among them is **Tamarindo Sportfishing** (☎ 653–0090) run by Randy Wilson, who has led the way in developing new fish-saving catch-and-release techniques that go as easy as is possible on the fish. Wilson has roamed and fished the Guanacaste waters for 25 years now, and he knows where the big ones lurk. His boat, the *Talking Fish,* is equipped with a marlin chair and a cabin with a shower. Full days run $875, half days $550.

Playa Langosta

㉙ *2 km (1 mi) south of Tamarindo.*

Playa Langosta is a leatherback turtle-nesting beach that is less protected than the beach at Tamarindo. Informal viewings with private guides are a lot cheaper than the more organized Playa Grande turtle tours, but eggs are being stolen in huge quantities, and the whole arrangement will most likely be formalized in the near future. Big, well-shaped river-mouth waves near the north end of the beach make it popular with surfers. An oversize casino-condo-hotel complex going up on the bluff overlooking the river mouth will forever change this gorgeous spot.

Lodging

$$$–$$$$ $$ \quad $$ **Sueño del Mar.** Langosta has great surf, turtle nesting at night, the
★ fantastic bird-watching estuary of the Río San Francisco, and American Susan Money's gorgeous little dream of a B&B, one of the prettiest in Costa Rica. Gather a group of friends and take the place over for a week—you'll love every minute. The adobe-style buildings house three double rooms with overhead fans and Balinese-style showers open to the sky. A small casita sleeps four, and has its own kitchen and veranda. Upstairs, the matrimonial suite offers even greater privacy. The complex has lovely gardens and intimate patios, and is decorated with hand-painted frescoes and colorful antique tiles; hammocks swing in the courtyard. Gourmet breakfast is served in the "community" room, where three-course dinners are held a couple of times a week. The lively

Ms. Money and her partner-husband, surfing forester Greg Mullins, will help arrange myriad trips. ✉ *Playa Tamarindo, Santa Cruz,* ☎ FAX *653–0284;* ✉ *Susan Money, 4 Mountainview Ct., Burlington, VT 05401,* ☎ FAX *802/658–8041. 3 rooms with bath, 1 suite, 1 casita. Dining room, horseback riding, snorkeling, surfing, boating, fishing, bicycles. No credit cards.*

En Route   To reach Playas Negra, Avellanes, and Junquillal, take the turn toward Tamarindo at the Huacas junction, then when you reach the village of Villarreal continue south rather than turning right toward Tamarindo. The road is in fairly good shape except for a few spots as you head down the Nicoya Peninsula. You make a right turn at the T junction a few miles south, and to reach Playa Avellanes (the 20-km/12-mi drive should take about half an hour) follow the signs to Cabinas Las Olas (☞ *below*). From here, questionably passable roads lead south to Playa Negra—sage drivers will only attempt it with four-wheel drive. Better to double back to the T junction on the main road from Villarreal, and head south again. After 21 km (12½ mi) you'll come to a junction with a left turn to Santa Cruz (a terribly potholed road) and a right to Paraiso and Junquillal. Turn right, and another 15 km (8 mi) of decent mixed dirt and paved road gets you to the hamlet of Paraiso. From here it's about 6 km (4 mi) north on a funky but passable dirt road to Playa Negra, and 2 km (1 mi) south on a better road to the north end of Junquillal, which stretches south uninterrupted for about 3 km (2 mi). This area can also be reached via the Río Tempisque ferry; follow the signs to Santa Cruz once you're off the boat. From Santa Cruz, take the first dirt road on the left, north of the bridge, and take it slow—it's a terrible road. Follow the signs to the Junquillal hotels, as they're the best directions you're going to get.

Playas Avellanes, Negra, and Junquillal

㉚   *About 40 km (25 mi) south of Tamarindo by road, probably half that distance as the crow flies (or the boat sails).*

Americans—surfers, at least—got their first look at Playa Negra in *The Endless Summer II,* which featured some dynamite sessions at this spectacular rock-reef point break. The waves are almost all rights, and most are beautifully shaped. A bit north of Negra, Avellanes is a beautiful half-mile stretch of pale golden sand with rocky outcroppings, a river mouth, and a mangrove swamp estuary. Locals claim there are eight surf spots when the swell is strong. Junquilla (pronounced hoon-key-*yall*), to the south, is a long, lovely stretch of uninterrupted beach with small surf and only one hotel on the beach side of the road. This is one of the quieter beaches in Guanacaste, and a real find for tranquillity seekers.

Lodging

$$$ 🏨 **Hotel Atumalal.** Set back off the beach at the south end of Junquil-
★   lal, Atumalal is a lovely resort that is perhaps a little too slick for its location. On the other hand, why not play tennis, slide into the pool, have an Italian dinner, then disco the night away close to a perfect beach in the middle of nowhere? The grounds are lovely, and the views of the sea from the main dining room behind the reception area are splendid. Breakfast is included in the price of a room, and amenities include good reading lights and plenty of hot water. ✉ *Apdo. 49, Santa Cruz,* ☎ FAX *653–0425. 23 rooms. Restaurant, 3 bars, refrigerators, pool, tennis court, dance club. AE, MC, V.*

$$$ 🏨 **Hotel Playa Negra.** For years, surfers and other adventurers have
★   roughed it at assorted motley lodges and cabinas in the area. All that changed with the 1996 opening of this hotel run by Lito Pedro Fer-

nandez. Behind the restaurant-bar facing the sea, a collection of round thatch-roofed cabinas sits among lawns and plantings. Cooled by ceiling fans, the cabinas are all bright pastels outside andbuilt-in sofas and beautiful tile bathrooms inside. The ocean here is good for swimming and snorkeling, with rock reefs providing shelter from the waves and creating tide pools and swimming holes. And for surfers, with a good swell running, this is paradise found. A large pool gives surf widows a place to relax, and a tennis court is in the works. The restaurant serves deft preparations of Latin and European dishes by the French and Costa Rican chefs. ⊠ *Go north on the dirt road out of Paraiso, follow signs carefully, as there are several forks in the road,* ☎ ⅨⅩ *382–1301; 293–0332 in San José. 10 cabinas. Restaurant, bar, pool, tennis court, horseback riding, volleyball. AE, MC, V.*

$$–$$$ 🏨 **Cabinas Las Olas.** Frequented primarily by surfers on holiday surf-tour packages from Brazil and Argentina, these spacious freestanding cabinas in an airy forest behind Playa Avellanes should also appeal to American surfers as well as bird-watchers, animal-lovers, and all manner of naturalists. The isolated location guarantees the presence of many monkeys and other critters. The three-meal restaurant, with an adjacent outdoor video bar, serves reasonably priced food. A wonderful elevated boardwalk leads from the cabinas through a protected mangrove estuary to Playa Avellanes, with its multiple surfing breaks and pristine sands. ⊠ *Apdo. 1404–1250, Escazú,* ☎ *233–4455,* ⅨⅩ *222–8685. 10 cabinas. Restaurant, bar, laundry service. AE, MC, V.*

$$–$$$ 🏨 **Guacamaya Lodge.** Up on the hill a few hundred yards off Playa
★   Junquillal (follow signs), the secluded Guacamaya offers expansive views and ideal bird-watching. Swiss brother and sister Alice and Bernie Etene have established a delightful compound, with flocks of visiting parrots in the mornings and a multitude of cranes visible in the estuary below. The three-meal restaurant is very reasonably priced. ⊠ *Apdo. 6, Santa Cruz,* ☎ ⅨⅩ *653–0431. 6 cabinas. Restaurant, bar, pool. No credit cards.*

$$–$$$ 🏨 **Hotel Iguanazul.** Situated on 100 acres on the bluff at the north end
★   of Playa Junquillal, the Iguanazul is an isolated beachfront resort that has it all: cabinas with bath and hot water, a swimming pool, a three-meal restaurant and bar, and 3 km (2 mi) of beach stretching south from the hotel. Junquillal is almost completely undeveloped—this is one of only half a dozen hotels in the area—and the beach is wonderful: better for swimming than surfing, great for walking, and occasionally nesting grounds for leatherback turtles. The hotel management will arrange endless tours, and offers karaoke nights and trips to local fiestas. The fabulous surf of Playa Negra is 10 minutes away. Ask for air-conditioning. ⊠ *No. 130–5150, Santa Cruz,* ☎ *653–0124,* ⅨⅩ *653–0123. 24 cabinas. Restaurant, bar, pool, volleyball. AE, MC, V.*

$$–$$$ 🏨 **Mono Congo Lodge.** Mono Congo translates as howler monkey, and the noisy but endearing creatures are plentiful here. The hard-working American owners have transformed 10 acres of barren cattle pasture into a little gem, with extensive plantings surrounding a handsome three-story hardwood structure housing a restaurant, comfortable seating areas, and four rooms. A separate cabina rents for slightly more. If the waves go flat, take a ride: the owners guide horseback tours. A pool should be open by press time. Good food, good waves, boards for rent, and rustic, comfortable accommodations with hot water on demand: a perfect spot for a surfer's dream holiday. ⊠ *Apdo. 177–5150, Santa Cruz,* ☎ *382–6926,* ⅨⅩ *680–0208. 4 rooms with bath, 1 cabina. Restaurant, pool, horseback riding. No credit cards.*

$ 🏨 **Hotel Playa Junquillal.** Highly recommended for low-budget wan-
★   derers in search of a secret spot, the Hotel Playa Junquillal is an old-fashioned, funky little resort, short on amenities but long on charm.

After all, with a 3-km (2-mi) stretch of beach in your front yard, you can do without amenities. The only hotel on the beach proper, it is run by a shifting cast of American partners, all very friendly and happy to share stories over cold beers. The restaurant sits on one side of the quasi-landscaped courtyard, and the cabinas (with hot water) sit on the other. ✉ *Apdo. 22, Santa Cruz,* ☎ ℻ *653–0432; May–Sept. contact Robin and Mike Lake,* ✉ *Box 67, Kyburz, CA 95720,* ☎ *916/659–0714. 4 cabinas. Restaurant. No credit cards.*

NICOYA PENINSULA A TO Z

Arriving and Departing

By Boat
See Getting Around, *below.*

By Bus
PUNTARENAS TO CABO BLANCO

Buses(☎ 222–0064) run from San José (C. 12 between Avdas. 7 and 9) to Puntarenas daily, every 30 minutes 5 AM–7 PM (2 hrs).

NICOYA AND THE TEMPISQUE RIVER DELTA REGION

Buses (☎ 222–2750) run from San José (C. 14 between Avdas. 3 and 5) daily to Nicoya (includes Río Tempisque ferry) at 6 AM, 8 AM, 10 AM, 12:30 AM, and 2 PM. Buses to Liberia at 6:30 AM, 10 AM, 1:30 PM, and 5 PM, same location. Daily buses (☎ 221–7202) to Santa Cruz leave from San José's Calle 14 between Avenidas 1 and 3 every hour from 7 AM to 1 PM and at 2 PM, 4 PM, and 6 PM.

CENTRAL NICOYA BEACHES: PUNTA ISLITA TO NOSARA

Buses (☎ 222–2750) leave San José (C. 14 between Avdas. 3 and 5) daily at 6 AM for the six-hour trip to Nosara. Buses (☎ 222–2750) leave from Calle 14 between Avenidas 3 and 5 for Sámara daily at 12:30 PM (4½ hrs).

LIBERIA AND THE NORTHERN NICOYA BEACHES

Seven buses (☎ 222–1650) leave daily (7 AM–8 PM) from San José's Calle 14 between Avenidas 1 and 3 for Liberia (4 hrs). For Playa del Coco, take bus daily at 8 AM and 2 PM from Calle 14 between Avenidas 1 and 3 (5 hrs). For Hermosa and Playa Panamá, a bus (☎ 666–1249) departs daily at 3:20 PM (5 hrs) from Calle 12 between Avenidas 5 and 7. Buses (☎ 221–7202) for Brasilito–Flamingo–Potrero leave daily from Calle 20 between Avenidas 3 and 5 at 8 and 10 AM, and 3 and 5 PM (6 hrs). For Tamarindo, a bus (☎ 222–2750) leaves daily at 3:30 PM from Calle 14 between Avenidas 3 and 5 (5½ hrs). A bus (☎ 221–7202) bound for Junquillal leaves every day at 2 PM from Calle 20 between Avenidas 3 and 5.

By Car
Road access to the northwest is by way of the paved two-lane Inter-American Highway (CA1), which starts from the top of Paseo Colón in San José.

By Plane
Sansa (✉ C. 24, between Avda. Central and Avda. 1, San José, ☎ 506/221–9414 or 506/441–8035, ℻ 506/255–2176) and **Travelair** (✉ Aeropuerto Internacional Tobías Bolaños, Apdo 8–4920, ☎ 506/220–3054 or 506/232–7883, ℻ 506/220–0413) fly to San José, Liberia, Tamarindo, Carrillo, Nosara, Punta Islita, and Tambor. **Lacsa** (✉ La Uruca, San José, ☎ 296–0909 reservations, 506/290–2727) also flies direct from Miami to Liberia twice a week (Wednesday and

Saturday), before continuing on to San José and has return flights to Miami Thursday and Sunday. Other carriers, both charter and commercial, were planning flights into Liberia at press time; call your travel agent for current details.

Getting Around

By Boat

Note that these schedules are subject to change, especially as relates to the high and low seasons. If possible call ahead to verify schedules.

PUNTARENAS TO CABO BLANCO

The Puntarenas–Playa Naranjo car ferry (☎ 661–1069) takes 1½ hours and departs daily at 3:15 AM, 7 AM, 10:30 AM, 2:50 PM, and 7 PM. The 1½-hour Puntarenas–Paquera ferry departs daily at 6 AM, 11 AM, and 3 PM, returning at 6 AM, 10:30 AM, 2:30 PM, and 7:15 PM. The Tambor ferry departs from Puntarenas daily at 4:15 AM, 8:45 AM, 12:30 PM, and 5:30 PM. A passenger-only ferry leaves Puntarenas daily at 6 AM, returning at 2:30 PM. Bus links and cabs are available at the Nicoya ends of the ferry lines. Pedestrian-only ferry service from Montezuma to Paquera and Puntarenas is also available; just ask around in town.

NICOYA AND THE TEMPISQUE RIVER DELTA REGION

The Tempisque car ferry crosses continuously and takes 20 minutes; lines can get very long in the dry season.

By Bus

PUNTARENAS TO CABO BLANCO

Buses run to Montezuma from Paquera daily at 8 AM and 5 PM, returning at 5:30 AM and 2 PM. There may be schedule changes and added routes since press time: the best place to check for the latest routes and times is the tourist office in San José.

CENTRAL NICOYA BEACHES: PUNTA ISLITA TO NOSARA

Bus service within the area includes the following: to Garza, Guiones, and Nosara from Nicoya bus station daily at 1 PM; to Sámara and Carrillo from Nicoya weekdays at noon, 3 PM, and 4:15 PM, and weekends at 8 AM.

LIBERIA AND THE NORTHERN NICOYA BEACHES

Buses to Flamingo and Brasilito from Santa Cruz run daily at 6:30 AM and 3 PM. Buses to Tamarindo from Santa Cruz depart daily at 8 PM, returning at 6:45 AM.

By Car

Paved roads run down the spine of the Nicoya Peninsula all the way to Playa Naranjo, with just a few unpaved stretches. Once you get off the main highway, the pavement holds out only so far, and then dirt, dust, mud, potholes, and other factors come into play. The roads to Playa Sámara and Playa del Coco are paved all the way; every other destination requires some dirt road maneuvering. If you're headed down to the coast via unpaved roads, be sure to get as much information as possible, in advance, regarding the condition of the roads you plan to travel. Take a four-wheel-drive vehicle if possible.

Contacts and Resources

Car Rentals

Sol Rentacar (⊠ In front of Hotel El Bramadero, ☎ 666–2222). **Budget** (⊠ 10 km / 6 mi west of airport, ☎ 223–3284 main office, San José).

Emergencies

In case of emergency, dial ☎ 911. **Ambulance** (☎ 221–5818). **Fire** (☎ 118). **Police** (☎ 117 in towns; 127 in rural areas). **Traffic Police** (☎ 227–8030).

Guided Tours

ADVENTURE

JeriLin Ruhlow uses the Hotel Oasis del Pacific (⊠ Apdo. 200–5400, Puntarenas, ☎ FAX 661–1555) in Playa Naranjo as a base for her riveting sea-kayaking trips along the coast and among the islands of the Golfo de Nicoya.

DAY TRIPS

Day trips to the idyllic Isla Tortuga in the Golfo de Nicoya are very popular, and **Calypso Tours** (⊠ Arcadas building, 3rd fl., Apdo. 6941–1000, San José, ☎ 233–3617, FAX 256–6767) has been doing them the longest. **Guanacaste Tours** (☎ 666–0306) is recommended for day trips from within the northwest to Santa Rosa, Palo Verde, Playa Ostional, Playa Grande by night (to see turtles), and Arenal (☞ Chapter 4); guides pick up tour participants from large hotels in the area.

SPECIAL-INTEREST TOURS

Tikal Ecoadventures (⊠ Avdas. 2, between Cs. 7 and 9, Apdo. 6398–1000, San José, ☎ 223–2811) runs highly informative weeklong tours that take in Parque Nacional Carara, Parque Nacional Manuel Antonio, the Lomas Barbudal reserve, Playa Grande, Parque Nacional Santa Rosa, and Arenal (☞ Chapter 4). The excellent **Horizontes** (⊠ 150 m north of Pizza Hut Paseo Colón, San José, ☎ 222–2022) specializes in more independent tours with as few as eight people, including transport by four-wheel drive, naturalist guides, and guest lecturers.

Visitor Information

The tourist office in San José (☞ Visitor Information *in* San José A to Z, *in* Chapter 2) has information covering Guanacaste. In Liberia, the **Casa de la Cultura** (⊠ 3 blocks from Central Plaza, ☎ 666–1606) has local tourist information. It is open Monday–Saturday 8–4.

6 Central Pacific Costa Rica

This may be one of Costa Rica's smallest regions, but it is endowed with disproportionate natural assets. Playas Jacó, Hermosa, and Manuel Antonio promise sparkling sun, surf, and sand, and the Reserva Biológica Carara and Parque Nacional Manuel Antonio hold rare, beautiful species. And since its so close to San José, it is the perfect destination if you are in a hurry to start your rest and recreation.

THE REGION SOUTHWEST OF SAN JOSÉ packs in most of the attractions that would draw you to Costa Rica: lush tropical forests, palm-lined beaches, and varied terrain for an array of outdoor activities. The region—its Reserva Biológica Carara in particular—is a transition zone between the tropical dry forest of the northwest and the wet forests of the nearby Southern Pacific coast. Since most of the region's woodlands were cut years ago, rolling green pastures and oil palm plantations dominate the landscape, offering unforgettable horseback riding. The Parque Nacional Manuel Antonio, synonymous with tropical paradise, protects an indented stretch of coastal rain forest, a backdrop for strands of idyllic white-sand beaches. Despite the fact that the region's protected areas are among the smallest in the country, they are vibrant habitats fostering an amazing variety of flora and fauna, including such endangered species as the scarlet macaw and the Central American squirrel monkey. The sea jostling Playas Jacó and Manuel Antonio hosts abundant marine life, affording awesome snorkeling and world-class sportfishing. Ideal conditions for surfing, sea kayaking, horseback riding, rafting, hiking, and bird-watching also abound in this region, within just 160 km (100 mi) of San José. The rainy season may last a little longer here than in the northwest, but the Central Pacific still enjoys plenty of sunshine.

Updated by
David
Dudenhoefer

Pleasures and Pastimes

Dining

Since the central Pacific zone is one of the most-visited parts of Costa Rica, it is only natural that it should have some excellent dining options. Manuel Antonio and Jacó have restaurants with some of the best food in the country, but by no means do they have the dining market cornered—some of the region's isolated lodges also serve delicious and tasty local food. Given the area's world-class fishing, it's no surprise that seafood—from fresh caught dorado and mahimahi to scrumptious crustaceans—is the forte among the area's best chefs

Lodging

The central Pacific's accommodations are as varied as its scenery; you can choose from beachside cement boxes to luxury hotels—the country's premier establishments among them—perched on verdant hillsides. Manuel Antonio hosts some of the country's most expensive accommodations, charging more than $150 for a double during high season, but nearby Quepos has rates to please backpackers. As a rule, prices drop 20%–30% during low season.

Outdoor Excitement

There is no shortage of outdoor diversions to choose from in this corner of the country. Several white-water rivers flow down from the Cordillera de Talamanca chain to the northeast: Ríos Parrita, Naranjo, and the less accessible Savegre. Horseback riding can be done just about everywhere, and two working ranches near Orotina that double as hotels have enough trails to keep you in the saddle for a week. Skin diving is good in the Manuel Antonio area, and the offshore sportfishing is among the best in the world. The region also has great surfing, sea kayaking, and ocean excursions ranging from wave-runner tours to dolphin-watching sunset cruises.

Exploring Central Pacific Costa Rica

Attractions in the central Pacific zone lie conveniently close to each other, which makes it easy to combine beach time with forest exploration, or country living with marine diversions. Every one of its destinations lies between two and four hours from San José by road. The paved coastal highway, or Costanera, heads southeast from Orotina to Tárcoles, Jacó, Hermosa, and Quepos. The flight from San José to Quepos is speedy, a mere half hour.

Numbers in the text correspond to numbers in the margin and on the Central Pacific Costa Rica map.

Great Itineraries

IF YOU HAVE 3 DAYS

Fly directly to ☷ **Quepos** ⑦ and hit the beach at ☷ **Manuel Antonio.** If you are driving, be sure to stop at **Reserva Biológica Carara** ② on your way to Manuel Antonio. Get up early the next day and explore ☷ **Parque Nacional Manuel Antonio** ⑧. Spend the afternoon either horseback riding or relaxing on the beach. Dedicate the third morning to river rafting, skin diving, or another tour, then catch an afternoon flight back to San José.

IF YOU HAVE 6 DAYS

Spend the first two nights at one of the ranches near ☷ **Orotina** ①, enjoying horseback riding, rafting, and bird-watching, and from there explore the **Reserva Biológica Carara** ②. On the third morning, head to either the ☷ **Tárcoles** ③ area or ☷ **Jacó** ④ to get your beach and surfing fix. On day four head south to ☷ **Manuel Antonio** or **Quepos** ⑦, spending day five fishing, skin diving, rafting, horseback riding, or lounging on the beach. Visit the **Parque Nacional Manuel Antonio** ⑧ early on day six, then return to San José after lunch. Since Quepos and Manuel Antonio have so much to offer, an alternative would be to fly straight there, and dedicate all five days to that diverse beach resort.

When to Tour Central Pacific Costa Rica

The weather in the central Pacific region follows the same dry- and rainy-season weather patterns common to the rest of the Pacific slope, which means lots of sun from December to May, frequent rain from September to November. Since you'll have to share the area with plenty of tourists during the dry months, consider touring the region during the low season. The weather actually tends to be perfect in July and August, with lots of sunny days and occasional light rain.

CENTRAL PACIFIC HINTERLANDS

Orotina, Reserva Biológica Carara, Tárcoles

Beaches may be this region's biggest draw, but the countryside hosts vast haciendas interspersed with patches of tropical wilderness where you might spy exotic wildlife from white-faced capuchin monkeys to baby blue herons, and estuaries where crocodiles lurk amidst the mangroves. Because it is an ecological transition zone, it has high biological diversity, making it great for bird-watchers and other nature enthusiasts.

Atenas

35 km (22 mi) west of San José.

National Geographic magazine once listed Atenas as one of the 12 places with the best climates in the world, and this is the little town's only

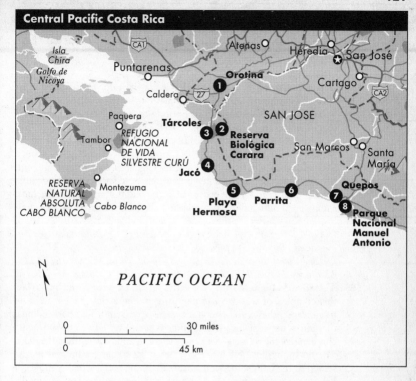

Central Pacific Costa Rica

Isla Chira
Golfo de Nicoya
Puntarenas
Atenas
Heredia
San José
Orotina ❶
Cartago
Caldera
27
SAN JOSE
Paquera
Tárcoles
❸ ❷
Reserva Biológica Carara
San Marcos
Santa María
Tambor
REFUGIO NACIONAL DE VIDA SILVESTRE CURÚ
❹
Jacó
RESERVA NATURAL ABSOLUTA CABO BLANCO
Montezuma
Cabo Blanco
❺
Playa Hermosa
Parrita
❻
Quepos
❼
❽
Parque Nacional Manuel Antonio

N

PACIFIC OCEAN

0 — 30 miles
0 — 45 km

claim to fame. In addition to having spectacular weather, Atenas is a pleasantly quiet, traditional community that few foreigners visit, despite the fact that it lies on the main route to the Central Pacific beaches. Some well-kept wooden and adobe houses are scattered around a small church and central plaza, and surrounding the town are coffee farms, cattle ranches, and patches of forest. Just to the west of Atenas, the road to Orotina winds its way down the mountains past breathtaking views.

Lodging

$$$ 🏨 **El Cafetal Inn.** The friendly owners of this B&B—a Salvadorean/Colombian couple—go out of their way to make their guests comfortable and help with travel plans. Their small two-story cement lodge is set on a hill amidst a coffee farm. The larger tower rooms have curved windows for panoramic views. Complimentary breakfast is usually served on the patio out back. Trails through the surrounding countryside make for perfect walking routes, and horseback tours can be arranged. This place is halfway between Grecia and Atenas, and the same distance from the airport as from San José. ✉ *Apdo. 105, Atenas, on highway 1 km (½ mi) west of Grecia, left just before bridge, follow signs,* ☎ *466–5785,* ℻ *466–7028. 10 rooms with bath. Restaurant, pool. AE, MC, V.*

Orotina

❶ *62 km (38 mi) southwest of San José.*

One of the central Pacific's oldest communities, Orotina is a laid-back commercial center and transportation hub in the heart of an important agricultural region. The town is centered around an attractive park shaded by tall tropical trees, with a modern church towering over its eastern end. The town market, a rickety building near the park, is a good place to pick up some of the fruits, such as mangoes, grown in the area. The main agricultural endeavor around Orotina, however, is cattle ranching; the two haciendas to the west of town that have been converted into hotels attract travelers.

Lodging

$$$ ⚇ **Dundee Ranch.** This 850-acre hacienda right up the road from Ha-
★ cienda Doña Marta (☞ *below*) is something between a dude ranch and a nature lodge. Two dozen tour options keep you busy, the most popular of which are horseback trips into the ranch's protected forest. You can actually see a bit of wildlife creeping near the rooms, but the wildest part of the ranch is the El Cañón del Río Machuca (Machuca River Canyon), where monkeys, macaws, iguanas, and toucans abound. The old ranch house and a newer building hold spacious, comfortable guest rooms with colorful bedspreads, air-conditioning, and ceiling fans; rooms open onto a portico surrounding a garden courtyard. In a shallow lagoon nearby are the resident waterfowl and crocodile. ⊠ *Apdo. 7812–1000, San José, 16 km (10 mi) west of Orotina, take Costanera toward Puntarenas, turn right at 3rd intersection, look for ABOPAC factory, then follow signs,* ☎ *428–8776 or 267–6222,* FAX *267–6229. 25 rooms with bath. Restaurant, pool, horseback riding. AE, MC, V.*

$$$ ⚇ **Hacienda Doña Marta.** Part cattle ranch, part romantic hideaway,
★ this complex of wooden *cabinas* surrounding a tiny pool shaded by *marañón* (cashew) and coconut trees is a real find. Bamboo ceilings, tile floors, expansive showers, and sweet country-style appointments characterize the rooms—each one different, and prettier than the next. The no-funny-business kitchen crew cooks stellar traditional meals, served in the handsome wood-beamed dining room where you'll find handmade pottery for sale. Horseback riding among acres of woods, cattle pastures, and mango trees is a must, as is early-morning bird-watching. ⊠ *Apdo. 463–1000, San José, 18 km (11 mi) west of Orotina; take Costanera toward Puntarenas, turn right at 3rd intersection, look for ABOPAC factory, then follow signs,* ☎ *253–6514 or 428–8126. 6 cabinas and 2 rooms. Dining room, pool, horseback riding. No credit cards.*

Reserva Biológica Carara

❷ *83 km (51 mi) southwest of San José.*

Situated between Costa Rica's drier northwest and more humid south, Reserva Biológica Carara (Carara Biological Reserve) (also ☞ Chapter 10) is part of an ecological transition zone, and consequently contains a great diversity of flora and fauna. Much of the 18-sq-mi reserve is covered in primary forest growing on steep slopes, the massive trees laden with vines and epiphytes. The relatively sparse undergrowth makes wildlife easier to see here than in many other parks—though animals are always tough to spot. If you're lucky, you might see boat-billed herons, blue-crowned motmots, scarlet macaws, roseate spoonbills, crocodiles, iguanas, coatis, and monkeys.

You'll find the first trail on the left shortly after the bridge that spans the Río Tárcoles. It leads to a horseshoe lagoon, which was abandoned as an oxbow lake by the meandering Tárcoles. It is now almost entirely covered with water hyacinths and is home to water birds such as the jacana, as well as large crocodiles. The main ranger station is several kilometers farther south, and next to it another trail heads into the forest. Remember that the earlier in the morning you get to there, the more likely you are to see the animals. ⊠ *CA1 from San José to*

In case you want to see the world.

In case you want to be welcomed there.

We're here to see that you're always welcomed at establishments everywhere. That's why millions of people carry the American Express® Card – for peace of mind, confidence, and security, around the world or just around the corner.

do more ®

Cards

In case you're running low.

We're here to help with more than 118,000 Express Cash locations around the world. In order to enroll, just call American Express before you start your vacation.

do more

Express Cash

And just in case.

We're here with American Express® Travelers Cheques and Cheques *for Two.*® They're the safest way to carry money on your vacation and the surest way to get a refund, practically anywhere, anytime.

Another way we help you...

do more

Travelers
Cheques

EYES AFLIGHT IN COSTA RICA

IF YOU VISIT A COSTA RICAN cloud forest, you'll probably have your eyes peeled for the resplendent quetzal, or the three-wattled bellbird, but if you're here between October and April, you'll actually be just as likely to see a Kentucky warbler. Experienced birders shouldn't be surprised to see that some of their feathered friends from home made similar vacation plans, but many of you probably never realized that when northern birds fly south for the winter, they don't all head to Miami.

Seasonal visitors are just part—about a quarter—of the amazing avian panorama in Costa Rica. More than 830 bird species have been identified here, more than the United States and Canada have between them—all in an area about half the size of Kentucky. The country is consequently a mecca for amateur ornithologists, who flock here by the thousands. Though the big attractions tend to be such spectacular species as the keel-billed toucan and scarlet macaw, it is the diversity of shape, size, coloration, and behavior that makes bird-watching in Costa Rica so fascinating.

The country's varied avian inhabitants range in size from the scintillant hummingbird, standing a mere 2½ inches tall and weighing just over two grams, to the long-legged jabiru stork, which reaches a height of more than 4 ft, and a weight of 14 pounds. The diversity of form and color ranges from such striking creatures as the showy scarlet macaw and the quirky purple gallinule to the relatively inconspicuous, and seemingly ubiquitous, clay-colored robin, which is, surprisingly enough, Costa Rica's national bird. These robins may look a bit plain, but their song is a melodious one, and since the males sing almost constantly toward the end of the dry season—the beginning of their mating season—local legend has it they call the rains, which play a vital role in a nation so dependent on agriculture.

Foreigners tend to ooh and aah at the sight of those birds associated with the tropics: parrots, parakeets, and macaws; toucans and toucanets; and the elusive but legendary resplendent quetzal. But there are many other equally impressive species aflight, such as the motmots, with their distinctive racquet tails, *oropéndolas* (golden orioles), which build remarkable hanging nests, and an amazing array of hawks, kites, and falcons.

On the color scale, the country's tanagers, euphonias, manakins, cotingas, and trogons are some of its loveliest plumed creatures, but none of them match the iridescence of the hummingbirds and their hyperactive cousins. Costa Rica hosts 51 members of the hummingbird family, compared to the just one species for all of the United States east of the Rocky Mountains. A bit of time spent near a hummingbird feeder will treat you to an unforgettable display of accelerated aerial antics and general pugnacity.

YOU JUST MIGHT FIND that the more you observe Costa Rica's birds, the more interesting they get. Bird-watching can be done everywhere in the country—all you need is a pair of binoculars and the field guide *A Guide to the Birds of Costa Rica,* by Stiles and Skutch. Wake up early, get out into the woods or the garden, focus those binoculars, and you'll quickly be enchanted by the beauty on the wing.

Atenas turnoff, turn left and follow signs for Jacó; on left after cross-ing Río Tárcoles. ☎ *$6.* ☉ *Daily 8–4.*

Tárcoles

❸ *90 km (56 mi) southwest of San José.*

Although the town of Tárcoles doesn't warrant a stop, it is the departure point for a boat tour up the Río Tárcoles. Two exceptional hotels are nearby, as is a spectacular waterfall set in a private nature reserve. If you pull over just after crossing the **bridge,** you can often spot exotic birds strutting and crocodiles lounging along the banks of the Río Tár-coles (bring your binoculars). The entrance to Tárcoles is on the west side of the road, just south of the Reserva Biológica Carara—across the highway is a dirt road that leads to the Hotel Villa Lapas and the waterfall reserve.

The **Manatial de Agua Viva** is a 600-ft waterfall in the heart of a pri-vate reserve across from Tárcoles. The waterfall flows into 10 natural pools, perfect for a refreshing dip after the hike into the reserve. The forest surrounding the waterfall is home to parrots, monkeys, scarlet macaws, and most of the other animals found in the adjacent Reserva Biológica Carara. A 2½-km (1½-mi) trail makes a loop through the woods, passing the waterfall and pools; it can take from 40 minutes to two hours to hike, depending on how much bird-watching you do. The entrance is 5 km (3 mi) from the coastal highway, up the same dirt road that leads to Villa Lapas. ☎ *$7.* ☉ *Daily 8–5.*

Lodging

$$$$ 🏨 **Villa Caletas.** Set amidst the rain forest atop a promontory, this el-
★ egant collection of villas built along lush slopes may seem remote, but it is only minutes from Jacó and Carara. Although the architecture is reminiscent of southeast Asia, guest rooms are decorated in the French style, with fine antiques and art, black furniture, and sweeping draperies. French is also the predominant influence in the cuisine, served in an attractive open-air restaurant. The cleverly designed pool appears to blend into the horizon. The entrance is on the west side of the road between Tárcoles and Jacó. ⊠ *Apdo. 12358–1000, San José,* ☎ *257–3653 or 382–5794,* ℻ *222–2059. 8 rooms with bath, 6 suites, 11 vil-las. Restaurant, bar, pool. AE, MC, V.*

$$$ 🏨 **Hotel Villa Lapas.** The grounds of this hotel lies, just a short drive from Carara and the waterfall reserve, are shaded by tall trees, with a stream flowing by, making it a great spot for bird-watching. A trail heads up the valley into the hotel's patch of protected forest. White bungalows with barrel-tile roofs and small porches hold two rooms each; those closest to the restaurant have views of the stream. Rooms have tile floors, wood ceilings, desks, and ceiling fans. The open-air restaurant overlooks the stream and forest and serves international cui-sine. Reservations are handled by Alegro Resorts. ⊠ *Apdo. 171–5400, Puntarenas, across from entrance to Tárcoles,* ☎ *663–0811,* ℻ *663–1516. 46 rooms with bath. Restaurant, bar, pool. AE, MC, V.*

Outdoor Activities and Sports

BOAT TRIPS

Río Tárcoles boat trips are run daily, and can be booked by tour op-erators (**Fantasy Tours,** ⊠ Best Western hotel lobby, ☎ 643–3032), or the receptionists of hotels in Jacó or the Tárcoles area.

COAST NEAR SAN JOSÉ
Jacó, Playa Hermosa, and Manuel Antonio

Along this short stretch of Pacific coast are some of Costa Rica's most accessible beaches and the popular Parque Nacional Manuel Antonio. Since its attractions lie just a few hours' drive from San José, it is a region where travelers who are short on time can get a quick overview of Costa Rica's rich natural splendor.

Jacó

❹ *108 km (67 mi) southwest of San José, 70 km (43 mi) north of Quepos.*

The relative proximity to San José, coupled with the attractiveness of its wide sandy bay, has contributed to Jacó's popularity as a resort. More than 50 well-dispersed hotels reside here, but most of them are hidden behind the palms, and because it is such a long beach, you may get the impression that the place is relatively quiet and undeveloped. But during high season, especially holidays, it can be bustling. If you do want fun in the sun and nightlife, this is the closest beach resort to the capital. Aside from sunbathing and surfing, you can rent bicycles and motor scooters to explore the countryside, go horseback riding, or take a tour to Reserva Biológica Carara or the Río Tárcoles.

The gray sand of Jacó's long, palm-lined **Playa Jacó** can burn the soles of your feet on a sunny afternoon. It's a popular spot with surfers due to the consistency of its waves, but riptides make the sea hazardous for swimmers when the waves are big. Those traveling with children may want to hit the **miniature golf course** on the town's main drag.

Dining and Lodging

$$ ✕ **Chatty Cathy's.** This small, second-floor restaurant in the heart of Jacó is the place to go for breakfast. The friendly Canadian owners serve an array of fast-breaking favorites—banana pancakes, bagels, bacon, hash browns, cinnamon buns—as well some tasty inventions of their own, and a small lunch menu. The name's no joke; she'll happily talk your ear off if you let her. ⊠ *Across from Rayo Azul supermarket,* ☎ *No phone. Reservations not accepted. No credit cards. Closed Mon., Tues., and Apr. No dinner.*

$$ ✕ **El Recreo.** El Recreo probably has Jacó's most extensive seafood menu—if it swims in the sea, they probably serve it. Sure there are a few meat and vegetable dishes on the menu, but it is dominated by tuna, lobster, shrimp, and mahimahi, all prepared in a variety of ways. Seating is beneath a big thatched roof overlooking Jacó's main street; a colorful marine mural covers the only wall. ⊠ *Across from Rayo Azul supermarket,* ☎ *643–1172. Reservations not accepted. AE, MC, V.*

$$ ✕ **Killer Munchies.** This popular restaurant on Jacó's main street has been feeding happy residents and travelers alike for years. The attractive open-air restaurant overlooks the street, and what packs 'em in is the food. The menu is eclectic—burritos and other Tex-Mex treats, a few pastas, and salads—but the big draw is the pizza, cooked in a wood-burning oven. ⊠ *300 yds south of the Best Western Hotel,* ☎ *643–3354. Reservations not accepted. No credit cards. No lunch weekdays, closed Tues.*

$$ ✕ **Villa Creole.** The restaurant at this quiet bed-and-breakfast ½ km (⅓ mi) inland from downtown Jacó is a popular dinner spot. The Belgian owners serve a fairly traditional selection of fine French cuisine, as well as interesting nightly specials and a theme dinner every Friday night. The restaurant itself is pretty simple—a few tables under a thatched roof—but the food is simply delicious. They offer take-out service for people staying in the beach hotels. ⊠ *500 yds east of Jacó center, Apdo. 76,* ☎ *643–3298. MC, V.*

$$–$$$$ ★ 🏨 **Hotel Club del Mar.** It's easy to forget you're in busy Jacó when you stay at this secluded spot on the southern extreme of the beach. Bungalows are shaded by giant trees, and iguanas lounge on the lawn. Handsome superior rooms have green tile floors, high ceilings, and wooden shutters that open onto porches or balconies. Smaller standard rooms in back have kitchenettes, sitting areas, and balconies; budget rooms are a bit cramped. The restaurant is not only one of the few in Jacó with an ocean view, it also serves some of the best food in town. ⊠ *Follow Costanera to Quepos, turn right at first street past service station, Apdo. 107–4023,* ☎ ℻ *643–3194. 18 rooms with bath. Restaurant, bar, pool. MC, V.*

$$$ 🏨 **Tangerí Chalets.** The first six rooms in these two-story cement buildings have ocean views, whereas the remaining eight overlook the hotel's lawn and two pools. All rooms have tile floors, high ceilings, two double beds, air-conditioning, and small balconies or porches. The eccentrically designed bungalows each have a kitchen, covered patio, and eight beds, perfect for a family or small group. ⊠ *Apdo. 622–4050, Alajuela, on main street, between Jacó center and Best Western,* ☎ *643–3001,* ℻ *643–3636. 14 rooms with bath, 10 bungalows. Restaurant, pool, basketball. AE, MC, V.*

$$–$$$ ★ 🏨 **Aparthotel Flamboyant.** This small, quiet, oceanfront hotel is a good deal, especially if you take advantage of the cooking facilities. All the rooms have kitchenettes, breakfast bars, tile floors, ceiling fans, and one double and one single bed. They also have small terraces with chairs overlooking the verdant pool area, where there's a grill for guests' use. It's all just a few steps from the beach, and Jacó's busy main strip. ⊠ *Jacó center, behind Flamboyant Restaurant, Apdo. 018, Puntarenas,* ☎ *643–3146,* ℻ *643–1068. 9 rooms with bath. Kitchenettes, pool. AE, MC, V.*

$$ 🏨 **Cabinas Alice.** Spread along a narrow oceanfront property, these cabinas open onto a lawn that doubles as a parking lot. The rooms closest to the beach are the best bets: they're bright, with newer kitchenettes, tiled floors, front porches, and lots of windows. Older rooms in back are a bit dark, but considerably less expensive. The modern, open-air restaurant serves good seafood and Costa Rican standards. ⊠ *Jacó, end of the first street south of Red Cross,* ☎ ℻ *643–3061. 22 rooms with bath. Restaurant, kitchenettes, pool. AE, MC, V.*

$$ 🏨 **Mar de Luz.** It may be a couple of blocks from the beach, and it doesn't look like much from the street, but Mar de Luz is a surprisingly pleasant place. The Dutch owners are dedicated to cleanliness and details, such as the grill next to the pool, the well-stocked kitchenettes, and air-conditioning. Pastel older rooms have two queen-size beds and small porches. Split-level newer rooms are a bit larger, with attractive stone walls, white tile floors, and windows overlooking the gardens. ⊠ *50 yds east of main road, across from Tangerí,* ☎ ℻ *643–3259. 20 rooms with bath. Kitchenettes, pool. MC, V.*

Nightlife and the Arts

During the high season, Jacó gets lively when the sun goes down. Cut loose at the popular disco **La Central** (☎ 643–3076), on the beach opposite Tienda La Flor. You can also dance at **Los Tucanes** (☎ 643–3226), next door to La Central. Those who prefer a seat and to watch a game should hit the **sports bar** by the Copacabana Hotel's pool.

Outdoor Activities and Sports

SURFING

Jacó has several excellent beach breaks, which are best around high tide. The town's reputation as a surfer's paradise has spread far and wide, and you'll consequently see dozens of surfboard-toting tourists. Several places rent surfboards, such as **Chuck's** (☎ no phone), on the main street just north of the Hacienda Restaurant. If you're going to spend more than a week surfing, it might be cheaper to buy a used board, and sell it before you leave.

Playa Hermosa

⑤ *113 km (70 mi) southwest of San José, 5 km (3 mi) south of Jacó.*

Just over the rocky ridge that defines the southern end of Jacó is Playa Hermosa, a swath of gray sand stretching off to the southeast as far as the eye can see. The northern end of Playa Hermosa is a popular spot with surfers; because of the beach's angle, it often has waves when Jacó and other spots are flat. But you don't have to be a surfer to enjoy Hermosa, a quiet alternative to Jacó. If you want to swim, keep in mind that dangerous rip currents are common when the waves are big.

Lodging

$$$ 🏨 **Fuego del Sol.** A colorful tropical garden surrounds the pool area of this modern beachfront hotel. There's a small, open-air sports bar by the pool, next to which is a simple restaurant with an ocean view. Rooms are in a two-story cement building; all have tile floors, ceiling fans, air-conditioning, and rain-forest wall paintings. Those upstairs have high wooden ceilings and balconies overlooking either the pool area or beach, and those downstairs have small terraces. ☎ 643–3737, FAX 643–3736. 20 rooms with bath. Restaurant, bar, pool, exercise room. AE, MC, V.

$$ 🏨 **Ola Bonita.** Just a few steps from the surf break, this two-story building with a barrel-tile roof is a nicer alternative to Hermosa's other low-budget hotels. Rooms have red-tile floors, white-stuccoed walls, simple kitchenettes, fans, and one bunk and one double bed. There's a tiny pool out front if you tire of the ocean. ⊠ Playa Hermosa, ☎ FAX 643–3990. 5 rooms with bath. Kitchenettes, pool. MC, V.

Outdoor Activities and Sports

HORSEBACK RIDING

If you tire of the surf and sand, **Hermosa Stables** (☎ 643–3808) runs a nice horseback tour into the nearby rain forest.

SURFING

Most people who stay at Playa Hermosa are there for this one thing. Because of the beach's angle, it almost always has waves, even when most other breaks are flat. The surf is best at high tide. Boards can be rented, purchased, and repaired at nearby Jacó (☞ *above*).

Parrita

⑥ *150 km (93 mi) southwest of San José, 46 km (28½ mi) south of Jacó, 24 km (15 mi) north of Quepos.*

Set in the heart of an African palm plantation, Parrita is a dusty town of painted wooden bungalows. First planted in 1945 by the United Fruit Company after their banana plantations were decimated by Panama disease, the palms are cultivated for their fruit, from which oil is extracted for margarine, cooking oil, scent, and soap. Though the town has little to offer travelers, a dirt road that heads west from the Costanera just south of town leads to **Playa Palo Seco,** an endless beach backed by palms and mangrove swamps.

Quepos

❼ *174 km (108 mi) southwest of San José, 70 km (43 mi) south of Jacó.*

With around 12,000 inhabitants, Quepos is the largest and most important town in this corner of the country. The town owes its name to the Indian tribe that inhabited the area when the first Spaniard, Juan Vásquez de Coronado, rode through the region in 1563. Though there is some controversy as to whether those Indians were called Quepos or Quepoa, it is known that they lived by a combination of farming, hunting, and fishing, until the violence and disease that accompanied the Spanish conquest wiped them out.

For centuries following the conquest, Quepos hardly existed, but in the 1930s, the United Fruit Company put it on the map, building a banana port there and bringing in workers from other parts of Central America to populate the area. The town thrived for a decade, but when Panama disease decimated the banana plantations around 1945, the fruit company switched to the less lucrative oil palms, and the area slipped into a prolonged depression. Only during the past decade have revenues from tourism and fishing lifted the town out of that extended slump, and it owes the renaissance of its natural beauty to nearby Parque Nacional Manuel Antonio (☞ *below*).

Dining and Lodging

$$–$$$ ✕ **El Gran Escape.** This unpretentious wooden building on Quepos' wa-
   ★   terfront street is the place to go for seafood. It's a favorite spot with sport fishermen—they've got a "you catch 'em, we cook 'em" policy—so you can be sure the fish is fresh. The menu ranges from broiled shrimp with a tropical sauce to catch of the day prepared any of a half dozen ways. They've got an impressive array of appetizers, including such unheard-of-in-these-parts items as crab cakes, as well as a good selection of burgers and Tex-Mex standards. And as if that weren't enough, there's a sushi bar upstairs. ⊠ *Waterfront,* ☎ *777–0395. Reservations not accepted. V. Closed Tues. and 2 wks in June.*

$$$ 🏨 **Costa Verde.** The builders of this place, near the end of the road to
   ★   Manuel Antonio, were careful to damage the forest as little as possible. The hotel is therefore surrounded by lush foliage, where you might spot squirrel monkeys, sloths, iguanas, and a variety of birds in the branches outside your room. Two types of rooms are spread through five buildings: smaller efficiencies, short on privacy, and spacious studios, with tile floors, larger beds, tables, chairs, and kitchenettes. All of them have ceiling fans, lots of screened windows, and large balconies shared between two rooms. An open-air restaurant serves good seafood and killer tropical drinks. ⊠ *Apdo. 106,* ☎ *777–0584,* 𝔽𝔸𝕏 *777–0560. 44 rooms with bath. Restaurant, bar, kitchenettes, 2 pools. AE, DC, MC, V.*

$$$ 🏨 **Villas Nicolas.** The more elevated of these attractive tiered apart-
   ★   ments—Mediterranean white with barrel-tile roofs—have wonderful views over the Pacific. The more private rooms at the bottom look out at the jungle, where there's usually some interesting creature stirring. Half the units have well-equipped kitchens; all have terra-cotta floors and large balconies furnished with wooden chairs and hammocks. Some interconnect to form larger units. Waterfalls unite separate pools. It's a tasteful, friendly place that has very competitive rates during the

low season. ⊠ *Apdo. 236,* ☎ *777–0481,* ⒻⒶⓍ *777–0451. 21 rooms with bath. Restaurant, pool. V.*

$ 🖬 **Hotel Malinche.** A block west of the bus terminal, in Quepos, this hotel has older rooms that are a bargain. They are simple but bright, with tile floors, bare white walls, small beds, fans, and small tiled baths. Some rooms have carpeting, air-conditioning, and hot water, but they cost about twice as much. ⊠ *Center of Quepos,* ☎ ⒻⒶⓍ *777–0093. 29 rooms with bath. MC, V.*

Nightlife and the Arts

The popular disco **El Arco Iris** is on the north side of the estuary. Large, glitzy **Maracas** is south of town, next to the docks. There is a casino in the **Hotel Kamuk** (☎ 777–0379) in Quepos.

Outdoor Activities and Sports

HORSEBACK RIDING

Lynch Travel (⊠ Quepos, ☎ 777–1170) has two horseback tours, a three-hour ride to a scenic overlook, and an all-day trip to the Catarata de Nara, a waterfall that pours into a natural swimming pool. **Costa Rica Adventure Travel** (⊠ Next to Si Como No hotel, Manuel Antonio, ☎ 777–0850) offers a more exclusive horseback excursion through the pristine rain forest of the Rain Maker private reserve.

SPORTFISHING

The Southwest's waters have some of the country's best deep-sea fishing, and Quepos is one of the best ports from which to head out. There are fewer boats trolling those waters and plenty of sailfish, marlin, wahoo, roosterfish, yellowfin tuna, and snapper. Charters are available out of Quepos: **Costa Rican Dreams** (☎ 777–0593), **Sportfishing Costa Rica** (☎ 257–3553 or 800/862–1003), and **Lynch Travel** (☞ *above*).

WHITE-WATER RAFTING

There are three white-water rivers near Quepos: the Parrita (class II–III), perfect if this is your first rafting trip, and the Naranjo (class III–IV), which requires some experience. The Parrita can be run in rafts from May till January, when it drops so low that it is only navigable in two-person inflatable "duckies." The Naranjo can only be descended from June to December. Both are run by **Iguana Tours** (☎ 777–1262). The third, and most beautiful river, is the Savegre (class II–III), which flows past plenty of rain forest and wildlife, and is navigated from June to March by **Amigos del Rió** (☎ 777–1531).

Ↄ If you're traveling with children, or have a keen interest in wildlife, you may want to visit the **Jardín Gaia,** a small zoo that rehabilitates former pets and injured animals and releases them back into the wild. The zoo holds mostly parrots and macaws that were confiscated by government wildlife officials, as well as monkeys that were electrocuted while playing on power lines. ⊠ *Left side of road to Manuel Antonio, 2½ km (1½ mi) from Quepos.* 🖬 *$5.* ☉ *Thurs.–Tues. 2–5.*

Parque Nacional Manuel Antonio

❽ *Park begins 5 km (3 mi) south of Quepos, 181 km (112 mi) southwest of San José, 77 km (48 mi) south of Jacó.*

It doesn't take long to figure out why the Parque Nacional Manuel Antonio (Manuel Antonio National Park, also ☞ Chapter 10), with its golden beaches and lush coastal forest, has become one of Costa Rica's most famous destinations. It is undeniably one of the country's most attractive parks, but it can get crowded during the high season, when you'll want to get there as early as possible. The parks service, for its part, has responded by placing a cap on the number of people allowed into the park on any given day and by closing it to visitors on Monday. Little more than a collection of hotels and restaurants itself, the town of **Manuel Antonio** is actually just a bedroom community of Quepos (☞ *above*).

Though the park is small—only 2½ sq mi—it protects a remarkable stretch of coast comprising three idyllic white-sand beaches backed by luxuriant forest. Though many of the biggest trees were knocked down by a hurricane in 1993, some impressively large bully, black locust, cow, kapok, and ficus trees survived. Mangrove swamps, marshland, and coral reefs contribute further to the park's biodiversity. Manuel Antonio is home to endangered Central American squirrel monkeys, as well as two- and three-toed sloths, green and black iguanas, white-faced monkeys, and agoutis, which are large jungle rodents. Be careful of the *manzanillo* tree (indicated by warning signs), whose leaves, bark, and fruit—which resemble apples—secrete a gooey substance that irritates the skin. Also, do not feed or touch the monkeys, which have seen so many tourists that they sometimes walk right up to them, and have bitten several overfriendly visitors.

Plan for sunbathing, swimming, snorkeling, hiking, and a respite at the picnic area; spending a morning or full day is advisable. To enter the park, you'll need to cross a narrow estuary, waist-deep at high tide, ankle-deep at low tide. The first beach after the ranger station, **Playa Espadilla Sur,** is the longest and least crowded, since it is rougher than the second beach. At its southern end is a tombolo (isthmus formed from sedimentation and accumulated debris) leading to a steep forested path that makes a loop on **Punta Catedral.** The lovely, palm-lined strand north of Espadilla Sur is **Playa Espadilla,** popular with sunbathers, surfers, volleyball players, and vacationing Tico families. Inexpensive beachfront restaurants are perfect for a cool drink while watching the waves go by. Unfortunately, there are deadly rip currents off this beach when the waves are big. To the east is the precipitous vegetation-crowned **Isla Mogote,** one of the park's 12 islands and site of pre-Columbian Quepos Indian burials. East of the tombolo is **Playa Manuel Antonio,** a small, sandy, and relatively safe swimming beach. At low tide you can see what little remains of a Quepos Indian turtle trap on the right—the Indians stuck poles in the semicircular rock formation there, which would trap turtles as the tide receded. This deep bay is a good snorkeling area, with coral formations a mere shell's toss from the beach. Walking even farther east you arrive at the rockier, more secluded beach of **Playa Puerto Escondido,** where people sometimes sunbathe nude. ☞ *$6.* ☉ *Tues.–Sun. 8–4.*

Dining and Lodging

$$–$$$ ✕ **Barba Roja.** This open-air restaurant with sweeping views over the Manuel Antonio shoreline has a reputation as lofty as its setting. The dining room is furnished with dark hardwoods and decorated with colorful prints. Food takes a close second to atmosphere; try the daily fish specials and excellent sandwiches at lunchtime. Desserts are delicious, and breakfasting is quite popular, but the view is never more impressive than at sunset. ☎ *777–0331. Reservations not accepted. V. No lunch Mon.*

$$–$$$ ✕ **Karolas.** Nestled in the forest just below the Barba Roja, with tables on two simple patios surrounded by greenery, Karolas makes up for its lack of an ocean view with the quality of its cuisine. The menu is limited, but features such varied choices as chili con carne and chicken cacciatore. Fresh fish and shrimp dishes are the specialties, as are homemade desserts—leave room for a piece of macadamia pie. At

night, this is easily Manuel Antonio's most attractive, intimate restaurant. They also serve breakfast. Reservations are recommended. ☎ 777–1557. V.

$$$$ ★ 🏨 **La Mariposa.** High on a promontory, Manuel Antonio's classiest hotel has the best view in town, perhaps in the country: a sweeping panorama of verdant hills, pale beaches, rocky islands, and shimmering Pacific. The main building is a white Spanish-style villa with an open-air dining room and pool area below. Older, split-level units are perched along the edge of the ridge, and have sitting rooms, balcony bedrooms, and conservatory bathrooms alive with plants. Newer one-level suites and deluxe rooms have hot tubs and cost slightly less. There are also a few rooms above the restaurant, which are smaller and less private. ☎ 777–0355, FAX 777–0050. *22 rooms and villas with bath. Restaurant, bar, pool. MC, V.*

$$$$ 🏨 **Si Como No.** This eco-friendly place uses solar power, energy-efficient air-conditioning systems, and very little hardwoods, and was designed to damage as little of the forest as possible. The result is an attractive inn surrounded by the rain forest, where monkeys and birds can often be spotted. Rooms are tasteful, with tile floors and stained-glass windows in the bathrooms; suites have small kitchens and balconies. Two suites join to make a villa, a good deal for two couples or a family. The blue-tiled pool has an artificial cascade flowing into it, a water slide, and swim-up bar. The hotel has a poolside grill, a formal restaurant serving fine Costa Rican cuisine, and a small movie theater. ☎ 777–1250; 800/237–8201 in the U.S., FAX 777–1093. *6 rooms with bath, 32 suites. 2 restaurants, 2 bars, pool, cinema. AE, MC, V.*

$$$$ 🏨 **Tulemar Bungalows.** The scenery surrounding these octagonal bungalows is impressive, and since the walls are almost completely made of windows, the rooms take good advantage of it. The bungalows are spacious, and each has a small kitchen, a sitting area with hideaway bed, and a large bath with tub. A paved road winds down past the pool and grill and through the forest to a small private beach, complete with a rustic bar and kayaks. The hotel provides transportation to and from the beach, but a walk down early in the morning makes for the perfect bird-watching expedition. ☎ 777–0580, FAX 777–1579. *14 bungalows. Bar, kitchenettes, pool, beach, boating. AE, MC, V.*

$$$ 🏨 **Hotel Playa Espadilla.** This small hotel a short walk from the beach and national park entrance has its own forest reserve. The owners' land was declared part of the park decades ago, but they were never paid for it, so they petitioned the government to create a private preserve. A two-story cement building holds simple rooms with tile floors, air-conditioning, and kitchenettes. There's a blue-tile pool and small bar under a barrel-tile roof in back, surrounded by a large lawn bordered by the reserve's thick foliage. They also have some cheaper cabinas nearby, which are smaller, older, and lacking air-conditioning. ☎ FAX 777–0903. *16 rooms with bath. Bar, kitchenettes, pool. AE, MC, V.*

$$$ 🏨 **Villas El Parque.** These wooden apartments are stacked up on the southern slope of the hill that separates Quepos from Manuel Antonio, offering breathtaking views of the national park and adjacent coastline. Rooms are bright and spacious, with large seaward balconies complete with chairs and hammocks. Two rooms can be connected to form a villa, a good deal for a family or two couples. A small pool below the rooms, next to the restaurant, is surrounded by the rain forest. ✉ Apdo. 111, Quepos, ☎ 777–0096, FAX 777–0538. *34 rooms with bath. Restaurant, bar, pool. AE, MC, V.*

$$–$$$ 🏨 **La Colina.** The new cement tower of this small B&B on the Quepos side of the Manuel Antonio hill holds the nicest rooms, with tile floors, ceiling fans, big windows, and balconies; two have air-conditioning. Smaller rooms without views are less expensive; there are also

two cozy apartments. There's a small split-level pool, next to which is the open-air restaurant under a thatched roof where you can enjoy the complimentary breakfast, a light lunch menu, and nightly dinner specials. The friendly American owners are happy to book tours and help you with travel arrangements. ☎ *777–0231,* FAX *777–1553. 11 rooms with bath, 2 apartments. Restaurant, bar, pool. AE, MC, V.*

$$ ☒ **Hotel Vela Bar.** A hundred yds back from the first Playa Manuel Antonio—left at the Bar del Mar—the bedrooms here have white stucco walls, terra-cotta floors, wooden beds, fans, and framed tapestries. The apartments (which sleep four) are a good value for groups. An open-air rotunda restaurant is a popular spot with nonguests, since it serves a good selection of vegetarian, meat, and fresh seafood dishes. ☒ *Playa Manuel Antonio,* ☎ *777–0413,* FAX *777–1071. 9 rooms with bath, 1 bungalow. Restaurant, bar. AE, DC, MC, V.*

Nightlife and the Arts

Most of Manuel Antonio's nightlife is found in Quepos (☞ *above*), which has several bars and two full-fledged discotheques. There is a casino in the **Hotel Divisamar,** across from the Barba Roja.

Outdoor Activities and Sports

HORSEBACK RIDING

Horses can be rented in Manuel Antonio from **Malboro Stables** (☎ 777–1108), which has a two-hour guided tour through the nearby forest. **Equus** (☎ 777–0001) can provide mounts and a guide to lead you through the forest and beach.

SEA KAYAKING

Iguana Tours (☎ 777–1262) runs sea-kayaking adventures to the islands of Parque Nacional Manuel Antonio, which requires a bit of experience when seas are high, and a mellower paddle to the mangrove estuary of Isla Damas, where you might see monkeys, crocodiles, and plenty of birds.

SWIMMING

Manuel Antonio's safest swimming area is the second beach in the national park, Playa Manuel Antonio, which also has great snorkeling conditions. When the surf gets big, rip currents are a serious problem on Playa Espadilla, the long beach before you come to the park. Riptides are characterized by a strong current running out to sea. The important thing to remember if you become caught in one of these currents is not to struggle against it, but instead swim parallel to shore. If you can't swim out of it, the current will simply take you out just past the breakers, where its power dissipates. If you conserve your strength, you can then swim parallel to shore a bit, and back into the beach. The best policy, however, is not to go in deeper than your waist if the waves are big.

SKIN DIVING

Playa Manuel Antonio, inside the national park, is a good snorkeling spot, as is Playa Biesanz, near the **Hotel Parador.** At press time, **Lynch Travel** (☎ 777–1170) was offering scuba diving around the islands in the national park, for experienced divers only.

Shopping

There is no shortage of shopping opportunities in this town, from the T-shirt vendors lining the road near the national park to the boutiques in the big hotels. There is little in the way of local handicrafts, so you'll find much the same things you would in San José, at slightly elevated prices. **La Buena Nota** (☎ 777–0345) is one of the oldest souvenir shops in town, with two locations: on the left as you enter Quepos, and on the right just past the top of the hill, between Quepos and Manuel Antonio.

CENTRAL PACIFIC COSTA RICA A TO Z

Arriving and Departing

By Bus

Buses to Orotina leave from San José's Coca-Cola bus station (✉ Calle 16 between Avdas. 1 and 3) daily at 8, 9:30, and 11:15 AM, and 12:30, 1:45, 2:45, and 4 PM. All buses heading toward San José can drop you off at the airport, but you need to ask the driver ahead of time. Buses to Jacó and Quepos (☞ Getting Around, *below*) can drop you off at Reserva Biológica Carara.

Buses (☎ 223–1109) from San José to Jacó leave from the Coca-Cola bus station daily at 7:15 AM, 10:30 AM, and 3:30 PM (2½-hr trip), returning at 5 AM, 11 AM, and 3 PM, with more frequent direct buses on weekends. Express buses depart San José from the Coca-Cola bus station for Quepos and Parque Nacional Manuel Antonio at 6 AM, noon, and 6 PM (2½-hr trip), returning at 6 AM, noon, and 5 PM.

By Car

The quickest way to reach the central Pacific is to take the Carretera Interamericana (Inter-American Highway, CA1) west past the airport to the turnoff for Atenas, turning left and driving through Atenas to Orotina. The coastal highway, or Costanera, heads southeast from Orotina to Tárcoles, Jacó, Hermosa, and Quepos, and is well marked and paved all the way.

By Plane

During the high season, **Sansa** (☎ 221–9414) has four flights daily between San José and Quepos. They also have one flight daily between Quepos and Tamarindo (☞ Chapter 5). **Travelair** (☎ 220–3054) has one flight daily between San José and Jacó and four flights daily to Quepos. Travelair also runs daily flights between Jacó and Tambor (☞ Chapter 5), and between Quepos and Tambor, Tamarindo, and Palmar Sur (☞ Chapters 4, 5, and 7).

Getting Around

By Bus

All buses traveling between San José and either Jacó or Quepos can drop you off at Orotina.

The short stretch of road between Quepos and Manuel Antonio is serviced by buses that leave Quepos every half hour from dawn till dusk, with a few more runs after dark. Buses leave Puntarenas for Quepos daily at 5 AM and 2:30 PM, returning at 10:30 AM and 3 PM (3 hrs); stopping at Hermosa and on the outskirts of Jacó. Buses to Quepos and Parque Nacional Manuel Antonio (☞ Arriving and Departing, *above*) can drop you off at Playa Hermosa. To explore the southern Pacific region (☞ Chapter 7), buses leave Quepos for Dominical daily at 9 AM, 1:30 PM, 4:30 PM, and 6:30 PM, returning at 6 AM, 2 PM, and 2:45 PM (2½ hrs).

By Car

The Costanera connects Orotina with the Reserva Biológica Carara, Tárcoles, Jacó, Playa Hermosa, and Quepos. It is well marked, and was in the process of being repaired at press time. The road between Quepos and Manuel Antonio National Park takes about 15 minutes to drive.

Contacts and Resources

Car Rentals
See Contacts and Resouces *in* San José A to Z, *in* Chapter 2

Emergencies
In case of an emergency, dial ☎ 911. **Ambulance** (☎ 221–5818). **Fire** (☎ 118). **Police** (☎ 911; 117 in towns; 127 in rural areas). **Traffic Police** (☎ 227–8030).

Guided Tours
Cruceros del Sur (✉ Across from Colegio Los Angeles, Sabana Norte, San José, ☎ 232–6672, FAX 220–2103) runs three- and six-day natural-history cruises along the central Pacific coast, visiting Parque Nacional Manuel Antonio. The *Undersea Hunter* (✉ San Rafael de Escazú, 600 m north and 50 m west of Rosti Pollos, ☎ 228–6535, FAX 289–7334). In Tarcoles, Victor Pineda leads an unforgettable **Crocodile Tour** (☎ 637–0426).

FROM SAN JOSÉ

A number of tours to the central Pacific can be arranged out of San José. **Cosmos Tours** (✉ 50 m north and 50 m east of Centro Cultural Norteamericano Coastarricense, ☎ 234–0607, FAX 253–4707). **Costa Rica Expeditions** (✉ Avda. 3 at Calle Central, San José, ☎ 222–0333, FAX 257–1665). **Horizontes** (✉ 150 m north of Pizza Hut Paseo Colón, ☎ 222–2022, FAX 255–4513).

CENTRAL PACIFIC HINTERLANDS

See Fantasy Tours, *below.*

COAST NEAR SAN JOSÉ

An array of tours are offered out of Jacó by **Fantasy Tours** (✉ Best Western Jacó Beach Hotel, ☎ 643–3032), the most popular being hiking in the Reserva Biológica Carara, a boat trip to a secluded beach nearby, crocodile watching on the Río Tárcoles, and the cruise to Isla Tortuga.

Costa Rica Adventure Travel (✉ Next toSi Como No Hotel, Manuel Antonio,, ☎ 777–0850), in Manuel Antonio, offers a variety of outdoor trips, including guided tours of the national park, a boat trip to a mangrove swamp, snorkeling from a private barge, sportfishing, and horseback riding or hiking in the Rain Maker private jungle reserve. In Quepos, **Lynch Travel** (✉ Quepos, ☎ 777–1170) offers several boat trips, horseback tours, river rafting, and sportfishing. **Iguana Tours** (✉ Across from soccer field, Quepos, ☎ 777–1262) specializes in sea kayaking and white-water rafting.

Visitor Information
The tourist office in San José (☞ Visitor Information *in* San José A to Z, *in* Chapter 2) has information on the central Pacific. **Costa Rica Adventure Travel** (☞ *above*) can both provide information and arrange excursions. In Quepos, **Lynch Travel** (☞ *above*) also provides information and travel help.

7 Southern Pacific Costa Rica

Diverse and wild, the southern Pacific zone is marked by the cloud forests of the Cordillera de Talamanca and remote Osa Peninsula beaches. Isolated national parks and private nature preserves, excellent nature lodges, and one of the finest botanical gardens in Latin America, plus sublime surfing, fishing, hiking, bird-watching, skin diving, and horseback riding, make this region seventh heaven for outdoor enthusiasts.

Updated by
David
Dudenhoefer

TRAVELERS TO THE SOUTHERN PACIFIC ZONE—a lush, tropical coastal plain overlooked by the highest mountain chain in the country, the Cordillera de Talamanca—should thank the national park system for preserving some of the most breathtaking natural areas in the country. Visitors to Parque Nacional Chirripó can climb Costa Rica's highest mountain and explore remote wilderness ranging from rugged forest to glacial lakes. On the Osa Peninsula, the creation of Parque Nacional Corcovado put something of a halt to the furious logging and gold mining that was destroying the rain forest. Corcovado contains a wide range of habitats, including large areas of swamp, deserted beaches, cloud forest, and luxuriant lowland rain forest, which provide habitat for most of the country's endangered species.

The southern Pacific zone has the most dramatic and diverse scenery and wildlife in Costa Rica, as well as excellent conditions for practicing a variety of outdoor sports. Some of Costa Rica's best surfing breaks, for example, as well as its second-best skin diving area can be found here. Anglers can fish the renowned Pacific waters, rafters can take on the rambunctious Río General, trekkers can climb Chirripó, and birdwatchers who head to the right spots are almost guaranteed glimpses of the country's two most spectacular birds: the brilliant quetzal and scarlet macaw. Botany lovers, too, will go gaga here, especially at the Wilson Botanical Garden near San Vito, with its spectacular displays of local and imported plant life.

Bordering the southern Pacific region of Costa Rica is the Chiriquí province of Panama, which has plenty of impressive scenery of its own, and considerably fewer tourists. The Cordillera de Talamanca, which extend east from Costa Rica into Chiriquí, contain dense cloud forest and scenic agricultural communities. Those tranquil mountain towns provide access to hiking, bird-watching, and white-water rafting to rival any found elsewhere in Costa Rica. If you have more than a few days to explore the region, you may want to consider venturing over the border for two or three days (☞ Chiriquí Province *in* Chapter 9).

Pleasures and Pastimes

Dining

The southern Pacific zone may not be renowned for its gourmet cooking, but you can actually enjoy some tasty meals here. Thanks to the prime fishing off the coast here, fresh seafood is a specialty. There is also plenty of fresh fruit available: apples, plums, and peaches are grown in the upper reaches of the Cordillera de Talamanca, whereas the lowlands hold vast pineapple plantations. If you're here between June and August, try *rambutans,* locally called *mamones chinos,* with red spiky shells protecting a succulent white fruit very similar to a litchi.

Lodging

The southern Pacific zone's accommodations are as diverse as its terrain. There are simple, low-budget oceanside *cabinas* (cottages), tranquil mountain retreats, and luxury hotels set amidst the greenery of the rain forest. Be aware that nature lodges may appear to be more expensive than they are in reality, since the price of rooms includes three hearty meals a day.

Outdoor Excitement

The southwest could be called an outdoorsy person's nirvana: horseback riding is done everywhere here; hikes range from one-day jaunts through private reserves to more demanding treks up Chirripó or into the Corcovado jungles. The water surrounding Isla del Caño is a lively habitat offering some of Costa Rica's best skin diving, and prime sportfishing is enjoyed off the entire southern Pacific coast. The surf here whips up into a half dozen breaks, and in the more tranquil waters of Golfo Dulce you can take sea kayaking excursions.

Private Nature Preserves

In addition to the southern Pacific zone's celebrated national parks, there are a growing number of private nature preserves, some of which run their own lodges. Dominical's Hacienda Barú, a 700-acre reserve, offers a number of ways to experience the rain forest, as does Lapa Ríos, on the southern tip of the Osa Peninsula, with its extensive protected rain forest. Cabinas Chacón, in San Gerardo de Dota, has a large cloud forest reserve crisscrossed by footpaths. Other private rain forest reserves include La Amistad Lodge, in the mountains above San Vito; Marenco Biological Station, to the north of Parque Nacional Corcovado; the area surrounding the Costa Rica Expeditions' tent camp and the southern edge of Corcovado; the Tiskita Jungle Lodge, in Pavones; and the forest reserve at Wilson Botanical Garden.

Exploring Southern Pacific Costa Rica

The southern Pacific zone comprises the western slope of the Cordillera de Talamanca, the Valle de El General, and the Osa Peninsula. There are are two routes into the region: the Costanera, or coastal highway, and the Carretera Interamericana (Inter-American Highway, CA2). To take the Costanera, drive west from San José, turn off the highway at the road to Atenas, and after Orotina, turn south, toward Jacó and Quepos. To get to the Valle de El General from the Inter-American Highway, drive east out of San José, and turn south outside Cartago. The CA2 heads high over the Cordillera de Talamanca, then descends down to and across the rolling hills of the Valle de El General, all the way to Panama. The Costanera runs into the CA2 at Palmar Norte, to the south of which is the turnoff for Puerto Jiménez. Though a faithful translation from the Spanish, "highway" is really a misnomer for these neglected two-lane roads.

The good news is that between the country's two domestic airlines, there are regular flights to the southern Pacific zone's most important destinations, and charter service to many of its more isolated spots. The great distance that separates the Osa Peninsula, Golfito, and San Vito from San José makes flying even more attractive, since a one-hour flight can save you six to eight hours behind the wheel or in a bus seat.

Numbers in the text correspond to numbers in the margin and on the Southern Pacific Costa Rica map.

Great Itineraries

IF YOU HAVE 3 DAYS

Fly straight to the Golfo Dulce–Osa Peninsula area, where comfortable nature lodges are in or near pristine wilderness in three distinct areas. You can fly direct to ▦ **Playa Pavones** ⑨ on a charter arranged by the Tiskita Jungle Lodge. Or, fly to Puerto Jiménez, a short drive from the nature lodges of ▦ **Cabo Matapalo** ⑫, and the Corcovado Lodge Tent Camp farther afield. The third option is to fly to Palmar Sur, where the taxi and boat trip to ▦ **Bahía Drake** ⑬ begins. Amazing as it may seem, a one-hour flight from San José and short trip by land or water will take you to some of the wildest and most beautiful spots in Costa Rica, any one of which deserves at least three days.

Southern Pacific Costa Rica

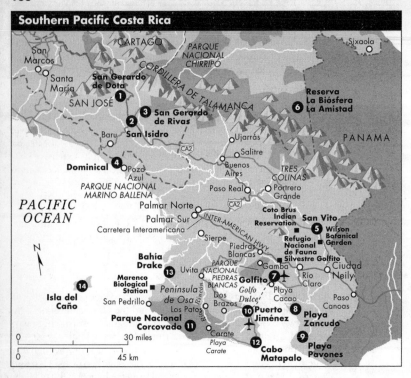

IF YOU HAVE 5 DAYS

Start by driving south on the Inter-American Highway (CA2), to the cool mountain air and cloud forests of ⊞ **San Gerardo de Dota** ①, the perfect place for hiking and bird-watching. On day two, you may want to make the hike down the Cerro de la Muerte, or simply explore the Dota Valley. On day three, head down out of the mountains to the coastal enclave of ⊞ **Dominical** ④. Spend day four and the morning of day five enjoying the waterfalls, nature reserves, and beaches of Dominical, before heading up the coast to the Central Pacific zone (☞ Chapter 6), and/or San José.

IF YOU HAVE 8 DAYS

Head south on the CA2 to ⊞ **San Gerardo de Dota** ①, for quetzal watching and hiking. On the second afternoon, work your way down to ⊞ **Dominical** ④, which deserves at least two nights. On the morning of day four, head to either ⊞ **Golfito** ⑦ or ⊞ **San Vito** ⑤, and from here you can continue on to **Reserva La Biósfera La Amistad** ⑥, ⊞ **Playa Zancudo** ⑧, or ⊞ **Playa Pavones** ⑨ on the following day. If you are so inclined, you can slip across the border into Panama for three days, to explore Chiriquí Province (☞ Chapter 9). Another alternative is to go from Dominical straight out to the rain forests and isolated beaches of the Osa Peninsula, either by driving or busing to ⊞ **Puerto Jiménez** ⑩ and ⊞ **Cabo Matapalo** ⑫, or by parking in Sierpe and taking a boat to ⊞ **Bahía Drake** ⑬.

When to Tour Southern Pacific Costa Rica

You'll experience the same wet- and dry-season weather patterns here as the rest of the Pacific. It rains considerably more here than in the Northwest during the rainy months, but during July and August, you may catch a week without any serious precipitation. The Osa Peninsula and Talamanca highlands are especially susceptible to downpours, making the region the last place you want to visit during the September-October deluge, when you'd have to be amphibian to be comfortable.

GENERAL VALLEY

From the Cordillera de Talamanca to the Golfo Dulce

The Valle de El General is bounded to the north by the massive Cordillera de Talamanca and to the south by the Golfo Dulce, or "Sweet Gulf." This region comprises vast expanses of highland wilderness and high-altitude *páramo* (a shrubby ecosystem) of Chirripó, and and isolated beaches and the lowland rain forest around Golfito and Playa Pavones

San Gerardo de Dota

❶ *80 km (50 mi) southeast of San José, 54 km (34 mi) north of San Isidro.*

Cloud forests, cool mountain air, pastoral imagery, and excellent bird-watching make San Gerardo de Dota one of Costa Rica's great overlooked destinations. You'll find San Gerardo in a narrow valley of the Río Savegre, 9 km (5½ mi) down a twisting track that descends abruptly to the west from the Carretera Interamericana. This tranquil and beautiful spot more closely resembles the Rocky Mountains than something you would expect to see in Central America. Hike down the waterfall trail, however, and the vegetation quickly becomes tropical again. The trail is steep and isn't for every traveler, but is well worth the effort for those up to it. Other activities include horseback tours and trout fishing, but most people are content to wander around the pastures and forests marveling at the valley's varied avian inhabitants.

The damp, epiphyte-laden forest of giant oak trees, now broken up by bare, stump-strewn patches, is renowned for its high count of quetzals, for many the most beautiful bird in the New World. Males are the more spectacular, with metallic green feathers, bright crimson stomachs, helmetlike crests, and long tail streamers especially dramatic in flight. Quetzals commonly feed on *aguacatillos* (small avocado-like fruits) in the tall trees scattered around the valley's forests and pastures. The people who run your hotel can usually point you in the direction of where the quetzals have been hanging out. Early morning is the best time to spot them.

Lodging

$$$–$$$$ 🏨 **Cabinas Chacón.** Nearly 30 years ago, Efrain Chacón and his brother bushwhacked their way through the mountains to homestead in San Gerardo. With hard work and business acumen, they built a successful dairy farm. Now a hotelier and staunch conservationist, Efrain aids researchers and takes visitors on tours of his extensive farm. The tours provide a wealth of information on natural and political history and nearly always include quetzal-spotting. The cabins are comfortable and clean, and the main house has a bar with a fireplace and a veranda. Meals are included. Efrain will pick up guests from anywhere in the country for a fee. ⊠ *Apdo. 482, Cartago,* ☎ 🖷 *771–1732. 20 cabinas. Restaurant, bar. AE, MC, V.*

$$$–$$$$ 🏨 **Trogon Lodge.** A collection of green cabins nestled in a secluded part
★ of an enchanting valley, the Trogon Lodge overlooks the cloud forest and boulder-strewn Río Savegre. Each cabin has two rooms with hardwood floors, colorful quilts, big windows, white-tile baths with hot showers, and small electric heaters for those chilly mountain nights.

Meals are served in a small dining hall and can be taken separately or as part of a package. The lodge can also provide a guide and/or transportation from San José. ⊠ *Apdo. 10980–1000, San José,* ☎ *222–5463 or 771–1266,* FAX *223–2421. 10 rooms with bath. Restaurant. AE, DC, MC, V.*

Outdoor Activities and Sports

HIKING

There are enough trails and country roads around San Gerardo de Dota to keep you hiking for days. A short trail heads through the forest above the Trogon Lodge, ending in a pasture, and Cabinas Chacón has miles of trails winding through their forest reserve (☞ Lodging, *above*). The best trail in the valley, however, is the one that follows the Río Savegre down to a **waterfall.** Follow the main road past Cabinas Chacón to a fork, where you veer left, cross a bridge, and head over the hill to a pasture, where it narrows to a footpath. The path becomes steep near the bottom and takes about three hours both ways. A longer, guided hike is offered by Cabinas Chacón: they'll drive you up to the páramo near **Cerro de la Muerte,** from where you spend all day hiking back down through the forest into the valley.

San Isidro

❷ *134 km (83 mi) southeast of San José, 205 km (127 mi) northwest of Golfito.*

San Isidro has no attractions of its own, but it's not a bad place to get stuck spending a night, since it has friendly inhabitants and a fairly agreeable climate. The second-largest town in the province of San José, San Isidro has a bustling market and colorful, grid-plan streets. The large central square is the town's hub, with a modern church towering to the east. A couple of blocks south is the market, where buses depart for San Gerardo de Rivas (☞ *below*), the starting point of the trail into Parque Nacional Chirripó. The regional office of the **National Parks Service** (☎ 771–3155) can provide information about Chirripó and reserve space in the park's cabin. Buses to the nearby beach town of Dominical leave from near the fire station.

Lodging

$$ 🏨 **Hotel del Sur.** This white, motel-style building with a red barrel-tile roof, 6 km (4 mi) south of town, is the most comfortable option here. Most of the rooms could use a paint job, and the carpeted ones are pretty musty—ask for one with a tile floor—but they're spacious, well furnished, and relatively inexpensive. Bungalows in back are good for families, and offer an escape from the drone of the highway; they have kitchenettes, bunks, and separate bedrooms. ⊠ *Apdo. 4–8000, San Isidro, Perez Zeledon,* ☎ *771–3033,* FAX *771–0527. 48 rooms with bath, 12 bungalows. Restaurant, bar, pool, sauna, tennis court, basketball, Ping-Pong. MC, V.*

Outdoor Activities and Sports

WHITE-WATER RAFTING

Boasting the country's longest white-water run, the Río General makes for a fun rafting or kayaking trip. The white water begins to the south of San Isidro, flowing through predominantly agricultural land before winding its way through a rocky canyon. A class III–IV river, the Río General can only be run during the wettest months (September–November), and is offered by the major rafting companies in San José (☞ Chapter 2) as a three-day camping expedition. Based in San Isidro, **Brunca Tours** (⊠ 75 m south of ICE, 1st fl., San Isidro, ☎ 771–3100) offers a one-day rafting trip on the river for most of the year, and trips on the nearby Río Coto when the General gets too low. Brunca Tours also offers guided trips to Chirripó and Reserva La Biósfera La Amistad, the hot springs near San Gerardo de Rivas, and Wilson Botanical Garden (☞ San Vito, *below*).

San Gerardo de Rivas

❸ *20 km (12 mi) northeast of San Isidro.*

The trail into **Parque Nacional Chirripó** (☞ Chapter 10), home of Costa Rica's highest peak, begins here. It's a grueling climb up to the park—6 to 10 hours, depending on your physical condition—so you should head out of San Gerardo with the first light of day.

Even if you aren't up for the hike into Parque Nacional Chirripó, San Gerardo de Rivas is a great place to spend a day. It's a quiet agricultural community with lovely views and an agreeable climate, where the outdoor options include hiking—on the trail up to Chirripó and others—and horseback riding. There are also small hot springs and a waterfall nearby. You can easily visit the area on a day trip from San Isidro, or overnight at one of the town's rustic lodges.

Dominical

❹ *22 km (14 mi) southwest of San Isidro.*

Fifty minutes to the southwest of San Isidro, Dominical, once a sleepy fishing village, is slowly being discovered. It still has a mere fraction of the tourists found at beaches like Tamarindo or Manuel Antonio, but it certainly isn't for lack of natural attractions. Dominical's magic lies in its combination of terrestrial and marine wonders: the rain forest grows right up to the beach at some points, and the sea offers world-class sportfishing and surfing. The beaches here are long and practically empty, perfect for strolling and shell collecting, but beware of rip currents when the waves are big. There are several good surf breaks in and around Dominical, which is why you'll see plenty of surfer dudes hanging around.

Parque Nacional Marino Ballena, 20 km (12 mi) to the southeast of Dominical, protects a gorgeous long beach, sandy point, and a collection of offshore islets. They weren't charging an entrance fee at press time, since there are so many ways to enter the park.

There is also plenty to see and do on land at Dominical. The area's steep hillsides are covered with lush forest, much of which is protected within private reserves. Several private nature reserves are trying to finance preservation of the rain forest through ecotourism by offering hiking and horseback tours. Two private reserves border spectacular **Cataratas de Nauyaca** (Nauyaca Waterfalls) a massive double cascade that is simply one of the country's most spectacular sights. The **Pozo Azul** is a considerably smaller waterfall in the jungle about 5 km (3 mi) south of town. Both are accessible by foot or on horseback (☞ Outdoor Activities and Sports, *below*).

Dining and Lodging

$$ ✕ **San Clemente Restaurant.** This is the local surfer hangout, most
★ crowded whenever it's too dark or too flat to catch a wave. Dozens of broken surfboards hang between the rafters and the corrugated metal roof, and there are plenty of photos of the sport's early years, including a little shrine to surfing legend the Duke. Satellite TV airs U.S. sporting events, and foosball and pool tables occupy most of the floor space; seating is in wooden booths, inside and out in the garden. Good

seafood (grilled outdoors at dinner), Tex-Mex burritos and nachos, veggie food, and inventive breakfast items are served. Next door is the local post office, surf shop, and laundromat rolled into one; they also arrange tours. A range of lodgings is available here (☞ *below*). ⊠ *Halfway along the main road,* ☎ ℻ 787–0055. AE, MC, V.

$$$ 🏨 **Villas Río Mar.** Upriver from the beach, this hotel on landscaped grounds is the fanciest in town. The adobe-style bungalows have thatched roofs, white-tile floors, and cane ceilings. The rooms and baths are on the small side, but each has a porch with a hammock, wet bar with refrigerators, and mosquito-net curtains. The restaurant sits beneath a giant thatched roof, with lots of plants and elegant table settings. ⊠ *Apdo. 1350–2050, San José,* ☎ *787–0052 or 257–1138,* ℻ *787–0054. 40 rooms with bath. Restaurant, bar, pool, tennis court, exercise room. AE, DC, MC, V.*

$$–$$$ 🏨 **Hacienda Barú.** These bungalows are part of a large private reserve, which makes it a great spot if you want to explore the rain forest. Bungalows are basic, with red cement floors and bare white walls, small kitchens, sitting rooms, and either two or three bedrooms (perfect for three or four people). You can spend an hour on a platform in the rain-forest canopy or overnight at a shelter in the heart of the forest. ⊠ *Selva Mar, 1,000 yds north of Dominical, Apdo. 215–8000, San Isidro, Perez Zeledon,* ☎ *771–4582 or 771–4579,* ℻ *771–1903;* ⊠ *AAA Express Mail, 1641 N.W. 79th Ave., Miami, FL 33126-1105. 6 bungalows. Restaurant, kitchenettes, hiking, horseback riding. AE, MC, V.*

$$ 🏨 **Pacific Edge.** The forest grows right up to this lodge, on a moun-
★ tain ridge south of town. The grounds, planted with flowers and fruit trees and aflight with plenty of birds and butterflies, lead through the forest to a stream and small waterfall. Four breezy, rustic-but-comfortable bungalows are surrounded with screened windows and have large, hammock-strung porches. Each one has a simple kitchen, which costs $5 a day to use, but the lodge's small restaurant, set under a thatched roof, serves great breakfasts and dinners, including some Thai dishes. The road up to Pacific Edge leaves the coastal highway 4 km (2½ mi) south of Dominical and requires four-wheel drive, but they will pick up guests in town. ⊠ *Apdo. 531–800, Dominical,* ☎ ℻ *787–0031 or 771–1903. 4 bungalows. Restaurant. MC, V.*

$–$$ 🏨 **Cabinas San Clemente.** With a great location just across the road
★ from the beach and a wide selection of accommodations, San Clemente has something for just about everyone. A two-story building overlooking a tropical garden holds the best rooms, which are spacious, bright, and well ventilated. They have hardwood floors, lots of screened windows, firm beds, and small tile baths. Buildings to the north and south hold less expensive rooms, which are smaller, darker, and warmer. Budget travelers can get a soft bed in communal quarters next to the restaurant (☞ *above*) for $8 a night; they also rent four three-bedroom beach houses. ⊠ *Dominical,* ☎ *787–0026,* ℻ *787–0055. 18 rooms with bath, 4 houses. Restaurant, bar, laundry service. AE, MC, V.*

Outdoor Activities and Sports

ECOTOURISM

Hacienda Barú (☞ Dining and Lodging, *above*) is definitely the best organized ecotourism operation in Dominical, offering such unusual tours as a trip into the rain-forest canopy, which entails being hoisted up to a platform in the crown of a giant tree, and a night spent in a shelter in the woods.

INNER TUBING

A popular excursion is to inner-tube trip down green **Río Barú,** which flows into the Pacific south of town; trips can be arranged through your hotel or at the San Clemente Restaurant (☞ Dining and Lodging, *above*).

Angling options range from expensive sportfishing charters to heading out in a small boat with a local fisherman. The folks at **Tropical Waters** (✉ 3½ km/2 mi north of Dominical on road to San Isidro, ☎ 787–0031) or the San Clemente Restaurant (☞ Dining and Lodging, *above*) can arrange trips.

The easiest way to get to Nauyaca Waterfalls is with **Don Lulo** (☎ 771–3187), 12 km (8 mi) north of town. He offers horseback trips to the falls that include swimming in the natural pools below the cascades and a hearty, typical Costa Rican lunch. Book through your hotel, Tropical Waters, or at the San Clemente Restaurant (☞ Dining and Lodging, *above*). The other option is through the private reserve of the **Bella Vista Lodge** (☎ 771–1903), which entails a longer horseback trek, but takes you through much more rain forest. To hike to **Pozo Azul,** head up the road toward the Bella Vista lodges, and when it begins to climb the hill, look for a trail down to the river on your right.

San Vito

❺ *267 km (166 mi) southwest of San José, 93 km (58 mi) northeast of Golfito.*

The charming little town of San Vito lies at an altitude of 3,150 ft, close to the Panama border. It owes its founding in 1952 to a government scheme whereby 200 Italian families were given grants to convert the rain forest into coffee, fruit, and cattle farms. After much initial hardship and wrangling over the size of the agreed grant, a relatively large modern town with some 40,000 inhabitants quickly sprang up. Since it lies near the **Coto Brus Indian Reservation,** San Vito is one of the few towns in Costa Rica where you might see Ngwobe, or Guaymí, Indians, who are easy to spot, thanks to the colorful dresses worn by the women. It's also a good place to enjoy some Italian food, but the real reason folks head to this corner of Costa Rica is to explore the nearby botanical garden.

Six kilometers (4 mi) south of San Vito is the extensive **Wilson Botanical Garden.** These 25 hillside acres were converted from a coffee plantation in 1961 by U.S. landscapers Robert and Catherine Wilson, who planted a huge collection of tropical species (today the gardens hold around 3,000 native species and 4,000 exotic species), including palms (an amazing 700 species), orchids, aroids, ferns, bromeliads, heliconias, and marantas, all linked by a series of neat grass paths. The property was transferred to the Organization for Tropical Studies (OTS) in 1973 and in 1983 became part of the **Reserva La Biósfera La Amistad** (☞ *below*). Destroyed by fire in 1994, the facilities, including the main building, have been completely rebuilt. The garden functions mainly as a research and educational center, but visitors and overnight guests (☞ Dining and Lodging, *below*) are welcome. Helpful booklets provide you with a self-guided tour. ✉ *Apdo. 73–8257, San Vito,* ☎ *773–3278,* ℻ *773–3665.* ⊡ *$8 full day, $5 half day.* ☉ *Daily 8–4.*

| OFF THE BEATEN PATH | **CIUDAD NEILY** – The 33 km (21 mi) of road that connects San Vito and Ciudad Neily is twisty and spectacular, with views over the Coto Colorado plain to the Golfo Dulce and Osa Peninsula beyond. Much of this steep terrain is covered with tropical forest, which makes it an ideal route for bird-watching and photography. |

Dining and Lodging

$ ★ ✕ **Pizzeria Liliana.** A simple, small-town restaurant near San Vito's central square, the Liliana serves large portions of good food at remarkably low prices. The decor is basic, with wooden tables and a bar at one end, but the pastas and pizzas are yummy. Go for the baked chicken or the steak with mushroom sauce if you aren't up for Italian. ⊠ *1½ blocks west of central square,* ☎ *773–3080. Reservations not accepted. V.*

$$$$ ★ ⊞ **Wilson Botanical Garden.** A row of 12 cabins lines a ridge in the heart of the garden, with hardwood floors, high ceilings, and large balconies. Four guest cabins have small sitting rooms and large windows. Two cabins are equipped for travelers using wheelchairs. Rates are high, but remember that you get three hearty meals a day with the room, and, besides, you are also helping to maintain the garden. Staying overnight is the easiest way to see the garden at dusk and dawn, a highly recommended experience. ⊠ *OTS, Apdo. 676–2050, San Pedro,* ☎ *240–6696,* ℻ *240–6783. 16 cabinas. Restaurant. AE, MC, V.*

$ ⊞ **Hotel El Ceibo.** The owner, Antonio, arrived here from Italy at age two, and he has some interesting stories about his early days in San Vito. His modern bedrooms are pleasant and clean—foam-rubber mattresses are their only drawback—and the bathrooms have powerful, hot showers. They are really quite a deal. Those in the back of the two-story buildings overlook a forested ravine. The airy restaurant, with its sloping wood ceiling, arched windows, and wine trolley, serves solidly good fare. ⊠ *San Vito, behind the Municipalidad,* ☎ ℻ *773–3025. 40 rooms with bath. Restaurant, bar. V.*

Shopping

An old farm house on the east side of the road between San Vito and the botanical garden houses a shop called **Cántaros** (⊠ 3 km/2 mi south of San Vito, ☎ 773–3760), which features crafts by local indigenous artisans, as well as ceramics from San José artists. Profits help support the adjacent children's library.

Reserva La Biósfera La Amistad

❻ *40 km (25 mi) northwest of San Vito.*

The Parque Nacional La Amistad (La Amistad National Park), at more than 765 sq mi, is by far the largest park in the country, but it is actually a mere portion of the vast Reserva La Biósfera La Amistad (Amistad Biosphere Reserve)—a collection of protected areas that stretches from southern Costa Rica into western Panama. The park itself covers altitudes ranging from 700 to 11,600 ft, with an array of ecosystems that holds two-thirds of the country's vertebrate species. Unfortunately, the national park is practically inaccessible, but a worthwhile excursion for the adventurous. The easiest part of the park to visit is the **Tres Colinas** sector, 23 km (14 mi) north of Potrero Grande, a small town just north of Paso Real, which is where the road to San Vito leaves the Carretera Interamericana. There is a ranger station in Potrero Grande, from where a four-wheel-drive-only road winds its bumpy way up into the mountains. Camping is allowed there; you have to reserve space at the regional office in San Isidro (☎ 771–3155).

Golfito

❼ *339 km (211 mi) southeast of San José, 58 km (36 mi) northwest of Paso Canoas, at the Panamanian border.*

Once a thriving banana port, Golfito was devastated when United Fruit pulled out in 1985 due to labor disputes, rising export taxes, and a diminishing Pacific banana market. The company had arrived in 1938 to supplement its diseased plantations in Limón, and Golfito became the center of activity, with a dock that could handle 4,000 boxes of bananas per hour and elegant housing for its plantation managers. To inject new life into Golfito, the government declared the town a duty-free port in 1990. The handful of shops called the **Depósito Libre** (Duty-free Zone) does much of its business during the month preceding Christmas, when it can be very difficult to find a room in Golfito, especially on weekends.

Golfito is beautifully situated overlooking a small gulf (hence its name) and is hemmed in by a steep bank of forest, all of which lies within protected areas. At the northwestern end is the so-called **American zone**, full of elegant stilted wooden houses where the expatriate managers lived, courtesy of United Fruit. With a golf course nearby, life here must have been more than bearable. The hills behind Golfito are covered with the lush forest of the **Refugio Nacional de Fauna Silvestre Golfito.** Adjacent is the **Parque Nacional Piedras Blancas,** which makes the Golfito area for great for bird-watching. Follow the main road northwest through the old American zone, past the airstrip and a housing project, where a dirt road heads into the rain forest—this is the best area to see birds. If you have four-wheel drive, you can follow that dirt track through the heart of Parque Nacional Piedras Blancas to the community of **La Gamba,** the Esquinas Rain Forest Lodge, and Villa Briceño, on the Carretera Interamericana. This back route can cut miles off a trip to or from the north, and it passes through a gorgeous patch of wilderness.

Although Golfito doesn't have a beach itself, **Playa Cacao** lies across the bay from town—just a five-minute boat ride. The beach has several restaurants and lodges, which make it a convenient option when the hotels in Golfito fill up. The old banana port can also serve as a base for trips to Playas Zancudo and Pavones—two remote and beautiful spots that can be reached by boat or by four-wheel-drive vehicle.

Lodging

$$ ⊡ **Hotel Las Gaviotas.** Just south of town on the water's edge, this hotel has wonderful views over the inner gulf. Bedrooms lead off a terrace overlooking the sea and have terra-cotta floors, white walls, firm beds, fans, and air-conditioning. Outside each room is a small veranda with two chairs. An open-air restaurant looks onto the pool, which has a terrace that is barely divided from the sea. ⊠ *Playa Tortuga, Apdo. 12, Golfito,* ☎ *775–0062,* ℻ *775–0544. 18 rooms with bath, 3 suites. Restaurant, bar, pool. AE, DC, MC, V.*

$ ⊡ **Jardín Alamedas.** This property's popular restaurant occupies the ground floor of a former administrator's house in what was once the banana company's American zone; its guest quarters are in a newer, cement building next door. The rooms are simple but clean, with tile floors, small baths, and too many beds. The restaurant's good food ranges from fried rice dishes to fresh seafood and several kinds of pastas. ⊠ *110 yds south of airstrip, Apdo. 9 Golfito,* ☎ *775–0126. 6 rooms with bath. Restaurant. AE, MC, V.*

Outdoor Activities and Sports

SPORTFISHING

There is some great fishing to be had out of Golfito, either in the Golfo Dulce or out in the open ocean. Waters are stocked with sailfish, marlin, and roosterfish during the dry months, and dolphin and wahoo during the rainy season, and excellent bottom fishing can be had any time of year. Contact **Roy Ventura** (☞ Outdoor Activities and Sports *in* Playa Zancudo, *below,* ☎ 775–0515, ℻ 775–0631).

Shopping

Duty-free bargains on such imported items as TV sets, stereos, linens, and tires are what draw most visitors to Golfito. You can shop in the **Depósito Libre,** but you won't find things that much cheaper than they are at home. To buy things in the Depósito you have to spend the night, which means you register in the afternoon, with your passport, and shop the next morning. Shopping here is sheer madness during December.

Playa Zancudo

❽ *32 km (20 mi) south of Golfito.*

Playa Zancudo, a long, palm-lined beach fronting a tiny fishing village, can be reached either by road or by hiring a boat at the municipal dock in Golfito. Zancudo has a good surf break, but it is nothing compared with Pavones. There are also some good swimming areas, and if you get tired of playing in the surf and sand, you can arrange a boat trip to the nearby mangrove estuary to see birds and crocodiles. Zancudo is also home to the area's best sportfishing operation.

Lodging

$$–$$$ 🏨 **Roy's Zancudo Lodge.** Most of the people who stay at Roy's are anglers on all-inclusive sportfishing packages, but the hotel is a good option for folks who've never caught anything more exciting than a cold. It's on the beach, with ample, verdant grounds surrounding a pool and open-air restaurant, where buffet breakfasts and dinners are served. Rooms have hardwood floors, firm beds, ceiling fans, air-conditioning, and ocean views; they can be rented on their own, or with the three meals and open bar included. ⊠ *Playa Zancudo, Apdo. 41, Zancudo,* ☎ *776–0008,* 𝖥𝖠𝖷 *776–0011. 14 cabinas. Restaurant, bar, pool. V.*

$$ 🏨 **Cabinas Sol y Mar.** This group of beachside cabins is a 20-minute walk south of where the boat from Golfito drops you off. The owners designed and built structures that look like polyhedral space modules, with elegant charcoal-clay tiles, wooden beds, and white canvas sofas. Boat transportation can be arranged from the dock if you call ahead. ⊠ *Playa Zancudo, Apdo. 87, Golfito,* ☎ *776–0014,* 𝖥𝖠𝖷 *776–0015. 4 cabinas, 1 house. Restaurant, bar. V.*

Outdoor Activities and Sports

SPORTFISHING

If you've got your own gear, you can do some good shore fishing from the beach or the mouth of the mangrove estuary, or hire one of the local boats to take you out into the gulf. **Roy Ventura** (⊠ Roy's Zancudo Lodge, Apdo. 41, Golfito, ☞ Lodging, *above,* ☎ 775–0515, 𝖥𝖠𝖷 775–0631) runs the best charter operation in the area, with 10 boats ranging in length from 22 to 32 ft. Packages include room, food and drink, and they can pick up customers in Golfito or Puerto Jiménez.

Playa Pavones

❾ *45 km (28 mi) south of Golfito.*

On the southern edge of the Golfo Dulce's mouth stands Pavones, a windswept beach town at the end of a dirt road. Famous among surfers for having one of the longest waves in the world, the area also boasts pristine beaches and virgin rain forest. It's far from everything, but there are ample attractions for adventurous travelers willing to make the trip.

Lodging

$$$$ 🏨 **Tiskita Jungle Lodge.** Peter Aspinall has planted 100 different fruit
★ trees from all over the world as a kind of research exercise into alternative exports for Costa Rica. For you he has built wooden cabins on

stilts, surrounded by screens and lush vegetation and equipped with rustic furniture and open bathrooms from which you can observe wildlife. Trails allow you to safely explore the jungle and the wide variety of wildlife lured by the fruit trees' fine pickings. Most people fly into the lodge, though you can reach it with a four-wheel-drive. ⊠ *Costa Rica Sun Tours, 4 km (2½ mi) north of Pavones, Apdo. 1195–1250, Escazú,* ☎ *255–2011,* ℻ *255–4410. 14 cabinas. Dining room, pool, hiking, horseback riding, snorkeling. AE, DC, MC, V. Closed Sept.–Oct.*

OSA PENINSULA

Puerto Jiménez, Corcovado National Park, and Bahía Drake

Some of Costa Rica's most spectacular scenery and striking wildlife are to be discovered on the Osa Peninsula, one third of which is covered by Parque Nacional Corcovado. A paradise for backpackers, who can hike into the park via any of three routes, Corcovado can also be visited on day trips from nearby nature lodges, most of which lie within private preserves that are home for much of the same wildlife you might see in the park. And to complement the peninsula's lush forests and pristine beaches, the sea that surrounds it holds great sportfishing and skin diving.

En Route   If you're coming from San José, you've got a seven-hour drive; take the Carretera Interamericana (CA2) south to Piedras Blancas, where you turn right for the rough road into the Osa Peninsula.

Puerto Jiménez

❿ *364 km (226 mi) southeast of San José.*

There isn't much to write home about in Puerto Jiménez, but it can be a convenient base for exploring some of the nearby wilderness. You won't be dodging any pigeons in this urban center, but you are likely to see scarlet macaws flying noisily over the rooftops or perched in the Indian almond trees. Its claim to fame is that it's the biggest town on the Osa Peninsula. Most people spend a night here either before or after visiting the Parque Nacional Corcovado (☞ *below*), as Puerto Jiménez has the best access to the park's two main trailheads.

The headquarters of the **National Parks Service** (☎ 735–5036) are at the southern end of town, opposite the Texaco gas station. This is where you check in before entering Corcovado, ask about hiking routes and present conditions, and arrange meals and lodging at the **Sirena ranger station.** During the dry season, you'll want to reserve park admission, meals, and accommodations well ahead of time, by calling and depositing money into an account in the Banco Nacional. A truck that carries hikers to **Carate** and its nearby beach leaves from the Mini Mercado El Tigre every morning at 6 AM (☞ Outdoor Activities and Sports *in* Parque Nacional Corcovado, *below*), and taxis in town can be hired to take you to the **Río Rincón,** near Los Patos. If you have a four-wheel-drive vehicle, it's just a 30-minute drive to **Dos Brazos,** and the Tigre sector of the park, which few hikers explore.

Puerto Jiménez also lies just 40 minutes from spectacular Cabo Matapalo (☞ *below*), where virgin rain forest meets the sea at a rocky point; it is also a good base for boat or sea-kayaking trips on the **Golfo Dulce,** or to one of the nearby mangrove estuaries and rivers.

Dining and Lodging

$ ✕🍽 **Restaurante Carolina.** It may not look like much, but this simple
★   restaurant in the heart of Puerto Jiménez is known to serve the best
food in town, especially fresh seafood. They also have a few small rooms
in back, making it a good spot for backpackers on their way in or out
of Corcovado. Rooms are your basic cement boxes, with private bathrooms and cold running water, but they are clean and convenient. The
daily truck to Carate leaves from in front of the restaurant. ⊠ *Center
of town, two blocks south of soccer field,* ☎ *735–5007. 5 rooms with
bath. Restaurant. No credit cards.*

$–$$ 🍽 **Cabinas Los Manglares.** Although fairly basic, this group of simple
white cabinas provides the most comfortable accommodation in Puerto
Jiménez itself. Cabins have tile floors, white walls, fans, tables, and small
wooden beds. Five of them stand by the parking lot, and five are scattered around a lawn on the other side of the mangroves, which are crossed
by a catwalk. A thatched roof covers the restaurant, which serves an
unexciting selection of meat and seafood dishes. You can see an amazing amount of wildlife in the mangrove forest that surrounds this small
lodge. ⊠ *Puerto Jiménez, across from the airport,* ☎ 📠 *735–5002.
10 cabinas. Restaurant, bar. No credit cards.*

Parque Nacional Corcovado

⓫   *There are three entrances to Corcovado: San Pedrillo to the north, Los
Patos to the east, and La Leona to the south. From Puerto Jiménez,
it's an hour with four-wheel drive to Carate, and 20 minutes to the
Río Rincón, which is a two-hour hike from Los Patos, but you'll have
to leave your car at a farm if you want to spend a night in the park.*

Comprising 168 sq mi, Parque Nacional Corcovado (Corcovado National Park) (☞ Chapter 10) is one of the largest and wildest protected
areas in the country. Much of the park is covered with virgin rain forest, where massive *espavel* and *nazareno* trees tower over the trails,
thick lianas hang from their branches, and animals such as toucans,
spider monkeys, scarlet macaws, and poison dart frogs abound. There
are no roads in the park, and the ones that approach it are dirt tracks
that require four-wheel-drive vehicles most of the year. Visitors to Corcovado often arrive by boat from Bahía Drake (☞ *below*) or Carate,
but the best way to explore the park is to sling on a backpack and hike
into the wilderness.

Lodging

$$$–$$$$ 🛖 **Corcovado Lodge Tent Camp.** It isn't easy to get here—the lodge is
★   best reached by air—but the effort is certainly worth it. Costa Rica Ex-
peditions owns the lodge, as well as the 400-acre forest reserve that
surrounds it and borders the park. The 20 tents, with two single beds
each, are pitched on wooden platforms just off the beach. There are
communal bathrooms and a bar-restaurant that serves family-style
meals. Resident naturalist guides will lead you through the jungle and
hoist you into the forest canopy to a platform 100 ft off the ground.
Bring a flashlight—there's electricity only a few hours each day—and
insect repellent. Charter planes depart from San José via Carate every
Wednesday and Friday; otherwise you can fly to Puerto Jiménez and
hire a taxi to Carate, and from here it's a 45-minute walk. ⊠ *Apdo.
6941–1000, San José,* ☎ *222–0333,* 📠 *257–1665. 20 tents without
bath. Restaurant, bar. AE, MC, V.*

Outdoor Activities and Sports
HIKING

Three hiking routes go into Corcovado, two of which begin near Puerto Jiménez, the other in Bahía Drake, which follows the coast down to San Pedrillo. You can hire a taxi in Puerto Jiménez to go to the Los Patos trailhead, or at least to the first crossing of the Río Rincón (from where you have to hike a few kilometers upriver to the trailhead). The beach route, via La Leona, starts in Carate, about 16 km (10 mi) southwest of Puerto Jiménez. A four-wheel-drive truck carries hikers to Carate every day, departing Puerto Jiménez at 6 AM and returning at 7:30 PM; for information call the Mini Mercado El Tigre (☎ 735–5075).

Cabo Matapalo

⑫ *16 km (10 mi) south of Puerto Jiménez.*

The southern tip of the Osa Peninsula possesses the kind of natural beauty that people are happy to travel halfway across the country to experience. Its ridges afford views of the blue Pacific, where schools of dolphin and whales may sometimes be spotted in the distance. The forest is tall and dense, its giant trees draped with thick lianas, branches covered with aerial gardens of bromeliads and orchids. The translation of Cabo Matapalo is "Strangler Fig Cape," a reference to the fig trees that germinate in the branches of other trees and eventually grow to smother them with their roots and branches. Strangler figs are common to the area, as they are nearly everywhere in the country, but Matapalo's greatest attractions are its rarer species, like the brilliant scarlet macaw and the *gallinazo* tree, which bursts into yellow blossom as the rainy season draws to an end.

A forested ridge extends east from Corcovado down to Matapalo, where the foliage clings to almost vertical slopes and waves crash against the black rocks below. This continuous forest corridor is protected within a series of private preserves, which means that Cabo Matapalo has most of the same wildlife as the national park—even the big cats. Most of the point itself lies within the private reserves of the area's two main hotels, and that forest is crisscrossed by footpaths, some of which head to tranquil beaches or to waterfalls that pour into small pools. On the eastern side of the point, the waves break over a platform that creates a perfect right that draws surfers from far away. The area also has excellent sea kayaking, and both the big hotels can arrange horseback excursions, guided tours to Corcovado, or deep-sea fishing.

Lodging

$$$$ 🏨 **Lapa Ríos.** More than one of Costa Rica's finest hotels, Lapa Ríos—
★ spread along a ridge surrounded by jungle—is part of an innovative conservation project. Owners Karen and John Lewis built the hotel as part of an effort to preserve a patch of endangered wildlife, and the profits help pay off the mortgage on the hotel's 1½-sq-mi nature reserve. Guests can explore that pristine wilderness on foot or horseback, accompanied by one of several resident naturalist guides on one of the eight tours, but the wildlife that can be spotted from the rooms and restaurant is simply amazing. Spacious and airy bungalows feature thatched roofs, hardwood floors, large balconies, and screened walls. A lookout and porch above the restaurant's giant thatched roof promise great bird-watching. The kitchen prepares some of the best food in the country, specializing in fresh seafood, fruit, and vegetables. ⊠ *Apdo. 100, Puerto Jiménez,* ☎ *735–5130,* 𝖥𝖠𝖷 *735–5179;* ⊠ *Box 025216, SJO 706, Miami, FL 33102-5216. 14 bungalows with bath. Restaurant, bar, pool, hiking, horseback riding. AE, MC, V.*

$$$–$$$$ ★   🏨 **Bosque del Cabo.** The tip of the point lies within the 200-acre grounds of this nature lodge, more than half nestled in primary forest and home to all kinds of wild critters. Comfortably rustic, wooden bungalows are scattered along the edge of a wide lawn, from where guests enjoy breathtaking views of the ocean. Each bungalow is slightly different, but they all have wood floors, private baths, solar energy, and porches with hammocks. Delicious meals are served family style in a simple, open-air and thatch-roofed restaurant. Trails wind down through the forest to two secluded beaches and a waterfall with a natural swimming pool. Distractions from the views include sportfishing, sea kayaking, bird-watching, and horseback riding. ✉ *Matapalo, Apdo. 15, Puerto Jiménez,* ☎ 𝔽𝔸𝕏 *735–5206. 7 bungalows with bath. Restaurant, pool. V.*

Bahía Drake

⑬   *40 km (25 mi) southwest of Palmar Sur, 10 km (6 mi) north of Corcovado.*

Bahía Drake (Drake Bay), to the north of Corcovado, was named after Sir Francis Drake, the British explorer who, legend has it, anchored here some 400 years ago. The only road into this isolated area is a muddy track that could swallow a Jeep, and apart from those who come on the occasional seaplane, the only arrivals are by boat via the Río Sierpe, or by hiking north out of Corcovado. Thanks to its inaccessibility, Bahía Drake remains wild and scenic, where the forest rises up behind the beaches and rocky points, and monkeys, ospreys, toucans, and macaws are common sights. The town of Drake is scattered along the bay, and its inhabitants earn their living by fishing, farming the hinterlands, or from tourism.

Several nature lodges stand at the southern end of the bay, near the Río Agujitas. They offer access to the area's luxuriant forests and rich marine resources. The forests around Drake host plenty of wildlife and can be explored on foot or horseback. Another popular diversion is to paddle up the Río Agujitas at high tide. Most of the lodges run guided tours to the San Pedrillo sector of Corcovado, where an ancient trail runs along the coast between Bahía Drake and San Pedrillo—it's about a three-hour hike. The ocean here is just as big an attraction as the rain forest, and the big lodges offer snorkeling and scuba trips to nearby Isla del Caño (☞ *below*) and deep-sea fishing.

Lodging

$$$$ ★   🏨 **Aguila de Osa Inn.** Just because you're out in the woods doesn't mean you have to rough it: each ridge-side room here has a unique hand-carved door, ceiling fans, colorful bedspreads, original art, and spacious tile baths with brass fixtures. The restaurant and bar sit under a thatched roof and have an impressive hardwood floor and ocean view. Meals are served family style, but the quality is comparable with that of San José's finest restaurants, and the fish has usually been caught that day by a guest. The inn's four-boat fleet and extensive tackle room coddle these sportfishermen, and the inn also runs scuba and snorkeling excursions to Isla del Caño, natural history tours to Corcovado, and horseback trips through the nearby forest. All meals are included. Transportation can be arranged in San José. ✉ *Apdo. 10486–1000, San José,* ☎ *296–2190,* 𝔽𝔸𝕏 *232–7722. 14 rooms with bath. Restaurant, bar, horseback riding, snorkeling, fishing. AE, MC, V.*

$$$$ 🏨 **Drake Bay Wilderness Camp.** One of the area's oldest lodges, the Wilderness Camp is just across the Río Agujitas from Aguila de Osa. Most of the people who stay here come to see the rain forest, but scuba diving and sportfishing are also offered. Cabins scattered around the

manicured grounds have cement floors, ceiling fans, and hot-water show-ers. Tent cabins with shared baths are less expensive. All meals and laundry service are included in the price. Horseback tours and canoe-ing on the Río Agujitas are offered, but the most popular excursions are to Corcovado and Isla del Caño. The camp can arrange trans-portation from Palmar Norte or San José. ⊠ *Apdo. 98–8150, Palmar Norte,* ☎ 📠 *771–2436, 256–7394. 20 cabinas, 5 tent cabins with-out bath. Restaurant, bar, horseback riding, boating. MC, V.*

$$$$ 🏨 **Marenco Biological Station.** Covering almost 20 sq mi of rain for-
★   est along the coast between Bahía Drake and Parque Nacional Cor-covado, Marenco is one of the country's first ecotourism enterprises. A series of well-marked trails winds through the forest, and resident naturalist guides are available to show you around. A series of breezy, simple wooden bungalows, smaller rooms, and an open-air dining hall all overlook the forest and ocean from a high ridge. Rooms have hardwood floors, thatched roofs, small bathrooms, and porches fac-ing the ocean. Daily excursions to Corcovado and Isla del Caño are offered; packages that include tours and transportation from San José are the best deal. ⊠ *Apdo. 4025–1000, San José, 11 km (7 mi) north of Bahía Drake,* ☎ *221–1594,* 📠 *255–1346. 25 rooms with bath. Dining room, hiking, horseback riding. MC, V.*

Isla del Caño

⑭ *19 km (12 mi) off the Osa Peninsula, due west of Bahía Drake.*

Most of the more than 1 sq mi of this uninhabited island, Isla del Caño, and its Reserva Biológica (biological reserve) are covered in evergreen forest containing fig, locust, and rubber trees. Coastal Indians used it as a burial ground, and the numerous bits and pieces unearthed here have prompted archaeologists to speculate about pre-Columbian long-distance maritime trade. The island's big attraction, however, is the sur-rounding ocean, which offers superb conditions for scuba diving and snorkeling. The snorkeling is excellent around the rocky points that flank the island's main beach, but certified divers will want to explore such nearby dive spots as Bajo del Diablo and Paraiso, where they are guaranteed to encounter thousands of big fish. Lodges in Bahía Drake (☞ *above*) offer day trips to Isla del Caño.

SOUTHERN PACIFIC COSTA RICA A TO Z

Arriving and Departing

By Bus

GENERAL VALLEY

Buses (☎ 222–2422) from San José to **San Isidro** leave daily from Musoc, next to the Coca-Cola Station (⊠ C. 16 at Avda. 1), departing hourly between 5:30 AM and 5 PM (3-hr trip), returning at the same times. Buses (☎ 223–5567) from San José to **Dominical** via Quepos leave from the Coca-Cola Station daily at 5:30 AM and 3 PM (6-hr trip), returning at 5:30 AM and 1 PM.

Buses (☎ 221–4214) from San José to **Golfito** depart from Avenida 18 between Calles 2 and 4 daily at 7 AM, 11 AM, and 3 PM (8-hr trip), returning at 5 AM and 1 PM. Buses (☎ 222–2750) from San José to **San Vito** depart from Calle 14 between Avenidas 3 and 5 daily at 5:45 AM, 8:15 AM, 11:30 AM, and 2:45 PM (7-hr trip).

OSA PENINSULA

Buses from San José to **Puerto Jiménez** leave from Calle 12 between Avenidas 7 and 9 (☎ 771–2550) at 6 AM and noon (8-hr trip), returning at 5 AM and 11 AM. Buses from San José to **Palmar Norte** depart from Calle 14 between Avenidas 5 and 7 (☎ 223–7685) daily at 5 AM, 7 AM, 10 AM, 1 PM, and 2:30 PM (6-hr trip); buses to Golfito, Puerto Jiménez, and San Vito also stop there. In Palmar Norte, you can hire a taxi to Sierpe, the port for boats to Bahía Drake.

By Car

The quickest way to reach the coastal highway, or Costanera, which leads past Jacó and Quepos (☞ Chapter 6) to Dominical and the rest of the southern Pacific zone, is to take the Carretera Interamericana (Inter-American Highway, CA1) west past the airport to the turnoff for Atenas, turning left and driving through Atenas to Orotina, where you head south on the coastal highway. The Southern Pacific can also be reached by taking the Inter-American Highway south, past Cartago and over the Cerro de la Muerte to San Isidro, Valle de El General, and the Osa Peninsula. Foggy conditions atop Cerro de la Muerte make it best to cross the mountains as early in the day as possible.

By Plane

Sansa (⊠ C. 24, between Avda. Central and Avda. 1, San José, ☎ 506/ 221–9414 or 506/441–8035, FAX 506/255–2176) has two flights daily from San José to Golfito; daily flights to Palmar Sur (for Bahía Drake), Puerto Jiménez, and Coto 47 (for Panama); and three flights weekly to San Vito. **Travelair** (☎ 220–3054) has daily flights to Golfito, Palmar Sur, and Puerto Jiménez. Both airlines also have daily flights from Quepos to Palmar Sur, which is the quickest way to move between the central and southern Pacific zones.

Getting Around

By Boat

A small ferry crosses the Golfo Dulce, leaving Puerto Jiménez at 6 AM and returning from Golfito at 11:30 AM. You can negotiate with the boat owners at the **Muelle Público,** a pier north of the gas station in Puerto Jiménez, for rides to Zancudo or the more distant Playa Pavones; it is cheaper, however, to find someone who is already headed that way. Bahía Drake is usually reached by boat from Sierpe, south of Palmar Norte.

By Bus

GENERAL VALLEY

From San Isidro, buses leave for Dominical at 5:30 AM, 1:30 PM, and 3 PM (1-hr trip); for San Gerardo de Rivas, the trailhead for Chirripó, at 5 AM and 2 PM.

OSA PENINSULA

From San Isidro, buses leave for Puerto Jiménez at 9 AM and 3 PM (5-hr trip). A truck for hikers leaves Puerto Jiménez daily at 6 AM for Carate, returning at 7:30 AM.

By Car

The coastal highway is a bit rough south of Dominical, but it can take you all the way to Palmar Sur. The Carretera Interamericana (CA2) also has some rough spots—watch out for those potholes—but is predominantly paved. From San Isidro, paved roads head northeast to San Gerardo de Rivas and west to Dominical. The Carretera Interamericana continues southeast from San Isidro to the turnoffs for San Vito, Puerto Jiménez, and Golfito, before reaching Paso Canoas and the border of Panama. The turnoff for the back road to Golfito (four-wheel drive only) is on the right at Villa Briceño; look for signs to La Gamba and the Esquinas lodge. The road from the Inter-American Highway into the Osa Peninsula was in rough shape at press time (four-wheel drive recommended).

By Plane

Aeronaves (☎ 775–0278), based in Golfito, offers a wide array of charter destinations. **Aerotaxi Alfa Romeo** (☎ 735–5178, FAX 735–5112) offers charter flights to Carate, Bahía Drake, Puerto Jiménez, Sirena ranger station, Tiskita Jungle Lodge, and anywhere else you want to go. You have to charter the whole plane, which is expensive, so it's best to fill it with the maximum capacity of five.

Contacts and Resources

Car Rentals

See Contacts and Resources *in* San José A to Z, *in* Chapter 2.

Emergencies

Ambulance (☎ 221–5818). **Fire** (☎ 118). **Police** (☎ 911; 117 in towns; 127 in rural areas). **Traffic Police** (☎ 227–8030).

Guided Tours

Out of San José, **Costa Rica Sun Tours** (☎ 255–3418) is the sole tour operator flying to (and owner of) the remote Tiskita Jungle Lodge (☞ Playa Pavones, *above*). **Costa Rica Expeditions** (✉ Avda. 3 at Calle Central, San José, ☎ 222–0333, FAX 257–1665). **Costa Rica Sun Tours** (✉ 200 m south of Toyota Paseo Colón, ☎ 255–2011, FAX 255–4410).

CRUISES

Cruceros del Sur (✉ Across from Colegio Los Angeles, Sabana Norte, San José, ☎ 232–6672, FAX 220–2103) runs three- and six-day natural-history cruises along the southern Pacific coast that visit Parques Nacional Manuel Antonio (☞ Chapter 6) and Corcovado and Reserva Biológica de Isla del Caño. They also offer 10-day skin-diving expeditions to distant Isla del Coco on the *Okeanos Agressor*. The **Undersea Hunter** (☎ 228–6535, FAX 298–7334) is a smaller vessel that runs similar expeditions to Isla del Coco.

HIKING TOURS

Brunca Tours (☎ 771–3100) offers hiking and nature tours to Chirripó and other areas, as well as white-water rafting on the Río General. In Dominical, **Hacienda Barú** (✉ 1 km/½ mi north of Dominical, ☎ 771–4582) has a number of guided hikes through the rain forest. **Costa Rica Expeditions** (✉ Avda. 3 at Calle Central, San José, ☎ 222–0333, FAX 257–1665) offers guided hikes out of its Corcovado Tent Camp, near Carate, on the southern edge of Corcovado National Park.

SEA-KAYAKING TOURS

In Puerto Jiménez, **Escondido Trex** (✉ Restaurante Carolina, Puerto Jiménez, ☎ 735–5210) organizes sea-kayaking tours that range from a sunset paddle to a one-week trip that explores the entire Golfo Dulce.

Visitor Information

The tourist office in San José (☞ Visitor Information *in* San José A to Z, *in* Chapter 2) has information. In Dominical contact **Tropical Waters** (✉ 3½ km/2 mi north of Dominical on road to San Isidro, ☎ 787–0031).

8 The Atlantic Lowlands and the Caribbean Coast

Inhabited by African-Caribbean, Spanish, and indigenous peoples, the Atlantic coastal plain contains dense jungles and wild outposts. Sprawling eastward from the rugged, verdant Atlantic slope of the Cordillera Central are the hot, sultry, and isolated Atlantic Lowlands. Along with its magnificent cloud and rain forests, the lowlands pack in coral-fringed beaches, easygoing towns, rapids-cut rivers, and enchanting national parks.

Updated by
Justin
Henderson

ADJACENT TO THE CARIBBEAN SEA and separated from the Central Valley by the lofty spine of the Cordillera Central and the Cordillera de Talamanca to the southeast, the Atlantic Lowlands lie between the provinces of Limón and Heredia, scenically dominated by sprawling banana plantations and thick tropical jungle. A widespread, largely untamed region, the Lowlands stretch from the east slope of the Cordillera Central up to the Sarapiquí area northeast of San José, home to the private Rara Avis and La Selva reserves, east through banana-growing areas, and down to the pristine beaches at Cahuita and Puerto Viejo de Limón on the southern Caribbean Sea. The region also stretches north to the Nicaraguan border, encompassing the coastal jungles and canals of Parque Nacional Tortuguero and Refugio Nacional de Fauna Silvestre Barra del Colorado.

Roughly a third of Limón province's population are Afro-Caribbeans, descendants of early 1800s turtle fishermen and the West Indians who arrived in the late 19th century to construct the Atlantic Railroad and then remained to work on banana and cacao plantations. Some 4,000 Jamaicans are reputed to have died of yellow fever, malaria, and snakebites during the construction of the first 40 km (25 mi) of railroad to San José. They were paid relatively well, however, and gradually their lot improved. By the 1930s many had obtained their own small plots of land, and when the price of cacao rose in the 1950s, they emerged as comfortable landowners employing migrant, landless Hispanics. However, until the Civil War of 1948, Afro-Caribbeans were forbidden from crossing to the Central Valley, for fear of upsetting the country's racial balance, and they were thus prevented from following work when, in the 1930s, United Fruit abandoned many of its blight-ridden plantations for green-field sites on the Pacific plain. Although Jamaicans brought some aspects of British colonial culture along with them, such as maypole dancing and cricket, these habits have long since given way to reggae and salsa, soccer and baseball. Many of the Atlantic coast Ticos are bilingual, speaking fluent English and Spanish, and to the south, around Puerto Viejo de Limón, you'll even hear some phrases that derive from the language of the indigenous peoples, among them the Kekoldi, the Bribri, and the Cabecar.

To the northeast is the Tortuguero region, whose centerpiece is Parque Nacional Tortuguero, where turtles arrive by the thousands to lay their eggs on the beaches. The occasional caiman can be spotted here, sunning on a bank or drifting like a log down a jungle waterway. And farther north still, sportfishing fans will find tarpon and snook aplenty to detain them off the shores of Barra del Colorado.

It's a short hop from Bribri, in the southern Cordillera de Talamanca, to the Río Sixaola bordering Panama; and just a few hours away are the Panamanian islands of the Bocas del Toro archipelago—islands difficult to reach from the population centers of Panama but an easy jaunt from the Atlantic side of Costa Rica. This quiet corner of Panama is home to the Parque Nacional Marina Isla Bastimentos, one of the great undiscovered diving spots in the Caribbean (☞ Bocas del Toro *in* Chapter 9).

A note on crime: During the 1990s some of the cocaine flowing from Latin America into the United States has spilled into the Puerto Viejo de Limón and Cahuita area, resulting in a drug-related crime problem. In the far north, close to the Nicaraguan border, Nicaraguan refugees have become rather aggressive in their efforts at squatting on and claiming land, some belonging to American and European investors. One does not wish to overemphasize difficulties in a country far safer than most, but they are real: two kidnappings of Europeans occurred in 1996. (Ransoms were paid, and no one suffered harm in the end.) If you are eager to experience Costa Rica's Caribbean beaches and jungles but wish to avoid the possibly more dangerous towns, head by boat or plane directly to Tortuguero or Barra del Colorado, or drive south through Puerto Viejo de Limón to savor the seaside jungle experience while being holed up in one of the many lodges, hotels, and tent camps that have opened along the road between Puerto Viejo de Limón and Manzanillo.

Pleasures and Pastimes

Dining
The number of upscale hotels, lodges, and restaurants opening in recent years has introduced a more varied international cuisine to the region. Yet much of the cooking along the Caribbean coast derives from old Jamaican recipes. *Rondon,* for example, is a traditional Jamaican stew that requires hours of preparation (notify your restaurateur well in advance). Rice and beans are flavored with coconut, meat is fried with hot spices to make *paties* (pies), and fish or meat, yams, plantains, breadfruit, peppers, and spices are boiled in coconut milk. Johnnycakes and *panbón* (a heavy spicy fruit bread) are popular baked goods. Various medicinal herbal teas are ubiquitous in the Lowlands. Seafood is, of course, readily available, as is a wide variety of fresh fruit.

Fishing
World-class tarpon and snook attract serious sportfishermen to the northern Caribbean shore in and offshore of the national parks of Tortuguero and Barra del Colorado. January through May is the best time for tarpon, August through November for snook.

Hiking and Jungle Boating
From the beach hiking of Parque Nacional Cahuita to the more leisurely jungle boat cruises arranged by the lodges near Parque Nacional Tortuguero, the opportunities for plunging into tropical jungle and rain forest abound in the Atlantic Lowlands. Farther inland on the eastern slope of the mountains, Braulio Carrillo's cloud- and rain-forested mountains offer scenic trails, and the private lowland reserves of La Selva and Rara Avis provide excellent jungle exploring. And in the southeast, the remote and little-touristed Reserva Biológica Hitoy Cerere contains a mix of difficult and easy hiking trails as the jungle climbs into the hills of the Talamanca range. Look for waterfalls, swimming holes, and an encyclopedic variety of Costa Rican flora and fauna.

Lodging
The Atlantic Lowlands have little in the way of luxury hotels, although in recent years a number of relatively upscale, self-proclaimed ecotourist lodges and other somewhat pricier accommodations have opened along the highway south of Puerto Limón and (especially) on the beach road south of Puerto Viejo de Limón. Nonetheless, most of the places to stay are either rustic *cabinas* (cottages) or nature lodges. Often isolated in the jungle and reached only by boat or strenuous hike, some of the lodges are rough, bare-essentials kinds of places; others verge on the luxurious. Given the difficulty inherent in getting supplies in to these luxe lodges, you will find that you'll have to pay a hefty price for the comforts of a hot shower and a cold beer in the jungle.

Snorkeling and Scuba Diving
Cahuita has Costa Rica's largest coral reef, and although it has been severely damaged by pollution, there is plenty still to admire. Other

dive spots include the coral reef at Isla Uvita off Puerto Limón, and the sea caverns off Puerto Viejo de Limón. The water is clearest during the dry season. In and around Parque Nacional Marina Isla Bastimentos near Bocas del Toro (☞ Chapter 9) in Panama, the snorkeling and diving are magnificent.

Surfing

Although some point breaks were badly affected by coastal uplift in 1991, other new ones were created—a left at Punta Cocles and a right at Punta Uva. Puerto Viejo de Limón's famous and formidable Salsa Brava is still ridable, but its spectacular waves are really only for the practiced and/or fearless surfer. Other, perhaps less hairy spots include Playa Negra, Cahuita, Playa Bonita north of Puerto Limón, and Isla Uvita, 20 minutes from Puerto Limón by boat. You must always beware of riptides. Off the coast of Panama are great reef breaks as yet to be discovered in the Bocas del Toro archipelago. December to March and June to August are the best times for surfing this coast.

Turtle-Watching

The Caribbean coast is one of the few places in the world where the green sea turtle nests. Great groups of them descend on Parque Nacional Tortuguero from July to October each year. Three other turtle species—the hawksbill, the loggerhead, and the giant leatherback—also nest in the park (☞ Close Up: Tican Turtles, *below*).

White-Water Rafting and Kayaking

The Atlantic side of the Cordillera Central is Costa Rica's white-water heartland. The Río Reventazón is the fiercest, with many class IV and V rapids suitable only for more experienced rafters and kayakers. The Río Pacuare, which runs parallel to it, has class III and IV rapids, ideal for adventurous beginners in guided boats, and passes through a spectacularly beautiful gorge en route to the lowland plain. At press time Costa Rica's national electric company, the ICE—under pressure from environmentalists and rafting companies—had shelved plans to employ hydroelectric dams on both the Pacuare and the Reventazón. For the moment, these irreplaceable natural treasures appear to be safe. According to local sources, the Pacuare dam would have submerged forever the river's awesomely beautiful gorge and its thrilling white water.

Exploring the Atlantic Lowlands and the Caribbean Coast

Below the cloud- and rain-forested mountains and foothills of the Cordillera Central and the Cordillera de Talamanca lie fertile agricultural plains, with the roadless jungles of Barra del Colorado and Tortuguero to the northeast. Significant remnants of primary tropical jungle are still evident in the flatlands of the agricultural plains. Although much of the land has been cleared and given over to farming and ranching, and most beaches are within walking distance of the road, vast expanses of this region are still inaccessible by car.

Numbers in the text correspond to numbers in the margin and on the Atlantic Lowlands and the Caribbean Coast map.

Great Itineraries

You need at least a week to cover this territory, but even three days are enough to sample the charms of Costa Rica's Caribbean side if you plan your time judiciously. In addition to the difficulties of getting around, it should be emphasized that the Atlantic Lowlands and the mountains above offer a wide selection of activities requiring different levels of physical endurance and commitment, ranging from seashore lounging to rain-forest trekking. If your time, energy, and willingness to put up with discomfort—mud, mosquitoes, and rain, for starters—are limited, you'll have to make choices. Another consideration is travel time. The Rara Avis preserve, for example, is a wonderful place to visit, but the difficulty in getting there—a two- to four-hour tractor haul into the park—explains the two-night minimum stay requirement. Reaching Parque Nacional Marina Isla Bastimentos in Panama takes roughly six hours from Puerto Viejo de Limón by way of a sequence of buses, taxis, and water taxis. At the end of a six-hour haul you might want to spend at least a couple of days in the Bocas del Toro (☞ Chapter 9) before facing the long trek back.

Be honest with yourself. Do you want to spend your vacation roughing it, slogging through virgin mud in Reserva Biológica Hitoy Cerere, or would you rather see the jungle from the comfort of a motorized launch, cruising through the canals of Parque Nacional Tortuguero, then finishing the day with a well-cooked meal at the elegantly rustic Tortuga Lodge? Similarly, Puerto Viejo de Limón is a fun, funky little town, but if you're not a surfer-hippie type—this town is swarming with twentysomething surfpunks and would-be Rastafarians these days—there's probably no reason to visit there for more than an hour or two, en route to one of the better hotels at Punta Uva or Punta Cocles.

A final note: keep in mind that there are two towns called Puerto Viejo on the Atlantic side of Costa Rica. One, Puerto Viejo de Sarapiquí, is a former river port that lies in the more northerly, inland section of the Lowlands; the other, Puerto Viejo de Limón, is on the coast not far from the border with Panama. Keeping these towns straight can be confusing, since locals often refer to both of them merely as "Puerto Viejo" without the clarifying "de Sarapiquí" and "de Limón." Plus there's plain Puerto Limón, often called Limón.

IF YOU HAVE 3 OR 4 DAYS AND LOVE THE BEACH

Hop on an early flight from San José to ☷ **Tortuguero** ⑥ or ☷ **Barra del Colorado** ⑦ for a jungle boat tour. Next morning take the boat down to Moín, and head south by car; or take the boat to Moín and then taxi from Moín to **Puerto Limón** ⑨, and take a bus or drive from Puerto Limón south to ☷ **Cahuita** ⑪ and/or ☷ **Puerto Viejo de Limón** ⑬. Relax on the beach or spend the day playing in the surf, snorkeling, and hiking through the Parque Nacional Cahuita. Camp at Puerto Vargas or stay a couple of nights in Cahuita, Puerto Viejo de Limón, Punta Uva, or farther south along the beach road, which terminates at the bird-filled jungles and deserted beaches of the **Refugio Nacional de Vida Silvestre Gandoca-Manzanillo** ⑭.

IF YOU HAVE 3 DAYS AND LOVE THE RAIN FOREST

Wake early in San José and drive or bus over the Carretera Guápiles, or Guápiles Highway, to hike **Parque Nacional Braulio Carrillo** ① or ride the **Rain Forest Aerial Tram**—get there early, since the people in the first gondolas into the forest will see the most wildlife. Then drive or bus to ☷ **Zona Protectora La Selva** ③ (it's a 2-km/1-mi walk from the road to the La Selva entrance, so pack light if you're taking public transportation) and spend the afternoon hiking its network of trails. Spend a night there (reservations essential), then move to one of the lodges in the ☷ **Puerto Viejo de Sarapiquí** ④ area, most of which offer horseback excursions into the jungle, hiking, rafting, and kayaking. Or, after a night at La Selva, you can leave early the next morning and bus or drive back to Las Horquetas to meet the 9 AM tractor, which will take you into ☷ **Rara Avis** ② for two days and nights (two-night minimum stay, reservations essential).

IF YOU HAVE 3 OR 4 DAYS AND WANT A MIX

An alternative with appeal for archaeology buffs would start with an early trip by car through Turrialba to the Monumento Nacional

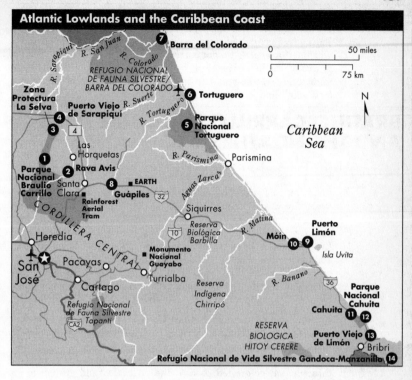

Atlantic Lowlands and the Caribbean Coast

Guayabo (☞ Chapter 3), Costa Rica's primary site for pre-Columbian ruins. From there the road follows the Río Reventazón east; stop at the Centro Agronómico Tropical de Investigación y Enseñanza (CATIE) to admire the grounds and the tropical plant research and to do some bird-watching. From there head down from the mountains to meet the main highway at Siquirres. Near **Guápiles** ⑧, make another stop at EARTH University to check out the alternative agricultural activities. Drive east, bypass **Puerto Limón** ⑨, and head south for two days of beach, jungle, surf, and sun at ⛺ **Cahuita** ⑪, ⛺ **Puerto Viejo de Limón** ⑬, and the kilometers of beaches between and beyond.

IF YOU HAVE 7 DAYS OR MORE

Explore any or all of the above however you find most congenial, then consider some variations: add an overnight rafting trip down the Río Pacuare, near Turrialba (☞ Chapter 3), or take a fishing trip out of **Barra del Colorado** ⑦ or **Tortuguero** ⑥; these can run one, two, or three days, or more. You might want to arrange to visit the Bribri, Cabecar, or Kekoldi Indian reservations in the hills west of **Puerto Viejo de Limón** ⑬ or hike into the remote Reserva Biológica Hitoy Cerere. Finally, if you love snorkeling amidst pristine coral reefs, block out two or three days to visit Bocas del Toro and Bastimentos Island National Marine Park in Panama (☞ Chapter 9). From Changuinola, two hours by water taxi and bus gets you to Bocas, and an eight-hour bus ride gets you back to San José.

When To Tour the Atlantic Lowlands and the Caribbean Coast

In three words: when it's dry. This realm absorbs 200 or more inches of rain a year, so unless you are planning to view the turtles laying eggs on the beach (each species has its own schedule), you'll want to avoid the worst of it. Chances are you'll be rained on no matter when you go, but your best bets for good weather are the Atlantic Coast's two short "dry" seasons—September and October and March and April—which unfortunately do not correspond to the dry season or the high tourist season in the rest of the country. If you don't mind the rain, go in the rainy season: you may be waterlogged your entire visit, but at least you'll find lower prices and few tourists.

BRAULIO CARRILLO NATIONAL PARK AND THE NORTHERN LOWLANDS

Rara Avis, La Selva, Puerto Viejo de Sarapiquí

The immense Parque Nacional Braulio Carrillo, northeast of San José, extends toward the Caribbean coast. The park protects virgin rain forest on either side of the highway to Guápiles; you can get some idea of it as you pass through on the highway, but inside is another world. Everywhere you look, green things sprout, twist, and bloom. Bromeliads and orchids cling to arching trees while white-faced monkeys and blue morpho butterflies creep, climb, and flutter. Adjacent to the park is the Rain Forest Aerial Tram, a private reserve, where you can explore the flora and fauna of the rain-forest canopy via gondolas.

After threading through Braulio Carrillo, the Guápiles Highway branches at Santa Clara, having completed its descent onto the Caribbean plain. To the southeast, the highway continues on to Puerto Limón and the Caribbean coast; to the north, the smoothly paved road leads through flat, deforested pasture and pockets of old growth forest toward two preserves, Rara Avis and La Selva. Continue farther north to reach the old river-port town of Puerto Viejo de Sarapiquí and the forest-clad hills of the eastern slope of the central mountains.

Parque Nacional Braulio Carrillo

❶ *30 km (19 mi) north of San José.*

In a country where deforestation has been and still is rife, Parque Nacional Braulio Carrillo (Braulio Carrillo National Park; ☞ Chapter 10) provides the rare opportunity to see dense primary tropical cloud forest as far as the eye can see. The park owes its foundation to the public outcry provoked by the construction of the highway through the region in the late 1970s, when the government bowed to pressure from environmentalists. With the highway running through it, the park's rain forest is the most accessible in Costa Rica for travelers from the San José area. Covering 171 sq mi, the park's extremely diverse terrain extends from 100 to more than 9,500 ft above sea level; the park reaches from the central volcanic range down the Atlantic slope to La Selva research station near Puerto Viejo de Sarapiquí. Six thousand tree species, 500 different birds, and 135 types of mammals have been cataloged here.

Braulio Carrillo's **Zurquí ranger station** is to the right of the road, a quarter mile before the Zurquí tunnel. Ascents start here and are steep, so the paths inevitably involve a lot of ups and downs. Note: before you head out on one of the trails, put on boots to protect yourself from the mud and possible snakes. The main 1½-km (1-mi) long trail through primary forest culminates in a *mirador* (vantage point); unfortunately the highway is included in the view. If you start early, preferably before 8 AM, you are more likely to avoid the mist that can obscure your view. Monkeys, tapirs, jaguars, kinkajous (a nocturnal tree-living, raccoonlike mammal), sloths, raccoons, margays (a small spotted cat similar to the ocelot), and porcupines all live in the forest, although most animals are very shy. Resident birds include the quetzal and the eagle. Orchids, bromeliads, heliconias, fungi, and mushrooms can be seen throughout. From the **Carrillo ranger station,** 22 km (14 mi) down the highway from Zurquí, the trails are less steep and make for an easier jaunt. For access to the 9,500-ft **Volcán Barva,** you need to start from Sacramento, north of Heredia. The walk to the crater takes two to three hours, but your efforts will be rewarded by great views. ☎ 283–8004 *for Sistemas de Areas de Conservación in San José; dial 192 for National Parks toll-free hot line.* 🎟 $6. ☉ Daily 7–4.

Rain Forest Aerial Tram

Adjacent to Parque Nacional Braulio Carrillo, a 1½-sq-mi preserve houses the Rain Forest Aerial Tram, a privately owned and operated engineering marvel consisting of a series of gondolas strung together in a modified ski-lift pulley system. (To lessen the impact on the jungle, the support pylons were flown into place by helicopter, with the chopper and pilot rented from neighboring Nicaragua's Sandinista Army.) The tram provides students, researchers, and tourists with a new way of seeing the rain-forest canopy—its spectacular array of epiphyte plant life and birds—from close above, hitherto possible only if you climbed the trees yourself. The founder, Dr. Donald Perry, developed a more primitive system of canopy touring at nearby Rara Avis. Of the two, this is the easier-to-use, commercialized version, and though purists might complain that it treats the rain forest like an amusement park ride, it is entertaining and educational—a great way to enlighten people about the beauty and value of rain forest ecology.

The 21 gondolas hold five people each, including a bilingual guide who is also a biologist. The guides are equipped with walkie-talkies so they can request brief stops for viewing or photography. The 2½-km (1½-mi) ride takes between 1 and 1½ hours, depending on the number of stops. There are simple day accommodations for researchers and students and a breakfast and lunch café on site. The price includes a biologist-guided walk through the area, for ground-level orientation before the tram ride. The walks commence at 6 AM, and the tram rides begin at 8 AM. San José pickups can be arranged, and there is a regular bus service (on the Guápiles line) every half hour. ☎ 257–5961, 🖷 257–6053 *for reservations.* 🎟 $47.50 guided walk and tram. AE, MC, V. ☉ Mon. 9–2, Tues.–Sun. 6–2.

Rara Avis

❷ *100 km (62 mi) north of San José.*

Toucans, sloths, green macaws, howler and spider monkeys, vested anteaters, and tapirs may be on hand to greet you when you arrive at Rara Avis, one of Costa Rica's most popular private reserves. Ecologist Amos Bien founded Rara Avis with the intent of combining research, tourism, and the sustainable extraction of forest products. Bilingual guides are on hand to take visitors along the muddy trails and canopy observation platforms and to help spot wildlife. Bring a camera: the reserve's lacy double waterfall is one of Costa Rica's most photographed sites. The site is open only to overnight guests.

The town of **Las Horquetas** is the jumping-off point for the 5-sq-mi private reserve. The 16-km (10-mi) trip from Horquetas to the reserve is accomplished in three hours on horseback, two to three hours by tractor (leaves daily at 8:30 AM), or one hour by Jeep, plus a rough 3-km (2-mi) hike up to the lodge proper. The trails are steep and rugged, but the flora and fauna along the way are remarkable. One note: some readers have complained that although the reserve itself is lovely, the guides and services were considerably less than what they had expected.

Lodging

$$$$ ⊞ **Rara Avis.** The Waterfall Lodge, named for the 180-ft waterfall nearby, contains hardwood-paneled rooms with chairs, firm beds, balconies, and hammocks. Despite the property's price range, these are rustic accommodations with minimal amenities. El Plástico Lodge used to be a prison and has coed bunk rooms and reductions for International Youth Hostel Federation members, students, and scientists. All rates include transport from Horquetas, guides, and three meals daily. Management requires a two-night minimum stay. ⊠ *Apdo. 8105–1000, San José, from Braulio Carrillo, turn left at signs for Puerto Viejo de Sarapiquí, travel 17 km (10½ mi) to town of Las Horquetas,* ☎ *710–6872, 253–0844, or 764–3131,* FAX *253–0844; 764–4187 reservations office in San José. 13 rooms, 8 with bath. Dining room. AE, MC, V.*

Zona Protectora La Selva

❸ *79 km (49 mi) northeast of San José, 6½ km (4 mi) south of Puerto Viejo di Sarapiquí.*

La Selva is a biologist's paradise, a 5¾-sq-mi reserve at the confluence of the Ríos Puerto Viejo and Sarapiquí, not far from the Rara Avis preserve. La Selva is a much more agreeable locale than Rara Avis for those who prefer to see wildlife without having to rough it—about 14 km (9 mi) north of the reserve is the beautiful Selva Verde Lodge (☞ Lodging, *below*). This **OTS (Organization for Tropical Studies)** biological research station is designed for scientists but welcomes visitors in the daytime and also offers basic lodging (☞ Lodging, *below*). Extensive and well-marked trails and swing bridges connect habitats as varied as tropical wet forest, swamps, creeks, rivers, secondary regenerating forests, and pasture. Exploring with the reserve's guides—who run informative 3½-hour nature walks and are some of the best in the country—is compulsory. You should reserve a walk and lunch (additional $5) ahead of time. The OTS van can transport visitors here from San José, or you can take a public bus.⊠ *OTS, Apdo. 676–2050, San Pedro, look for sign for La Selva Biological Station, west side of road, 6½ km/4 mi south of Puerto Viejo,* ☎ *766–6565; 240–6696 in San José.* ⌑ *$20 nature walk.* ☉ *Walks 8AM and 1:30 PM*

Lodging

$$$ ⊞ **La Selva Lodge.** Some of the region's other lodges offer more comfort for the money, but none can match La Selva's tropical nature experience. Accommodations are in dorm-style rooms with large bunk beds, ceiling fans, tile floors, and lots of screened windows. The restaurant, something like a school cafeteria, serves decent food but has a very limited schedule (reserve ahead). Lodging for $60 includes three meals and a guided nature walk. ⊠ *OTS, Apdo. 676–2050, San Pedro,* ☎ *766–6565; 240–6696 in San José, Restaurant. AE, MC, V.*

$$$ ⊞ **Selva Verde Lodge.** This expanding rancho-style complex is on the edge (across the Río Sarapiquí) of a ¾-sq-mi private reserve of tropical rain forest and caters primarily to retirees on natural-history tours. The river lodge stands on stilts over the Río Sarapiquí. All the buildings have wide verandas strung with hammocks, and bedrooms come with polished wood paneling, fans, and mosquito blinds. Activities include fishing, horseback riding, boat trips, rafting, mountain biking, canoeing, and guided walks. The rates include three meals per day in the hotel restaurant. ⊠ *Apdo. 55, Chilamate, Heredia, 7 km (4½) mi west of Puerto Viejo de Sarapiquí in Chilamate,* ☎ *766–6077 or 240–*

6696 reservations office in San José, FAX *766–6011. 54 rooms, 47 with bath. Restaurant, library. MC, V.*

Puerto Viejo de Sarapiquí

④ *6½ km (4 mi) north of La Selva.*

During the last century Puerto Viejo de Sarapiquí was a thriving river port and the only link with the Refugio Nacional de Fauna Silvestre Barra del Colorado and Parque Nacional Tortuguero. Fortunes nose-dived with the construction of the coastal canal from the town of Moín, and today Puerto Viejo bears a slightly run-down air. The activities of the Contras also made this a dangerous zone during the 1980s, but with the political situation now improved, boats once again ply the old route up the Río Sarapiquí to the Río San Juan on the Nicaraguan frontier; from here you can travel downstream to Barra del Colorado or Tortuguero. We haven't tried this route, but it sounds like an interesting trip. There's really not much here to grab the attention of tourists, although a couple of companies such as Desafío and Sunset Tours (☞ Guided Tours *in* Atlantic Lowlands and the Caribbean Coast A to Z, *below*) now offer river tours, with up to class III rapids, plus there is plenty of wildlife in the area.

Dining and Lodging

$$$ ✕🏨 **Rancho Leona.** This roadside ranch has small rustic dormitories with shared bath built to accommodate customers on package kayaking tours. Owners Ken and Leona Upcraft have opened the restaurant—serving very cheap, tasty food—to the public and say they'll put you up if there's room. With dazzling works of stained glass crafted in the adjacent studio, the restaurant has a varied menu with Italian specialties like eggplant parmigiana and chicken cacciatore and numerous vegetarian dishes. Activities include kayaking on the Sarapiquí, hiking to a beautiful 30-ft waterfall, and river swimming. ✉ *La Virgen de Sarapiquí, Heredia, 17 km (10½ mi) southwest of Puerto Viejo,* ☎ FAX *761–1019. 5 rooms without bath. Restaurant, library. No credit cards.*

$$$ 🏨 **El Gavilán Lodge.** The lodge, the erstwhile hub of a fruit and cattle
★ farm, is two stories high and fronted by a veranda. Comfortable bedrooms have white walls, terra-cotta floors, fans, and decorative *artesanía* (crafts). Beautiful manicured gardens run down to the river, and colorful tanagers (a brightly colored woodland bird) and three types of toucan feast in the citrus trees. The food, *comida típica* (typical Costa Rican fare), earns its good reputation. As do most, you can come here as part of a tour, with pickup in San José, for horseback jungle treks and boat trips up the Río Sarapiquí toward the Río San Juan and the border with Nicaragua. ✉ *Apdo. 445–2010, Zapote, San José, a few km southeast of Puerto Viejo; watch for the sign on the road southeast of Puerto Viejo de Sarapiquí,* ☎ *234–9507,* FAX *253–6556. 13 rooms with bath. Dining room, hot tub, fishing. AE, MC, V.*

$$–$$$ 🏨 **Islas del Rió.** A reasonable option for Río Sarapiquí travelers, this little lodge about 10 km (6 mi) west of Puerto Viejo keeps rooms in the main building or in cement cabinas. A spacious open-air restaurant offers basic fare. The greatest feature is the Río Sarapiquí, rushing past in the "backyard." Hikes, horseback trips, and meals are included in the price of a room; rooms with bath have hot water. ✉ *Bajos de Chilamate, on the road between Puerto Viejo de Sarapiquí and Las Virgen,* ☎ *233–0366,* FAX *233–9671,* ☎ FAX *710–6898. 12 rooms, 9 with bath. Restaurant, hiking, horseback riding. No credit cards.*

$$ \qquad $$ ☒ **Hotel Bambu.** Unlike most of the region's isolated properties, this hotel is right in the heart of the little town of Puerto Viejo de Sarapiquí. The upstairs rooms are nothing special, simple but comfortable, with private baths, hot water, and TVs. A dense cluster of tall bamboo stalks climbs like Jack's beanstalk out of the hotel's garden, providing shade for a new bar and restaurant serving Costa Rican–style Chinese food at reasonable prices. ☒ *Apdo. 151–A–2100, on main street across from the town square/soccer field, Guadeloupe ,* ☎ *766–6005,* FAX *766–6132. 11 rooms with bath. Restaurant, bar. MC, V.*

TORTUGUERO AND BARRA DEL COLORADO

Tortuguero means "turtle region," and this area, tucked into northeastern Costa Rica, remains one of the world's prime spots for viewing the awesome life cycle of sea turtles. The stretch of beach between the Colorado and Matina rivers was first mentioned as a nesting ground for sea turtles in 1592, in a Dutch chronicle, and due to the area's isolation—there isn't a road here to this day—the turtles were able to get on with their nesting virtually undisturbed for centuries. By the mid-1900s, however, the harvesting of eggs and catching of turtles had increased to such an extent that the turtles faced extinction. In 1963 an executive decree regulated the hunting of turtles and the gathering of eggs, and in 1970 the government established the Parque Nacional Tortuguero (☞ Chapter 10). The area is also home to watery Refugio Nacional de Fauna Silvestre Barra del Colorado.

Parque Nacional Tortuguero

❺ *50 km (31 mi) northwest of Puerto Limón .*

Tortuguero National Park's claim to fame is its turtle nesting: at various times of the year, green, hawksbill, loggerhead, and giant leatherback turtles lumber up the beaches here and deposit their eggs for safe keeping—a fascinating natural ritual to witness (☞ Close Up: Tican Turtles, *below*). Freshwater turtles inhabit the rivers at Tortuguero, as do crocodiles, which are most prevalent in the Río Agua Fría, and the endangered *vacas marinas,* or manatees. Manatees consume huge quantities of aquatic plants, and are endangered mainly because their lack of speed renders them easy prey for hunters. You might catch glimpses of tapirs (watch for these in the jolillo groves), jaguars, anteaters, ocelots, howler monkeys, collared and white-lipped peccaries, raccoons, otters, skunks, and coatis. Some 350 species of birds and countless butterflies—the iridescent blue morpho one of them—inhabit the area.

Deep in the Tortuguero jungle, the **Canadian Organization for Tropical Education and Rainforest Conservation** has set up a small station, where a couple of volunteers are running a butterfly farm, cataloging plants and animals, and exploring sustainable forest practices.

Tortuguero

❻ *There are no roads to Tortuguero; flying time from San José airport 30 mins; 3 hrs by boat from Moín.*

To the north of Parque Nacional Tortuguero, the hamlet of Tortuguero, with its 600 inhabitants, two churches, three bars, and two souvenir shops, is a pleasant little place to spend an hour or two if you are in the area for more than a day. Be sure to visit the headquarters of the Caribbean Conservation Corporation, check out the information kiosk

TICAN TURTLES

COSTA RICA'S TURTLE visitations are renowned in the world of eco-tourism. On both the Pacific and Atlantic-Caribbean coasts, an array of species make their predictable but no-less-amazing annual visits to beaches, many set aside to protect them. Alas! In spite of this protection, the endangered classifications, and the earnest ecologists and well-meaning people looking after them, turtle populations remain seriously threatened: poachers have for generations harvested the eggs—a rumored aphrodisiac—and/or the meat and shells; beachfront development, with bright lights, can disorient the turtles; and long-line fishermens' nets entangle the turtles, causing them to drown.

Nesting turtles come ashore at night, plowing an uneven furrow with their flippers to propel themselves to the high-tide line, beyond which they use their hind flippers to scoop out a hole in which to lay their eggs. A couple of months later, the hatchlings struggle out of the nests and make their perilous journey to the sea.

On the east coast, four species of turtles nest at Parque Nacional Tortuguero: the green turtle, hawksbill, loggerhead, and the giant leatherback. Green turtles reproduce in large groups from July to October. A green turtle lays eggs on average every two to three years and produces two or three clutches each time. In between, they feed as far afield as Florida and Venezuela. Small in comparison with their peers, hawksbills are threatened by hunters because of their shells, a transparent brown much sought after to make jewelry in countries like Japan. Loggerheads, as their name implies, have outsized heads and shorter fins, and make rare appearances at Tortuguero. The giant leatherback is the largest of all turtle species; individu-

als grow up to 6½ ft long, and can weigh in at up to 1,000 lbs. They have a tough outer skin instead of a shell, hence the name. From mid-February through April, leatherbacks nest mainly in the southern sector of Tortuguero.

Olive ridleys are the smallest of the sea turtles—the average carapace, or hardback shell, is 21–29 inches—and the least shy. During mass nestings, or *arribadas*, thousands of olive ridley turtles take to the Pacific shores at night, plowing the sand as they move up the beach sniffing for the high-tide line.

It is estimated that 200,000 of the 500,000 turtles that nest each year in Costa Rica choose Playa Nancite, a gray-sand beach in Guanacaste's Parque Nacional Santa Rosa, backed by dense hibiscus and button mangroves. It is the world's only totally protected olive ridley turtle arribada. Easier to reach is the Ostional refuge, near Nosara on the Nicoya Peninsula. Locals harvest the eggs in the early stages of the arribada—visits run from August to December and peak in September and October—for the later arrivals invariably destroy the earlier nests.

MORE ACCESSIBLE IS Playa Grande, on Nicoya, stamping ground of the mammoth, ponderous, and yet exquisitely dignified leatherback turtles from November to April. Parque Nacional Marino Las Baulas was created specifically to protect the leatherbacks, who also show up in smaller numbers at Playas Langosta and Junquillal.

To help save these gentle giants, you can volunteer with turtle research and protection. *See* Close-Up: Volunteer Vacations, *in* Chapter 10.

on the park, turtles, wildlife, and so on in town center, and take a stroll along the 32 km (20 mi) of beach—although swimming here is not recommended due to strong riptides and the presence (although, according to locals, no one has ever actually been attacked) of large numbers of nurse sharks and barracuda.

The **Caribbean Conservation Corporation** (CCC) opened a Visitor's Center and Museum in Tortuguero in late 1994. Actor Cliff Robertson narrates the video history of the area, and the exhibits include excellent animal photos as well as detailed discussions of what's going on in the area, ecologically speaking, and what one can do to help. There's a souvenir shop next door, and at least one other store in Tortuguero sells locally produced crafts. ⊠ *Apdo. 246–2050, Att: Tortuguero, San Pedro, from beach walk north along path and watch for sign,* ☎ *710–0547; 224–9215 San José office.* ⊙ *Daily 10–noon, 2–5:30.*

For the committed ecotourist, the **Casa Verde Green Turtle Research Station** (⊠ By the airport, across the canal from Tortuga Lodge, ☎ 352/373–6441 in the U.S.) has camping areas as well as dormitory-style quarters with a communal kitchen. If you're interested in a deeper involvement in the life of the turtles, you can arrange a stay through the CCC.

OFF THE BEATEN PATH	**COASTAL CANALS** – The jungle life seen during a three-hour boat trip through the combination of natural and man-made canals between Tortuguero and Moín is awesome, a kind of real-life amusement park adventure ride. As you swoop through the sinuous turns of the natural waterways, your driver-guide will spot monkeys, snakes, caiman, mud turtles, sloths, and dozens of different birds, including flocks of bright, noisy parrots, kingfishers, aracaris, and assorted herons. The densely layered greenery is highlighted by brilliantly colored flowers—and the visual impact is doubled by the jungle's reflection in the mirror-smooth surface of the water. You should definitely plan on either leaving or arriving by boat.

Dining and Lodging

$$$$ ✕🏨 **Mawamba Lodge.** This lodge is the perfect place to kick back and relax. Once whisked from Moín in a fast launch (2½ hours), you stay in comfortable rustic cabinas with hot water baths, garden views, and fans, and dine in the spacious dining room. All-inclusive packages include guided tours of the jungle, canals, and turtle-laying beaches, all meals, and transfers. ⊠ *Apdo. 10980–1000, San José, 1 km (½ mi) north of Tortuguero on ocean side of canal,* ☎ *710–7282; 223–2421 reservations office in San José,* FAX *222–5463. 36 cabinas. Dining room, pool, conference room. MC, V.*

$$$ ✕🏨 **Tortuga Lodge.** Costa Rica Expeditions owns this thatched river-
★ side lodge, surrounded by lush lawns, orchids, and tropical trees and renowned for its tarpon and snook fishing. The second-largest tarpon ever caught in Costa Rica, weighing 182 pounds, was reeled in here in 1987. The bedrooms are comfortable, with fans, mosquito blinds, and hot water. A couple of short hiking trails from the property lead into the nearby jungle, where you might see bright-red poison dart frogs and other critters. The mosquitoes can be voracious; wear repellent and long sleeves. Considering most of the restaurant ingredients are flown in, the chefs do an excellent job producing voluminous quantities of hearty, well-prepared food. The lodge is across the river from the airstrip, 2 km (1 mi) from Tortuguero. Most guests come as part of a tour. ⊠ *Apdo 6941–1000, San José, 20 mins north by boat from Parque Nacional Tortuguero or 35 mins by plane from San José,* ☎ FAX

710–6861; ☎ *257–0766 reservations office in San José,* FAX *257–1665. 25 rooms with bath. Bar, dining room, fishing. AE, MC, V.*

$$ ✕⊟ **El Manatí.** The friendly owners, Fernando and Lilia Figuls, adopted the indigenous rough-hewn wood-and-cane architectural style when they carved this comfortable lodge out of the jungle. The sparkling-clean wood-paneled rooms have firm beds, mosquito screens, and fans. The terraces look across a narrow lawn to the river, where you can kayak and canoe. Chestnut-beaked toucans, poison arrow frogs, and three types of monkey hang out in the jungle looming behind the rooms. The Figuls are currently working with the legendary guides Modesto and Fran Watson on tour packages. Call the Watsons (☎ FAX 226–0986) for further information and to book a two- or three-day trip aboard their *Riverboat Francesca.* ✉ *Across river, about 1 km (½ mi) north of Tortuguero,* FAX *239–0911. 8 rooms with bath. Dining room, Ping-Pong, boating. No credit cards.*

Barra del Colorado

❼ *25 km (16 mi) northwest of Tortuguero.*

Farther up the coast is the ramshackle hamlet of Barra del Colorado, a sportfishing paradise characterized by stilted, plain wooden houses, dirt paths, and no motorized land vehicles, although some locals have added outboard motors to their hand-hewn canoes. Bordered in the north by the Río San Juan and the frontier with Nicaragua is the vast 350-sq-mi **Refugio Nacional de Fauna Silvestre Barra del Colorado** (☞ Chapter 10), really the only area attraction for nonanglers. Approach is by air or boat from San José or Tortuguero, and transport once you get there is almost exclusively waterborne; there are virtually no paths in this swampy terrain. Apart from the route via Tortuguero, you can come from Puerto Viejo de Sarapiquí up the Ríos Sarapiquí and San Juan. The list of species that you are likely to see from your boat is virtually the same as that for Tortuguero; the main difference here is the greater feeling of being more off the beaten track.

Dining and Lodging

$$$$ ✕⊟ *Rain Goddess.* Dining, lodging, and everything else is self-contained on Dr. Alfredo López's 65-ft-long *Rain Goddess,* a small floating luxury hotel that travels up the Río San Juan and around the Barra del Colorado area, offering guests an opportunity for nature cruising and deep-sea fishing—there are two seaworthy fishing and excursion boats in tow—depending on their own preferences. The emphasis is on fishing, but the amenities include first-class food, hot showers, air-conditioning, handcrafted furnishings, color TV with a video library, and covered decks. Five- to seven-day packages include van pickup in San José for transfer to speedboat at Puerto Viejo de Sarapiquí, and a fast trip downriver to the *Rain Goddess,* waiting on the Río San Juan. Note that if you use a credit card, you are charged a 7% fee. ✉ *Apdo. 850–1250, San José,* ☎ *231–4299 San José office; 800/308–3394 in the U.S.,* FAX *231–3816. Sleeps 12 in 6 staterooms. AE, MC, V.*

$$$$ ✕⊟ **Río Colorado Lodge.** This jungle lodge caters almost exclusively to sportfishing folk on its modern fleet of 16- and 23-ft sportfishing vessels. Lodge bedrooms have twin beds with patterned bedspreads, paneled ceilings, white curtains, and basket lamp shades. Expensive all-inclusive tours include the flight here from San José, all meals, and fishing. The lodge also offers fly-in, boat-out nature tour packages, including Parque Nacional Tortuguero tours at lower prices. *Apdo. 5094–1000, San José, 35-min flight from San José via Travelair,* ☎ *232–8610 San José office; 800/243–9777 in the U.S.,* FAX *231–5987. 18 rooms with bath. Restaurant, bar, fishing. AE, MC, V.*

COASTAL TALAMANCA

The quickest route from San José to the Atlantic coast runs through the magnificent cloud forest of Parque Nacional Braulio Carrillo before reaching the Caribbean Sea and the lively—and sometimes dangerous—port town of Puerto Limón. The 160-km (100-mi) trip along the Carretera Guápiles, or Guápiles Highway, to the coast takes about 2½ hours, with all going well—the highway, carved out of mountainous jungle, is susceptible to landslides. Make sure it's not blocked before heading out.

As the highway descends and straightens toward Guápiles, you will enter Limón province, where cloud forest gives way to banana plantations and partially deforested pastureland (and the highway gives way to potholes). This region is also home to farms producing cocoa, exotic export plants, and macadamia nuts. Many of the crystal-clear green rivers running through the area have bathing pools. After passing through villages with names like Bristol, Stratford, and Liverpool, you arrive in the provincial capital, Puerto Limón.

Guápiles

8 *60 km (38 mi) east of San José on the Carretera Guápiles.*

There may not seem to be many reasons to stop in the Guápiles area—the town itself is off the main road—other than weariness or the need for a fast gas and food fix. However, this farm and forest area, home to several major biological research facilities as well as commercial tropical plant producers, might be worth another look. It is a kind of crossroads: more or less equidistant are the palm beaches of the Caribbean shore, the jungles to the north, and the rain-forested mountains looming in the west. For this reason it isn't a bad place to linger for a day or two, day tripping in any of three directions.

Dining and Lodging

$$ ✕ **The Ponderosa.** This lively restaurant features, you guessed it, a variety of steak dishes and noncarnivorous entrées. Although the grill chef tends to oversalt the meat, the range of beefy selections for $5–$10 is impressive: filet mignon, sirloin, T-bone, and sirloin tips with jalapeños are but a few. There's a full bar, souvenir shop, and live music on weekends. Rumor has it the place rocks on Saturday nights. With photographs of Ben Cartwright and the boys, maps of the Ponderosa, and other Bonanza memorabilia, '60s TV buffs should feel right at home. ✉ *East of San José on Carretera Guápiles, near Braulio Carrillo, about 5 km (3 mi) east of the turnoff for Los Horquetas, Rara Avis, La Selva, and the northern zone,* ☎ *710–7144. MC, V.*

$$–$$$ 🏠 **Hotel Rio Palmas.** Call it a hacienda motel. Proximate to EARTH (☞ *below*), the Rio Palmas grabs your eye as you're speeding by on the Carretera Guápiles, thanks to the red-tiled roof topping its charming open-air restaurant. Behind an arched, whitewashed entry gate, one-story whitewashed cabinas with tile roofs wrap around a central courtyard with a fountain and plants. Rooms with bath (and hot water) have TVs. Exotic plantings abound, in fact, as the hotel is on an ornamental plant farm. The management can arrange hikes, farm and jungle tours, and horseback rides to private waterfalls. ✉ *Carretera Guápiles,* ☎ *760–0305,* FAX *760–0296. 32 rooms and cabinas, 24 with bath. Restaurant, pool, hiking, horseback riding. AE, MC, V.*

EARTH (Escuela de Agricultura de la Region Tropical Humeda)

15 km (9 mi) east of Guápiles.

Agriculture and ecology buffs will want to check out the Escuela de Agricultura de la Region Tropical Humeda, a nonprofit research center emphasizing hands-on involvement in the study and production of less pesticide-dependent bananas and other forms of sustainable agriculture as well as medicinal plants. (You'll find EARTH's elegant collection of stationery and other paper products made from banana stems in many tourist shops.) A banana plantation and a forest reserve with nature trails are on the property, which is on the Carretera Guápiles a few kilometers east of Guápiles. You are welcome to stay in the university's 50-person lodging facility, replete with private baths, hot water, and ceiling fans, for $20–$30, which includes the use of a swimming pool and exercise equipment. Costa Rica Expeditions (☎ 222–0333, ℻ 257–1665) offers a one-day guided tour package for $69. ☎ 255–2000, ℻ 255–2726.

En Route If you are bypassing Puerto Limón entirely, and heading south to Cahuita and Puerto Viejo de Limón, a right turn 3 km (2 mi) shy of Puerto Limón will take you on an alternate route—a smooth new road that weaves through the hills. Look for the white road sign that indicates a right turn to Sixaola and other points south.

Puerto Limón

⑨ *130 km (81 mi) southeast of Parque Nacional Braulio Carrillo, 100 km (62 mi) southeast of Guápiles.*

Puerto Limón's promontory setting, overlooking the Caribbean, is inherited from an ancient Indian village, Cariari, which lay close to the Isla Uvita, where Christopher Columbus lay anchor on his final voyage in 1502. The colorful Afro-Caribbean flavor of Costa Rica's most important port (population 50,000) gives many visitors their first glimpse of life on Costa Rica's east coast. Puerto Limón is a lively if shabby town with a 24-hour street life. The wooden houses are brightly painted, but the grid-plan streets bear a somewhat worn appearance, largely due to the damage caused by the 1991 earthquake. Street crime, including pick-pocketing and night muggings, is common in this port town, and staying overnight is not recommended.

On the left of the highway as you enter Puerto Limón is a large **Chinese cemetery**; Chinese made up a large part of the ill-starred railroad construction team that worked here. Follow the railroad as far as the palm-lined **promenade** that runs around the Parque Vargas. From the promenade you can see the raised dead coral left stranded by the quake. Nine hoffman's two-toed sloths live in the trees of **Parque Vargas**; ask a passerby to point them out, as sighting them requires a trained eye. From the park, find the lively **market** on Avenida 2, between Calles 3 and 4, where you can buy fruit for the road ahead.

Dining and Lodging

Puerto Limón is a run-down, crime-prone town these days, and a hard sell to wary travelers, but the hotels along the beachfront bluffs north of town deserve to prosper.

$–$$ ✕ **Springfield.** Protected from the street by a leafy conservatory, this Caribbean kitchen whips up tasty rice and bean dishes. Decor consists of wood paneling, red tablecloths, and a white tile floor. Bring your dancing shoes: the huge dance floor out back creaks to the beat of soca, salsa, and reggae on weekends. ⊠ *On road north from Puerto Limón* *to Portete, left opposite hospital,* ☎ *758–1203. Reservations not accepted. AE, MC, V.*

$$$ 🏨 **Hotel Maribú Caribe.** Perched on a cliff overlooking the Caribbean
★　Sea, between Puerto Limón and Portete, these white, conical thatched
huts have great views, air-conditioning, and hot water. Green lawns,
shrubs, palm trees, and a large, kidney-shape pool dominate the lovely
gardens. The poolside bar does away with the need for any added exertion. ✉ *Apdo. 623–7300, San José, Carretera to Portete,* ☎ *758–
4010,* FAX *758–3541. 52 rooms with bath. Restaurant, bar, snack bar,
pool. AE, MC, V.*

$$$ 🏨 **Hotel Matama.** If you're coming from San José and planning to catch
an early boat north out of Moín, this is a great spot to get your first
taste of the Caribbean. The property is across the street from the
beach, 2 km (1 mi) up the road from the Maribú Caribe (☞ *above*).
A new pool has been installed by the bar and the grounds are gorgeously
landscaped throughout with botanical trails. The open-air restaurant
offers lovely views of the gardens. Rooms have phones, air-conditioning, and TVs. ✉ *Apdo. 606, Limón,* ☎ *758–1123, 758–4409,
or 758–1797,* FAX *758–4499. 12 rooms with bath. Restaurant, bar, pool,
meeting room. AE, MC, V.*

Moín

❿ *5 km (3 mi) north of Puerto Limón.*

The docks at Moín are a logical next stop from neighboring Puerto
Limón, especially if you want to take a boat north to explore the
Caribbean coast. Possibly you can also negotiate a waterway–national
park tour with a local guide, and if you're lucky or made a call in advance you'll find the man considered the best guide on the Caribbean
coast. His name is Modesto Watson (☞ Guided Tours *in* Atlantic
Lowlands and the Caribbean Coast A to Z, *below*), and he is legendary
for his bird- and animal-spotting skills as well as his howler monkey
calls.

En Route　As you head south from Puerto Limón, the Caribbean character of the
Atlantic Lowlands becomes powerfully evident, in the surf rolling
shoreward on your left; in the hot, humid stir of the Caribbean trade
winds; in the laid-back pace of the people you meet. This is tropical
Central America, and it feels like another country, its slow, somewhat
sultry atmosphere far removed from the business and bustle of San José.
The coast is lined with gorgeous black- and white-sand beaches fringed
with palm trees. Way offshore, you can see white-water breaks where
the waves crash over coral reefs. Following the nearly ruler-straight coastline, the road is smooth and well paved, with indents and curves mirroring the coastal geography, and the occasional bank of dead coral
exposed above the surface. Passing through cleared forests of banana
plantations and stands of primary jungle, you'll now and then cross a
rebuilt bridge reaching over a slow green river, its peaceful waters belying the fierce flooding that has washed out the lowland bridges—those
that survived the big earthquake—time and time again. By late 1997,
however, all the bridges were in decent shape, but the road itself is pocked
with enormous potholes and unpaved stretches. Don't dare drive fast,
and keep your eyes on the road. Some of these holes are big enough
to swallow an entire wheel, and if you hit one going too fast you'll probably destroy your car's suspension, or get a flat tire at best. Watch carefully for the left turn to Cahuita about 44 km (27 mi) out of Puerto
Limón; it is quite easy to miss. Turn right at the end of the first of three
entrance roads to get to Cahuita's main drag.

Cahuita

⑪ *44 km (27 mi) southeast of Puerto Limón.*

Dusty Cahuita, its main dirt street flanked by wooden-slat cabins, is a backpackers' holiday town with something of a druggy reputation, a hippie hangout with a dash of Afro-Caribbean spice tossed in. The town's reputation as a dangerous drug haven is only partially deserved; like Puerto Viejo de Limón, Cahuita has its share of junkies, but they are not perceived by locals as a threat. Nor should they be by tourists. The turquoise **Salón Vaz** in Cahuita emits lively reggae, soca, and samba 24 hours a day; the assemblage of dogs dozing on its veranda sums up the laid-back pace of life here. Turn left at the main intersection for the **Turística Cahuita** information center (☎ 755–0071); Joaquín Fuentes can set you up with a variety of adventures, including tours to the canals, Indian reservations, and mountains; river rafting and kayaking; and bike and snorkeling-equipment rentals. They can also reconfirm flights and make reservations. At the southern end of Cahuita's main street is the start of **Parque Nacional Cahuita** (☞ *below,* and Chapter 10).

Dining and Lodging

$$ ✕ **Edith Soda y Restaurant.** Miss Edith is revered for her outrageous
★ Caribbean cooking, vegetarian meals, and herbal teas for whatever ails you. Don't expect to get anything in a hurry; most of her dishes are made to order. But her rondon and smoked chicken are worth the wait. Her restaurant is on an easy-to-miss side street at the north end of town, near the *guardia rural* (police station). ⊠ *From bus station, follow main road north, turn right at police station,* ☎ *No phone. No credit cards. Closed Tues. No lunch Sun.*

$$ ✕ **Vista del Mar.** The main attraction of this open-air, aluminum-roof eatery is its proximity to Parque Nacional Cahuita. After a hard day of sunbathing, you need walk only about 10 steps past the park exit to sample the Vista's intriguing selection of Chinese-influenced Costa Rican casados (plates of white rice, beans, fried plantains, salad, cheese, and meat) and seafood dishes. The *pescado en salsa* (fish in sauce) is always fresh and delicious. ⊠ *South of bus stop, next to park entrance,* ☎ *755–0008. AE, MC, V.*

$$$ 🏨 **Aviarios del Caribe.** Luís and Judy Arroyo have built this lodge and
★ bird-watching sanctuary from the rubble of the 1991 earthquake. More than 285 species of bird have been spotted on the property, many with the help of the telescope on the wide second-floor deck. Spacious guest rooms have white walls, blue tile floors, and fresh flowers. Buttercup, the resident three-toed sloth, oversees the proceedings from her spot on the couch of the airy sitting room–library, and Koko the crocodile will arrive on demand to tangle with birds over morsels of cheese. For $3 you can hike the wildlife refuge, and $30 will get you an unforgettable 3½-hour riverboat wildlife-watching tour with Luís as your guide. ⊠ *Apdo. 569–7300, Puerto Limón, head south from city and follow hotel signs on Río Estrella delta, 9 km (5 mi) north of Cahuita,* ☎ 𝖥𝖠𝖷 *382–1335. 5 rooms with bath. Breakfast room, hiking. MC, V.*

$$$ 🏨 **Hotel Jaguar.** This hotel on Playa Negra provides the roomiest
★ digs—375-sq-ft singles, 540-sq-ft doubles—and some of the classiest cooking around. Naturally ventilated white cabinas have high ceilings, queen-size wooden beds, mosquito blinds, solar-heated water, and terra-cotta floors. You'll be delighted by the fruit trees and the virtual menagerie of exotic birds on the 17-acre grounds; pick up the guidebook detailing the botanical garden's trails, plants, and animals. With

goodies from their herb garden, the owners turn out a most popular recipe, *dorada en salsa de hierbas* (dorado fish in an herb sauce). Call ahead for possible transportation from Puerto Limón. ✉ *Apdo. 7046–1000, San José, from football field, 326 yds to the north; across from Playa Negra,* ☎ *755–0238; 226–3775 San José office,* FAX *226–4693 in San José. 45 cabinas. Restaurant, bar, pool, hiking. MC, V.*

$$$ 🏨 **Magellan Inn.** The owners sailed the seas for 20 years before land-
★ ing here around 1990 to build this group of bungalows, perhaps the most elegant around. Graced with tile-floored terraces facing a pool and gardens growing atop an ancient coral reef, the white-walled rooms have original artwork, custom-made wooden furniture, and ceiling fans. Feast on intensely flavored French and Creole seafood specialties in the charming Casa Creole, a freestanding coral-pink concoction with an outdoor dining room. Don't miss the house pâté or the homemade ice creams. The hotel's enticing open-air bar rocks to great blues and jazz recordings in the evenings, and mellows with classical music at breakfast. ✉ *Apdo. 1132, Puerto Limón, 2 km (1 mi) north of Cahuita at far end of Playa Negra,* ☎ FAX *755–0035. 6 rooms with bath. Restaurant, bar, pool. AE, DC, MC, V.*

$$–$$$ 🏨 **Atlántida Lodge.** Atlántida's main assets are its attractively landscaped grounds, the beach across the road, and its large swimming pool. The rooms have new tile floors, beds replete with headboards and night tables, and terraces with chairs. The guest rooms encircle a thatched restaurant that provides breakfast with the price of the room. You can also cook your own food. The managers cultivate a younger and trendier ambience than neighboring Jaguar's. ✉ *Next to soccer field at Playa Negra,* ☎ *758–0115,* ☎ FAX *755–0213. 30 rooms with bath. Restaurant, pool, hot tub, massage, meeting rooms. AE, MC, V.*

$$ 🏨 **El Encanto B&B.** Just north of town on the beach road, this 1996 property includes three tastefully designed, comfortable bungalows set in a lovely garden. Amenities include queen-size beds, ceiling fans, hot water, and secure parking. The California-born owners, Mike and Karen Russell, offer a hearty vegetarian breakfast with the price of a room. ✉ *Apdo. 1234, Limón,* ☎ FAX *755–0113. 3 bungalows. MC, V.*

$$ 🏨 **Kelly Creek Hotel-Restaurante.** Andres and Marie-Claude de Alcala, from Madrid, have transformed the Kelly Creek Hotel-Restaurante into a wonderful budget lodging option. Separating Cahuita from the national park, the handsome wooden hotel sits on the creek bank across a short pedestrian bridge from the park entrance. Four spacious hardwood-finished guest rooms feature beds big enough to sleep a small army. Señor de Alcala barbecues meat and fresh fish on an open-air grill, and also serves paella and other Spanish specialties. Caiman come to the creek bank seeking snacks, and the monkeys, parrots, jungles, and beaches of the national park are just a few yds away—as is the lively little center of Cahuita town. ✉ *Next to the national park entrance, Cahuita ,* ☎ *755–0007. 4 rooms with bath. Restaurant. AE, MC, V.*

Parque Nacional Cahuita

⑫ *Northern entrance at south edge of Cahuita. Main entrance is at Puerto Vargas, 5 km (3 mi) south of Cahuita en route south to Puerto Viejo de Limón.*

Parque Nacional Cahuita (Cahuita National Park) starts at the southern edge of Cahuita. Lush rain forest extends to the brink of the completely undeveloped curving white-sand beach that stretches for 3 km (2 mi). A 7-km (4½-mi) trail follows the coastline within the forest to Cahuita point, encircled by a 1-sq-mi coral reef. Blue parrot fish and angelfish weave their way among the various equally colorful species of coral and sponge. The reef escaped the 1991 earthquake with little damage, but biologists are worried that the coral has stopped growing due to silt and plastic bags washed down the Río Estrella from banana plantations upstream. Catch a glass-bottom-boat tour operating out of Cahuita to visit this aquatic garden. Visibility is best in September and October. To snorkel independently, swim out from the beach on the Puerto Vargas side. Five kilometers (3 mi) south of Cahuita on the left is the road to Puerto Vargas, the ranger station, and the camping area. ✉ *$6 voluntary fee requested at Cahuita entrance.*

A hiking trail extends as far as **Puerto Vargas,** the park's main headquarters. Along the trail, you might spot howler and white-faced monkeys, coatis, armadillos, and raccoons. Some stretches of beach have much worse currents than others; ask the rangers at Puerto Vargas for advice. Campsites carved out of the jungle dot the beach here.

Outdoor Activities and Sports

BICYCLING

You can bike through the national park, but the trail gets pretty muddy at times, and you'll encounter logs, river estuaries, and other obstacles. Nevertheless, mountain bikes are a good way to get around on the dirt roads and trails surrounding Cahuita, Puerto Viejo de Limón, and points south. They can be rented at a number of different places in the region, such as **Turistica Cahuita** in Cahuita. Near the convergence of the two beach roads, this friendly storefront tourist info and travel office makes reservations, rents surfboards, bicycles, and snorkeling gear, and arranges horseback and other tours. ATEC (☞ Outdoor Activities and Sports *in* Puerto Viejo de Limón and Points South, *below*) does the same and more down the road in Puerto Viejo de Limó.

HIKING

If you stay in Cahuita, you can take a bus or catch a ride into Puerto Vargas and hike back around the point in the course of a day. If you camp at Puerto Vargas, you can also hike south along the beach to Puerto Viejo de Limón and bus or taxi it back to the park. Be sure to bring plenty of water, food, and sunscreen.

SNORKELING

Parque Nacional Cahuita's reefs comprise just one of several high-quality dive spots in the area. Snorkeling gear can be rented in Cahuita or Puerto Viejo de Limón or through your hotel. Most hotels will organize dive trips. Or contact the ATEC office (☞ Outdoor Activities and Sports *in* Puerto Viejo de Limón and Points South, *below*) in the middle of Puerto Viejo de Limón or Aquamor in Manzanillo to make arrangements. It's a good idea to work with a guide because the number of good dive spots is limited, and they are not necessarily easily accessible.

En Route   Watch for the left turn for Puerto Viejo de Limón 8 km (5 mi) before Bribri; the last 6 km (4 mi) are unpaved and slow going. Drive accordingly. The deeply pocked dirt road leads south from Puerto Viejo de Limón to Punta Cocles and Punta Uva; the road ends in Manzanillo.

Puerto Viejo de Limón and Points South

⑬   *16 km (10 mi) south of Cahuita.*

Puerto Viejo de Limón was once quieter than Cahuita, but no more: it's turned into one of the hot spots on the international surfpunk circuit. The muddy, colorful little town is swarming with surfers, New Age hippies, beaded and spangled punks, would-be Rastafarians of all colors and descriptions, and wheelers and dealers both pleasant and otherwise. It used to be that most of the kids came here with only one thing on their mind: surfing. Today, a lot of them seem to be looking for a party, with or without surf. (Nevertheless, the waves are at their best between December and April and again in June and July.) Some locals bemoan the loss of their town's innocence, as the ravages of crack cocaine and other evils have surfaced, but only in small doses: this is still a fun town to trip through, with a great variety of hotels, cabinas, and restaurants in every price range. Heading south from Puerto Viejo de Limón to Punta Cocles and Punta Uva, you'll find some of the region's first luxurious tourism developments and interesting ecotourist lodges, new in the last few years.

One other note: multiple phone lines finally made it into Puerto Viejo de Limón and points south in 1996. As of this writing, many of the local numbers listed below are new. Things move slowly in Talamanca, and so numerous hotels in the area are still negotiating phone lines and credit-card contracts; telephone numbers and credit cards accepted are subject to change.

Dining and Lodging

$$–$$$ ✕ **The Garden.** Transplanted to Costa Rica from Trinidad by way of
★ Toronto, the Garden's owner-chef, Vera Mabon, incorporates her Indian heritage into her beautifully prepared and presented Asian-Caribbean food. Charming and colorful decor—candlelight, linen, and flowers—complements the pleasant, competent staff and the round, wood- and thatch-roofed open-air building buried in a flowering garden. The Cabinas Jacaranda, on the same property, also belong to Vera Mabon. Vera won't take plastic, but will take traveler's checks. ⊠ *Near the beach, follow signs,* ☎ *No phone. No credit cards.*

$$–$$$ ✕ **Salsa Brava** Once a breakfast place called the Juice Joint, the café at Salsa Brava—with sublime surf vistas—has taken on the famed surfing spot's name. Counter service is very casual, or grab a seat at the funky roadside tables for breakfast from 6 AM to noon and barbecued fresh fish and meat dinners from 6:30 to 10 PM. ⊠ *Salsa Brava,* ☎ *No phone. No credit cards.*

$–$$ ✕ **Bambú.** This funky little waterfront bar serves world-class cocktails with a view of the world-class surf of Salsa Brava. ⊠ *Outside of town on ocean road,* ☎ *No phone. No credit cards.*

$ ✕ **Elena Brown Soda y Restaurant.** Unpretentious, shady, and calm, Elena's place serves tasty fresh fish dishes. ⊠ *Along road from Puerto Viejo de Limón to Punta Uva,* ☎ *No phone. No credit cards.*

$$$ ✕⌂ **Shawandha Lodge.** Shawandha's refined, beautifully designed, and
★ spacious bungalows nestle in remote jungle settings well back from the road through Punta Uva. Every single bathroom, replete with gorgeous tile work, has been designed by French ceramicist Filou Pascal. Bungalows feature elegant hardwood construction, custom-designed furniture, and large verandas with hammocks. In the kitchen of the open-air restaurant, a well-known local chef who goes by the name of Madame Oui Oui lovingly crafts her distinctive French-Caribbean cuisine; a hearty breakfast is included in the price of a room. The adjacent salon is a great place to hang out and meet fellow adventurers. A white-sand beach protected by a coral reef lies 200 yds away. The hotel offers all regional tours and activities. ⊠ *On the road to Manzanillo, south of Puerto Viejo, look for signs across the road from the beach,* ☎ *750–0018,* ⊠ *750–0037. 12 bungalows. Restaurant, hiking, horseback riding, snorkeling, surfing, boating. No credit cards.*

$$$ ✕⛺ **Yaré.** The sound of the jungle is overpowering, especially at night, as you relax in your charming, brightly painted cabina. The cabinas have fans, hot water, and private baths. The in-house restaurant is open for breakfast, lunch, and dinner. The owner organizes all kinds of tours. ✉ *4 km (2½ mi) on right side of road to Manzanillo,* ☏ FAX *750–0106 or 284–5921;* ☏ *232–7866 San José office. 10 rooms with bath, 8 cabinas. Restaurant, horseback riding, fishing. AE, MC, V.*

$$–$$$ ✕⛺ **El Pizote Lodge.** El Pizote observes local architectural mores while
★ offering more than most in the way of amenities. Rooms have polished wood paneling, reading lamps, mirrors, mats, firm beds, and fans. Some rooms share a bathroom; others, in individual huts, have their own. A two-room bungalow accommodates six people. The restaurant serves breakfast, dinner, and drinks all day. Guanabana and papaya grow on the grounds; hiking trails lead off into the jungle. ✉ *Apdo. 230–2200, on right side of road into Puerto Viejo,* ☏ *750–0088; 221-5915 in San José,* FAX *223–8838 in San José. 8 rooms without bath, 6 bungalows with bath. Restaurant, bar, pool, volleyball. MC, V.*

$$–$$$ ✕⛺ **Hotel La Perla Negra.** The owners' previous experience as designers is evident in the fine construction of this handsome, two-story wooden structure across a tiny dirt road from Playa Negra, between Parque Nacional Cahuita and Puerto Viejo. The three-meal restaurant features grilled meats and fish; a spacious, inviting pool lies between the building and the beach. ✉ *North of Puerto Viejo on Playa Negra,* ☏ *750–0011,* FAX *750–0014. 24 rooms with bath. Restaurant, pool. No credit cards.*

$$$–$$$$ ⛺ **Palm Beach Resort** The most southerly major project on the Manzanillo road, this new beachfront hotel is the better half of a grandiose resort whose owners fell on hard times, sold off half the property, and scaled down their initial vision. The unfortunate other half still stands next door, but fortunately the Palm Beach Resort turns its back on it, instead facing the sea across one of the finest beaches on the Caribbean coast. Not surprisingly, since it does lie within the borders of the wildlife refuge, the opportunities for animal and bird-watching, surfing, kayaking, fishing, and snorkeling are virtually boundless. Every room has an ocean view, along with air-conditioning, TV, whirlpool bath, and telephones. ✉ *Apdo. 6942–1000, San José,* ☏ *750–0049; 255–3939 in San José,* FAX *255–3737 in San José. 20 rooms with bath. Restaurant, coffee shop, pool. AE, MC, V.*

$$$ ⛺ **Almonds & Corals.** Buried in a dark, densely atmospheric beachfront jungle within the Refugio Nacional de Vida Silvestre Gandoca-Manzanillo near the end of the road that runs south from Puerto Viejo to Manzanillo, Almonds & Corals takes tent camping to a new level, for the "campsites" are freestanding platforms raised on stilts and reached by stairs. Each is protected by a peaked roof, enclosed by mosquito netting, and contains electric lamps, fans, beds, hammocks, and a private (cold water) bath. Sited to maximize privacy, all are linked by raised boardwalks illuminated by kerosene lamps. A fine, three-meal restaurant is tucked into the greenery halfway to an exquisite, secluded beach. The 35-sq-mi wildlife refuge surrounds the property; your wake-up call will be provided by howler monkeys and gossiping parrots. ✉ *Apdo. 681–2300 ,* ☏ *272–2024 or 272–4175,* FAX *272–2220. 20 tent cabins with bath. Restaurant, beach. AE, MC, V.*

$$$ ⛺ **Villas del Caribe.** Right on the beach north of Punta Uva, the Del
★ Caribe's multiroom villas are commodious and comfortable, if somewhat pedestrian in design. Each contains a blue tile kitchen with stove and refrigerator, a small sitting room with low-slung couches, a plant-filled bathroom, and a patio. Upstairs are one or two spacious bedrooms with a wooden deck offering views of the Caribbean. Although

they serve coffee at the reception counter, the nearest restaurant is several hundred yds away—that may not seem far, but when it rains it pours, and the road is unlit and full of potholes. But if you bring your own edibles you're set, since the hotel rents all kinds of water-sports equipment and will arrange any kind of tour. ⊠ *Puerto Viejo, Limón,* ☎ *233–2200,* FAX *221–2801. 12 villas. Kitchenettes. AE, DC, MC, V.*

$$–$$$ 🏨 **Cariblue Bed & Breakfast.** Cariblue's finely crafted all-wooden bungalows are spaciously arrayed on the edge of the jungle across the road from the splendid black- and white-sand beaches of Punta Cocles. Paths meandering through a gently sloping lawn shaded with several enormous trees link the cabinas with the main rancho-style building, where the youthful Italian owners serve continental breakfast, included in the price of the room. Expansive verandas and beautiful bathroom tile work await you.⊠ *South of Puerto Viejo on the road to Manzanillo,* ☎ FAX *750–0057. 6 cabinas. Breakfast room. No credit cards.*

$$–$$$ 🏨 **Miraflores Lodge.** It's not difficult to tell that this was a flower farm before a hotel was built on the property in 1990. The collection of bromeliads and heliconias and the intricate landscaping are a dead giveaway. The buildings, designed in the indigenous style, with peaked thatched roofs and cane walls, make you feel as if you're off the tourist trail—while proprietor Pamela Carpenter makes you feel like you're right at home. ⊠ *Playa Chiquita, Puerto Viejo, Limón,* ☎ *750–0038; 233–2822 in San José. 10 rooms, 5 with bath. Breakfast room. No credit cards.*

$$ 🏨 **Casa Verde.** This German-run collection of cabinas is one of the finest moderately priced properties in Puerto Viejo itself. Set back a few blocks from the waterfront hustle, the comfortable cabinas offer handsomely furnished porches sporting hammocks, hardwood finishes, ceiling fans, and plentiful hot water. Lush plantings screen the cabinas from the street and enhance the jungly atmosphere. Look for the signs as you mosey down "main" street along Puerto Viejo's waterfront. No restaurant is on the premises, but half a dozen are within a five-minute walk. ⊠ *Apdo. 1115, Puerto Limón,* ☎ *750–0015,* FAX *750–0047. 14 rooms, 6 with bath. Laundry service. AE, MC, V.*

$$ 🏨 **Playa Chiquita Lodge.** Elevated a few feet above the damp jungle floor and 100 yds back from the beautiful, secluded Chiquita beach near Punta Uva, these wooden cabinas are tastefully furnished, with spacious verandas. As of early 1998, a new spa with a hot tub was near completion. The lodge is popular with bird-watchers, so at night you can swap sightings. The property is run by German-born Wolf Bissinger and his talented Talamancan-born partner, Wanda Patterson-Bissinger, who also edits and writes the region's homegrown newspaper, *Talamanca Voice.* ⊠ *10 km (6 mi) from Puerto Viejo on left side of road,* ☎ *233–6613,* FAX *223–7479,* ☎ FAX *750–0062. 11 cabinas. Restaurant, bar. No credit cards.*

Outdoor Activities and Sports

ECOTOURISM

Founded in 1990, **ATEC** (Asociación Talamanqueña de Ecoturismo y Conservación, or Talamanca Association for Ecotourism and Conservation) operates out of a small office in the middle of Puerto Viejo di Limón. ATEC plays an increasingly important role in the ecotourism movement in Talamanca. The agency's office also serves as a fax and phone center, a post office, and a general information center for the town and the region. Under ATEC's auspices the following tours and activities can be pursued: Afro-Caribbean culture and nature walks; indigenous culture and nature walks; rain-forest hikes; coral reef snorkeling or fishing trips; bird and night walks; adventure treks; and myriad others. ATEC is also an excellent source for information on volunteer vacations, a vacation devoted to volunteering (for which you often pay!), in the region. Remember, ATEC is not a profit-making tourist agency but a grassroots organization promoting ecotourism in Talamanca; the idea is to encourage tourism through small-scale, locally owned businesses—tour guides, cabinas, restaurants, and so on. Of the money collected for tours booked through ATEC, 15%–20% goes to local organizations and wildlife refuges. Even if you're not using their services, they could use a donation. ⊠ *ATEC, Puerto Viejo de Talamanca, Limón,* ☎ *750–0158.* ☉ *Daily 8–8, except for lunch.*

SURFING

Surfing is the name of the game in Puerto Viejo. There are a number of breaks here, the most famous being **Salsa Brava.** Salsa Brava breaks rather far offshore and there are some tricky currents and reefs to maneuver just to get out there. It's a hollow, primarily right-breaking wave over a shallow reef; when it gets big, it is one gnarly wave. If Salsa Brava is too big, or not big enough, check out the breaks at **Punta Uva, Punta Cocles,** or **Playa Chiquita.** For a **wave conditions forecast,** call 220–2026 all over the country. The operators claim about an 80% success rate, which isn't too bad; the cost is about 50¢ per minute. Boogie boarders and bodysurfers will also dig the beach-break waves to be found at various spots along this tantalizingly beautiful coast.

Refugio Nacional de Vida Silvestre Gandoca-Manzanillo

⑭ *15 km (9 mi) south of Puerto Viejo de Limón, via Punta Uva to Manzanillo.*

The Refugio Nacional de Vida Silvestre Gandoca-Manzanillo (Gandoca-Manzanillo Wildlife Refuge) protects orey and jolillo swamps, 10 km (6 mi) of beach where four species of turtle lay their eggs, and almost 1¼ sq mi of cativo forest and coral reef (☞ Chapter 10). The Gandoca estuary is a nursery for tarpon and a wallowing spot for crocodiles and caimans. The administrators of the park, Benson and Florentino Grenald, can tell you more and recommend a local guide. If you ask when you enter Manzanillo village, residents will point you toward them. In Manzanillo, try a seafood dinner at **Restaurant Maxie's.** Locals and expatriates alike swear by the freshness of Maxie's fish, especially the lobsters—and the prices can't be beat.

From the frontier with Panama, retrace your steps to the main road and head southwest through Bribri to Sixaola, the border town. Indian reserves in the area protect the domains of the Bribri, Cabecar, and Kekoldi Indians.

Outdoor Activities and Sports

WATER SPORTS

For surfing, sea, river, and estuary kayaking, and especially snorkeling and scuba diving trips out of Manzanillo, **Aquamor** (☎ 750–0093 or 228–9513) is the place to go. The Manzanillo-based business, run by Katrina Larkin and her mixed Tico-American family, will also transport and guide snorkelers and divers down to the magnificent reefs of Bocas del Toro in Panama.

OFF THE BEATEN PATH **RESERVA BIOLÓGICA HITOY CERERE –** The remote 35-sq-mi Hitoy Cerere National Park occupies the head of the Valle de la Estrella. The park's limited infrastructure was badly damaged by the 1991 quake, whose epicenter was precisely there. Paths that do exist are very overgrown due to their limited use—visitors scarcely ever get here. Jaguars, tapirs, peccaries, porcupines, anteaters, and armadillos all live in the forest, along with more than 115 species of birds. Watch for the so-called Jesus Christ lizards, which walk on water. The moss-flanked rivers have clear bathing pools and spectacular waterfalls. To get there, take a Valle de la Estrella bus from Puerto Limón and get off at Finca Seis; hire a Jeep and you'll be able to get within 1 km (½ mi) of the reserve for $5. Check beforehand with the park service in San José if you want to stay overnight. ☎ 283–8004.

THE ATLANTIC LOWLANDS AND THE CARIBBEAN COAST A TO Z

Arriving and Departing

By Bus

PARQUE NACIONAL BRAULIO CARRILLO AND THE NORTHERN LOWLANDS

Buses from San José to Guápiles will drop you off in Parque Nacional Braulio Carrillo; they depart every half hour between 7:30 AM and 7 PM from Calle 12 between Avenidas 7 and 9 (45-min trip). Buses go to Río Frío and Puerto Viejo de Sarapiquí (stopping at Rara Avis and La Selva) via Braulio Carrillo from Avenida 9 and Calle 12; they depart daily at 8 AM, 10 AM, 11:30 AM, 1:30 PM, 3:30 PM, and 4:30 PM (2-hr trip). Alternately from the same location to the same destination, buses go via Vera Blanca—not passing through Braulio Carrillo—at 8 AM, noon, and 3 PM (4-hr trip).

COASTAL TALAMANCA

Bus service to the Atlantic Lowlands from San José includes daily service to Puerto Limón from Avenida 3 between Calles 19 and 21 (☎ 223–7811 or 257–0895) every half hour between 5:30 AM and 7 PM (2½-hr trip). Service to Cahuita and Sixaola runs from Avenida 11 between Calles Central and 1 (☎ 257–8129) daily at 6 AM, 1:30 PM, and 3:30 PM (4-hr trip). Alternatively, the direct bus runs at 10 AM and 4 PM from the same location. Buses to Puerto Viejo de Limón and points south depart at 3:30 PM and Sundays at 8 AM from Calle 1 and Avenida 11 (☎ 257–8129) (4 ½-hr trip).

By Car

PARQUE NACIONAL BRAULIO CARRILLO AND THE NORTHERN LOWLANDS

The Carretera Guápiles passes the Zurquí and Quebrada González sectors of the **Parque Nacional Braulio Carrillo,** whereas the Barva sector lies to the north of Heredia. The roads in the Sarapiquí area of the Atlantic Lowlands are mostly paved, with the usual rained-out dirt and rock sections—road quality depends on the time of year, the last pass of the infrequent road crews, or the amount of rain dumped by the latest tropical storm.

COASTAL TALAMANCA

The paved two-lane Carretera Guápiles runs from Calle 3 in San José to Puerto Limón, a distance of about 160 km (100 mi).

By Plane

TORTUGUERO AND BARRA DEL COLORADO

Travelair (✉ Aeropuerto Internacional Tobías Bolaños, Apdo. 8–4920, ☎ 506/220–3054 or 506/232–7883, FAX 506/220–0413) flies from San José to Tortuguero and Barra del Colorado daily, with flights departing at 6 AM. **Sansa** (✉ C. 24, between Avda. Central and Avda. 1, San José, ☎ 506/221–9414 or 506/441–8035, FAX 506/255–2176) flies to Barra del Colorado on Tuesday and Thursday through Saturday at 6 AM. Several tour companies, such as **Costa Rica Expeditions** (☎ 222–0333, ⓕⓐⓧ 257–0766) offer regular or charter flights into Tortuguero and/or Barra del Colorado in conjunction with stays in their lodges in the area.

COASTAL TALAMANCA

Currently neither of the two domestic airlines flies to Puerto Limón on a scheduled basis, although a charter is possible because there is a good landing strip just south of town.

Getting Around

By Boat

From Puerto Viejo de Sarapiquí, boats ply the old route up the Río Sarapiquí to the Río San Juan on the Nicaraguan frontier; from here you can travel downstream to Barra del Colorado or Tortuguero, but departure times vary—contact El Gavilán Lodge (☞ Puerto Viejo de Sarapiquí, *above*) or negotiate your own deal dockside. Many private operators will take you from the docks at Moín, just outside of Puerto Limón, to Tortuguero, but there is no scheduled public transportation. Modesto Watson (☞ Guided Tours, *below*), an eagle-eye Miskito Indian guide, will take you upstream if he has room on his boat. You can hire boats to travel between Tortuguero and Barra del Colorado, but prices are quite high.

By Bus

Buses leave from in front of Distribuidora Tropigas Victor Chin on the west side of Calzado Mary in Puerto Limón for Cahuita, Puerto Vargas, Puerto Viejo de Limón, and Sixaola daily at 5 AM, 8 AM, 10 AM, 1 PM, 4 PM, and 6 PM (1 hr to Cahuita, 1½ hrs to Puerto Viejo de Limón). There is sporadic bus service to Manzanillo from Puerto Viejo de Limón on both local buses and buses coming through Limón to San José.

By Car

TORTUGUERO AND BARRA DEL COLORADO

There are no roads to Tortuguero (☞ By Boat, *above*).

COASTAL TALAMANCA

South of Puerto Limón, a paved road goes for about 40 km (25 mi) to Cahuita, then past the Cahuita turnoff, and proceeds for roughly 16 km (10 mi) toward Puerto Viejo de Limó. The paved main road turns inland and heads up to Bribri and Sixaola a couple of kilometers before it reaches Puerto Viejo, but the dirt road remains navigable as far as Punta Uva year-round (and Manzanillo during the dry season). Four-wheel drive is always preferable, but for the most part the major roads in this region are passable by any kind of car. Watch out for potholes and unpaved sections—they can appear on any road, at any time, without marking or warning. Driving in Costa Rica requires perpetual vigilance.

Contacts and Resources

Car Rentals

See Contacts and Resources *in* San José A to Z, *in* Chapter 2.

Emergencies

In just about any emergency you can dial ☎ 911, but here are some additional useful numbers: **Ambulance** (Cruz Roja, ☎ 128). **Fire** (Bomberos, ☎ 118). **Police** (☎ 117 in towns; 127 in rural areas). **Traffic Police** (☎ 227–8030).

Guided Tours

PARQUE NACIONAL BRAULIO CARRILLO AND THE NORTHERN
LOWLANDS

Both **Desafio** (⊠ Apdo. 37–4417, La Fortuna SC, ☎ 479–9464, FAX
479–9178) and **Sunset Tours** (☎ 479–9415, FAX 479–9099) based in
La Fortuna (☞ Chapter 4) run tours to Puerto Viejo de Sarapiquí.

PARQUE NACIONAL TORTUGUERO

Parque Nacional Tortuguero tours are usually packaged with one- or
two-night stays in local lodges. **Cotur's** (⊠ Paseo Colón and Cs. 34 and
36, San José, ☎ 233–0155) offers three-day, two-night tours, including bus and boat transport from San José to the Jungle Lodge in Tortuguero for $230. **Mawamba** (⊠ San José, ☎ 223–2421) offers a slightly
more expensive version of the same tour, with the nights spent at the
Mawamba Lodge, or a less expensive version with nights at Cabinas
Sabina. **Costa Rica Expeditions** (⊠ C. Central and Avda. 3, San José,
☎ 222–0333, FAX 257–1665) flies you directly to their rustically
charming Tortuga Lodge for three days, two nights, for about $300.
Fran and Modesto Watson (☎ FAX 226–0986) know the history and
ecology of the area best. Among others they offer a two-day, one-night
tour on their *Riverboat Francesca,* with overnight at Laguna or Ma-
nati Lodge ($144–$157 including meals and transfers).

PUERTO VIEJO DE LIMÓN AND POINTS SOUTH

The **ATEC** office (⊠ Across from Soda Tamara, Puerto Viejo de Limón,
☎ 798–4244) offers tours to local Indian preserves as well as every
destination in the area. Some of their special interest tours include "Sustainable Logging," "Yorkin Indigenous Tour," and assorted bird-
watching, turtle-watching, indigenous culture, and other ecologically
oriented trips. Most of the hotels in the Puerto Viejo area will organize tours of almost any kind—hikes, horseback, bicycle, fishing, and
so on. We recommend working with ATEC or other local people, because locally based tourism is in the sustainable mode.

Atlántico Tours (contact ATEC, ☞ *above*), based in Puerto Viejo, offers tours to Tortuguero and Barra del Colorado as well as more local
tours of Parque Nacional Cahuita, Reserva Biológica Hitoy Cerere, Refugio Nacional de Vida Silvestre Gandoca-Manzanillo, and other destinations. They also rent surfboards, bicycles, kites, and snorkeling gear.

Visitor Information

The **tourist office** in San José has information covering the Atlantic Lowlands (☞ Contacts and Resources *in* San José A to Z, *in* Chapter 2).
The **ATEC** (☎ FAX 798–4244) office in Puerto Viejo de Limón is a great
source of information on local tours, guides, and interesting activities.

9 Excursions to Panama

You may wish to head farther south—either to the verdant valleys and mountains of Chiriquí Province or to the islands of the Bocas del Toro archipelago in the Caribbean Sea. In Chiriquí, you can explore lush cloud forests, run raging rivers, or climb Volcán Barú. In Bocas del Toro you'll find stunning coral reefs, palm-lined beaches, and a tumbledown provincial capital.

THE AMERICAN VISION OF PANAMA is usually restricted to the canal Teddy Roosevelt dug there, a dictator named Manuel Noriega, and the invasion George
Updated by
David
Dudenhoefer
Bush launched to put Noriega behind U.S. bars. Are we myopic, or merely uninformed? Probably a bit of both. If we just look beyond that controversial canal, we'll discover vast expanses of jungle that hold amazing biological diversity, proud and colorful indigenous cultures that preserve centuries-old traditions, idyllic islands with coral reefs a shell's toss offshore, and exuberant mountain forests filled with colorful birds and other interesting creatures. And since Panama has only just started to receive the attention it deserves, you won't have to share its attractions with hordes of tourists.

The western half of the country offers several destinations well worth visiting. Tranquil Chiriquí Province, for example, has two small agricultural communities set in lush valleys, surrounded by dense cloud forests, with a massive, extinct volcano towering over them. The isolated islands of the Bocas del Toro archipelago, on the other hand, feature long, deserted beaches lined with coconut palms and washed by aquamarine waters that hold an incredible diversity of marine life.

Pleasures and Pastimes

Dining

Western Panama is unlikely to ever become an epicurean mecca, but the region does have a few excellent restaurants and many inexpensive eateries. Panamanian food tends to be a bit greasy, but the kitchens of the mountains of Chiriquí adhere to a more northern—though still fried—style of cooking. A few restaurants here specialize in food from other parts of the world.

Plenty of fresh seafood is lured from the sea near Bocas del Toro, and though the local cooks aren't terribly inventive about how they prepare it, a few foreigners who are have moved into the neighborhood. In addition to the local fare, you'll also find good Chinese and Italian food on the islands. Remember that, unlike in Costa Rica, there is no service charge included in the bill at a Panamanian restaurant, so 10% gratuity is expected.

Festivals

The annual Feria Internacional in David, a commercial exposition worthy of avoiding, takes place in late March. Boquete's extensive fairgrounds on the east bank of the Río Caldera is the site of the annual Flower Festival. Held in mid-January, it is a colorful but noisy affair with performances of folk music and dancing and lots of loud disco music. The Feria del Mar, on the beach north of Bocas del Toro in late September, is sort of a Caribbean version of Boquete's flower festival.

Lodging

Since tourism has yet to take off in Panama, there is a relatively small selection of accommodations available in the western provinces. Nevertheless, Chiriquí has several of Panama's nicest hotels. The region's most charming inns are nestled in its stunning mountain valleys, and one of them is set in the middle of the forest. Although you can usually show up and find a room, reservations are necessary during Panamanian holidays (☞ When to Tour Panama, *below*).

Undiscovered so far, Bocas del Toro doesn't offer a whole lot of options with hotel rooms, although the up-market room selection is slowly expanding in that largely low-budget town. The two oldest inns are in former banana company houses, which are somewhat ramshackle, but quite charming and recommended. An even less spoiled alternative to the town of Bocas is nearby Bastimentos, just across the bay, which is just starting to get into the tourism business.

National Parks

Chiriquí's two national parks, Volcán Barú and Parque Internacional La Amistad, both lie within the binational Reserva de la Biósfera La Amistad (La Amistad Biosphere Reserve), a collection of protected areas that together cover the better part of the Cordillera de Talamanca range. Although most of Parque Internacional La Amistad—contiguous with the Costa Rican park of the same name—lies within the province of Bocas del Toro, Chiriquí offers the best access to this protected area. The two sectors of the park accessible from Cerro Punta consist of cloud forest, which is home to the emerald toucanet, resplendent quetzal, three-wattled bellbird, nearly a dozen types of hummingbirds, and several hundred other avian species. Parque Nacional Volcán Barú covers the northern slope and upper reaches of Panama's only volcano, the peak of which affords views of two oceans, on those rare clear mornings. That park is home to much of the same wildlife found in La Amistad, which it borders, as well as the rare volcano junco, a bird that can only be found near the summit. A four-wheel-drive-only road winds its way up to the top of the volcano from Boquete, and a footpath heads up the other side, beginning near Bambito and Volcán. There is also a footpath through the cloud forest on the volcano's northern side, which connects the tiny agricultural outposts of El Respingo and Alto Chiquero, above Cerro Punta and Boquete respectively.

Skin Diving

Whether you prefer the simplicity of snorkeling, or are an experienced scuba diver itching to get back into the depths of the big blue, Bocas del Toro has what you're looking for. The islands' points, cays, and submerged reefs in this vast lagoon host an array of marine life, ranging from lugubrious sea turtles to hyperactive tropical fish. In the ocean off Panama's Caribbean coast are almost 75 different species of coral and an even greater variety of sponges, around which lurk countless vibrantly colored invertebrates, rays, lobsters, and fish species.

White-Water Rafting

Two rambunctious rivers wind their ways down out of the Chiriquí highlands, providing excellent conditions for white-water rafting year-round. The Río Chiriquí, which pours down from the Lago di Fortuna, to the northeast of David, is a class-III river during the dry season, surmountable even if you have no rafting experience. During the wettest months, October–December, the water level rises and the river gets wilder, with some of the rapids becoming class IV. The Chiriquí Viejo, which begins in the mountains above Cerro Punta and flows through the western end of the province, provides an invigorating class-IV white-water trip really only appropriate for people with some rafting experience.

Exploring Panama

Numbers in the text correspond to numbers in the margin and on the Chiriquí Province and the Bocas del Toro Archipelago map.

Great Itineraries

The Panamanian province of Chiriquí lies just a short trip from San Vito and Golfito, and though it's an eight-hour drive from San José, you can get there in just over an hour if you fly. It takes about five hours to reach Bocas del Toro from Cahuita or Puerto Viejo de Limón—via a sequence of bus, taxi, and water taxi—and about nine hours from San José. After that long a haul, you'll want to spend at least a couple of days in either Chiriquí or Bocas del Toro before heading back. Luckily there's plenty to keep you busy.

IF YOU HAVE 3 DAYS FOR CHIRIQUÍ
If you have three days in Chiriquí, you won't want to spend too much time in **David** ①. Head straight for the mountain air of ⊞ **Boquete** ②, which has a good selection of accommodations. Get up early the next morning, either for bird-watching or the predawn drive up Volcán Barú, to catch the sunrise from the summit. You can stay the second night in Boquete, or make the trip to ⊞ **Cerro Punta** ⑤, which is higher and thus cooler. Whether you spend one or two nights in Cerro Punta, you'll definitely want to explore the forests of Parque Internacional La Amistad. White-water rafting trips are available out of both towns; other diversions include horseback riding, hiking, and mountain biking.

IF YOU HAVE 3 DAYS FOR BOCAS DEL TORO
Spend your first day wandering through the town of ⊞ **Bocas del Toro** ⑥; if you have enough time, rent a bike and ride out to Playa Bluff. Be sure to arrange a boat excursion for the next day. On day two, wake up early and head for either the long beach on ⊞ **Isla Bastimentos** ⑦, or the Cayos Zapatillas. On day three, enjoy either the boat trip to Isla de Pajaros and nearby Boca del Drago, or a visit to an indigenous community, either on a nearby island or on the mainland.

When to Tour Panama
Since Panama's history has differed considerably from Costa Rica's, each country has its own political holidays, but the two countries share religious holidays. You'll want to make reservations well ahead of time for travel during most holidays, especially the last week of December, Holy Week (the week before Easter Sunday), and Carnival Week, which takes place approximately six weeks before Holy Week.

The massive Cordillera de Talamanca range divides western Panama into Atlantic and Pacific slopes, and the weather can differ considerably between its two provinces. Chiriquí experiences its nicest weather during the December–May dry season and enjoys some sunny days in July and August. It rains pretty much year-round in Bocas del Toro, though the province often experiences mini dry seasons September–October and March–April. However, since most of that region's rain falls at night, it's a pleasant place to visit just about any time of year.

CHIRIQUÍ PROVINCE

The province of Chiriquí is a land of rolling plains, green mountain valleys, raging rivers, and luxuriant forests. It is dominated by the peaks of the Cordillera de Talamanca, which extends southeast from Costa Rica into Panama, defining the province's northern edge. The range's upper slopes are cloaked in thick cloud forest, kept wet by the mist that the trade winds regularly push over the continental divide. That mist not only keeps the landscape green, it creates the perfect conditions for viewing rainbows, and feeds countless streams and boulder-strewn rivers. Two valleys set high on either side of Volcán Barú—the country's highest peak—offer cool mountain climates and close exposure to nature, while the rolling lowlands are hot, and almost completely deforested.

Much of the province is home to cowboys and Indians—vast haciendas cover the better part of the lowlands, and Indian villages pepper the eastern highlands—whereas such agricultural communities as Bo-

Chiriquí Province and the Bocas del Toro Archipelago

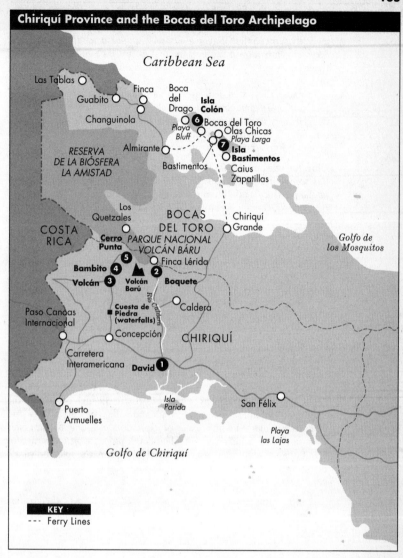

quete, Volcán, and Cerro Punta are dominated by the descendants of European immigrants. The province consequently reflects Panama's varied cultural spectrum, which includes half a dozen indigenous ethnicities, a mestizo majority, and the descendants of immigrants from all corners of the world.

Most immigrants came to Chiriquí via the Panama Canal area, which was an important route of transit long before the U.S. government started digging that famous ditch. Countless travelers and tons of cargo have crossed the Panamanian isthmus during the last five centuries, first via mule trains, then the railway, and finally, the canal. Some of the foreigners who ended up in the country were contract laborers who never went home, some were businessmen drawn by the opportunities that interoceanic transit represents, and others were simply travelers who got sidetracked. Though most of those immigrants stayed in the center of the country, some drifted west to the province of Chiriquí.

During the colonial era, Chiriquí was still the realm of Indians, who belonged to dozens of ethnicities, but whom the Spanish invaders collectively dubbed the Guaymí—a name that has stuck to this day. The Spaniards introduced cattle to the region, and as ranching took hold, the area's forests receded. During the last century, banana and sugar plantations were established in the lowlands, and the rich soil of the mountain valleys was dedicated to more lucrative crops, such as coffee, fruit, and vegetables. This agricultural development meant that Indian territory shrank considerably—the majority of Chiriquí's indigenous inhabitants now live in the mountains to the east—but it turned the province into a fairly affluent, independent region.

Chiriquí's distance from the Panamanian capital and canal probably has something to do with the independent nature of the Chiricanos, as the province's inhabitants are called. Most Chiricanos are farmers or ranchers, though the city of David profits from a bit of industry and commerce. They're hard-working, traditional people, with a rich heritage of folklore. You may be lucky enough to enjoy some of the local folk music and dancing, and you're almost certain to hear the popular Panamanian "típica" music, which is similar to the Colombian "cumbia," but is notable for its use of accordions and ululating vocals. You're also likely to encounter Ngwóbe, or Guaymí, Indians; some own farms in the area, but most just head there to work as agricultural laborers. Though Ngwóbe men might be hard to distinguish from nonindigenous Panamanians, the women are unmistakable, thanks to the long, colorful dresses they wear.

Although exposure to the local culture can enrich any visit, most people are drawn to Chiriquí by its natural assets. There are several islands and deserted beaches in and along the Golfo de Chiriquí, but the region's greatest attractions lie to the north, in the high country of the Talamanca mountain range. The highland valleys of Cerro Punta and Boquete are blessed with regular precipitation and some of Panama's most fertile soil, which has led to their development as agricultural centers. Both communities boast refreshingly cool climates, splendid views, plenty of outdoor diversions, and accommodations to fit every budget.

The mountains above these two towns retain much of their forest canopy, which makes them excellent areas for bird-watchers, or for anyone who enjoys nature. The area's forests are home for more than 400 species of birds, including such spectacular specimens as the blue-crowned motmot, resplendent quetzal, long-tailed silky flycatcher, and other colorful feathered creatures with complicated names. Those highland forests are luxuriant year-round thanks to the clouds that regularly float over the mountaintops and into the valleys. The abundant mist combines with the afternoon sun to make rainbows such a common sight in the area that the locals tend to ignore them. It is possible to drive up long-extinct Volcán Barú, the country's highest peak, in a four-wheel-drive vehicle, but there are dozens of trails through the area's forests that are accessible only to hikers and horses. Hiking and horseback excursions are available out of the highland towns, and two of the rivers that wind down those mountain valleys are currently navigated by professional white-water rafting outfitters.

David

❶ *37 km (23 mi) east of the border with Costa Rica.*

This provincial capital has little to offer travelers, but it is practically unavoidable, since it is the local transportation hub. The town is the political and economic center for a vast agricultural area, with banks, rent-a-car companies, and a small airport. Not only do the province's scattered inhabitants head here to take care of business, Costa Ricans sometimes travel to David on shopping trips, since most imported items are considerably cheaper in Panama than in Costa Rica. The busy boulevards near town center are consequently lined with a variety of modern shops and other businesses. If you wander past some of the clothing and department stores, you may notice the peculiar habit Panamanian salesmen have of clapping, shouting about the merchandise, and walking along next to passersby, telling them to come into the store and buy something.

Though David was founded almost four centuries ago, no buildings survive from the colonial era; there's hardly anything left from that last century. It is a fairly modern, grid-plan city, centered around the shady Parque Cervantes and skirted by the Carretera Interamericana (Inter-American Highway). It is not a terribly attractive place, and its lowland location creates steamy temperatures. Mountain communities to the north feature more pleasant climates and scenery. However, David can be a convenient base for such day trips as white-water rafting, a boat tour of the mangroves and islands of the Golfo de Chiriquí, or a day hike on Los Quetzales Trail, which heads through the forest on the northern slope of Volcán Barú.

If you have some extra time in David, you may want to visit the **Museo José de Obaldía,** which has exhibits about the region's pre-Columbian cultures and colonial history. ⊠ *Avda. 8 Este and C. A Norte,* ☎ *507/ 775–7839.* ▨ *$1.* ◷ *Tues.–Sat. 8:30–4:30.*

OFF THE
BEATEN PATH

GOLFO DE CHIRIQUÍ – If sun, sand, and clear waters are what you crave, consider an excursion on the Golfo de Chiriquí, the vast gulf to the south of the province. **Isla Parida,** a large island about 50 km (30 mi) south of the coast lined with idyllic white-sand beaches and aquamarine waters, can be visited on excursions out of David. The only hotel on Isla Parida, **Las Paridas** (☎ 507/774–8166), offers day trips out to the island, which include lunch at their hotel. They'll pick you up at Pedregal, the port just south of David, as early as you want, and get you back there late in the afternoon. They can take up to four people, and charge $240 for the group. They also offer overnight packages in their rustic beach hotel. The gulf also features world-class sportfishing; charters can be booked through the **Marina de Pedregal** (☎ 507/721–0071) or **Marco Devilio** (☎ 507/775–3830).

Dining and Lodging

$$–$$$ ✕ **Mar del Sur.** The best seafood in David is served at this Peruvian
★   restaurant, owned by the same people who run San José's popular Machu Picchu. It is on the north end of town, a few blocks from the bus station, in a former home. The dining area has tile floors, wooden ceilings, arched doorways, and a few posters and paintings of Peru hanging on the walls. Appetizers include seviche, *chicharón de calamar* (deep-fried squid), and *papas a la huancaina* (boiled potatoes in a cream sauce). Entrées, like the *picante de langostinos* (prawns in a spicy cream sauce) and the corvina prepared six different ways, are delicious. ⊠ *Behind Fe de Doleguita supermarket,* ☎ *507/775–0856. AE, MC, V. Closed Sun. and daily 3–6.*

$–$$ ✕ **Churrascos Place.** This open-air restaurant, one block from Parque Cervantes, serves a good selection of inexpensive food and is open 24 hours a day. Plants line two sides of the restaurant, which has a red-tile floor, a high sloping roof, and a bar on one end. The menu is pretty basic, with several cuts of beef, fish fillets, rice with chicken, soups, and sandwiches. Main dishes come with a simple salad. ⊠ *Avda. 2 Este and C. Central,* ☎ *507/774–0412. AE, MC, V.*

$–$$ ✕ **Pizzería Hotel Nacional.** Across the street from the venerable Hotel Nacional, in the same building as the hotel's discotheque, this place serves some decent pizza and an ample selection of meat, seafood, and pasta dishes. The decor is pretty basic, but it's clean, air-conditioned, and the service is good. ⊠ *Avda. Central and C. Central,* ☎ *507/775– 1042. AE, MC, V.*

$$–$$$ 🏨 **Hotel Nacional.** This stately building was long David's best hotel,
★ but the Nacional slipped into a state of dilapidation during the 1980s and early 1990s. It was sold in 1995, however, and the new owners have stepped in. Guest rooms have firm beds, bright tile floors, air-conditioning, Formica dressers, and satellite TV. Superior rooms in back are larger, and most have picture windows that overlook the pool area. The ample facilities make the Nacional a relatively busy spot in this sleepy town. ⊠ *Avda. Central and C. Central,* ☎ *507/775–2222,* 𝖥𝖠𝖷 *507/775–7729. 75 rooms with bath. Restaurant, 2 bars, pool, casino, cinema. AE, DC, MC, V.*

$$ 🏨 **Hotel Fiesta.** Just east of town, the slightly down-at-the-heels Fiesta is a one-story affair, with rooms surrounding a large swimming pool. But the Fiesta is clean and quiet, except when they host conventions and other events. Rooms are on the small side, with colorful bedspreads, thin carpeting, tiled baths, and satellite TV. The hotel's large, air-conditioned restaurant serves an ample selection of international dishes. ⊠ *North side of Inter-American Hwy., 1 km (½ mi) east of town,* ☎ *507/775–5454,* 𝖥𝖠𝖷 *507/774–4584. 55 rooms with bath. Restaurant, pool. AE, MC, V.*

$ 🏨 **Hotel Iris.** This central hotel offers basic, clean accommodations at budget rates. The rooms all have tile floors, telephones, fans, decent beds, and hot-water baths; those with air-conditioning and TV cost a few dollars more. A small restaurant off the lobby serves basic Panamanian fare. Ask for a room facing the street or all the way in back, since these rooms have large windows that make them cooler and brighter. ⊠ *C. A Norte, across from Parque Cervantes,* ☎ 𝖥𝖠𝖷 *507/775– 7233. 62 rooms with bath. Restaurant. MC, V.*

Outdoor Activities and Sports

SWIMMING

To escape the heat, head to the *balneario* (swimming hole) just north of town, across the bridge from the *cervecería* (brewery) on the road to Boquete. This simple swimming hole in the Río David has a small waterfall pouring into it and an open-air bar nearby; it's packed on weekends and holidays, but usually quiet the rest of the week.

Boquete

❷ *38 km (24 mi) north of David.*

Boquete is a pleasant little town of wooden houses and colorful gardens that sits 3,878 ft above sea level, in the verdant valley of the Río Caldera. For much of the year the trade winds blow over the mountains and down through that valley, often bringing a mist that keeps the area green year-round and makes rainbows a common sight. The mountains above town still have plenty of trees on them, which makes it a great place for bird-watching, and the roads and trails that head into those hills can be explored on foot, mountain bike, horseback, or four wheels.

Thanks to its rich soil, Boquete has become an important agricultural center, famous for its coffee, oranges, flowers, strawberries, and apples. The combination of good farming conditions and a pleasant climate have led many Europeans and North Americans to settle here over the years, which is why you'll see plenty of fair-skinned people and architecture that differs significantly from that of the lowlands. You'll also probably see Ngwóbe, or Guaymí Indians, some with farms in the valley, but most of whom migrate there from the eastern half of Chiriquí to work the orange and coffee harvests, which together span from September to April. Tidy homes and abundant blossoms make the town of Boquete a nice place for a stroll; a short loop can be made by heading north till you come to a fork in the road, where you veer right, passing the Hotel Panamonte, and crossing the Río Caldera. Turn right after crossing the river and follow it south, past the flower-filled fairgrounds, to another bridge, which you cross to get back to the town square.

The real attraction of this area lies a bit higher than Boquete. The road to the top of **Parque Nacional Volcán Barú** (Volcán Barú National Park) begins in town, heading west from the main road, two blocks north of the blue-and-white church. A large sign marks the route one block north of the main road; it is paved for the first 7 km (4½ mi), after which it becomes a rough and rocky dirt track that requires four-wheel drive for the 14 km (9 mi) to the summit. Since the routes to the summit are poorly marked, and the hike takes the better part of a day, it is best to hire a guide (☞ Outdoor Activities and Sports, *below*). 🕮 *$5.*

Other possible diversions include bird-watching, horseback riding, or mountain biking in the hills above town, a hike through the forest to several waterfalls, white-water rafting, or a visit to the hot springs and pre-Columbian petroglyphs in the nearby village of **Caldera.**

Dining and Lodging

$$–$$$ ✕ **Ristorante Salvatore.** Despite its Italian name, the menu here isn't much different from what you'll find at most Panamanian restaurants. They do serve pizza, and a couple of pasta dishes, but the selection is dominated by the standard meat dishes and a surprising seafood selection. The restaurant occupies the ground floor of a corner building, with small wooden tables set both inside and on a narrow cement porch. ✉ *1 block north of Hotel Rebequet,* ☎ *507/720–1857. No credit cards. Closed Mon.*

$–$$ ✕ **La Casona Mexicana.** Run by a local woman who lived in Mexico
★ for many years, this colorful place serves a limited selection of popular Toltec taste treats. The burritos are pretty standard, but the tacos are made with soft corn tortillas, whereas the tostadas and sopas have fried tortillas. It is set in an attractive old wooden house, the interior of which has been painted wild colors and decorated with Mexican souvenirs. It's on the left side of the main road as you enter town. ✉ *Avda. Central,* ☎ *No phone. No credit cards.*

$$$ 🏨 **Panamonte.** This charming country inn on a quiet street near the
★ Río Caldera seems oddly out of place: you would expect to find it in rural New England but not in Central America. The Collins family, of North American origin, has been pleasantly surprising guests since they opened the hotel in 1946. A two-story wooden building painted baby blue holds a lobby adorned with a small collection of colonial art, an elegant restaurant, and several guest rooms; a yellow house across the street has a few more rooms, while newer cement units in back are more spacious and private, but not nearly as charming. The restaurant is known for serving the best food in the region, and a large bar in back has a fireplace and views of the garden. The hotel rents horses and mountain bikes, and the in-house tour company, Río Monte, offers bird-watching on the family farm, sunrise on Barú's summit, and a coffee tour. ✉ *Avda. 11 de Abril, right at fork after town,* ☎ *507/720–1327,* FAX

507/720–2055. 19 rooms with bath. Restaurant, bar, horseback riding, mountain bikes. AE, MC, V.

$$–$$$ 📷 **Villa Marita** A relatively new addition to Boquete's accommodation selection, Villa Marita is in the hills above town. The bungalows, or *cabañas,* have attractive interiors and are bright and homey, with plenty of local hardwoods and windows overlooking the surrounding verdure. Each one has a bedroom, kitchenette, and couch that folds out into an extra bed. ✉ *Alto Lino, 5 km (3 mi) north of Boquete,* ☎ *507/720–1309. 7 bungalows. Kitchenettes. AE, MC, V.*

$$ 📷 **Hotel Rebequet.** This small hotel on a quiet corner two blocks east of the main road is an excellent option for people who like to cook, since it has cooking facilities and a dining area for the use of guests. Rooms surround a small courtyard and are relatively large, with parquet floors, windows, wood ceilings, blue-tile baths, TVs, and small refrigerators. ✉ *C. 6 Sur,* ☎ *507/720–1365. 9 rooms with bath. No credit cards.*

$–$$ 📷 **Pensión Topas.** The rooms in this small lodge, owned by a young
★   German couple and set in the corner of the owners' backyard, are spacious and attractive, with tile floors, big windows, firm beds, and original paintings and posters hanging on the walls. Four of them open onto a covered terrace overlooking the yard and a small pool, with a couple of tables where you can enjoy an optional German breakfast. A smaller, less-expensive room with a bathroom is in the back of the house. Turn right after the gas station, then right at the first corner. ✉ *Behind Texaco station,* ☎ *507/720–1005. 5 rooms, 1 without bath. Pool. No credit cards.*

$ 📷 **Pensión Marilos.** The small, clean rooms in this family-run lodge
★   are the best deal in Boquete and perhaps the entire country. They all have tile floors and windows, and all but two have private baths. The *pensión* is on the corner of two quiet side streets, a few blocks south of the central park. ✉ *C. 6 Sur,* ☎ *507/720–1380. 7 rooms, 5 with bath. No credit cards.*

Outdoor Activities and Sports

BIRD-WATCHING

The forested hills above Boquete are the perching grounds for abundant and varied avian life, which includes such colorful critters as collared redstarts, emerald toucanets, sulfur-winged parakeets, and about a dozen species of hummingbirds and their relatives. The area is also one of the best places in the world to see the legendary resplendent quetzal, reputed to be one of the most beautiful birds in the world, which are most easily observed from January to May. The cattle pastures, coffee farms, and orchards that surround town actually facilitate birding, since birds are easier to see when they leave the forest and enter wide open areas. The Panamonte (☞ Dining and Lodging, *above*) has tours to **Finca Lérida,** the family farm, where you're practically guaranteed to see a quetzal during the dry season. The waterfall hike offered by Expediciones Tierras Altas also passes through prime quetzal territory. The trip to the top of **Volcán Barú** takes you to higher life zones that have bird species you won't see around Boquete.

HIKING

There are plenty of hiking routes near Boquete, some of which can also be explored on horseback or mountain bike. The two paved loops above town can be hiked, but be aware that the loop reached by veering left at the fork is considerably longer and steeper. It also passes more forest and spectacular views.

The **Sendero los Quetzales,** the footpath to Cerro Punta, is reached by following the road to Alto Chiquero. The trail heads through the forest along Río Caldera, crossing it several times, and then over a ridge to El Respingo, in the hills above Cerro Punta. The 6-km (4-mi) hike is easier if you start in Cerro Punta, and a guided trip offered by **Expediciones Tierras Altas** (☎ 507/720–1342) includes transportation to El Respingo and pickup at Alto Chiquero. If you want to do the hike on your own, you should catch one of the first buses to David, then bus to Cerro Punta, and hire a four-wheel-drive taxi to take you to El Respingo. The trail isn't marked, and you should keep your eyes open for a left turn in a clearing about 1½ km (1 mi) into it, shortly after which you should turn right, at a gate, where the trail heads back into the forest. You should arrange to have a taxi pick you up in Alto Chiquero in the evening.

The hike to the summit of **Volcán Barú** is considerably more demanding, more than twice as long, and much steeper. You'll want to leave a car, or arrange to be dropped off and picked up, at the entrance to the national park, 14 km (9 mi) from the summit. Bring lots of water and warm, waterproof clothing for any hike, but especially for the trek up Barú. **Expediciones Tierras Altas** (☞ *above*) offers guided hikes up Barú, as well as a much easier tour on a farm above town, where hikers visit several waterfalls hidden in the forest. **Río Monte Tours** (☎ 507/720–1327) also arranges hiking trips up Barú. For those who aren't up to making the hike, they can also take you up in a Jeep to watch the sunrise from the summit.

Volcán

❸ *60 km (36 mi) northwest of David, 16 km (10 mi) south of Cerro Punta.*

A windy little town at a crossroads, Volcán is spread along the road on a plain to the south of Barú, in an area that lost its forests long ago. The highland towns of Boquete, Bambito, and Cerro Punta are all so close to the volcano that you can't see it in its entirety from any of them. From Volcán, however, you can often admire that massive peak and the mountains beyond it, weather permitting. Like Bambito and Cerro Punta, Volcán was largely settled by immigrants from Switzerland and Yugoslavia during the early part of this century. It's a good place to stay if you intend to hike up the volcano's southern side—you'll want to get up before dawn if you're attempting that grueling ascent.

There are some small lakes known as Las Lagunas several kilometers south of Volcán, which are surrounded by some of the last bits of standing forest in the area, but they're too far to walk to, and the last stretch of road is too rough for anything but a four-wheel-drive vehicle. Though it's often windy, Volcán tends to be warmer than either nearby Bambito or Cerro Punta, which can get very chilly at night, so it's a good place to stay if you didn't pack warm clothes. If you don't hike up the volcano, you'll want to use Volcán as a base for day trips to the Cerro Punta area, which has much more to see and do.

OFF THE
BEATEN PATH

CUESTA DE PIEDRA WATERFALLS – There are several waterfalls in a valley below Cuesta de Piedra, a small community on the road to Volcán, about 20 km (12 mi) north of Concepción. Since the cascades are in a restricted area belonging to the national electric institute, IHRE, you can only visit them with a guide from Cuesta de Piedra, who can be hired through the **Restaurante Porvenir** (☎ 507/770–6088); talk to Eneida or Leonel, and be prepared to haggle over the price. If you're driving, the **Mirador Alanher**, on the left side of the road shortly after Cuesta de Piedra, is a good place to stop for a *batido* (fruity milk drink)—papaya or *zarzamora* (blackberry) are the usual flavors—hot chocolate, or coffee. Be sure to climb the stairs to the *mirador* (lookout).

Lodging

$$ ⊞ **Hotel Dos Ríos.** Some of the rooms in this two-story wooden build-
★   ing west of town face the volcano. It is definitely Volcán's nicest hotel:
Large rooms have wood floors, walls, and ceilings, with windows on
the volcano side and small tile baths in back. Two larger suites on the
far end of the building have sitting areas and lots of windows and are
well worth the extra $6; the one upstairs has the best view of Barú. A
large restaurant in front serves basic meat and seafood dishes, and the
bar next door is a bit on the ugly side, but a large window lets you
gaze at the volcano while you sip your martini. The hotel can arrange
early-morning transport to the foot of the volcano and a guide to the
summit. ⊠ *2 km (1 mi) west of Volcán,* ☎ *507/771–4271. 14 rooms
with bath, 2 suites. Restaurant, bar. AE, MC, V.*

Bambito

❹   *6 km (4 mi) north of Volcán, 10 km (6 mi) south of Cerro Punta.*

Not really a town to speak of, Bambito consists of a series of farms
and homes scattered along the narrow valley on the western side of
Volcán Barú that the Río Chiriquí Viejo winds down. Sheer rock walls,
trees clinging to steep hillsides, and suspension bridges spanning the
boulder-strewn river punctuate the impressive terrain. The trade winds
whip down through the valley for much of the dry season, which
keeps it fairly cool, but it gets more sun than the Cerro Punta area.
Small coffee and vegetable farms line much of the road, and several
roadside stands sell local vegetables and fruit preserves. It's a lovely
spot, and is an excellent base for exploring the mountains around Cerro
Punta or rafting on the Río Chiriquí Viejo, since it has one of the coun-
try's best hotels.

Lodging

$$$$ ⊞ **Hotel Bambito.** This full-service, luxury resort has a great location
★   at the entrance to the Bambito Valley, and all its rooms overlook a mas-
sive rock wall draped with foliage that towers over the Río Chiriquí
Viejo. Rooms have hardwood floors, high ceilings, picture windows,
large tile baths, and satellite TV. Junior suites feature balconies, and
master suites have bedroom lofts—several of them also have tubs. A
small exhibit of pre-Columbian art and a fireplace are in the lobby,
next to which is a spacious, plush restaurant and cocktail lounge. The
large, heated pool is enclosed in a sort of greenhouse; there is also a
simple gym and lighted tennis courts. The hotel has motor scooters and
mountain bikes, and nature guides can take you bird-watching and hik-
ing in the nearby national parks. ⊠ *Bambito,* ☎ *507/771–4265,* FAX
*507/771–4207. 37 rooms with bath, 10 suites. Restaurant, bar, pool,
spa, 2 tennis courts, hiking, horseback riding, mountain bikes. AE, DC,
MC, V.*

Cerro Punta

❺   *78 km (48 mi) northwest of David, 16 km (10 mi) north of Volcán.*

This bowl-shape valley embraced by the Cordillera de Talamanca is
the remnant of a crater of a gigantic volcano, and its dark, volcanic
soil is consequently some of the most fertile in the country. That soil
has been a mixed blessing: it is a boon for farmers, but it has also led
them to deforest most of the valley. Nevertheless, Cerro Punta has some
splendid pastoral scenery, with a patchwork of vegetable farms, some
clinging to steep slopes, and an extensive ranch that raises dairy cat-
tle and thoroughbred horses. Several foliage-clad rocky formations tower
over the rolling landscape, and the upper slopes of the mountains that

ring the valley still retain most of their forest cover. Since the trade winds regularly push clouds over the continental divide and into the valley, Cerro Punta is often swathed in mist, which keeps everything green year-round, and makes for frequent rainbow sightings.

Cerro Punta is considerably higher than Boquete, and can consequently get rather chilly when the sun goes down or gets stuck behind the clouds. It sometimes drops down near 40°F at night, which means you'll want to bring warm clothes and a waterproof jacket. The cool climate no doubt played a part in the decision of many Swiss and Yugoslavian families to settle here earlier this century. That European influence is reflected in some of the valley's architecture and the complexions of many of its inhabitants. You may also see full-blooded Ngwóbe, or Guaymí, Indians in Cerro Punta, most of whom are temporary farm laborers.

The pastoral landscapes, distant mountains, colorful farmhouses, and abundant flowers of Cerro Punta are impressive enough, but if you are interested in birds, or in hiking, you have even more reason to head here. The paved road that enters the valley makes a small loop, with several dirt roads branching off it, heading farther up into the mountains. These dirt roads follow small streams past farms and patches of forest, which make them ideal routes for bird-watching. There are also several footpaths into the mountains around town.

Two trails head into the forest near the park headquarters of **Parque Internacional La Amistad.** La Amistad is a 20-minute drive along a dirt track that heads into the mountains above Cerro Punta. Turn left after the Hotel Cerro Punta, and left at the next intersection, then follow that road to the park, keeping left after you drive through the gate; the road is rough, but a good driver can get to the ranger station in any kind of car. You can also hire a four-wheel-drive taxi to take you to the park entrance (it should cost about $3). The **Hotel Bambito** (☎ 507/771–4265) can arrange guided tours to the park.

Another way to explore that park's forest is to visit the privately managed reserve of **Los Quetzales** (☞ Dining and Lodging, *below*) which lies up a four-wheel-drive road from the neighborhood of Guadelupe. Visitors must be accompanied by one of the reserve's guides, who charge each person $3 per hour, but they can take you to waterfalls and may help you spot a quetzal.

Dining and Lodging

$　✕ **Mama Lola.** Sandwiches, milk shakes, and homemade desserts are the specialties of this tiny restaurant down the hill from Cerro Punta's main intersection. The restaurant has lots of windows, and small Formica tables and benches attached to the walls. The limited menu includes basic burgers and the *pie grande* (big foot), sort of a French bread pizza. For dessert, try some *dulce de zanahoria* or *plátano* (carrot or banana cake), fresh yogurt, or one of a variety of fruit shakes. ⊠ *C. Central,* ☎ *507/771–2053. No credit cards. Closes daily at 7.*

$$　▥ **Los Quetzales.** The two spacious cabins inside this private 600-acre
★　cloud-forest reserve are in the area where the Volcán Barú and La Amistad parks meet. Both two-story cabins stand on a ridge in the midst of the forest; each one has several beds, a kitchen, balconies, a wood stove—no electricity—a shower with a gas heater, and kerosene lanterns. They are a good deal if you have four or more people, but are a bit expensive for one couple. A simple cement duplex at the edge of the forest holds two apartments, each of which has two bedrooms, one bath, a well-stocked kitchen, and a fireplace. The best deal for single travelers and couples is the main hotel, outside the reserve, with mod-

ern rooms with hardwood floors and windows overlooking the surrounding countryside. There's also a small restaurant upstairs, and a bakery and pizzeria downstairs. The reserve has several trails, one of which leads to a waterfall, and plenty of birds; the reserve provides guides, rubber boats, and rain gear. ⊠ *Altos de Guadelupe,* ☎ 507/771–2182, ℻ 507/771–2226. *11 rooms with bath, 2 cabins, 2 apartments. Restaurant, pizzeria, sauna, exercise room, hiking, horseback riding. MC, V.*

$–$$ 🏨 **Hotel Cerro Punta.** This small lodge across from the old gas station features great views of farms and distant peaks, simple rooms, and hearty food. Rooms are on the small side, with worn wooden floors, picture windows, and tiled baths. The restaurant serves basic food; daily specials are the best bet. The grounds are planted with flowers, which attract a steady stream of hummingbirds. ⊠ *C. Principal,* ☎ ℻ 507/771–2020. *10 rooms with bath. Restaurant, bar. MC, V.*

Outdoor Activities and Sports

BIRD-WATCHING

Although the valley's floor and lower slopes have been almost completely deforested, Cerro Punta is surrounded by mountain forests, and that high-altitude wilderness is home to a large and diverse avian population. The region's varied feathered friends can be spotted all around the bowl-shape valley, especially near the streams and rivers that flow into and out of it. Several roads head off the main loop around the valley's floor, and all of them lead to prime birding territory. The trails into the national parks offer access to the vast expanses of wilderness that border the valley, but the best birding area in Cerro Punta is probably the private Los Quetzales nature reserve. One birder spotted 45 species from the balcony of one of the reserve's cabins during a four-day stay and noted that quetzals abound there.

HIKING

There's a decent selection of trails that head into the mountains around Cerro Punta, ranging from short paths through the woods to the six-hour trek around the back of Volcán Barú to Boquete. There are several trails through the cloud forests of **Parque International La Amistad,** both near the ranger station and within the private reserve of Los Quetzales. The most challenging, and rewarding, hike out of Cerro Punta is the 6-km (4-mi) trek over the northern slope of **Volcán Barú,** from El Respingo to Alto Chiquero, high in the hills above Boquete. The most challenging aspect of that expedition, however, may be getting back to Cerro Punta, which lies about four hours by bus from Boquete. The last buses from Boquete and David leave at 6 PM, which means it's safer to make that hike while based in David, since it gives you a couple of more hours to get back to your hotel.

Chiriquí A to Z

Arriving and Departing

BY BUS

Several buses make the trip between San José and Chiriquí every day, but be warned that it is a 10-hour trip between the Costa Rican capital and David, and the road was extremely rough at press time. **Tracopa** (☎ 506/221–4214) has daily buses from San José to David, departing San José from Avenida 18 between Calles 2 and 4 at 7:30 AM; and departing David daily from Avenida 5 Este and Calle A Sur (Tracopa in David, Panama, ☎ 507/775–0585) at 8:30 AM. **Tico Bus** (☎ 506/221–8954) has daily service between San José and Panama City, departing San José from next to the Iglesia de la Soledad at 10 PM and passing David around 9:30 AM the next day. Buses from Panama sometimes pick up extra passengers at the border, from where they depart at around 8 PM. **Panaline** (☎ 506/255–1205) runs the same route in newer buses for a bit more money, leaving San José at 1 PM, which gets them into David around 10 PM.

BY CAR

Since you can't cross an international border with a car rented in Costa Rica, the only way to drive to Panama is with a private car. The Carretera Interamericana (Inter-American Highway, CA2) enters Panama at Paso Canoas, about 15 km (9 mi) before the turnoff to Volcán and Cerro Punta, and about 37 km (23 mi) before David.

BY PLANE

The Panamanian airline **Aeroperlas** (☎ 506/440–0093 San José; 507/721–1195 David) has five flights a week between San José and David, with quick connections to Bocas del Toro, Panama City, and a dozen other destinations within Panama. Those flights depart David Monday–Friday at 8:15 AM, returning from San José at 8:45 AM. Another quick, and less-expensive, way to travel between Chiriquí and San José is to take one of the daily **Sansa** (☎ 506/221–9414) flights to Coto 47 (☎ 506/783–3275), an airstrip in an oil palm plantation a 20-minute drive from the border town of Paso Canoas. If you fly to Coto 47, you'll want to call and arrange to have a taxi from **Paso Canoas** (☎ 506/732–2355) meet you at the airstrip. When traveling back to San José, try to confirm your reservation the day before. Another option is to fly either Sansa or **Travelair** (☎ 506/296–1102) to Golfito, where taxis and buses to the border abound.

Getting Around

BY BUS

Buses travel regularly between David and the following destinations: Paso Canoas (Costa Rican border) every 20 minutes from 5 AM to 7 PM (1-hr trip); Cerro Punta, Bambito, and Volcán, every 30 minutes from 5 AM to 6 PM (2-hr trip); Boquete, every 30–60 minutes from 5 AM to 6 PM (90-min trip).

BY CAR

Renting a car is an excellent way to explore Chiriquí, since most roads are in good repair and there are several rental companies in David. It also costs a lot less to rent a car in Panama than it does in Costa Rica. The road to Boquete heads straight north out of David, no turns required. To reach Volcán, drive west on the Carretera Interamericana to the town of Concepción—a collection of modern buildings 24 km (15 mi) west of David—where you turn right. The road to Bambito and Cerro Punta, on the right in Volcán, is well marked.

BY PLANE

Aeroperlas (☎ 506/440–0093 San José; 507/721–1195 David) flies several times a week between David, Changuinola, and Bocas del Toro and schedules daily flights between those three towns and Panama City.

Contacts and Resources

CAR RENTALS

Car-rental companies (all of which offer four-wheel-drive vehicles) with offices in David include the following: **Hertz** (✉ Avda. 20 at C F Sur, ☎ 507/775–6828), **Budget** (✉ Avda. 7 Oeste at C. F Sur, ☎ 507/775–1667), **Dollar** (☎ 507/774–3385), **Avis** (☎ 507/774–7075), **National** (☎ 507/774–3462).

EMERGENCIES

Panama's health-care standards are quite high for such a poor country, and David has a large **hospital** (☎ 507/775–4221). The following are important numbers:**Ambulance** (☎ 507/775–2161). **Fire department** (☎ 103). **Police** (☎ 104).

Expediciones Tierras Altas (☎ 507/720–1342), in Boquete, offers a variety of day trips in that area, including bird-watching, hiking, Jeep trips up Volcán Barú, and visits to the nearby hot springs and pre-Columbian sites of Caldera. **Río Monte Tours** (☎ 507/720–1327), also in Boquete, offers much the same tours as Expediciones Tierras Altas. **Panama Expedition** (☎ 507/771–4265, ext. 119), across from the lobby of the Hotel Bambito in Bambito, offers a variety of excursions. **Panama Rafting** (☎ 507/774–1236) runs trips down the province's white-water rivers. **Chiriquí River Rafting** (☎ 507/774–0204; 225–8949 Panama City) is a specialist in rafting trips.

International calls can be made at the INTEL office (⊠ C. C Norte and Avda. Cincuentenaria).

The **regional tourist office** (⊠ Avda. 3 de Noviembre and C. A Norte, David, ☎ 507/775–5120), which is on the second floor of a corner building across from Parque Cervantes, is open weekdays 8:30–4:30.

THE BOCAS DEL TORO ARCHIPELAGO

The isolated cluster of islands known as the Archipelago of Bocas del Toro—in the northwest corner of Panama, in a province of the same name—holds some spectacular scenery, a wealth of natural assets, and a laid-back, Caribbean atmosphere. The province includes a large piece of the mainland as well, but this part of mainland Panama is nothing special—it's the Chiquita Republic, an area virtually blanketed with banana plantations. The real interest for travelers lies offshore, on the islands where you'll find the capital city, also called Bocas del Toro.

The archipelago was "discovered," or at least visited, by Christopher Columbus in 1502. The islands' original inhabitants were Guaymí Indians, and they're still around in isolated villages and intermingled with African-Caribbeans and Hispanics in the larger towns. The language, too, is an interesting mix, called Guari-Guari, which combines English and Indian dialects. After the first Europeans appeared, several of the islands in the chain evolved into supply and repair stations for the shipping industry, which explains the names of at least two of them: Bastimentos translates as "supplies," which is why the ships landed there. And Carenero refers to "careening"—heeling a ship over on one side to effect repairs on the other side.

The capital island, Isla Colón (after Cristóbal Colón, or Christopher Columbus), and the little city upon it, Bocas del Toro, founded in 1826, along with the other nearby islands in the chain, comprised a thriving community for many decades. At one point Bocas del Toro (the source of its own odd name, which translates as "mouths of the bull," is lost in legend) was the third largest city in Panama, and there was talk of making it the capital. It was the hub of the banana business in the early days of that industry, and elegant wooden houses belonging to the banana kings lined the town's waterfronts and main streets.

With the advent of the Panama Canal, everything in Bocas del Toro changed. Although the nearby mainland town of Almirante is today a shipping port for the banana plantations that cover much of the Panamanian mainland in this area, the islands of Bocas del Toro and their once-thriving capital town lost importance, and in time the banana kings left town. According to local lore, when they did so, their former employees moved in and took over the town, resulting in a very confused situation regarding deeded property ownership, which may eventually play havoc with those looking to exploit the area for tourism.

The recent resurgence of interest in Bocas del Toro may have had very bureaucratic beginnings: thousands of foreigners living in Costa Rica on tourist visas have to leave the country for 72 hours every 90 days, and nearly all of them eventually make it to Bocas. These temporary refugees quickly discover that the islands are a very cool place: offbeat, out of the way, with great beaches, cheap rooms and food, excellent diving, and mellow local people. Now the word is very much out. Dozens of Americans and Europeans now inhabit the islands, either hiding out from the world or nudging into place the beginnings of a tourist-industry framework. Developers are beginning to swarm, and several projects are underway. We recommend a tour soon if you want to experience the area before it gets seriously developed.

Isla Colón

❻ *21 km (13 mi) north of Chiriquí Grande.*

A look at a map of the archipelago shows what an odd piece of geography Isla Colón is. The town of **Bocas del Toro,** sometimes called Bocas Town, sits on a little head of land, connected to the main body of the island by a narrow neck, or isthmus, that is at most a hundred yds wide. The town's slow fade into disrepair and obscurity was hastened by several fires and the disastrous earthquake of 1991, which wrecked many of the buildings in town and left many others teetering precariously. Dozens of buildings in Bocas Town would be condemned anywhere in the United States. As you ascend a tilting staircase to a restaurant or hotel room, you have the feeling that you're entering an amusement-park fun house. Still, many of the older buildings in Bocas del Toro are lovely, if dilapidated, with carved porch rails, fretwork, and trim, and the town is worth wandering through. Check out the classic, beautifully kept, circa-1926 **fire engine** in the fire-department garage.

Another strange element: a couple of hundred yds offshore from the Hotel Las Brisas, there's a **little sunken island** that slid a few feet below water during the 1991 earthquake. The entire island is underwater, but parts of it lie in water less than a foot deep. You can paddle a kayak or swim out there and walk around; there's even an underwater tennis court.

During the annual **Feria,** which is usually held in September, Panamanians crowd into Bocas Town by the thousands (there's a car ferry service from Chiriquí Grande, down the coast, and nearby Almirante). Along the right side of the isthmus road that connects Bocas with the rest of Isla Colón are dozens of simple structures housing beer shacks, restaurants, and exhibits during the Feria, which stand empty the rest of the year. Behind those shacks is the **town beach,** which is unfortunately sometimes littered. The island has much nicer beaches, though you'll want to rent a bike or hire a taxi to visit them.

If you follow the road for several kilometers, veering right at the fork, you'll reach **Playa Bluff,** a long swath of golden sand backed by thick foliage and washed by aquamarine waters. Four species of endangered sea turtles nest here from March to September; local guides may be able to take you to observe them. (☞ Outdoor Activities and Sports, *below*).

If you veer left at the fork, you'll head through the middle of the island to the other side, where there's a little village called **Boca del Drago.**

Between the two villages called Bocas, the island is mainly jungle. The rain forest covering much of the island is home to such animals as armadillos, pacas, several types of frogs, boa constrictors, two- and three-toed sloths, raccoons, coatis, and monkeys. Thankfully, the islands of Bocas have no poisonous snakes. At the center of the island is a large grotto worth a stop—bring a flashlight!

Bocas Town is a good place to catch a boat out to the real draw of these islands: the diving in and around **Parque Nacional Marina Isla Bastimentos.** There are dozens of great diving and snorkeling spots, especially around the two **Cayos Zapatillas,** and the richness and variety of the sea life—the diversity of sponges and coral, for starters—is amazing. At press time, Panama's **Institute of Renewable Natural Resources (INRENARE),** had begun charging a $10 admission fee for the Cayos Zapatillas, which should be paid at their office on First Street in Bocas Town before leaving for the cays. Since that fee increases the cost of an excursion considerably, most of the boat drivers in Bocas are taking people to comparable dive spots in the region, such as **Punta Hospital,** and **Olas Chicas,** on Isla Bastimentos.

Dining and Lodging

$$ ✕ **La Ballena.** In a simple cement building behind the municipality, La
★ Ballena—the name means "The Whale"—is a colorful, friendly little place. Christmas lights brighten up the entrance at night, and the interior has old bottles, bamboo, candles and bright colors on the wall and furniture. They've usually got good music playing on the stereo, and there are a few tables in front that overlook one of this sleepy little town's somnambulant side streets. The Italian owners prepare what is probably the best food in town, concentrating on fresh seafood and pasta. They also rent bicycles, arrange tours, and provide information. ⊠ *Avda. F between Cs. 3 and 2,* ☎ *No phone. No credit cards.*

$$ ✕ **Le Pirate.** This airy wooden building sitting over the water on Boca's main drag is the island's most attractive restaurant. The front half has a long bar and a few tables, but on a clear night, the deck in back is a great place to hang out, if only just for drinks. Meals there are complemented by the view out over the water, and the sound of the water lapping against the dock. They offer a small selection of seafood, and a few meat and pasta dishes. ⊠ *C. 3,* ☎ *507/757–9025. MC, V.*

$ ✕ **Anciflor.** This red and white kiosk on a little wedge of a park where Calles 1 and 3 come together is a popular hangout for locals, who head there for tasty pastries and hearty lunch specials, or to simply sip cool fruit drinks and gossip. It's a bit cramped inside, with a couple of large tables that people often end up sharing, but there's also a small bar outside. This is a good place to grab a light breakfast—empanadas (meat pies) and cakes—or dessert. ⊠ *Cs. 1 and 3,* ☎ *No phone. No credit cards. Closed Sun.*

$ ✕ **Kun Ju.** In a small wooden box of a building perched over the water where Calle 3 meets Calle 1, this places serves basic Chinese food at very reasonable prices. The menu includes wonton soup, roast pork or chicken, and several types of chow mein, chop suey, and *arroz frito* (fried rice). ⊠ *Cs. 1 and 3,* ☎ *No phone. No credit cards. Closed Wed.*

$–$$$ ▥ **La Coralina.** This rather elegant, hacienda-like guest house is the only place, other than the Mangrove Inn (☞ *below*), that is not in town. Instead, you'll find it on a forested hill with an ocean view on the road that leads to Playa Bluff. It's a fairly new building meant to have the look of an old Spanish hacienda, and it does have a certain charm due to the hardwood floors, high ceilings, and ocean views. Two rooms upstairs share a bath—the one in front has an ocean view—while a larger room downstairs has a private bath with a tub. There are also several rudimentary rooms in back for considerably less money, or you can camp on the grounds for $5. The owners will pick you up or run you into town for $2. ☒ *Paunch Beach,* ☎ ℻ *507/757–9458. 6 rooms with shared bath. No credit cards.*

$$ 🏨 **Hotel Laguna.** With its carved wooden balconies and sidewalk café, ★ the Hotel Laguna looks like it was transported from a village in the Alps and dropped into the heart of Bocas. At press time, it had the town's newest and most upscale accommodations, with such previously unheard of amenities as orthopedic mattresses, hot water heaters, and air-conditioning. Rooms have lots of wood, modern, black fixtures, closets, and small windows—those downstairs have tile floors; those upstairs, hardwood floors. The brightest, and nicest ones are the suite and the one standard room facing the street. ☒ *C. 3 between Avdas. D and E,* ☎ *507/757–9091,* ℻ *507/757–9092. 11 rooms with bath, 1 suite. Restaurant, bar. MC, V.*

$$ 🏨 **Mangrove Inn.** A short boat trip from town takes you to this collection of buildings propped over the water at the edge of a mangrove ★ forest. Primarily a dive resort, with all the equipment and a resident dive master, the inn is just a short swim from a decent reef. Dive packages include meals and boat transportation to the province's best dive sites. It's a good spot even if you just want to snorkel, swim, and relax. Blue-and-white wooden cabins have bunks, double beds, and small baths. A large, open-air restaurant and bar serves only daily specials. Everything sits over the water, and is connected via a series of docks. ☒ *General delivery,* ☎ ℻ *507/757–9594. 6 cabins with bath. Restaurant, bar, snorkeling, dive shop. No credit cards.*

$ 🏨 **Hotel Bahía.** This grand old building right across the street from the old banana-company dock once housed the company's main offices. It was converted to a hotel three decades ago, and has seen some hard times, but is still a sturdy, decent-looking place. Rooms are large, with high ceilings, but a bit dark and musty. Nevertheless, they're clean, and are decorated in a most eclectic manner. More expensive VIP rooms have air-conditioning and TV. The open-air restaurant out front is run by the town's only family of Kuna Indians. ☒ *C. 3 and Avda. A,* ☎ ℻ *507/757–9626. 22 rooms with bath. No credit cards.*

$ 🏨 **Hotel Las Brisas.** Built on stilts over the water on north end of Calle ★ 3, Las Brisas may look a bit shabby—it's in a ramshackle 50-year-old building—but it has a great location and friendly owner and staff. You can kayak out to the sunken island or across the channel to Carenero, or have your boatman pick you up for a ride to the national marine park or other snorkeling and diving spots. The rooms are pretty basic, but comfortable, with private baths and hot-water showers. Those in the old wooden building across the street are a bit larger, with two or three beds packed into each one, for budget travelers. ☒ *Avda. Norte at C. 3,* ☎ ℻ *507/757–9248. 27 rooms with bath. Boating, bicycles. AE, V.*

$ 🏨 **Hotel Scarlet.** Actually, it's cartoon-panther pink. The interior of this new cement building is much easier to look at, though it's not going to win any decorating awards. Rooms are fairly sterile boxes, with tile floors, small baths, and TV sets, but they're clean, and cheap. ☒ *C. 4, 1 block north of Bahía restaurant,* ☎ *507/757–9290. 12 rooms with bath. No credit cards.*

$ 🏨 **Pensión Delicias.** Above the restaurant of the same name, the Delicias has a collection of basic rooms, most of which have several beds packed into them. Some have private baths, some share baths. More money buys privacy and hot water. They also have a collection of two-level huts on Playa Bluff with hammocks, enclosed sleeping areas up top, a communal shower, and a small restaurant. Called "Camping Guaymí," it's quite rustic, but is a gorgeous spot; they provide cheap

transportation once daily. ⊠ C. 3, ☎ 507/757–9318. 8 rooms, some
without bath. No credit cards.

Outdoor Activities and Sports

SNORKELING AND SCUBA DIVING

There are three dive centers on the island, and at least half a dozen
people who take visitors on snorkeling excursions. Though you might
not encounter as many fish and big marine life here as in other parts
of the world, Bocas has a great variety of corals—almost 75 different
species—sponges, and small invertebrates. You're also likely to see lots
of rays, colorful tropical fish, and sometimes, sea turtles or even dolphins. The most famous spot is the reef around the **Cayos Zapatillas,**
with excellent conditions. **Punta Hospital** has an impressive coral and
sponge garden that extends down a steep wall into the blue depths.
Olas Chicas, on the northern coast of Isla Bastimentos, is another excellent spot, and excursions there often offer the added treat of a fresh
fish or lobster lunch prepared by Polo, who lives there. If you stay in
Bocas, it's cheaper to bike or hike out to the reef off Paunch, or better yet, the point on the far end of Playa Bluff.

Bocas Water Sports (⊠ C. 3, ☎ 507/757–9541) offers a variety of boat
dives and nonscuba excursions, including trips to their Red Frog camping area on a beach on Isla Bastimentos (☞ below). The **Mangrove
Inn/Turtle Divers** (⊠ C. 3, ☎ FAX 507/757–5954) offers a different excursion every day. It has its own hotel and dive center, the Mangrove
Inn, just south of town, and offers trips to about a dozen dive spots,
as well as inexpensive certification courses. **Starfleet Eco-Adventures**
(⊠ C. 1, ☎ FAX 507/757–9630) offers scuba and snorkeling excursions
on a private catamaran, and inexpensive certification courses. You can
also negotiate a ride to any of the area's attractions with one of the
dozens of freelance boatmen in and around town, though you'll need
to get a small group together to make it affordable. Dive trips usually
cost about $15 per person if you go with a group, though those to the
Cayos Zapatillas run about $25 per person.

SURFING

Isla Colón's Playa Bluff and Playa Paunch—a meager beach on the road
to Bluff—have good surfing spots when the ocean gets undulant. When
the waves get big, there is good surfing over the reef around the northern tip of Isla Carenero and at several spots on Isla Bastimentos, which
has long, deserted beaches.

TURTLE-WATCHING

For information about turtle-watching, ask at the **Mangrove Roots Shop,**
on Calle 3, or at **ANCON,** next door to the Hotel Las Brisas. When turtle-watching, be as quiet as possible, use flashlights as little as possible, and don't ever shine lights at or take photos of the turtle's face.

Isla Bastimentos

❼ 24 km (15 mi) north of Chiriquí Grande.

A large part of Isla Bastimentos lies within the boundaries of **Parque
Nacional Marina Isla Bastimentos** (Isla Bastimentos Marine National
Park), which protects an important sea turtle nesting beach and a significant expanse of rain forest that is home for plenty of birds, an abundance of colorful poison dart frogs, and various other interesting
creatures. **Playa Larga,** the long beach in the park, is an important nesting area for several species of sea turtles, which arrive there at night
from March to September to bury their eggs in the sand. Unfortunately,
that beach is almost impossible to visit at night, which makes Playa
Bluff, on Isla Colón, the best option for turtle-watching.

You might want to visit the little village of **Bastimentos,** also called "Old Bank," on the southwestern end of the island, whose Guari-Guari speaking residents are very friendly. It's a funky little town, with hundreds of small houses packed together on a hillside overlooking a quiet bay. Among other things, Bastimentos is the home of the region's most popular calypso band, the Beach Boys, who actually perform more regularly in Bocas. It's a tranquil, unspoiled spot, with a few small hotels that provide interesting alternatives to staying in the Bocas.

A 40-minute hike across the island on a muddy path leads to a lovely, palm-lined beach. It is just one of several gorgeous beaches that line the island's northern shore, all but one of which lie outside the national park. There are also several points around which you'll find good snorkeling when the sea is calm, including one of the best dive spots in the region, **Olas Chicas.** From there it takes almost four hours to walk east to the Playa Larga, which marks the beginning of the national park.

The only way to get to Parque Nacional Marina Isla Bastimentos is by boat. Boats head over to the community of Bastimentos pretty regularly, leaving from the dock next to the Commercial Chow Ku store. If you catch a boat that's already heading there, you can usually get a ride for $1, but if you hire one, it may cost $2 or $3.

Lodging

$ **El Pelicano.** On a tiny beach at the eastern end of town, this new place consists of a couple bungalows perched on the hillside, each of which has three rooms and a common bath, and a spacious bar and restaurant built out over the water under a high, thatched roof. The beach is hardly big enough to be called that, but a short swim from shore is a small reef that offers decent snorkeling, and the owners can arrange boat trips to more distant dive spots. The restaurant is the best on the island. ⊠ *Bastimentos,* ☎ *No phone. 6 rooms without bath. Restaurant, bar. No credit cards.*

$ **Pensión Bastimentos.** Housed in a wooden building over the water, this place makes up for what it lacks in privacy and amenities with friendly service. Rooms are simple, but comfortable—only one has a private bath—and the deck out back has a lovely view. The owner, Ila Robinson, will cook pretty much what you want, if it's available. She can also arrange trips, as well as fishing. ⊠ *Bastimentos,* ☎ *No phone. 4 rooms, 1 with bath. Restaurant. No credit cards.*

Bocas del Toro A to Z

Arriving and Departing

BY BOAT

Water taxi is the most common means of transport between Almirante, Bocas del Toro, and Chiriquí Grande. Water taxis make the 20-min trip between Almirante and Bocas del Toro approximately every hour from 6 AM to 6 PM. There are two companies, about 100 yds apart in Almirante, and boats leave once they fill up, so it is worthwhile to check both and sign up at the one that has more people waiting. In Bocas, taxis leave from a dock near the police station on Calle 1, and from the dock next to Le Pirate Restaurant, and it is good to check both spots to find out when the next boat leaves.

The free **"workingman's ferry"** leaves Bocas every day early in the morning and returns in the evening. There are also several water taxis per day between Almirante and Chiriquí Grande, which stop in Bocas if three or more people want to get on or off there. Otherwise you have to take an additional taxi to and from Almirante. They are run by the same two companies that provide service between Almirante and Bocas, and the schedule varies according to demand (check ahead). A daily **car ferry** runs between Chiriquí Grande, Almirante, and Bocas (no ferry to Bocas on Tuesday), but the ferry trip between Bocas and Chiriquí Grande takes four hours.

BY BUS

There's a daily, relatively direct bus from San José, Costa Rica, to **Changuinola,** Panama. This direct bus leaves at 10 AM from Calle 14, between Avenidas 5 and 7; it's an eight-hour trip. From Changuinola, you can take a bus or cab to the port of Almirante, where water taxis (☞ By Boat, *above*) run hourly to Bocas del Toro. Several daily buses (☎ 506/257–8129) also travel between San José and the border town of **Sixaola.** These buses depart San José (Avda. 11, between Cs. 1 and Central) at 6 AM, 8 AM, 1:30 PM, and 3:30 PM; they pick up passengers in Cahuita 3½ hours later, and at the entrance to Puerto Viejo 20 minutes after that; they arrive at Sixaola seven hours after departing San José. Buses leave Sixaola for San José at 5 AM, 7:30 AM. 9:30 AM, and 2:30 PM. There's also a bus from Puerto Viejo to Sixaola. From Sixaola, you hike across the railroad bridge into the Panamanian town of Guabito, where you can catch a bus or taxi to nearby Changuinola, or better yet, hire a taxi directly to the port of Almirante. A cab from Sixaola to Almirante can cost $10–$20, so you're best off sharing it with other travelers.

BY PLANE

The Panamanian airline **Aeroperlas** (☎ 507/757–9341) has daily flights between Bocas and Panama City, and five flights per week between Bocas del Toro, Changuinola, and David. Flights to David leave at 6:30 AM weekdays and connect to direct flights to San José. Flights to Panama City leave daily at 8:30 AM; Sunday at 5 PM.

Getting Around

BY BIKE

There are several places to rent bicycles in town—Hotel Las Brisas, Hotel Laguna, and La Ballena Restaurant (☞ Dining and Lodging *in* Isla Colón, *above*)—which is a good way to reach the island's beaches.

BY BOAT

This is the main mode of transportation in this area. Individually chartered, motorized dugouts are the usual means of interisland travel, although there's at least one sailboat for charter in town. Ask around the docks and town to find the kind of boat you're interested in chartering. Boats to Bastimentos leave fairly regularly from the dock next to the Commercial Chow Ku store, and charge $1 per person.

BY CAR

You won't see much in the way of auto traffic here, although there is a van-size taxi that makes a few trips a week to Bocas del Drago, at the other end of the island. You can hire a cab to drive you to Bocas del Drago and wait for you, or to take you to the closer Playa Bluff, and pick you up at an agreed-upon hour. It's possible to rent a car in Changuinola and bring it over on the car ferry, but it isn't recommended, because most spots can only be reached by boat.

Contacts and Resources

BANKS

A branch of the **Banco Nacional de Panama** is across the street from the government office buildings by Parque Simón Bolívar; they'll cash traveler's checks, but can't give credit card advances. The currency is the American dollar, also called the balboa.

The **Fire Department** (☎ 0 + 103) is on the corner of Calle 1 and North Avenue. The **Police Station** (☎ 0 + 104) is next to the ferry-arrival dock on Calle 3. **Hospitals** (✉ Bocas, ☎ 507/757–9201; Changuinola, ☎ 507/758–8295; Centro Medico Paitilla, Panama City, ☎ 507/263–6060).

GUIDED TOURS

Three dive shops and several local fishermen offer one-day excursions to the Cayos Zapatillas, Punta Hospital, Olas Chicas, and other popular snorkeling spots. Day trips can be arranged through the Hotel Las Brisas or La Ballena Restaurant on Isla Colón.

Turtle Divers (☎ FAX 507/757–9594) offers boat trips to Isla de Pajaros, Boca del Drago, and a Teribe Indian village in the rain forest, and a visit to a Guaymí Indian village. **Starfleet Eco-Adventures** (☎ FAX 507/757–9630) offers a snorkeling excursion on a private catamaran and hiking on Isla Bastimentos. **Bocas Water Sports** (☎ 507/757–9541) offers a variety of excursions, including trips to their Red Frog camp on Isla Bastimentos.

TELEPHONES

Information (☎ 507/757–9257). **International operator** (☎ 0 + 106). There is a **public telephone** in Parque Simón Bolívar; there are also public phones in the Bahía Hotel and by the fire department, on Calle 1.

VISITOR INFORMATION

The **Immigration Office** is in the Government House, a large cement building overlooking the town square, which is called Parque Simón Bolívar. The **Panamanian Tourist Board (PAT)** has an air-conditioned office a few doors down Calle 3 from the ferry dock, where they answer and hand out brochures. **Bocas del Toro** also has a web site (www.bocas.com), which is regularly updated. To visit Parque Nacional Marina Isla Bastimentos you need to pay the $10 fee and get a permit at the **INRENARE office** (✉ C. 1, ☎ 507/757–9244).

10 National Parks and Biological Reserves

A selective primer to the best of Costa Rican and Panamanian protected areas—where to find the wildlife, the spectacular flora, and the reef and volcanoes.

By David
Dudenhoefer
and Justin
Henderson

AN ALMOST UNFATHOMABLE WEALTH OF natural assets. The breathtaking scenery of the two countries, for example, encompasses barren mountain peaks, lush forests, and vibrant, multihued coral reefs. Equally fantastic is the native wildlife population, more species of plants and animals than scientists have been able to count.

Moreover, the governments of both nations have had the foresight to protect a significant portion of that ecological wealth within national parks and biological preserves. There are also wildlife refuges, forest reserves, and Indian reservations where the flora and fauna benefit from some degree of protection. This conservation effort is particularly remarkable when you consider that Costa Rica and Panama are relatively poor countries with limited resources. Just three decades ago, there was hardly a protected area in either nation. Today Costa Rica's parks cover about 13% of the national territory, and Panama's national parks and reserves cover 17% of their national territory, although the Panamanian areas tend to be less protected than those in Costa Rica.

During the first decades of those nations' park systems, conservationists raced against rampant deforestation to protect as much of the country's vital wildlands as possible. Parks were created and maps were drawn, but protecting the flora and fauna within them turned out to be a daunting task for the underfunded government agencies responsible for conservation. Thanks to the foresight of local conservationists, and ample assistance from abroad, those parks and reserves now contain examples of nearly all the ecosystems that exist in the region: mangrove estuaries, lowland rain forests, tropical dry forests, pristine beaches, coral reefs, cloud forests, caves, freshwater swamps and lagoons, active volcanic craters, transition forests, and various marine ecosystems.

The Costa Rican Ministry of the Environment and Energy (MINAE) and the Panamanian Institute of Renewable Natural Resources (INRENARE) are now concentrating on consolidating management of the parks and improving their infrastructure. Though the tropical flora and fauna they preserve is nothing short of spectacular, Panamanian and Costa Rican national parks have set in place very little infrastructure compared with protected areas in northern nations. Many of the parks require four-wheel drive to reach them, only a few have paved roads, and some can only be visited by boat, on horseback, or on foot. Most parks still don't have visitor centers, and trails often aren't always well marked.

Costa Rica is facing a new conservation challenge—controlling the crowds that flock to its most famous protected areas. Some Costa Rican parks receive so many visitors during the high season that it can be worth your while to head to less popular protected areas, where you'll be treated to a more private and natural experience. In addition to the national parks, there are a growing number of private nature reserves that are open to the public, many of which have their own lodges. Nearly all tour companies offer trips to the national parks and reserves, although certain ones have more experience in ecological tourism.

Responsible Tourism

In Costa Rica and Panama, economic pressures still cause people to cut down trees and hunt endangered animals. Citizens of both those countries are slowly coming to realize that conservation pays, and when you visit one of those parks or reserves, you are sending a positive message to both that government and the marketplace. But your contribution to the protection of the wilderness that you visit can go well beyond the payment of entrance fees. Whether you travel on your own or with a tour group, make sure your visit benefits the people who live near the wilderness areas: use local guides or services, visit local restaurants, and buy local crafts or fruits. To ensure that these areas will be preserved for future generations, you can also make donations to local conservation groups. A few foreign environmental organizations, including Conservation International, the Nature Conservancy, and the World Wide Fund for Nature, are also aiding ecological efforts in Costa Rica and Panama.

Viewing Wildlife

Although the protected areas contain some spectacular scenery and wildlife, including such endangered species as jaguars, tapirs, and giant anteaters, don't be disappointed if you don't come face to face with one of these animals. Despite their frequent appearances in advertisements and brochures, jaguars, for example, are practically impossible to see in the wild, given their scarcity, shyness, and nocturnal schedules. Don't give up hope, though: if you take the time to explore a few protected areas, you're almost certain to spy some monkeys, iguanas, sloths, parrots, toucans, and dozens of other interesting critters.

Travelers are often surprised by how difficult it can be to spot animals in the rain forest. The low density of mammals combined with the fact that thick vegetation often obstructs your view, means that you have to be patient and attentive to see things. River trips can provide some excellent animal observation, and because the tropical dry forest is less overgrown, it is one of the best life zones for animal observation.

Visitor Information and Admission Fees

In August, 1994, Costa Rica's Environment Ministry raised the cost of entry for foreign visitors into all national parks, biological reserves, and national monuments from less than $2 to $15, a decision that infuriated many in the tourism industry. The country's environment minister claimed the high fee increase was needed to accomplish two important goals: raising the money to effectively patrol the parks and improve infrastructure, and decreasing the traffic into some of the more heavily visited parks. Money was raised, and visitation decreased, but representatives from the country's tourism sector insisted the high fees were hurting that vital industry, and in 1996, the price of admission to national parks was reduced to $6 per day. The Panamanian government currently charges entrance fees ranging from $3 to $10.

For specific information on Costa Rican parks and protected areas, call the **Environment Ministry's national park information line** (☎ 192), which is attended by well-informed, bilingual operators who can quickly answer most questions. For more specific requests, such as reserving camping or cabin space, call the regional office of the conservation area in which the park in question is located. Numbers for specific offices can be found in the regional chapters of this guide, or can be obtained from the main office of the country's **National System of Conservation Areas** (☎ 506/283–8004).

In Panama, **INRENARE** can send written permission to visit a park and can contact a local guide for you if you fax the main office in Paraíso, outside Panama City (☎ 507/232–4325, FAX 507/232–4083). It is, however, easiest to simply go to the park: rangers are always happy to help visitors, who are still pretty scarce.

CENTRAL VALLEY: AROUND SAN JOSÉ

Since the Central Valley was one of the first parts of Costa Rica to be settled and is now home to more than half of its burgeoning population, Mother Nature has had to retreat to the region's mountaintops and a few isolated river valleys.The parks have good access, with paved, albeit somewhat potholed, roads leading to all of them, and most are accessible for people who can't walk far. Because the floor and lower slopes of the Central Valley are covered with coffee plantations, cities, and towns, the region's parks are predominantly high-elevation, cloud forest ecosystems—extremely luxuriant and often shrouded in thick mist. (☞ Chapter 3 *for additional information.*)

Parque Nacional Volcán Irazú

Parque Nacional Volcán Irazú, or Irazú Volcano National Park, protects little more than the summit of Volcán Irazú (11,260 ft), Costa Rica's highest. The landscape at the top of the crater is bleak but beautiful, still scarred from the volcano's violent eruptions between 1962 and 1965, when several feet of ash covered the Central Valley. It's best to head up Irazú as early in the morning as possible, before the summit becomes enveloped in clouds, so you can catch a glimpse of its cream-of-asparagus-color crater lake and, if you're lucky, views of nearby mountains and of either the distant Pacific or Caribbean. There are no trails or visitor center at the summit, but a paved road leads all the way to the top, past pastoral landscapes that resemble the Alps more than what you'd expect to see in Central America.

Refugio Nacional de Fauna Silvestre Tapantí

The Río Grande de Orosí flows through the middle of Refugio Nacional de Fauna Silvestre Tapantí (Tapantí National Wildlife Refuge), a protected cloud forest that covers the mountain slopes at the southern end of the Valle de Orosí. The emerald waters of that boulder-strewn river pour into some brisk but inviting swimming holes near the park's picnic area. There's a modest visitor center by the entrance, and 1½ km (1 mi) up the road is a parking area with trails that head into the woods on both sides of the street. The Sendero Oropéndola trail leads to two loops, one that passes the picnic and swimming areas and another that winds through the forest nearby. The trail across the road does a loop along a forested hillside, and La Pava trail, 2½ km (1½ mi) farther up on the right, leads down a steep hill to the riverbank. Several kilometers farther up the road from La Pava is a view of a long, slender cascade on the far side of the valley. Camping isn't permitted.

Monumento Nacional Guayabo

Although the ruins here don't compare with those of Guatemala and Mexico, Monumento Nacional Guayabo (Guayabo National Monument) is Costa Rica's most important archaeological site. Most of the original buildings were made of wood, so today only their bases remain. Rangers give guided tours (in Spanish) of the ruins, which include stone roads and a communal well fed by a pre-Columbian aqueduct. On your own, you can hike along a trail that loops through the surrounding rain forest, where you can do some bird-watching. Camping is permitted near the ranger station. Guayabo is closed to visitors on Monday.

NORTHERN GUANACASTE AND ALAJUELA

The several parks in the province of Guanacaste protect some of the last remnants of the Mesoamerican tropical dry forest that once covered the Pacific lowlands from Costa Rica to the Mexican state of Chiapas. Because Spanish colonists found the climate on the Pacific slope of the isthmus more hospitable than its humid Atlantic side, most of the development that followed the conquest of Central America took place at the cost of the Pacific forests, and today hardly any wilderness remains on that half of the land bridge. The protected dry forests of Guanacaste are, consequently, of extreme importance to conservationists. And the institution of new parks in Costa Rica is a work in progress: Volcán Tenorio is now protected in its own national park, but no infrastructure exists as of yet.

As the daily rain deluges subside in December, the lush landscape enters a transition: as the dry season progresses, most of the trees drop their foliage and the region resembles a desert. Many trees flower during the dry season, however, and the yellow, white, and pink blossoms of the *tabebuia* add splashes of color to the leafless landscape.

Because of the sparse foliage and partial deforestation, Costa Rica's dry forest parks are some of the best places in the country to see wildlife. Many animals native to North America are common in Guanacaste's protected areas—white-tailed deer, coyotes, magpie jays, diamondback rattlesnakes—but they are also home to predominantly South American animals, such as collared peccaries, armadillos, parrots, and broad-beaked hawks called caracaras.

Perhaps due to the wide-open spaces one encounters in the Northwest, the region's parks tend to lie away from bus routes, which means you're better off visiting most of them in a rental car or on tours. (☞ Chapter 4 *for additional information.*)

Parque Nacional Juan Castro Blanco

On the upper level of the Atlantic plain, where foothills mark the transition from the coastal lowland to the central mountains, most of the once-jungle-covered land has been cleared for cattle and dairy farming. There are, however, a number of biological preserves here, plus the Parque Nacional Juan Castro Blanco. East of Ciudad Quesada, locally known as San Carlos, the 55-sq-mi park was created to protect large tracts of virgin forest around the headwaters of the Platanar, Tora, Aguas Zarcas, Tres Amigos, and La Vieja rivers. There are no facilities of any kind in the park at present.

Refugio Nacional de Vida Silvestre Caño Negro

The river trip at Refugio Nacional de Vida Silvestre Caño Negro (Caño Negro National Wildlife Refuge) can be an interesting alternative to the Tortuguero canal trip. Another lowland rain-forest reserve, Caño Negro has suffered severe deforestation over the years, but most of the Río Frío remains lined with trees, so the boat trip up the river to the reserve provides an opportunity to see a variety of wildlife. The lagoon at the heart of the reserve also attracts numerous waterfowl from November to January. Caño Negro is most easily accessed from the Nuevo Arenal–La Fortuna area.

Parque Nacional Rincón de la Vieja

Parque Nacional Rincón de la Vieja, or Rincón de la Vieja National Park, was created to protect the upper slopes of the volcano, with forests that stay greener than those in the drier lowland and a series of steam geysers, bubbling mud pots, hot springs, and several cascades. This extensive protected area has entrances at Hacienda Santa María and Las Pailas. There's a camping area by the old farmhouse of Santa María, and a 2-km (1-mi) hike away is Bosque Encantado, where the Río Zopilote pours over a cascade in the forest, forming an enticing pool. Three kilometers (2 mi) farther is a hot sulfur spring and 4 km (2½ mi) beyond that are boiling mud pots and fumaroles in an area called Las Pailas. Respect the fences, and don't get too close to the mud pots; their edges are brittle, and several people have slipped in and been severely burned. The trail to the summit heads into the forest above Las Pailas, but it's a trip for serious hikers, best done in the dry season (and by those prepared for cold weather at the top). The Rincón de la Vieja Mountain Lodge offers horseback tours of the park. The lodge has its own network of trails, and it has turned a sulfur spring into a rock-lined, hot-water bathing pool.

A less strenuous option for visiting the park is to hike the 3-km (2-mi) loop where you will see fumaroles, a *volcáncito* (baby volcano), and Las Pailas, a series of bubbling mud pots. Along the trail you might also see armadillos, howler monkeys, and semidomesticated, raccoonlike coatis looking for handouts (which you should ignore: a cardinal rule of wildlife encounters is not to feed the animals).

Parque Nacional Santa Rosa

Parque Nacional Santa Rosa, or Santa Rosa National Park, is one of the country's most impressive protected areas. The dry forest that covers much of the park draws biologists and nature lovers, and whereas one of the park's beaches (Nancite) is a vital nesting area for the olive ridley sea turtle, the beach next to it (Naranjo) is well-known among the surfing cognoscenti for its world-class waves.

The forested slopes of Volcán Orosí, protected within Parque Nacional Guanacaste, can be seen from the Carretera Interamericana (Inter-American Highway) as you approach the entrance to Santa Rosa. A couple of kilometers after you enter Santa Rosa, a scenic overlook on the right offers the first good look at the park's dry forest. La Casona, an old farmhouse and former battle site, houses a small museum with exhibits about the area's ecology and the battle between ill-equipped Costa Ricans and American mercenary William Walker. A small nature trail loops through the woods near La Casona, and a large camping area is nearby. The road that passes the campground heads to Playa Naranjo, a spectacular, pristine beach with great animal watching and surfing. There is a camping area at Playa Naranjo, but no potable water, and it can only be reached in a four-wheel-drive vehicle or by taking a 12-km (7-mi) hike from La Casona. Be aware that Santa Rosa's campgrounds sometimes fill up during the dry season, especially in the first week of January and Holy Week (Palm Sunday–Easter Sunday).

If you don't have time to go to Playa Naranjo, there are two good animal-watching trails that head off the road before it becomes too steep for anything but four-wheel-drive vehicles. The Patos Trail, on the left a few kilometers after the campgrounds, heads through the forest past a water hole and several scenic overlooks. A kilometer (½ mi) farther down the road on the right is a short trail that leads to an overlook from which you can see distant Playa Naranjo, and the massive Witches Rock, which stands offshore.

Nancite, to the north of Naranjo, is an important turtle-nesting beach. The *arribadas* (mass nestings) that Nancite is famous for can also be seen at Refugio Nacional de Fauna Silvestre Ostional, near Nosara.

Parque Nacional Guanacaste

East of the Carretera Interamericana but contiguous with Parque Nacional Santa Rosa and comprising a mosaic of ecologically interdependent protected areas, parks, and refuges, the Parque Nacional Guanacaste, or Guanacaste National Park, stretches to the cloud forests atop Volcán Cacao. Although the park is still in fragments, the ultimate goal is to create a single, enormous Guanacaste megapark that will accommodate the natural migratory patterns of myriad creatures, from jaguars to tapirs. There are 300 different birds and more than 5,000 species of butterflies in the park. Camping is reportedly possible at the biological stations, and there are a couple of very rustic lodges; call ahead to the Santa Rosa Park Headquarters (☎ 506/695–5598).

NICOYA PENINSULA

On the sun-drenched Nicoya Peninsula, washed-up California dudes cruise the tubes along endless golden beaches, while monkeys howl in the dry tropical forests, coatimundis caper, and turtles ride in on the evening high tide to deposit their eggs into the sand in one of the world's most fascinating biological epics.(☞ Chapter 5 *for additional information.*)

Parque Nacional Palo Verde and Reserva Biológica Lomas Barbudal

Parque Nacional Palo Verde (Palo Verde National Park) and Reserva Biológica Lomas Barbudal (Lomas Barbudal Biological Reserve) protect some significant expanses of dry forest, and because both areas receive fewer visitors than Santa Rosa, they offer a more natural experience. Palo Verde's major attraction is the swampland, which becomes the temporary home for thousands of migratory birds toward the end of the rainy season. An important part of these lagoons lies near the ranger station, where a raised platform has been built for birdwatchers. From December to March you can spot dozens of species of aquatic birds in the area, including several kinds of herons, ducks, wood storks, and elegant roseate spoonbills.

Palo Verde's forests are alive with species inhabiting Santa Rosa, and the road that leads to the ranger station from the town of Bagaces passes some wooded patches where you're bound to spot birds and mammals if you drive slowly. There are also trails that head away from the ranger station—one short path into the hills behind it, and a longer one that goes to the river. The road south from Bagaces is long and rough and passes a lot of pasture before it gets to the park. An alternative route between Palo Verde and the Carretera Interamericana passes through Lomas Barbudal—meaning it traverses more forest—though it's a longer haul. The ranger station in Lomas Barbudal stands by the Río Cabuya, which has a small swimming hole nearby, and the road that crosses the stream becomes a trail that winds around the forested hillside. The road that heads north from Lomas is pretty bad, but it's only 15 km (9 mi) to the highway. Camping is permitted at Palo Verde.

VOLUNTEER VACATIONS

IF YOU'RE AN ASPIRING ecotourist hoping to spend vacation time productively, Costa Rica may be the place for you. A number of international and local environmental groups have programs allowing visitors—ranging from good-intentioned amateurs to scientists-in-training—to get involved. But bear in the mind that these volunteer activities often ask for more than your time and energy: you'll pay for the privilege of tracking nesting turtles, or counting caterpillars, or monitoring the mating dance of the manakins.

The mother of all volunteer programs has got to be Earthwatch, the worldwide environmental organization that emphasizes research—the hard science essential to making valid environmental arguments. In Costa Rica alone, the following Earthwatch programs, lead by experts in each field, were slated for 1998.

"Dancing Birds," staging area: Monteverde Cloud Forest Preserve. Observation and radio tracking of long-tailed and other manakins, small Neotropical birds whose singing and dancing courtship rituals form part of a complex social system. "Costa Rican Caterpillars," staging area: La Selva Reserve. Collection and observation of La Selva's estimated 5,000 species of caterpillars. "Costa Rica's Dry Forest," staging area: Guanacaste Conservation Area. Observing and marking plant, insect, and animal life in the tropical dry forest. "Costa Rica's River Wildlife," staging area: Tortuguero. Research and local community training in manatee ecology, caiman and crocodile ecology and status, environmental education in the local schools, and development of a local environmental scout program.

"Costa Rican Sea Turtles," staging area: Playa Grande, Guanacaste. Tracking and counting nesting leatherbacks, along with significant nesting data.

Participants are asked to pay from $1,500 to $1,700 (in addition to airfare to San José) for meals and rustic but comfortable accommodations. Contact **Earthwatch Institute** (⌗ 680 Mt. Auburn St. Box 9104, Watertown, MA 02272–9104, ☎ 800/776–0188, FAX 617/926–8532, http://www.earthwatch.org/).

Many local Costa Rican organizations offer similar opportunities. ATEC, based in Puerto Viejo de Talamanca, offers one- to two-week tours that entail, among other things, gathering data on leatherbacks nesting in the Gandoca-Manzanillo Wildlife Refuge; and patrolling and protecting nesting leatherbacks in the Pacuare Nature Reserve. Contact **ATEC** (⌗ Puerto Viejo de Talamanca, Puerto Limón, ☎ 750–0188, e-mail: tecmail@sol.racsa.co.cr).

ANOTHER ORGANIZATION that has done a lot of work on behalf of the turtles is the Caribbean Conservation Corporation. Volunteers work with researchers documenting sea turtle activities as well as observing and counting Neotropical bird populations. The CCC charges $1,500 to $2,000 for one- to two-week sessions. The CCC runs a Visitor's Center and Museum in Tortuguero, exhibiting excellent animal photos and hosting detailed discussions of what's going on in the area. Contact the **CCC** (⌗ 4424 N.W. 13th St., Suite A-1, Gainseville, FL 32609, ☎ 800/678–7853, FAX 352/375–2449, http://www.cccturtle.org/).

Parque Nacional Barra Honda

Rocky hills that contain an extensive network of caves dominate Parque Nacional Barra Honda (Barra Honda National Park), an area of protected dry forest. Local guides lower spelunkers into the caverns using ropes and a climber's ladder—a descent into darkness that is not for the fainthearted but is rewarding for the adventurous. If you're not up for the drop, you can trek into the forest-covered hills, full of wildlife and where scenic overlooks offer views of the Golfo de Nicoya and surrounding countryside. The Cascada Trail begins near the ranger's office and makes a loop near the caves that should take two or three hours to walk; serious hikers will want to continue on to the Boquete Trail, which, together with the Cascada Trail, takes the better part of a day to hike down and back. A community tourism association provides guides and climbing equipment and runs a simple restaurant and lodge, called Las Delicias, by the park entrance. Camping is permitted.

Parque Nacional Marino Las Baulas

Another important turtle nesting beach is Playa Grande, protected within Parque Nacional Marino Las Baulas (Las Baulas Marine National Park), near Tamarindo. Las Baulas, dedicated in 1991 and officially made a park in 1995, is visited by thousands of leatherback turtles—the world's largest—every year during the October–March nesting season. The adjacent Tamarindo wildlife refuge, although under some developmental pressure, protects a mangrove estuary that is an excellent bird-watching area. Just south of Tamarindo and accessible by dirt road is the Río San Francisco, with its own estuary system. Beyond this river lies Playa Langosta, added to the protected-areas list but as of yet not nearly as well organized as Las Baulas (turtle tours are less formal and less expensive). The San Francisco estuary is rich in bird life and (unlike the Tamarindo wildlife refuge) free of motorboats. Playa Langosta, like Playa Grande–Las Baulas, is a leatherback turtle nesting site.

CENTRAL PACIFIC COSTA RICA

Thanks to its proximity to San José, the Central Pacific has two of the country's most popular protected areas, both of which receive lots of visitors. Those areas are also home for plenty of wildlife, including such endangered species as the scarlet macaw and squirrel monkey. Try to get to the refuges as early in the morning as possible.(☞ Chapter 6 *for additional information.*)

Reserva Biológica Carara

The Reserva Biológica Carara (Carara Biological Reserve), on the road between Puntarenas and Playa Jacó, protects one of the last remnants of a transition zone between the dry forests of the northern Pacific lowlands and the humid forests of the southwest. Its tall trees don't drop their foliage during the dry season, but the sylvan scenery is much less luxuriant than what you'll encounter farther south. Carara is one of two areas in the country where you can see scarlet macaws, which are easiest to spot in the early morning or late afternoon. The Río Tárcoles, which defines the park's northern border, is a good place to see crocodiles, and you may also encounter monkeys, coatis, and an array of birds as you explore the reserve's forests.

Carara's proximity to San José and Jacó has made it one of the country's most popular protected areas, which means tour buses arrive here on a daily basis in the high season. For independent travelers, the presence of tour buses usually means that most of the animals have been frightened deeper into the forest, but if you catch Carara when there are few visitors—very early or late in the day—you can see a lot. The trail that starts near the ranger station makes a loop through the forest that should take an hour to hike. A longer trail, several km to the north, is better for animal-watching, but cars parked at the trailhead have been broken into. Camping isn't permitted at Carara.

Parque Nacional Manuel Antonio

The popularity of Parque Nacional Manuel Antonio, or Manuel Antonio National Park, is not surprising when you contemplate its exuberant forests, idyllic beaches, and coral reefs. But the assets of that beautiful patch of wilderness may have made the area too popular for its own good. The road between the town of Quepos and Manuel Antonio is lined with hotels, and when their guests head to the park, its magic wanes. In an attempt to manage the crowd, the parks service only allows 600 visitors to enter per day, which means you might not get in during the afternoon in high season. It is also closed Monday.

Because it is a relatively small, protected area, Manuel Antonio isn't home to a great deal of wildlife, but it is one of only two areas of the country, together with Corcovado, where you can see squirrel monkeys. It is also a good place to see agoutis, sloths, and capuchin monkeys, which have been fed by visitors, and get so close that they sometimes bite people who attempt to pet them. A tropical storm that hit Manuel Antonio several years ago toppled many of the park's largest trees. There is also plenty to see in the park's coves, which hold submerged rocks, coral formations, and abundant marine life.

The park entrance is on the beach just across a little estuary (don't swim there—it's polluted) from the end of the road. A trail heads through the forest just behind the beach, but you can also walk on the sand. Another trail that does a loop on Punta Catedral, the steep point at the end of the beach, offers a good look at the rain forest. The second beach, on the other side of the point, is in a deep cove safe for swimming and has good snorkeling. From the simple visitor center here, one trail leads to the nearby cove of Puerto Escondido and a lookout point beyond; a second, the Perezoso, heads back through the forest to the park's entrance. Camping is not permitted.

SOUTHERN PACIFIC COSTA RICA

The southwest is a vast and wild region, where the ecosystems range from the reefs off Isla del Caño to the highland *páramo* (a landscape of shrubs and herbs) of Chirripó peak. This is one of the best regions to see wildlife such as scarlet macaws, spider monkeys, toucans, and coatis, and the forests those animals live in are equally spectacular. (☞ Chapter 7 *for additional information*.)

Parque Nacional Chirripó

Surrounding the Parque Nacional Chirripó (Chirripó National Park) is a wild and scenic area different from what you'll find anywhere else in the country. It is also so remote that there is no easy way in; hikers usually spend one night in San Gerardo de Rivas, which has several inexpensive lodges. From San Gerardo, it's a grueling climb up to the park—6–10 hours. There is a cabin near the top, but you will need to bring food and water, a camp stove, a good sleeping bag, and warm clothes. It's best to head out of San Gerardo with the first light of day. You first hike through pastures, then forests, and then the burnt remains of forest fires. You'll want to spend at least two nights at the cabin, since you have to hike up from there to explore the peaks, glacier lakes, and *páramo*—a highland ecosystem common to the Andes that consists of shrubs and herbaceous plants. Trails lead to the top of Chirripó and the nearby peak of Terbi.

Camping isn't allowed at Chirripó, and reservations for space to spread your sleeping bag out in the cabin must be through the Environment Ministry's San Isidro regional office (☎ 506/771–3155). If there is space available for the dates you want to visit the park, they will tell you the number of an account in the Banco Nacional into which you must deposit admissions and lodging fees to confirm your reservation. The cabin holds only 40 people, so reservations must be made well ahead of time during the dry season. Be prepared for very cold weather on top.

Parque Nacional Corcovado

A pristine expanse of wilderness covering one-third of the Osa Peninsula, Parque Nacional Corcovado (Corcovado National Park) safeguards virgin rain forest, deserted beaches, jungle-edged rivers, and a vast, inaccessible swamp. Corcovado is home to boa constrictors, jaguars, anteaters, tapirs, and if you're lucky enough to come face to face with one of these rare creatures, it is most likely to happen here. You will definitely see flocks of scarlet macaws, troops of spider monkeys, colorful poison dart frogs, toucans, and agoutis.

The easiest way to visit the remote park is on a day trip from one of the lodges in the nearby Bahía Drake (Drake Bay) area, but if you have a backpack and strong legs, you can spend days deep within its wilderness. Bunks are available at the Sirena station—you'll need a good mosquito net and sheets—where you can also buy meals, but you have to reserve and pay for everything ahead of time. Only 35 people are allowed to camp at any given ranger station, so you usually have to register and prepay for your time in the park well ahead of time. Call the Environment Ministry's Puerto Jiménez regional office (☎ 506/735–5036), and if there is space available for the dates you want to visit the park, they will tell you the number of an account in the Banco Nacional into which you must deposit admissions and other fees to confirm your reservation.

There are several trails into the park, along the beach starting from La Leona or San Pedrillo ranger stations, or through the forest from Los Patos ranger station. Although hiking is always tough in the tropical heat, the forest route is easier than the beach hikes, which can be done only at low tide. The longer hike between San Pedrillo and Sirena can be undertaken only during the dry season, because the rivers become too high to cross during the rainy months. You can hire a boat in Sierpe to take you to San Pedrillo or Bahía Drake; from Drake it's a three-hour hike to San Pedrillo. You can hire a taxi in Puerto Jiménez to take you most of the way to Los Patos, and shared taxis leave every morning at 6 for Carate, which is a short hike from La Leona. It's an all-day hike between any two stations. There is potable water at every station, but don't drink stream water. Be sure to bring plenty of insect repellent, sunblock, rain gear, a pair of good boots, first-aid kit, and either a mosquito net and sheets, or a tent and sleeping bag. Finally, try to pack light.

ATLANTIC LOWLANDS AND THE CARIBBEAN COAST

The parks of the Caribbean coast—with a humid, greenhouse-like climate and lush vegetation—are the kind of wilderness one would expect to see upon hearing the word "jungle." In these Atlantic forests live South American species you won't find in the rest of Costa Rica—poison dart frogs, the crab-eating raccoon, and the great green macaw.

The Atlantic region's most popular protected areas are its coastal parks, where the rain forest meets the beach. You'll find marine wonders as well as the flora and fauna of the jungle. Aside from the surf and sand, the prime natural attractions along the southern Caribbean coast are coral reefs, whereas the northern beaches are famous for the sea turtles that come here by night to lay their eggs in the sand.

The protected areas on the Caribbean side have the added convenience of being close to good dining and lodging. And the trip there can be an adventure in its own right, since the Atlantic Highway passes through the heart of Parque Nacional Braulio Carrillo, and the boat trip up the canals to Tortuguero is one of the best opportunities to see wildlife in Costa Rica. (☞ Chapter 8 *for additional information.*)

Parque Nacional Braulio Carrillo

This amazing, accessible expanse of pristine wilderness is one of Costa Rica's largest protected areas (171 sq mi). Stretching from the misty mountaintops north of San José to the Atlantic Lowlands, Parque Nacional Braulio Carrillo (Braulio Carrillo National Park) protects a series of ecosystems ranging from the cloud forests covering the park's upper slopes to the tropical wet forest of the Magsasay sector. The Carretera Guápiles, the main route to the Atlantic coast, cuts through one of Braulio's most precipitous areas, passing countless breathtaking views of the rugged landscape. There is a ranger station just after the Zurquí Tunnel, where a short trail loops through the cloud forest. Another trail leads into the forest to the right about 17 km (10½ mi) after the tunnel, where it follows the Quebrada González, a stream with a cascade and swimming hole, into the rain forest. The vegetation is beautiful around the highway, and you may see a few of the 350 bird species that inhabit the park. (Although Braulio is home to most of the mammals found in Costa Rica, they tend to avoid the forest near the highway.) There are no camping areas in this part of the park.

Hikers will want to explore the Volcán Barva sector of Braulio Carrillo, with its trail that leads through the cloud forest to two crater lakes. Camping is allowed at the Barva ranger station, which is far from any traffic and thus is a good area to spot birds and animals. Quetzals can be seen in the area during the dry season, which is the only time you'll want to camp there, but it's a good place for a morning hike just about any time of year. Stay on the trail when hiking anywhere in Braulio; it's easy to get lost in the cloud forest, and the rugged terrain makes wandering through the woods very dangerous.

Parque Nacional Cahuita

The near 1-sq-mi coral reef that surrounds Punta Cahuita is a natural treasure, and the Parque Nacional Cahuita (Cahuita National Park) was set up to protect its 35 species of coral and even greater number of sponges and seaweeds, which provide food and refuge for the myriad colorful tropical fish and crustaceans. The reef alone would be ample attraction for visitors; most, however, come for Cahuita's luxuriant coastal forest and idyllic palm-lined beaches, which have stepped, seemingly, straight out of a travel poster.

The 7-km (4½-mi) path that winds in and out of the forest along the beach, from the town of Cahuita around the point to Puerto Vargas, offers a good look at the park's coastal and jungle wonders. The hike can be completed in a few hours. The forest and swamps are home to troops of monkeys, kingfishers and herons, sloths, snakes, crabs, and lizards. The beach nearest the town of Cahuita has a regular riptide, so wait to do your swimming until you're farther into the park, where the beach curves toward the point. This is also a good snorkeling area, although the best diving is off the point. Sadly, the park's coral reef is slowly being killed by sediment, run off from deforested areas such as the banana plantations in the nearby Valle de Estrella. This process was intensified by the earthquake of 1991, as many riverbank trees in the nearby jungle foothills were downed by the quake, exposing riverbank soil to the erosive effect of tropical deluges, and sending trees, soil, leaves, shrubs, and everything else seaward. After the quake, local divers estimated that the reef was 80% dead, but don't despair: there is still good snorkeling to be had. Just use a local guide to find the best reefs, and don't dive for a few days after it rains when the water is sure to be murky.

Refugio Nacional de Vida Silvestre Gandoca-Manzanillo

Although less pristine than Parque Nacional Cahuita, Refugio Nacional de Vida Silvestre Gandoca-Manzanillo (Gandoca-Manzanillo National Wildlife Refuge) stretches along the southeastern coast from the town of Manzanillo to the border of Panama, offering plenty of rain forest and many good dive spots. Because of weak laws governing the conservation of refuges and the value of coastal land in the area, Gandoca-Manzanillo has suffered steady environmental degradation over the years and continues to be developed. For now, the easiest way to explore it is by hiking along the coast south of Manzanillo, which also has some good snorkeling offshore. You can hike back out the way you came in, or arrange in Puerto Viejo to have a boat pick you up at Monkey Point (a three- to four-hour walk from Manzanillo) or Gandoca (six to eight hours). Boat trips to dive spots and beaches in the refuge can also be arranged in Puerto Viejo, Punta Uva, and Manzanillo.

Parque Nacional Tortuguero and Refugio Nacional de Fauna Silvestre Barra del Colorado

Parque Nacional Tortuguero (*tortuga* means turtle) was created to protect the sea turtles that nest by the thousands on its beach. The park comprises a variety of ecosystems, including lowland rain forest, estuaries, and swampy areas covered with *yolillo* palms. The park's palm-lined beach stretches off as far as the eye can see; you can wander here alone, but rip currents make swimming dangerous and there are rumors of sharks. This spectacular beach is even more intriguing at night, when four species of endangered sea turtles nest there. If you want to watch them, contact your hotel or the parks office to hire a certified local guide. (You won't be permitted to use a camera on the beach and flashlights must be covered with red plastic, since the lights may deter the turtles from nesting.)

The jungle-lined canals that lead to Tortuguero have been called the Amazon of Costa Rica, and the boat trip up to the park, which leaves from the docks at Moín, is an excellent opportunity to see the area's wildlife, including several species of kingfishers and herons, sloths, monkeys, and crocodiles. Hire a dugout canoe with guide to explore some of the rivers that flow into the canal; these waterways contain less boat traffic and often have more wildlife. You can also continue up the canals to the Refugio Nacional de Fauna Silvestre Barra del Colorado (Barra del Colorado National Wildlife Refuge), an immense protected area that is connected with the park via a biological corridor. Barra del Colorado is less visited, and it protects significant expanses of wilderness.

PANAMA

Panama's national park system protects an array of ecosystems as impressive as Costa Rica's, but since Panamanian tourism lags far behind that of its neighbor nation, the country's parks tend to have rather limited infrastructure. The good thing is that you don't have to share Panama's protected areas with the kinds of crowds that sometimes descend on Costa Rican parks. Panama's Renewable Resources Institute, INRENARE (☎ 507/232–4325, FAX 507/232–4083), recently introduced entrance fees of between $3 and $10, depending on the park.

The Cordillera de Talamanca extends from eastern Costa Rica into western Panama, and much of that massive range is protected within a series of parks and reserves that together form the Reserva de la Biósfera La Amistad (La Amistad Biosphere Reserve, ☞ *below*). Although most of the biosphere reserve covers the mountain range's Atlantic slope, its most accessible areas are found on the Pacific side, and several of those are in the mountains of western Panama. The trails and roads that wind into the mountains of Chiriquí, Panama's southwest province, not only pass unforgettable panoramas, they lead to luxuriant cloud forests inhabited by quetzals, toucans, tiny venomous toads, and other colorful creatures.

Although most of the isolated Bocas del Toro Archipelago remains covered with jungle, and much of that jungle is protected within national parks, forest reserves, and Indian reservations, the majority of it is barely accessible. Although adventurers with jungle gear and time to spare may want to head back into mountain refuges such as the Reserva Forestal Palo Seco (Palo Seco Forest Reserve), the Reserva Indígena Teribe (Teribe Indian Reservation), and the Atlantic sector of Parque Internacional La Amistad, most tourists will have to settle for the region's most accessible protected area, Isla Bastimentos. (☞ Chapter 9 *for additional information on the areas covered below.*)

Volcán Barú

Volcán Barú (Barú Volcano), an 11,450-ft, long-extinct peak, dominates the Chiriquí countryside, inviting hiking and bird-watching enthusiasts to ascend. The upper slopes and summit of that massive volcano are protected within Parque Nacional Volcán Barú, which comprises significant patches of cloud forest and a rugged peak. The cloud forest is home to a wealth of bird life, including three-wattled bellbirds and resplendent quetzals, whereas the heights are home for the rare volcano junco. There are two routes to the summit: a footpath that winds up the western slope from near the town of Volcán, and a road (you'll need a four-wheel-drive vehicle for this) that heads up the eastern slope from Boquete. A dirt trail also leads through the forest between Cerro Punta and Boquete, along the volcano's northern slope, which makes for a good one-day hike. There are no visitor facilities at the summit, and although camping is allowed, you'll need plenty of water and warm clothes—it freezes regularly up top.

Parque Nacional Marino Isla Bastimentos

Parque Nacional Marino Isla Bastimentos (Isla Bastimentos National Marine Park), centered around Isla Bastimentos in Panama's Bocas del Toro province, is a pristine jewel of a park, comprising coral reefs, white-sand beaches, and dozens of small cays and islets. Among the things to do and see there are fantastic skin diving, beachcombing, lots of wildlife, sea-turtle nesting beaches, and an as-yet-unexplored potential for windsurfing and surfing. Although there are communities on its western and eastern ends, most of Isla Bastimentos remains covered with lush forests that are home to ospreys, iguanas, parrots, and tiny poison dart frogs. The long, palm-lined beaches of its northern coast are as beautiful as they are ecologically important, and the waters to the south and west of the island hold some extensive coral reefs.

The best area for skin diving within the park is in the waters that surround the Cayos Zapatillas—two atolls to the southeast of Isla Bastimentos. When the ocean is calm, the visibility is quite good around the Cayos, where you'll discover an impressive array of sponges and corals, including some immense brain coral formations. This colorful coral garden is home for countless tropical fish, which range from tiny angels to larger parrot and trigger fish, and a great diversity of rays. The caves at the reef's edge often hold massive snappers, drums, moray eels, and, sometimes, sleeping sharks. And if you take the time to look closer you may discover delicate starfish, shrimp, octopuses, and an array of other interesting invertebrates.

But the Cayos are beautiful enough above the water to please people who have no desire to don a mask and snorkel. Its pale beach, lined with lanky coconut palms and washed by aquamarine waters, belongs on postcards and travel posters and in dreams dreamt during northern winter nights. The long beach on Isla Bastimentos is equally impressive, though more difficult to visit, and from April to September it is visited by nesting sea turtles on a nightly basis. That beach is backed by thick forest, home to a wealth of wildlife, which adventurous travelers may want to take the time to explore. Isla Bastimentos and the Cayos Zapatillas can be reached by boat from the regional capitol of Bocas del Toro, a pleasant town with a small selection of lodges and a few decent restaurants.

Parque Internacional La Amistad

The single largest protected area within the Reserva de la Biósfera La Amistad is Panama's Parque Internacional La Amistad, which covers more than 775 sq mi, extending from cloud forests down to sultry lowland jungles. The name Amistad, which means friendship in Spanish, refers to its role as half of a binational park—it is contiguous with Costa Rica's Parque Nacional La Amistad, which is slightly smaller than its Panamanian twin and more difficult to visit. The ranger station at Las Nubes, in the hills above Cerro Punta, is the park's main entry point. It is a quiet spot at the edge of the forest, with a couple of houses and a grassy area where you can camp. A 2-km (1-mi) trail does a loop through the forest near the ranger station, and a second trail heads up over a ridge, which affords views of the Cerro Punta valley, to a nearby waterfall; it takes about two hours to hike there and back. If you spend a night or two there, you may be able to accompany one of the rangers up Cerro Picacho, a four- to five-hour hike deep into the forest.

11 Portrait of Costa Rica

A Biological Superpower

A BIOLOGICAL SUPERPOWER

COSTA RICA MAY LACK oil fields and coal deposits, but the country is not without its natural assets. Its ecological wealth includes fertile volcanic soil, sun-swathed beaches, massive trees whose thick branches support elevated gardens of orchids and bromeliads, and hundreds of colorful bird species—the kind of priceless commodities that economists have long ignored. International bankers may wonder how this tiny nation ended up with so pretentious a name as "Rich Coast," but many a barefoot Indian, grizzled biologist, and binocular-toting tourist understands where the republic's wealth lies hidden.

Costa Rica's varied forests hold a treasure trove of flora and fauna, so vast and diverse that scientists haven't even named many of the plant and insect species found within them, and of the species that have been identified, few have been thoroughly studied. Those forests are among the most diverse and productive ecosystems in the world—though tropical forests cover a mere 7% of the Earth's surface area, they hold more than half the planet's plant and animal species—and few countries offer better exposure to the biological treasures of tropical nature than Costa Rica.

About half the size of the state of Kentucky, Costa Rica covers less than 0.03% of the planet's surface, yet it contains nearly 5% of its plant and animal species. The diversity of the country's flora and fauna can be summed up with statistics: it contains at least 9,000 plant species, more than 1,100 varieties of orchids, in excess of 2,000 different kinds of butterflies, and at least 850 bird species (more than exist in the United States *and* Canada). But such numbers don't begin to convey the awe one feels when staring up the convoluted trunk of a centennial strangler fig, listening to the roar of a howler monkey reverberate through the foliage, or watching a delicate hummingbird drink nectar from a multicolored heliconia flower.

This nation's rich and varied tropical nature is as beautiful as it is intriguing, and as complicated as it is fascinating. It may be hard to comprehend the richness and complexity of the country's forests at first glance—the overwhelming verdure of the rain forest can give the false impression of uniformity—but once you begin to examine the pieces of that great green puzzle, you come to understand why scientists have dubbed Costa Rica a "biological superpower."

That biological diversity is the result of the country's tropical location—on a slip of land connecting North and South America—its varied topography, and the many microclimates resulting from those mountains, valleys, and lowlands. But to understand why Costa Rica is such a biologically important place today, we need to look back into prehistory, and envision a world that human eyes never saw, but which scientists have at least partially reconstructed.

Just a Few Dozen Millennia Ago

In geological terms, Costa Rica is relatively young, which explains why precious few valuable minerals can be found beneath its soil. Five million years ago, the patch of land we now call Costa Rica didn't even exist. In those days, North and South America were separated by a canal the likes of which Teddy Roosevelt—the father of the Panama Canal—couldn't have conjured up in his wildest dreams. In the area now occupied by Panama and Costa Rica, the waters of the Pacific and Atlantic Oceans flowed freely together for unfathomable millennia. Geologists have named that former canal the Straits of Bolívar, after the Venezuelan revolutionary who wrested much of South America from Spain.

Far beneath the Straits of Bolívar, the incremental movement of tectonic plates slowly completed the Central American isthmus. Geologists speculate that a chain of volcanic islands appeared in that gap around 30 million years ago. A combination of volcanic activity and plate movement caused those islands to grow and rise from the water, eventually forming a connected ridge. The land bridge was completed approximately 3 million years ago, closing the interoceanic canal and opening a biological corridor between the Americas.

Because several tectonic plates meet beneath Central America, it has long been geologically unstable, experiencing occasional earthquakes, frequent tremors, and regular volcanic eruptions. Although being hit by one of those natural disasters can't help but seem a curse, there actually wouldn't be a Costa Rica if it weren't for such phenomena. What is today the country's best soil was once spewed from the bowels of the volcanoes that dominate the landscape, and the jarring adjustments of adjacent tectonic plates actually pushed most of the national territory up out of the sea. A recent example of this upward movement was the 7.2 earthquake of 1991, which thrust Costa Rica's southern Caribbean coastline up several feet, leaving portions of coral reefs high and dry. Shallow coral platforms that surrounded the points of Limón and Cahuita were thrust from the water, adding as much as 30 yards of land to some oceanfront property. Although that quake was a devastating natural disaster that damaged or destroyed almost half the homes along the Caribbean coast, it was but a tiny adjustment in the incremental tectonic process that created the country.

The intercontinental connection completed 3 million years ago had profound biological consequences, since it both separated the marine life of the Pacific and Atlantic Oceans and simultaneously created a pathway for interchange between North and South America. Though hardly the kind of lapse that a geologist could get excited about, 3 million years is a long time by biological standards, and the region's plants and animals have changed considerably since the inter-American gap spanned. Whereas evolution took different paths in the waters that flank the isthmus, organisms that had evolved on separate continents were able to make their way into the opposite hemisphere, and the resulting interaction determined what lives in the Americas today.

Mind-Boggling Biodiversity

Costa Rica's amazing biological diversity is in many ways the result of that intercontinental exchange, but the country's flora and fauna actually adds up to more than what has passed between the continents. Although it is a biological corridor, the isthmus also acts as a filter, which makes it home to many species that couldn't complete the journey from one hemisphere to the other. The rain forests of Costa Rica's Atlantic and southwest lowlands, for example, comprise the most northerly distribution of such southern species as the crab-eating raccoon and a dreaded jungle viper known as the bushmaster. The tropical dry forests of the northern Pacific slope, on the other hand, define the southern limit for such North American species as the white-throated magpie jay and the Virginia opossum. In addition to species whose range extends only as far as Costa Rica, and those whose range extends through the country into both North and South America, such as the white-tailed deer and the gray hawk, Costa Rica's many physical barriers and microclimates have fostered the development of indigenous plants and animals, such as the mangrove hummingbird and mountain salamander.

What all this biological balderdash means to a visitor to Costa Rica is that they might spot a North American pale-billed woodpecker and a howler monkey—of South American descent—in the branches of a rain tree, which is native to Central America. And then there are the tourists—migrants, that is—such as the dozens of northern bird species that winter in Costa Rica, among them the Tennessee warbler, western tanager, and yellow-bellied sapsucker.

In addition to the birds that winter in Costa Rica, you'll no doubt recognize some of the plants, such as the orchids and impatiens that grow wild in the country, but cost a pretty penny at the garden shop back home. Costa Rica has plenty of oak trees, squirrels, and sparrows, but most of the country's flora and fauna looks decidedly tropical. Not only are such common plants as orchids, palms, and ficuses unmistakably tropical, but many of the country's animals are distinctly Neotropical—that which is only found in the American tropics—such as sloths, poison dart frogs, toucans, and monkeys with prehensile tails.

This varied wildlife is spread through an array of ecosystems, which biologists have divided into a dozen "life zones," but which actually consist of a biological continuum almost too diverse for classification. Though the flora and fauna found in any given life zone are determined by various physical conditions, the two most important are altitude and rainfall. Although average temperatures change very little in the tropics through the course of the year, they do change a good bit during the course of the day, especially in the mountains. The Costa Rican highlands stay consistently cooler than the lowlands, which means you can spend a morning sweating in a sultry coastal forest, then drive a couple hours into the mountains, where you will need a warm jacket.

In a more temperate area of the world, the cold weather hits the mountaintops a month or two before the lowlands, but Old Man Winter eventually gets his icy grip on everything. In the tropics, the only places where it freezes is atop the highest mountains, so high-altitude flora tends to be completely different from that in even nearby valleys. Altitude also plays a substantial role in regulating humidity, since clouds accumulate around mountains and volcanoes, providing regular precipitation as well as shade, which slows evaporation. These conditions are perfect for the luxuriant cloud forests that cover the upper slopes of many mountains. In general, the higher you climb, the more lush the vegetation will be, except for the peaks of the highest mountains, which often protrude from the cloud cover, and are consequently fairly arid.

Though you may associate the tropics with rain, precipitation in Costa Rica varies considerably depending on where you are and when you're there. This is a result of its mountainous terrain and regional weather patterns. A phenomenon called rain shadow—when one side of a mountain range receives much more rain than the other—plays an important ecological role in Costa Rica. Four mountain ranges combine to create an intercontinental divide that separates the country into Atlantic and Pacific slopes. Thanks to the trade winds, the Atlantic slope receives much more rain than the Pacific. The trade winds steadily pump moisture-laden clouds southwest over the isthmus, where they encounter warm air or mountains, which make them rise. As the clouds rise, they cool, and become less able to hold moisture, which causes them to dump most of their liquid luggage on the country's Caribbean side.

During the rainy season, which runs from mid-May to December, the role of the trade winds is diminished, as regular storms roll off the Pacific Ocean and soak the western side of the isthmus. Though it rains all over Costa Rica during these months, it often rains more on the Pacific side of the mountains than on the Atlantic. Come December, the trade winds take over again, and hardly a drop falls on the western side until May. The dry season is most intense in the country's northwest corner, where the forests acquire a desert visage during the dry months, as most trees drop their foliage. That region, known as Guanacaste, quickly regains its verdure once the rains return in May, which marks the beginning of a springlike season that Costa Ricans nonetheless refer to as winter.

Climate variation within the country results in a mosaic of forests—from those that receive only a few feet of rain each year to those that soak up several yards of precipitation annually. The combination of humidity and temperature helps determine what grows where, but whereas some species have very restricted ranges, others seem to thrive just about anywhere. Plants such as strangler figs and bromeliads grow all over the country, and animals such as the collared peccary and coati—a long-nosed cousin of the raccoon—can live just about anywhere human beings let them. Other species have extremely limited ranges, such as the mangrove hummingbird, which is restricted to the mangrove forests of the Pacific coast, and the volcano junco, a gray sparrow that can only be found around the highest peaks of the Cordillera de Talamanca.

The Jungle Out There

The diversity of scenery found in Costa Rica is one of the things that makes it such an interesting country to visit, but the landscape that visitors most want to see is the tropical rain forest. The protected areas of the Atlantic and southern Pacific lowlands hold tracts of virgin rain forest where massive tropical trees tower more than 100 ft over the forest floor. The thick branches of those jungle giants are covered with an abundance of epiphytes (plants that grow on other plants, but aren't parasites) such as ferns, orchids, bromeliads, mosses, vines, and aroids. The arboreal garden of the canopy is where most of the forest's plant and animal species are found.

Although life flourishes in the canopy, the intense sunlight that quickly dries the tree-tops after downpours results in a recurrent water shortage. Plants that live there have consequently developed ways to cope with the aridity. Many orchids have thick leaves that resist evaporation and spongy roots that can quickly soak up large amounts of water when it rains. Tank bromeliads have a funnel shape that enables them to collect and hold water at the center of their leaves. Those plants act as miniature oases, attracting arboreal animals, which drink from, hunt at, or, like certain insect larvae and tree-frog tadpoles, live in their pools. In exchange for the vital water, the waste and carcasses of these animals provide the plant with valuable nutrients, which are also scarce in the canopy.

Many animals spend most or all of their time in the canopy, which can be frustrating for people who head to the jungle wanting to see wildlife. By peering through binoculars, you might glimpse the still, furry figure of a sloth or the brilliant regalia of a parrot. It's definitely hard to miss the arboreal acrobatics of monkeys, who leap from tree to tree, hang from branches, throw fruit or sticks, and generally make spectacles of themselves. For a closer look at the canopy, you may want to visit the Rain Forest Aerial Tram, near the Atlantic Highway, or spend some time in a tree platform at Hacienda Barú in Dominical, or the Corcovado Lodge Tent Camp, both in the southern Pacific.

Because little sunlight reaches the ground, the rain-forest floor is a dim, quiet place, with not nearly as much undergrowth as in those old Tarzan movies. Still, many plants—from aroids to palm trees—have adapted to this shady world. The light level inside a virgin rain forest is comparable to that found in the average North American living room or shopping mall, and some of the plants that grow there look familiar to visitors from the north, since those species have become popular houseplants. The vegetation isn't always sparse, though: whenever an old tree falls there's a riot of growth as an excess of plants fight over the newfound sunlight.

Few travelers are disappointed by the tropical forest, but some are frustrated by the difficulty of spotting wildlife. Hikers occasionally encounter such earthbound creatures as the coati or the agouti, a terrier-size rodent that resembles a giant guinea pig, and in most areas you're likely to see iridescent blue morpho butterflies, hyperactive hummingbirds, brightly colored poison dart frogs, and tiny lizards that stand guard on tree trunks. Most animals, however, spend much of their time and energy trying not to be seen, and the thick foliage aids them in that endeavor. An untrained eye can miss the details, which is why a naturalist guide is invaluable. In addition to spotting and identifying flora and fauna, a good guide can explain some of countless relationships that weave those plants and animals together in one of the planet's most complex ecosystems.

The rain forest is characterized by intense predation. Its inhabitants dedicate most of their time and energy to two essential tasks: finding their next meal, and avoiding being eaten in the process. Whereas animals tend to keep from being eaten by hiding or fleeing, plants have developed defenses such as thorns, prickly hairs, and toxic substances that make their leaves less than appetizing. Because of the relative toxicity of most of the rain-forest foliage, many insects eat only a small portion of a leaf before moving on to another plant, so as not to ingest a lethal dose of any one poison. The consequence of this can be seen by staring up into the canopy—almost every leaf is full of little holes.

Camouflage is also a popular defense of animals, and there are plenty of amazing insects that have evolved to look like the leaves, bark, moss, and leaf litter that abound in the tropical forest. Some bugs have adopted the colors of certain flowers, or even the mold that grows on plants. Though they are a chore to spot, the few camouflaged critters that you discover are invariably intriguing.

Some creatures go to the opposite extreme, and actually advertise with bright colors. Although some colors are meant to help animals find a mate amid the mesh of green, others serve as a warning to potential predators. Some species of caterpillars, for example, are not only immune to the toxins of the plant on which they live, they actually sequester that poison within their bodies, which makes them toxic as well. In certain areas, you may see brightly colored frogs hopping around the forest floor. Their skins are laced with such poisonous secretions that some Indian tribes use them to make their darts and arrows deadly. The typical warning pattern mixes bright colors with black, a coloration that conveys a simple message to predators: eat me and die.

A popular trick for scaring off predators is mimicry. Certain edible caterpillars look like venomous ones, and some harmless serpents have markings similar to those of the deadly coral snake. Such acts of deception often reach amazing levels of intrigue. The cocoons of certain butterflies not only resemble the head of a viper, but if disturbed, they begin to move back and forth just as a snake's head would. One large butterfly has spots on its wings that look like eyes, so when it opens them, it resembles an owl, and another butterfly species is identical to a wasp.

In addition to avoiding predators, plants and animals must compete with other species that have similar niches—the biological equivalents of jobs. This competition has fostered cooperation between noncompetitive organisms. Plants need to get their pollen and seeds distributed as far as possible, and every animal requires a steady food supply, which brings us to everybody's favorite subject: the birds and the bees.

Although butterflies and bees do most of the pollinating up north, tropical plants are pollinated by everything from fruit flies and hummingbirds to beetles and bats. The flowers of such plants are often designed so that the nectar is readily available to their pollinators but protected from freeloaders. The beautiful hibiscus flower is designed to dust a hummingbird's forehead with pollen and collect any pollen that's already there, while the tiny bird drinks the nectar hidden deep in its base. That flower is too long for a butterfly, and the nectar is held too deep for a bee to reach, but no system is perfect; you may spot a bananaquit—a tiny bird with a short beak—biting holes in the bases of hibiscus flowers to drink their nectar without ever getting near their pollen.

The intense competition for limited resources that characterizes the rain forest keeps trees growing taller, roots reaching farther, and everything mobile working on some way to get more for less. The battle for light has sent most of the foliage sky high, whereas the battle for nutrients has caused the process of decay and recycling that follows every death in the forest to take place at breakneck pace. One result of this high-speed decomposition is that most of the nutrients in a rain forest are found within living things, whereas the soil beneath them retains very few essential elements. As a consequence, rain-forest soils tend to be nutrient-poor and less than ideal for farming.

Tropical Nature Works Overtime

Though the rain forest is what most people imagine when they think of the tropics, Costa Rica has other types of forests that are equally diverse and well worth visiting. The tropical dry forests of the northwest lowlands are similar to rain forests during the rainy season, but once the daily deluges subside, the dry forest undergoes a profound change. Most trees lose their leaves, and some of them simultaneously burst into full, colorful flower. Such trees as the yellow-blossomed buttercup tree and the pink tabebuia brighten up the arid landscape of northwest Costa Rica during the dry season. The dry forest contains many of the plants, animals, and exclusive relationships found in the rain forest, but it is also home to species often associated with the forests and deserts of Mexico and the southern United States, such as cacti, coyotes, and diamondback rattlesnakes. Because they aren't as dense as rain forests, it can be easier to spot animals in dry forests. This is especially true during the dry season, when the foliage is sparse, and animals often congregate around scarce water sources and trees in fruit or flower.

The upper reaches of many mountains and volcanoes are draped with cloud forests, which are even more luxuriant than rain forests. They are the epitome of lushness—so lush that it can be difficult to find the bark on a cloud-forest tree for all the growth on its trunk and branches. Plants grow on plants that grow on still other plants: vines, orchids, ferns, aroids, and bromeliads are everywhere, and mosses and liverworts cover the vines and leaves of other epiphytes. Because of the steep terrain, the trees grow on slightly different levels, and the canopy is less continuous than that of a lowland rain forest. More light reaches the ground, so there is plenty of undergrowth, including prehistoric-looking tree ferns, a wealth of flowering plants, and "poor-man's umbrellas," which consist of little more than a few giant leaves.

Cloud forests are home to a multitude of animals, ranging from delicate glass frogs, whose undersides are so transparent that you can see many of their internal organs, to the spectacular quetzal—a bird that was considered sacred by the ancient Mayas. The male quetzal has a crimson belly and iridescent green back, wings, and tail feathers, which can grow longer than 2 ft. Those tail feathers float behind the quetzal during flight; a splendid sight that no doubt inspired its ancient name: "the plumed serpent." Although the tangle of foliage and almost constant mist make it difficult to see much of the cloud forest's wildlife, you should still catch glimpses of such colorful birds as the emerald toucanet, collared redstart, and various kinds of hummingbirds.

The almost constant mist prevents the cloud-forest canopy from facing the water shortage that often plagues a lowland rain forest. In fact, the cloud forest's canopy is usually soaking wet. During most of the year, a moisture-laden mist moves through the cloud forest, depositing condensation on the vegetation. This condensation causes a sort of secondary precipitation, with droplets forming on the epiphytic foliage and falling regularly from the branches to the forest floor. Cloud forests thus function like giant sponges, soaking up the humidity from the clouds and sending it slowly downhill to feed the streams and rivers that many regions and communities depend on for water.

Atop high ridges, and near the summits of volcanoes, the cloud forest has been transformed by the steady, strong winds, which topple tall trees and regularly break off branches. The result is a collection of small, twisted trees and bushes known as an *elfin forest*. On the upper slopes of the Cordillera de Talamanca—the country's highest range—the cloud forest gives way to the *páramo,* a high-altitude ecosystem composed of shrubs, grasses, and hardy herbs. Most of those plants are common in the heights of South America's Andes, and the Costa Rican páramo defines their most northerly distribution.

On the other extreme, along both the country's coasts, are river mouths and estuaries that hold extensive mangrove forests. Regularly flooded, primeval-looking profusions, mangrove forests grow in tidal zones all over the tropics. Many of the trees in those inundated forests grow propped up on stilt roots, which keep their leaves out of the saltwater, and help them absorb carbon dioxide when the tide is high. Those roots also provide protection for a variety of small fish and crustaceans, and they are often covered with barnacles, mussels, and other shellfish.

Mangrove forests are fairly homogeneous, with stands of one species of tree stretching off as far as the eye can see. They are also extremely productive ecosystems that play an important role as estuaries. Many marine animals, such as shrimp, spend the early stages of their lives in mangrove estuaries, whereas other species, such as certain kinds of snappers, are born and die there. Mangroves are vital to the health of the ocean beyond them and are attractive sites for animals that feed on marine life, especially fish-eating birds, such as cormorants, herons, pelicans, and ospreys.

The forests that line the Caribbean canals, along the northeast coast, are dominated by the water-resistant *yolillo* palm. This area is home to many of the same animals found in the rain forest, such as monkeys, parrots, and iguanas, as well as river dwellers such as turtles, otters, and anhingas. A boat trip up the canals is thus an excellent opportunity to observe wildlife, as are similar excursions on such jungle rivers as the Río Frío and the Río Sarapiquí. Seasonal swamps such as Caño Negro and the *lagunas* of Palo Verde, which disappear during the dry months, are also excellent areas to see birds. There is also a vast swamp in the heart of Parque Nacional Corcovado, which never dries up, but is virtually impenetrable because of the thick, thorny vegetation surrounding it.

In addition to its varied forests, Costa Rica has 1,224 km (760 mi) of coastline, which consists of beaches separated by rocky points. Although those points are home for a variety of marine life, most of the country's beaches are important nesting spots for endangered sea turtles. And submerged in the sea off both coasts are extensive coral reefs, inhabited by hundreds of species of colorful fish, crustaceans, and other interesting invertebrates. With its vertiginous biological diversity, the coral reef could well be the marine equivalent of the rain forest.

Where Have All the Jungles Gone?

Considering it is home for such remarkable biodiversity, you would expect a trip through Costa Rica to consist of natural panoramas packed with a wealth of flora and fauna. It soon becomes clear, however, that the region's predominant landscapes are not cloud and rain forests, but the coffee and banana plantations that have replaced them. The country's pre-Columbian cultures may have revered the jaguar and the harpy eagle, but today's inhabitants seem to put more stock in less-illustrious beasts: the cow and the chicken.

During the past 40 years, more than two-thirds of Costa Rica's original forests were destroyed, cut at a rate of between 140 sq mi and 295 sq mi per year. Forests have traditionally been considered unproductive land, and their destruction was for a long time synonymous with development. During the 1970s and 1980s, international and domestic development policies fueled the destruction of large tracts of wilderness. Fortunately, Costa Rican conservationists became alarmed by that deforestation, and in the 1970s they began creating what has since grown to become the region's best national parks system.

In addition to protecting vast expanses of wilderness—between 15% and 20% of the national territory—the Costa Rican government has made progress in curbing deforestation outside the national parks. The rate of destruction has dropped significantly, but poaching and illegal logging continue to be serious problems that, if they aren't corrected, will eventually wipe out many important species and wild areas.

Deforestation not only spells disaster for the jaguar and the eagle, it can also have grave consequences for human beings. Forests absorb the rains and release water slowly, playing an important role in regulating the flow of rivers, which is why severely deforested regions often suffer floods during the rainy season and drought during the dry months. A forest's tree cover also prevents topsoil erosion, thus keeping the land fertile and productive, and in many parts of the country, erosion has left once-productive farmland almost worthless. Finally, hidden within the country's flora and fauna are countless unknown or under-studied substances that could eventually be extracted to cure diseases and serve humankind. The destruction of Costa Rica's forests is a loss for the entire world.

Responsible Tourism

With each passing year, more and more Costa Ricans are coming to realize how valuable and endangered their country's remaining wilderness is. Costa Ricans visit their national parks in significant numbers, and they consider those protected areas vital to the national economy, both for the natural resources they preserve and their role as tourist attractions. Local conservationists, however, are still a long way from achieving their goal of involving the communities that surround the country's parks in their protection.

Costa Ricans who cut trees and hunt endangered animals usually do so out of economic necessity, and, unfortunately, the people who live near protected areas are often the last to benefit from the tourism that wilderness attracts. When you visit a park or reserve, your entrance fee helps pay for the preservation of Costa Rica's wildlife. But you can also make your visit beneficial to the people who live nearby by hiring local guides, horses, or boats; eating in local restaurants; and buying things (other than wild animal products, of course) in local shops.

You can go a few steps further by making donations to local conservation groups or to such international organizations as Conservation International, the Nature Conservancy, the Rainforest Alliance, and the World Wildlife Fund, all of which support important conservation efforts within Costa Rica. It is also good to stray from the beaten path: visit private preserves and stay at lodges that contribute to environmental efforts and nearby communities. By making your visit beneficial to grassroots conservation efforts, you can become part of the global effort to save the planet's tropical ecosystems, and thus help to ensure that the treasures you traveled so far to see remain intact for future generations.

— David Dudenhoefer

INDEX

Looking for a different kind of vacation?

Fodor's makes it easy with a full line of international guidebooks to suit a variety of interests—from adventure to romance to language help.

At bookstores everywhere.
www.fodors.com

WHEREVER YOU TRAVEL, *H*ELP IS NEVER FAR AWAY.

From planning your trip to

providing travel assistance along

the way, American Express®

Travel Service Offices are

always there to help.

American Express Travel Service Offices are found in central locations throughout Costa Rica.

Travel

http://www.americanexpress.com/travel